D1285439

DEAT
WOLV

LOGAN, THE WOLVERINE,
IS DEAD...

BUT NOT EVERYONE KNOWS IT.

WORD HAS BEEN SPREADING SLOWLY
BUT NO ONE'S SURE WHAT'S TRUE
AND WHAT'S RUMOR.

THE WOLVERINE IS A LEGEND.
AND LEGENDS LIVE FOREVER.

DEATH OF WOLVERINE: THE LOGAN LEGACY. Contains material originally published in magazine form as DEATH OF WOLVERINE: THE LOGAN LEGACY #1-7. First printing 2015. ISBN# 978-0-7851-9259-6. Published by MARVEL WORLDWIDE, INC., a subsidiary of MARVEL ENTERTAINMENT, LLC. OFFICE OF PUBLICATION: 135 West 50th Street, New York, NY 10020. Copyright © 2014 and 2015 Marvel Characters, Inc. All rights reserved. All characters featured in this issue and the distinctive names and likenesses thereof, and all related indicia are trademarks of Marvel Characters, Inc. No similarity between any of the names, characters, persons, and/or institutions in this magazine with those of any living or dead person or institution is intended, and any such similarity which may exist is purely coincidental. **Printed in the U.S.A.** ALAN FINE, EVP - Office of the President, Marvel Worldwide, Inc. and EVP & CMO Marvel Characters B.V.; DAN BUCKLEY, Publisher & President - Print, Animation & Digital Divisions; JOE QUESADA, Chief Creative Officer; TOM BREVOORT, SVP of Publishing; DAVID BOGART, SVP of Operations & Procurement, Publishing; C.B. CEBULSKI, SVP of Creator & Content Development; DAVID GABRIEL, SVP Print, Sales & Marketing; JIM O'KEEFE, VP of Operations & Logistics; DAN CARR, Executive Director of Publishing Technology; SUSAN CRESPI, Editorial Operations Manager; ALEX MORALES, Publishing Operations Manager; STAN LEE, Chairman Emeritus. For information regarding advertising in Marvel Comics or on Marvel.com, please contact Niza Disla, Director of Marvel Partnerships, at ndisla@marvel.com. For Marvel subscription inquiries, please call 800-217-9158. **Manufactured between 1/2/2015 and 2/9/2015 by R.R. DONNELLEY, INC., SALEM, VA, USA.**

10 9 8 7 6 5 4 3 2 1

H OF ERINE

THE LOGAN LEGACY

ISSUE #1
WRITER
CHARLES SOULE
ARTIST
OLIVER NOME
COLORIST
JOHN KALISZ
COVER ART
**OLIVER NOME
& SONIA OBACK**

ISSUE #2
WRITER
TIM SEELEY
ARTIST
ARIELA KRISTANTINA
COLORIST
SONIA OBACK
COVER ART
**ARIELA KRISTANTINA &
SONIA OBACK**

ISSUE #3
WRITER
KYLE HIGGINS
ARTIST
JONATHAN MARKS
COLORIST
LEE LOUGHRIDGE
COVER ART
**JONATHAN MARKS
& JOSE VILLARRUBIA**

ISSUE #4
WRITER
MARGUERITE BENNETT
ARTIST/COLORIST/
COVER ART
JUAN DOE

ISSUE #5
WRITER
RAY FAWKES
ARTIST
ELIA BONETTI
COLORIST
BRETT SMITH
COVER ART
**GERARDO SANDOVAL
& DAVID CURIEL**

ISSUE #6
WRITER
JAMES TYNION IV
ARTIST
ANDY CLARKE
COLORIST
DAN BROWN
COVER ART
ALEX GARNER

ISSUE #7
WRITER
CHARLES SOULE
PENCILER
PETER NGUYEN
INKER
SANDU FLOREA
COLORIST
**JOHN KALISZ
& BRETT SMITH**
COVER ART
**RAFAEL
ALBUQUERQUE**

LETTERER
**VC'S JOE
CARAMAGNA**
EDITORS
**KATIE KUBERT
& MIKE MARTS**

COLLECTION EDITOR:
ALEX STARBUCK
ASSISTANT EDITOR:
SARAH BRUNSTAD
EDITORS, SPECIAL PROJECTS:
**JENNIFER GRÜNWALD
& MARK D. BEAZLEY**
SENIOR EDITOR, SPECIAL PROJECTS:
JEFF YOUNGQUIST
SVP PRINT, SALES & MARKETING:
DAVID GABRIEL

EDITOR IN CHIEF:
AXEL ALONSO
CHIEF CREATIVE OFFICER:
JOE QUESADA
PUBLISHER:
DAN BUCKLEY
EXECUTIVE PRODUCER:
ALAN FINE

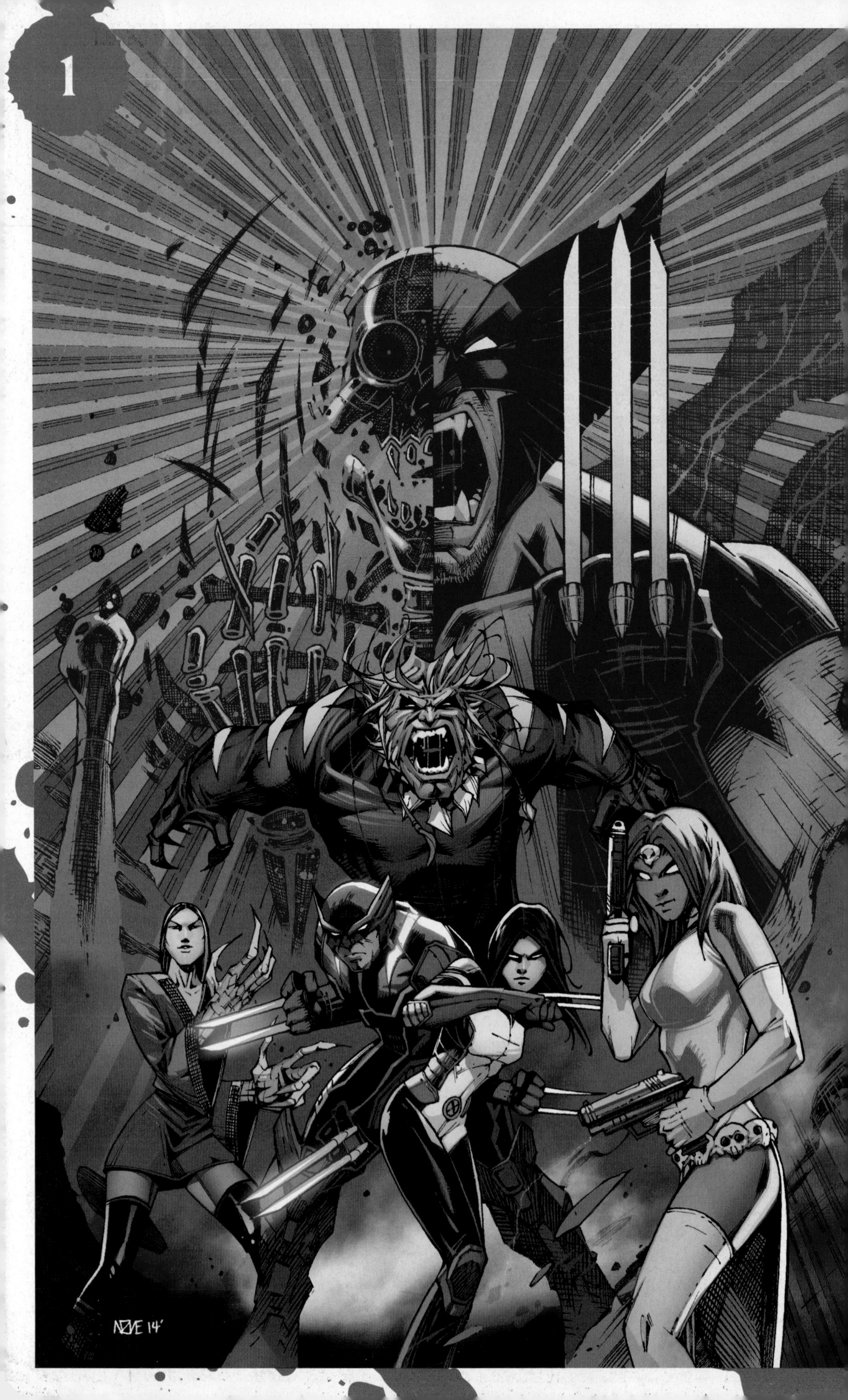
1
NZVE 14'

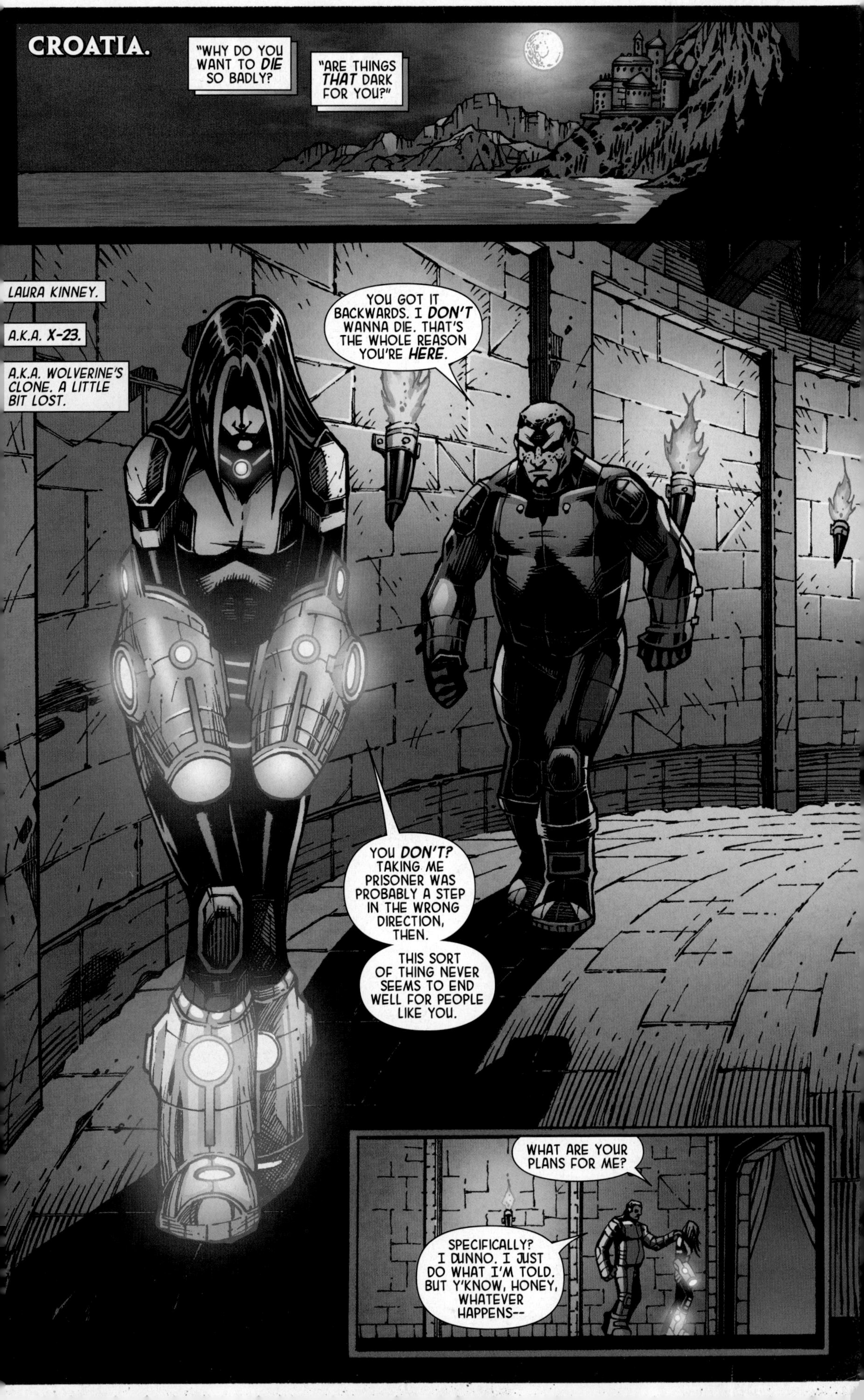
CROATIA.
"WHY DO YOU WANT TO DIE SO BADLY?
"ARE THINGS THAT DARK FOR YOU?"
LAURA KINNEY.
A.K.A. X-23.
A.K.A. WOLVERINE'S CLONE. A LITTLE BIT LOST.
YOU GOT IT BACKWARDS. I DON'T WANNA DIE. THAT'S THE WHOLE REASON YOU'RE HERE.
YOU DON'T? TAKING ME PRISONER WAS PROBABLY A STEP IN THE WRONG DIRECTION, THEN.
THIS SORT OF THING NEVER SEEMS TO END WELL FOR PEOPLE LIKE YOU.
WHAT ARE YOUR PLANS FOR ME?
SPECIFICALLY? I DUNNO. I JUST DO WHAT I'M TOLD. BUT Y'KNOW, HONEY, WHATEVER HAPPENS--

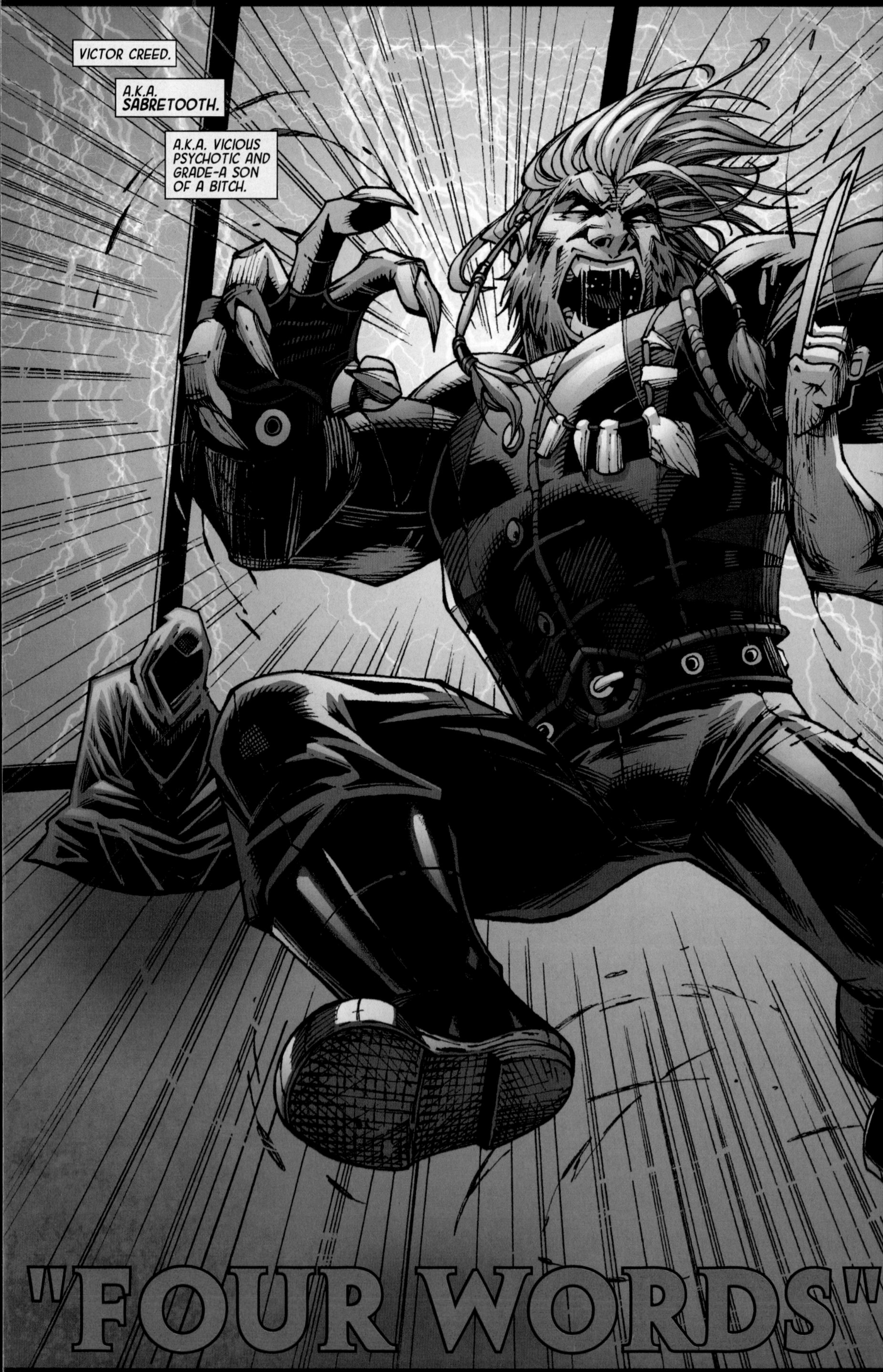
VICTOR CREED.
A.K.A. SABRETOOTH.
A.K.A. VICIOUS PSYCHOTIC AND GRADE-A SON OF A BITCH.
"FOUR WORDS"

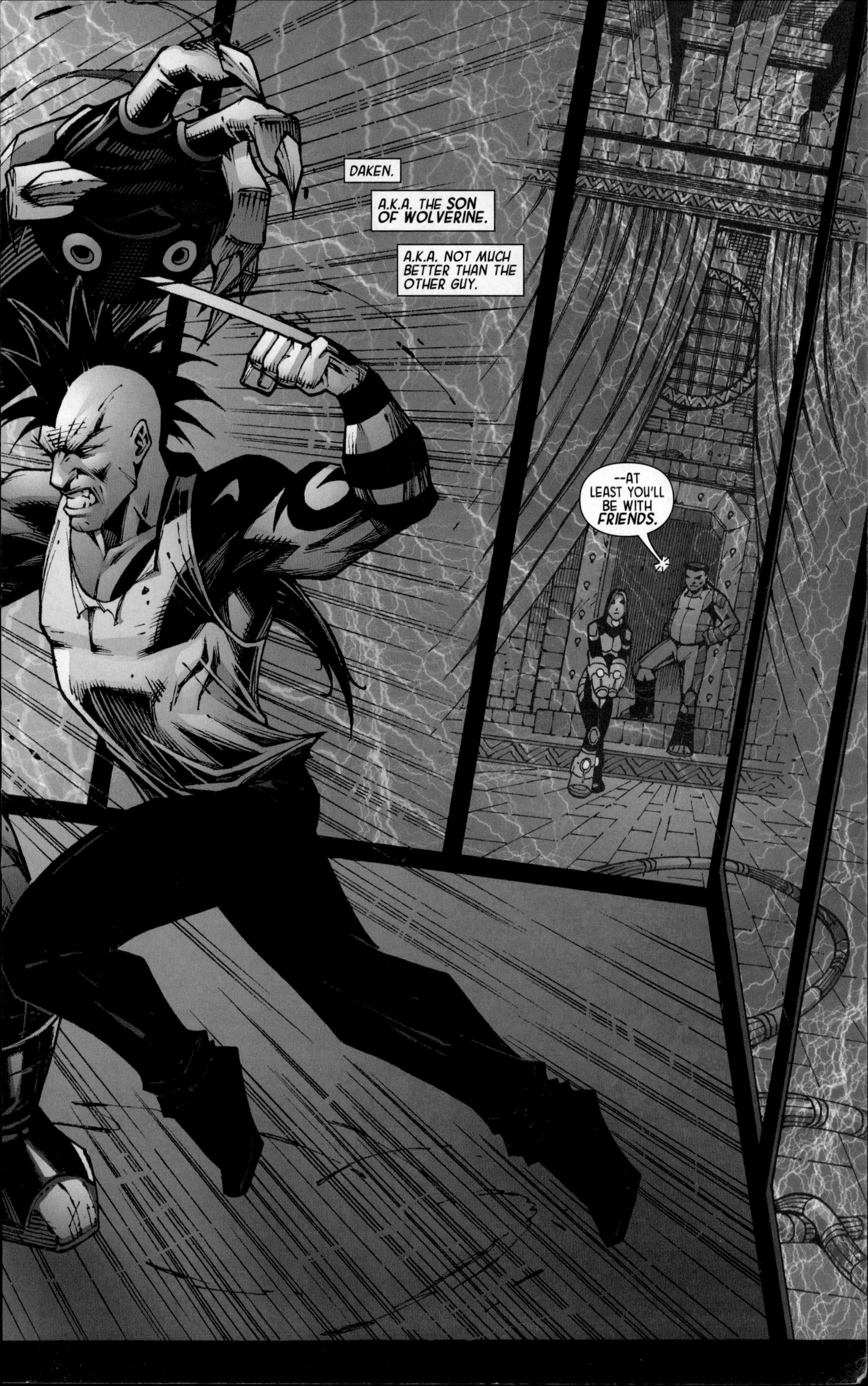
DAKEN.
A.K.A. THE SON OF WOLVERINE.
A.K.A. NOT MUCH BETTER THAN THE OTHER GUY.
--AT LEAST YOU'LL BE WITH FRIENDS.

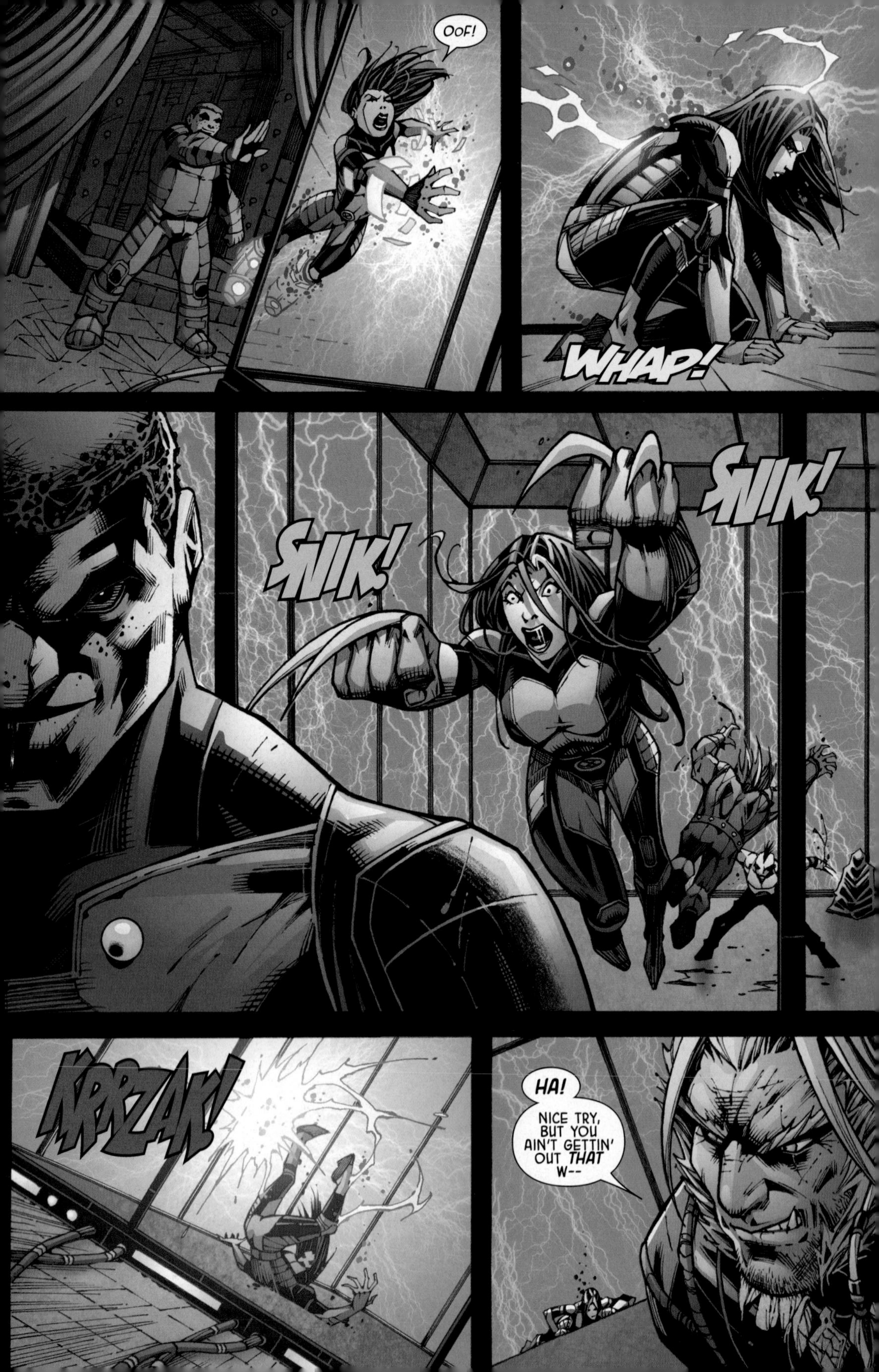
OOF!
WHAP!
SNIK!
SNIK!
KRRZAK!
HA!
NICE TRY, BUT YOU AIN'T GETTIN' OUT *THAT* W--

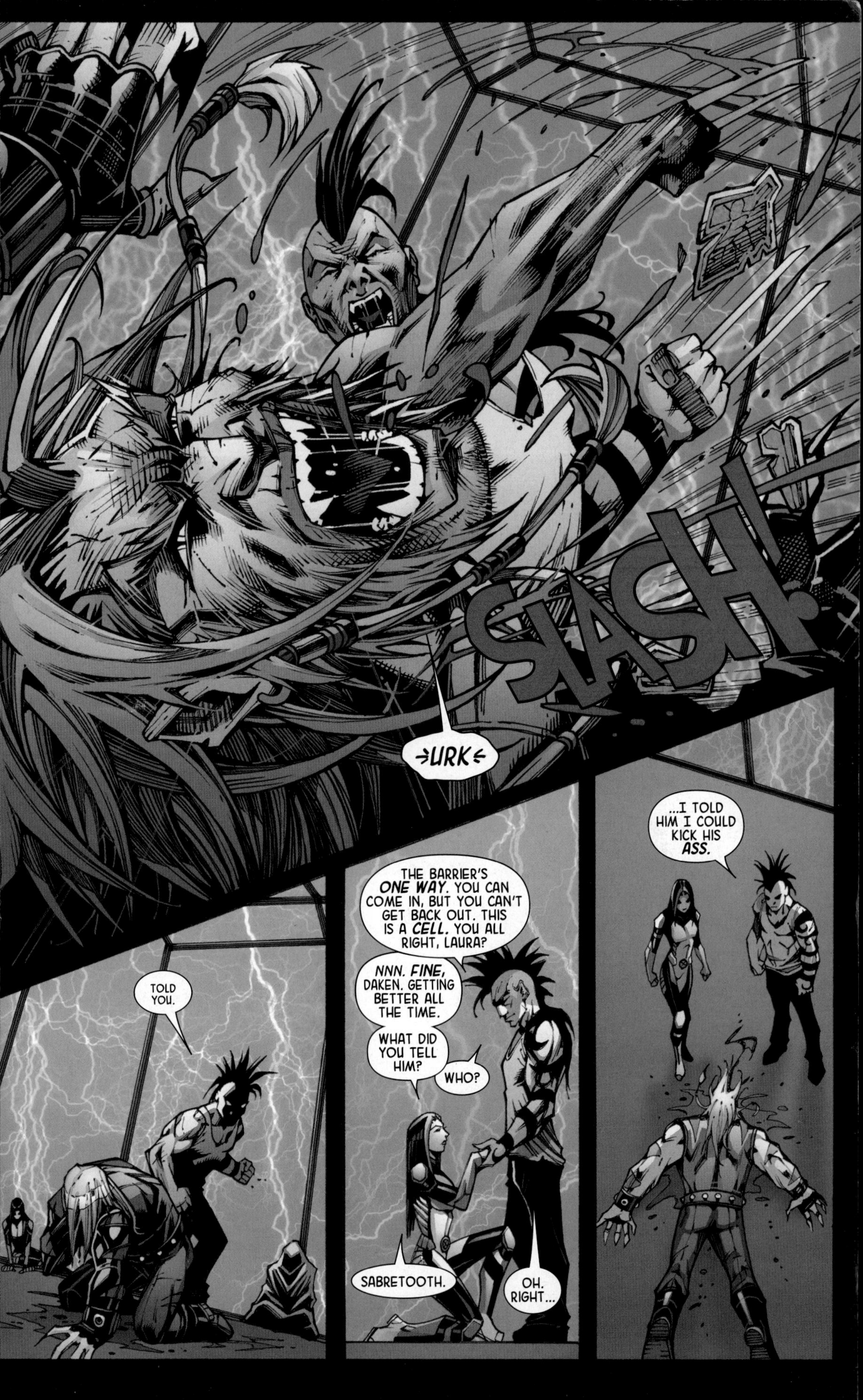
SLASH!
URK
TOLD YOU.
THE BARRIER'S ONE WAY. YOU CAN COME IN, BUT YOU CAN'T GET BACK OUT. THIS IS A CELL. YOU ALL RIGHT, LAURA?
NNN. FINE, DAKEN. GETTING BETTER ALL THE TIME.
WHAT DID YOU TELL HIM?
WHO?
SABRETOOTH.
OH. RIGHT...
...I TOLD HIM I COULD KICK HIS ASS.

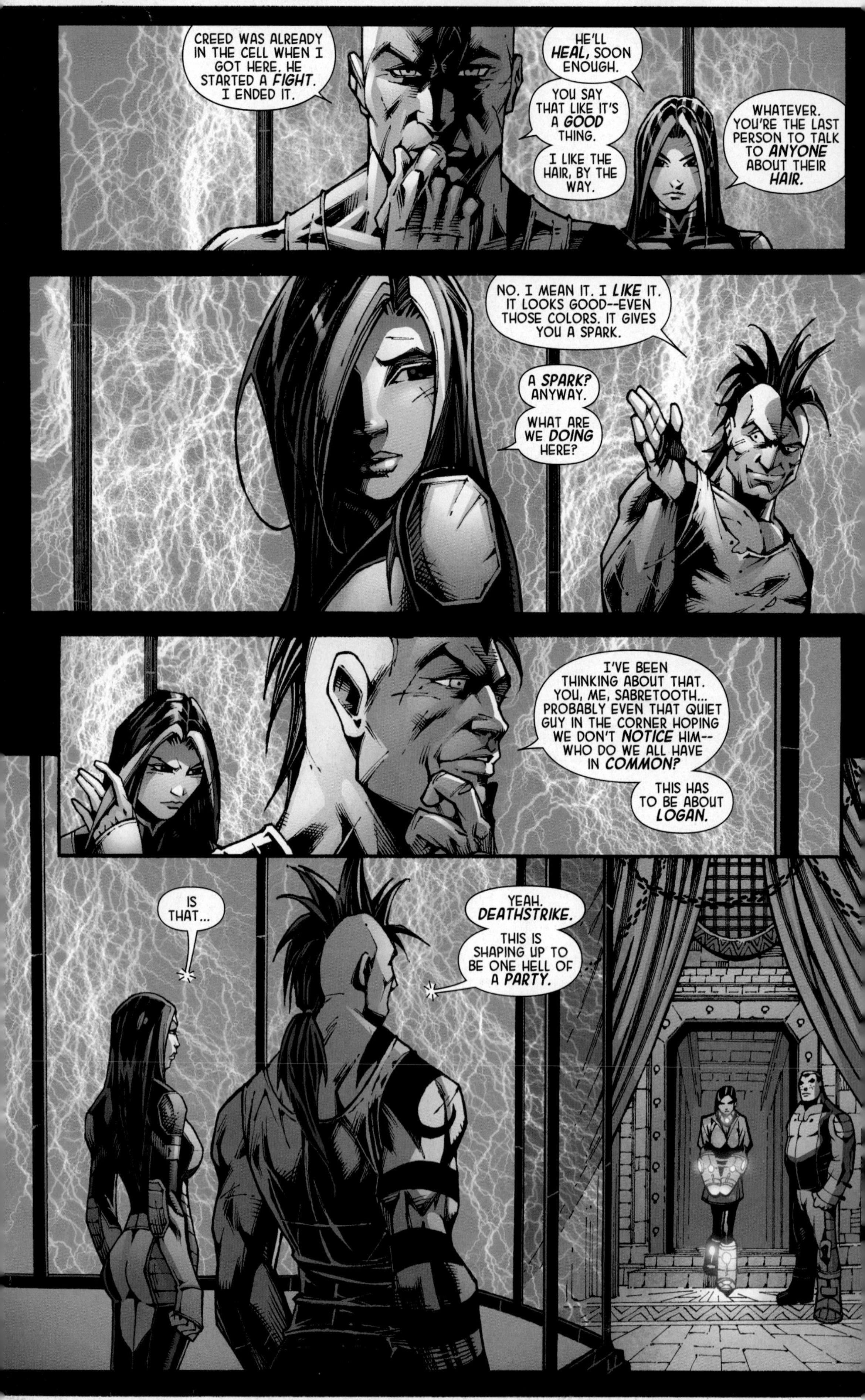
CREED WAS ALREADY IN THE CELL WHEN I GOT HERE. HE STARTED A *FIGHT*. I ENDED IT.
HE'LL *HEAL*, SOON ENOUGH.
YOU SAY THAT LIKE IT'S A *GOOD* THING.
I LIKE THE HAIR, BY THE WAY.
WHATEVER. YOU'RE THE LAST PERSON TO TALK TO *ANYONE* ABOUT THEIR *HAIR*.
NO. I MEAN IT. I *LIKE* IT. IT LOOKS GOOD--EVEN THOSE COLORS. IT GIVES YOU A SPARK.
A *SPARK?* ANYWAY.
WHAT ARE WE *DOING* HERE?
I'VE BEEN THINKING ABOUT THAT. YOU, ME, SABRETOOTH... PROBABLY EVEN THAT QUIET GUY IN THE CORNER HOPING WE DON'T *NOTICE* HIM-- WHO DO WE ALL HAVE IN *COMMON?*
THIS HAS TO BE ABOUT *LOGAN.*
IS THAT...
YEAH. *DEATHSTRIKE.*
THIS IS SHAPING UP TO BE ONE HELL OF A *PARTY.*

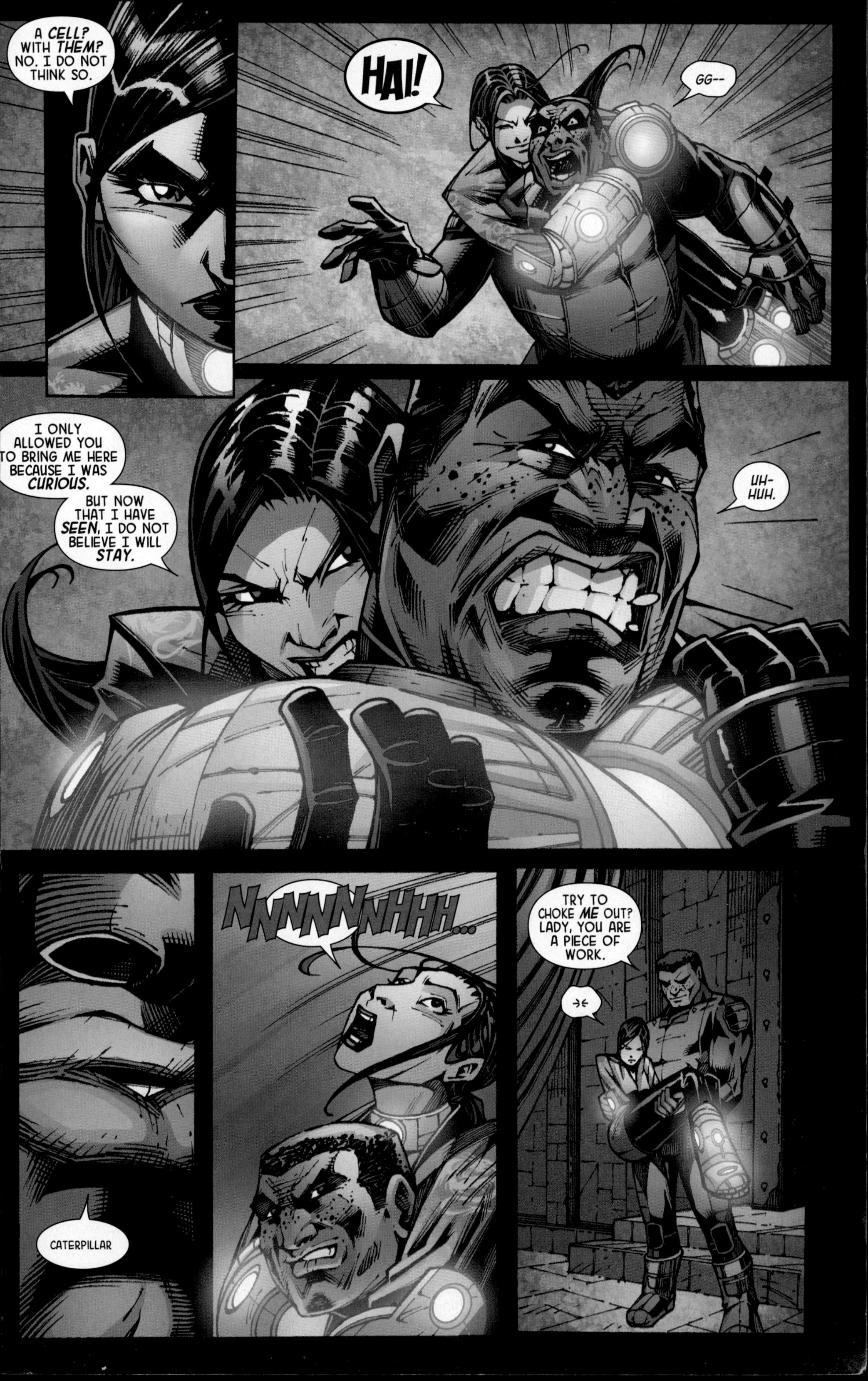
A CELL? WITH THEM? NO. I DO NOT THINK SO.
HAI!
GG--
I ONLY ALLOWED YOU TO BRING ME HERE BECAUSE I WAS CURIOUS.
BUT NOW THAT I HAVE SEEN, I DO NOT BELIEVE I WILL STAY.
UH-HUH.
CATERPILLAR
NNNNNNHHH...
TRY TO CHOKE ME OUT? LADY, YOU ARE A PIECE OF WORK.

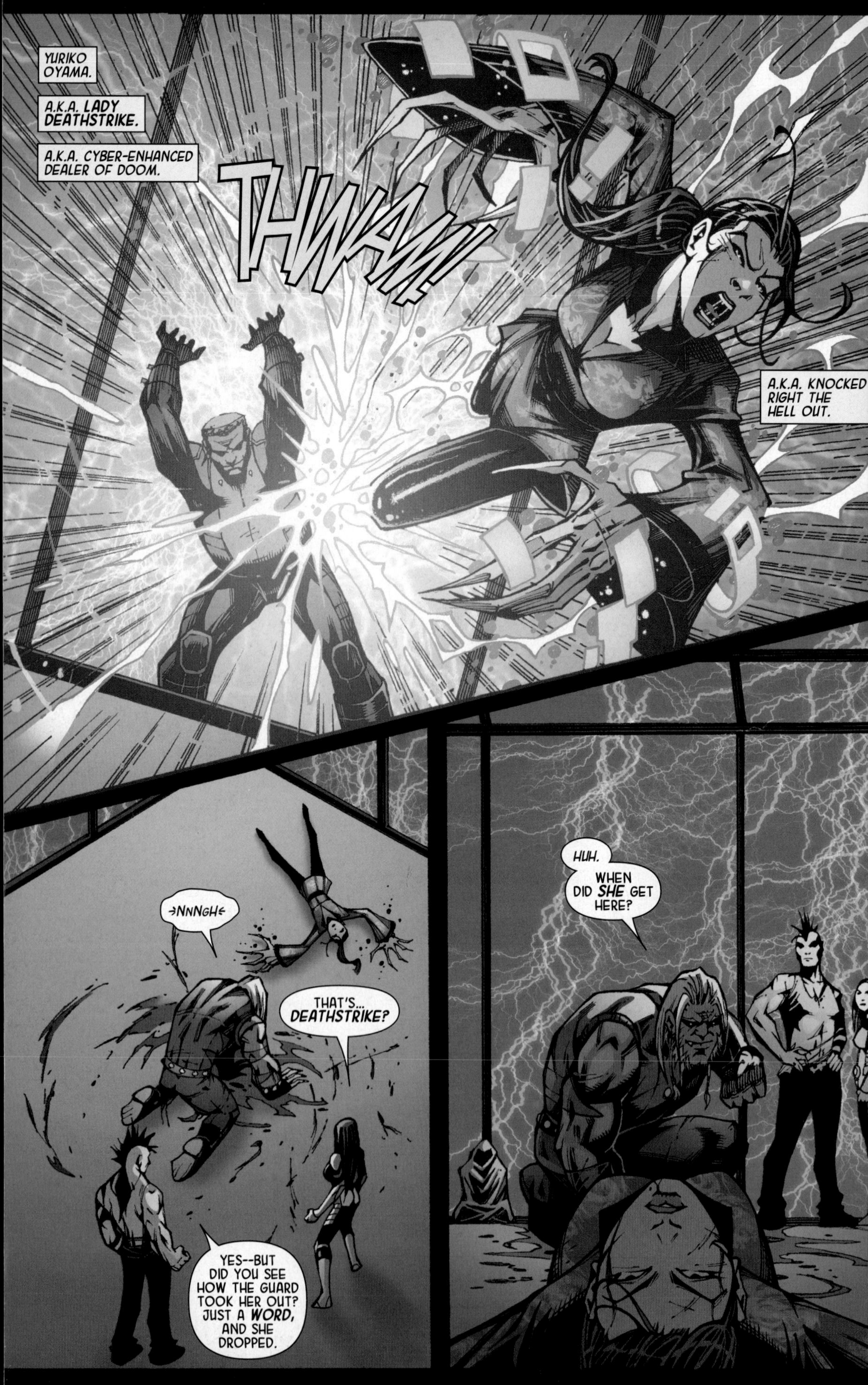

YURIKO OYAMA.
A.K.A. LADY DEATHSTRIKE.
A.K.A. CYBER-ENHANCED DEALER OF DOOM.
THWAM!
A.K.A. KNOCKED RIGHT THE HELL OUT.
›NNNGH‹
THAT'S... DEATHSTRIKE?
YES--BUT DID YOU SEE HOW THE GUARD TOOK HER OUT? JUST A WORD, AND SHE DROPPED.
HUH.
WHEN DID SHE GET HERE?

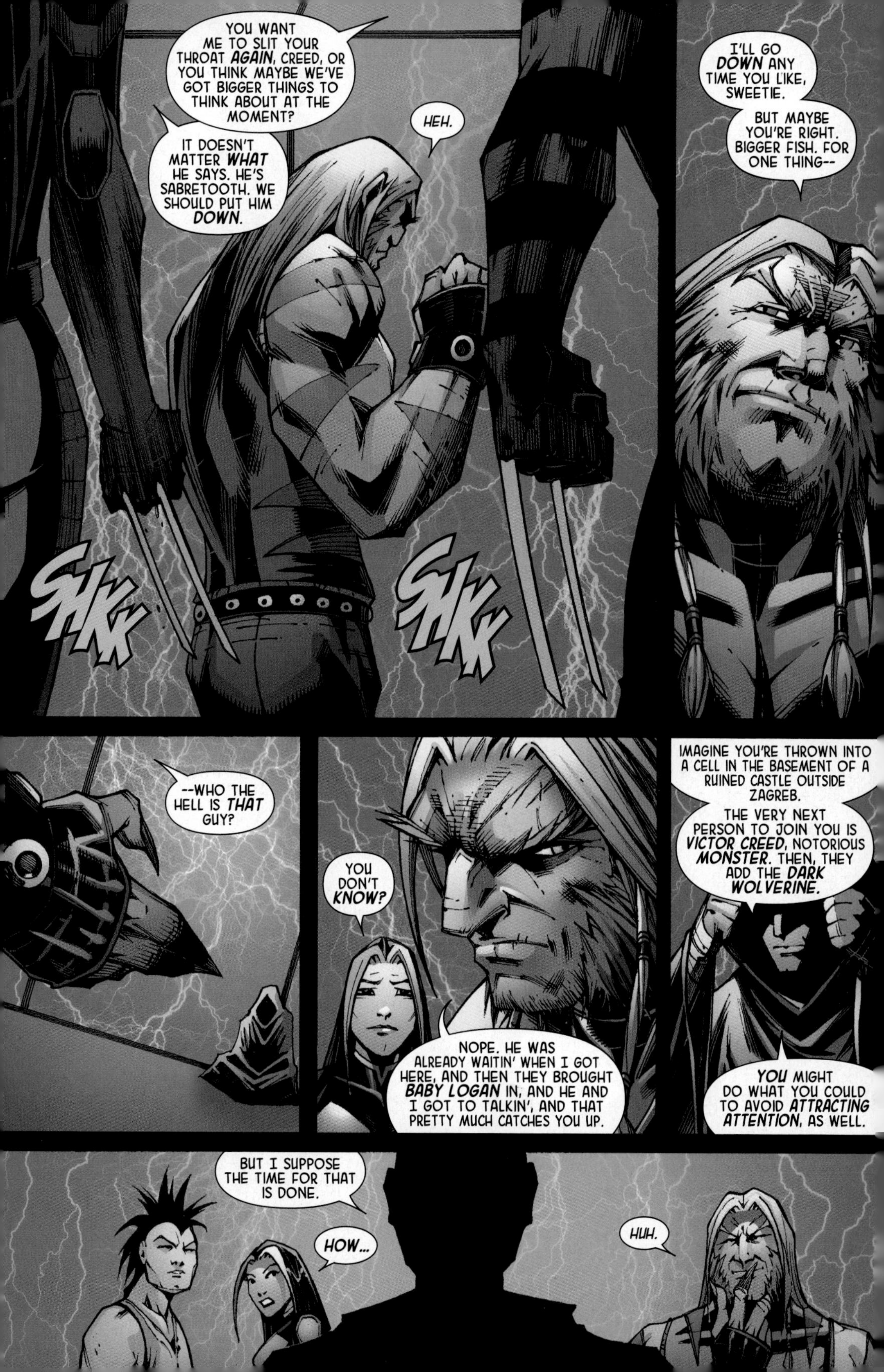
YOU WANT ME TO SLIT YOUR THROAT AGAIN, CREED, OR YOU THINK MAYBE WE'VE GOT BIGGER THINGS TO THINK ABOUT AT THE MOMENT?
IT DOESN'T MATTER WHAT HE SAYS. HE'S SABRETOOTH. WE SHOULD PUT HIM DOWN.
HEH.
SHKK
SHKK
I'LL GO DOWN ANY TIME YOU LIKE, SWEETIE.
BUT MAYBE YOU'RE RIGHT. BIGGER FISH. FOR ONE THING--
--WHO THE HELL IS THAT GUY?
YOU DON'T KNOW?
NOPE. HE WAS ALREADY WAITIN' WHEN I GOT HERE, AND THEN THEY BROUGHT BABY LOGAN IN, AND HE AND I GOT TO TALKIN', AND THAT PRETTY MUCH CATCHES YOU UP.
IMAGINE YOU'RE THROWN INTO A CELL IN THE BASEMENT OF A RUINED CASTLE OUTSIDE ZAGREB.
THE VERY NEXT PERSON TO JOIN YOU IS VICTOR CREED, NOTORIOUS MONSTER. THEN, THEY ADD THE DARK WOLVERINE.
YOU MIGHT DO WHAT YOU COULD TO AVOID ATTRACTING ATTENTION, AS WELL.
BUT I SUPPOSE THE TIME FOR THAT IS DONE.
HOW...
HUH.

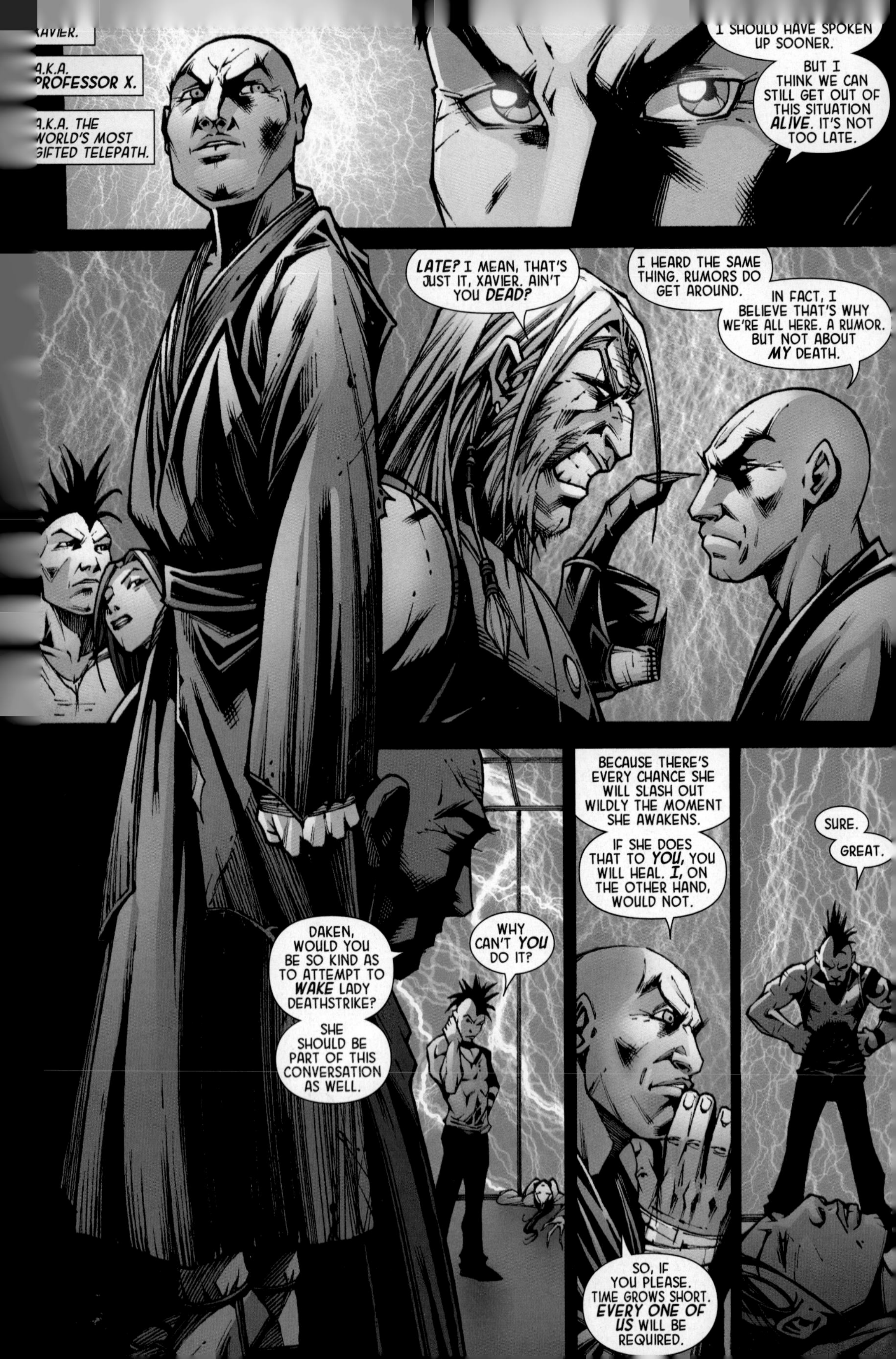
XAVIER.
A.K.A. PROFESSOR X.
A.K.A. THE WORLD'S MOST GIFTED TELEPATH.
I SHOULD HAVE SPOKEN UP SOONER.
BUT I THINK WE CAN STILL GET OUT OF THIS SITUATION ALIVE. IT'S NOT TOO LATE.
LATE? I MEAN, THAT'S JUST IT, XAVIER. AIN'T YOU DEAD?
I HEARD THE SAME THING. RUMORS DO GET AROUND.
IN FACT, I BELIEVE THAT'S WHY WE'RE ALL HERE. A RUMOR. BUT NOT ABOUT MY DEATH.
DAKEN, WOULD YOU BE SO KIND AS TO ATTEMPT TO WAKE LADY DEATHSTRIKE?
SHE SHOULD BE PART OF THIS CONVERSATION AS WELL.
WHY CAN'T YOU DO IT?
BECAUSE THERE'S EVERY CHANCE SHE WILL SLASH OUT WILDLY THE MOMENT SHE AWAKENS.
IF SHE DOES THAT TO YOU, YOU WILL HEAL. I, ON THE OTHER HAND, WOULD NOT.
SO, IF YOU PLEASE. TIME GROWS SHORT. EVERY ONE OF US WILL BE REQUIRED.
SURE.
GREAT.

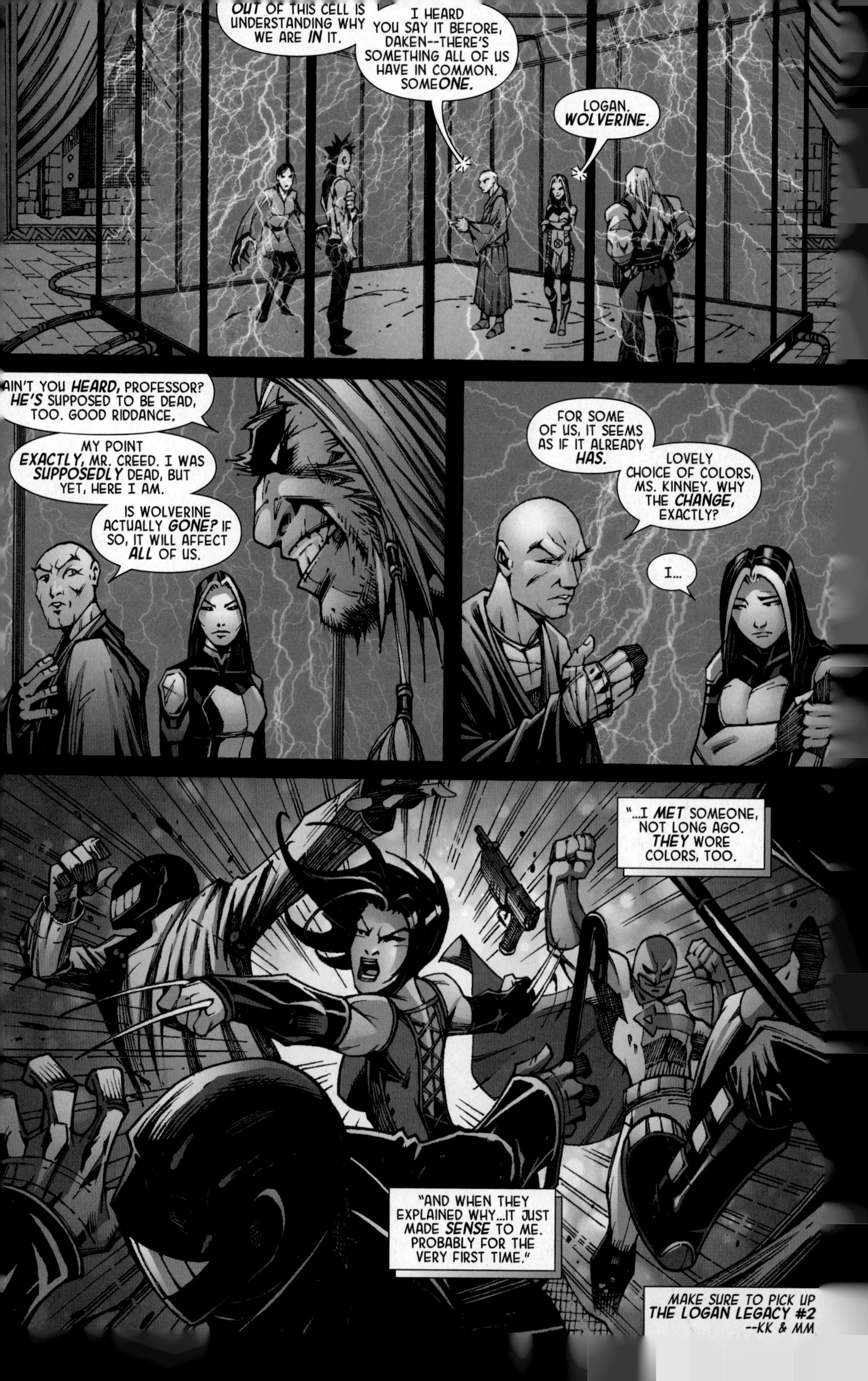
OUT OF THIS CELL IS UNDERSTANDING WHY WE ARE IN IT.
I HEARD YOU SAY IT BEFORE, DAKEN--THERE'S SOMETHING ALL OF US HAVE IN COMMON. SOMEONE.
LOGAN. WOLVERINE.
AIN'T YOU HEARD, PROFESSOR? HE'S SUPPOSED TO BE DEAD, TOO. GOOD RIDDANCE.
MY POINT EXACTLY, MR. CREED. I WAS SUPPOSEDLY DEAD, BUT YET, HERE I AM.
IS WOLVERINE ACTUALLY GONE? IF SO, IT WILL AFFECT ALL OF US.
FOR SOME OF US, IT SEEMS AS IF IT ALREADY HAS.
LOVELY CHOICE OF COLORS, MS. KINNEY. WHY THE CHANGE, EXACTLY?
I...
"...I MET SOMEONE, NOT LONG AGO. THEY WORE COLORS, TOO.
"AND WHEN THEY EXPLAINED WHY...IT JUST MADE SENSE TO ME. PROBABLY FOR THE VERY FIRST TIME."
MAKE SURE TO PICK UP THE LOGAN LEGACY #2
--KK & MM

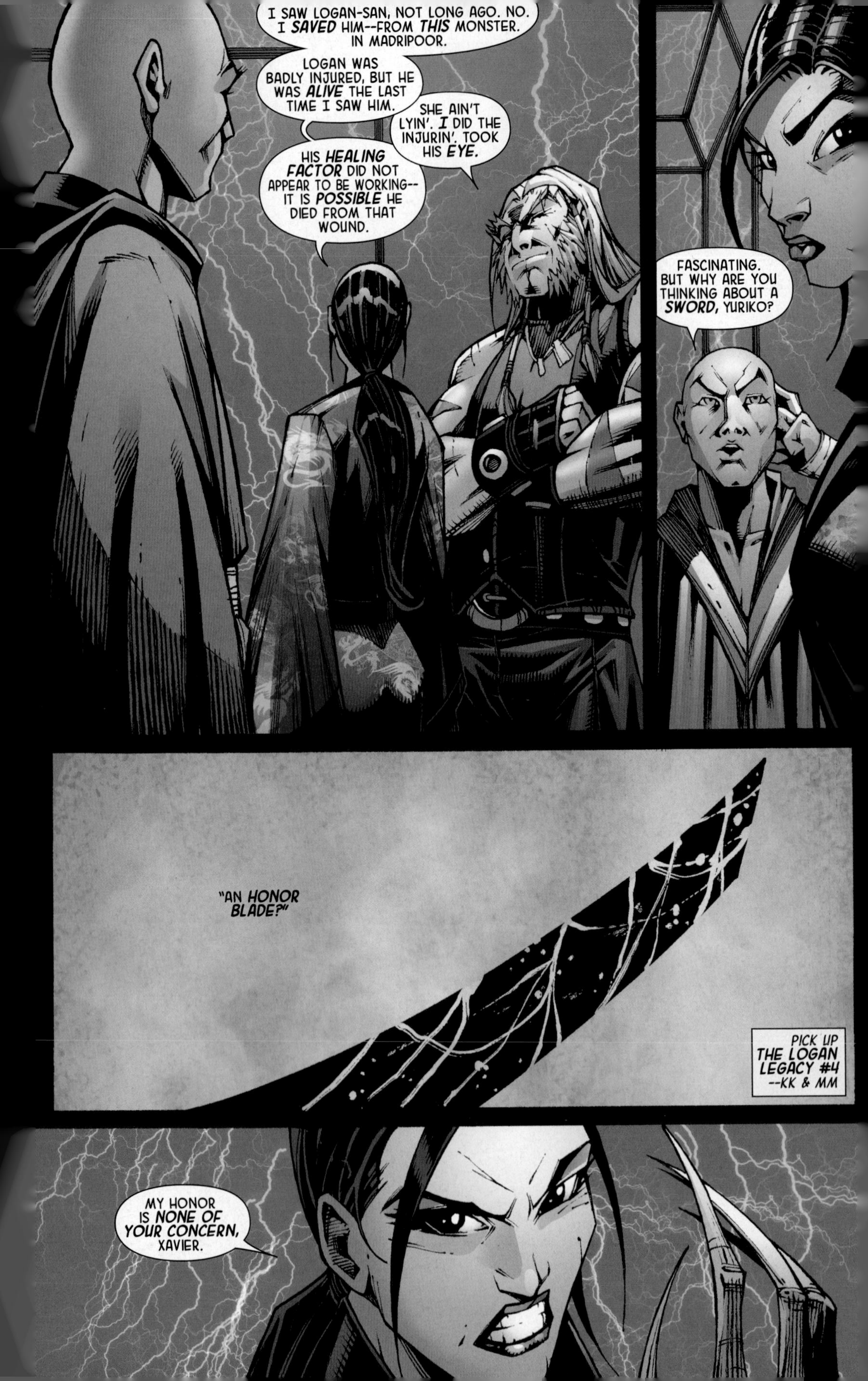
I SAW LOGAN-SAN, NOT LONG AGO. NO. I SAVED HIM--FROM THIS MONSTER. IN MADRIPOOR.
LOGAN WAS BADLY INJURED, BUT HE WAS ALIVE THE LAST TIME I SAW HIM.
SHE AIN'T LYIN'. I DID THE INJURIN'. TOOK HIS EYE.
HIS HEALING FACTOR DID NOT APPEAR TO BE WORKING-- IT IS POSSIBLE HE DIED FROM THAT WOUND.
FASCINATING. BUT WHY ARE YOU THINKING ABOUT A SWORD, YURIKO?
"AN HONOR BLADE?"
PICK UP THE LOGAN LEGACY #4 --KK & MM
MY HONOR IS NONE OF YOUR CONCERN, XAVIER.

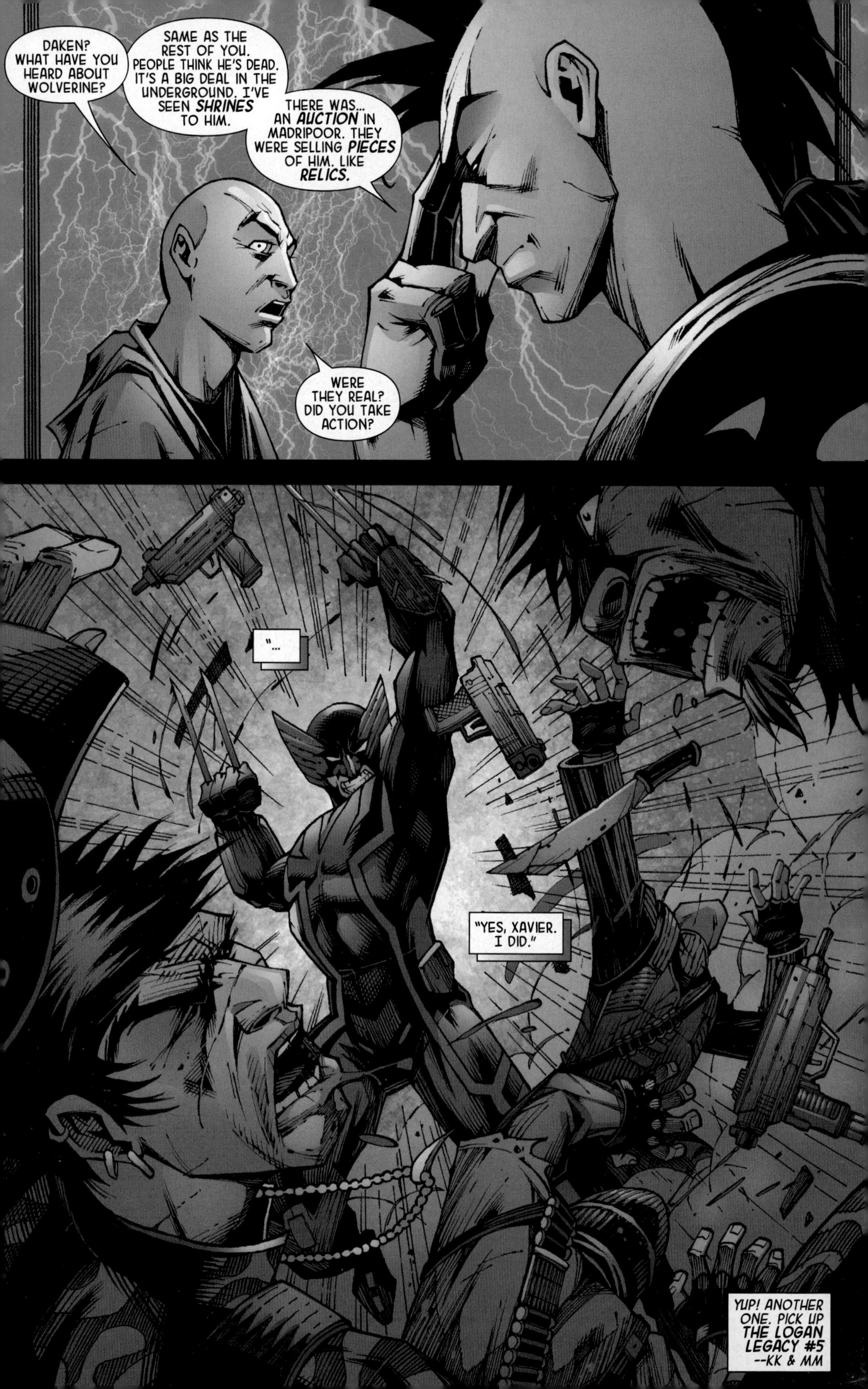
DAKEN? WHAT HAVE YOU HEARD ABOUT WOLVERINE?
SAME AS THE REST OF YOU. PEOPLE THINK HE'S DEAD. IT'S A BIG DEAL IN THE UNDERGROUND. I'VE SEEN SHRINES TO HIM.
THERE WAS... AN AUCTION IN MADRIPOOR. THEY WERE SELLING PIECES OF HIM. LIKE RELICS.
WERE THEY REAL? DID YOU TAKE ACTION?
"...
"YES, XAVIER. I DID."
YUP! ANOTHER ONE. PICK UP THE LOGAN LEGACY #5 --KK & MM

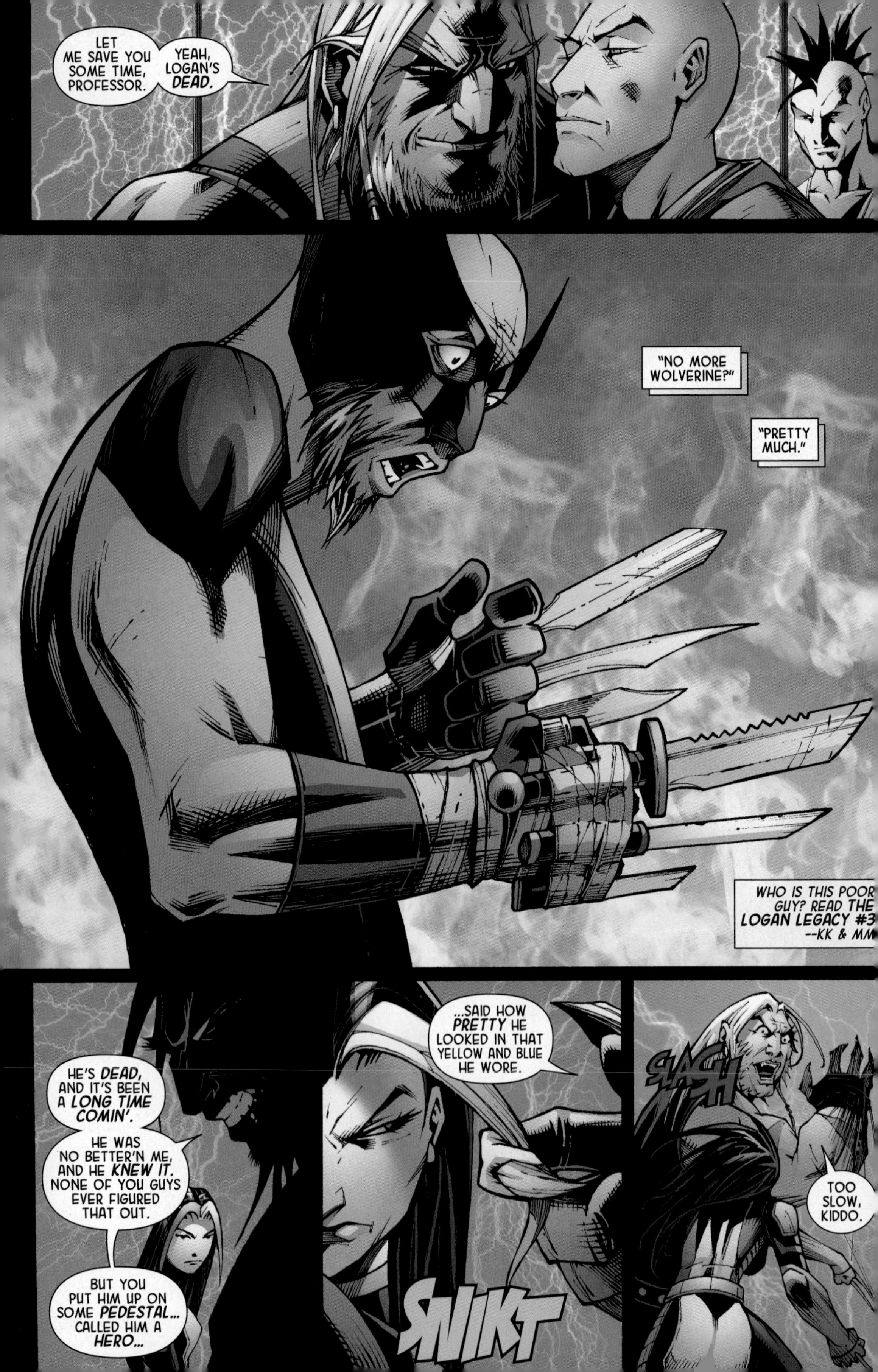

LET ME SAVE YOU SOME TIME, PROFESSOR.
YEAH, LOGAN'S *DEAD.*
"NO MORE WOLVERINE?"
"PRETTY MUCH."
WHO IS THIS POOR GUY? READ **THE LOGAN LEGACY #3** --KK & MM
HE'S *DEAD,* AND IT'S BEEN A *LONG TIME COMIN'.*
HE WAS NO BETTER'N ME, AND HE *KNEW IT.* NONE OF YOU GUYS EVER FIGURED THAT OUT.
BUT YOU PUT HIM UP ON SOME *PEDESTAL*... CALLED HIM A *HERO*...
...SAID HOW *PRETTY* HE LOOKED IN THAT YELLOW AND BLUE HE WORE.
SNIKT
SLASH
TOO SLOW, KIDDO.

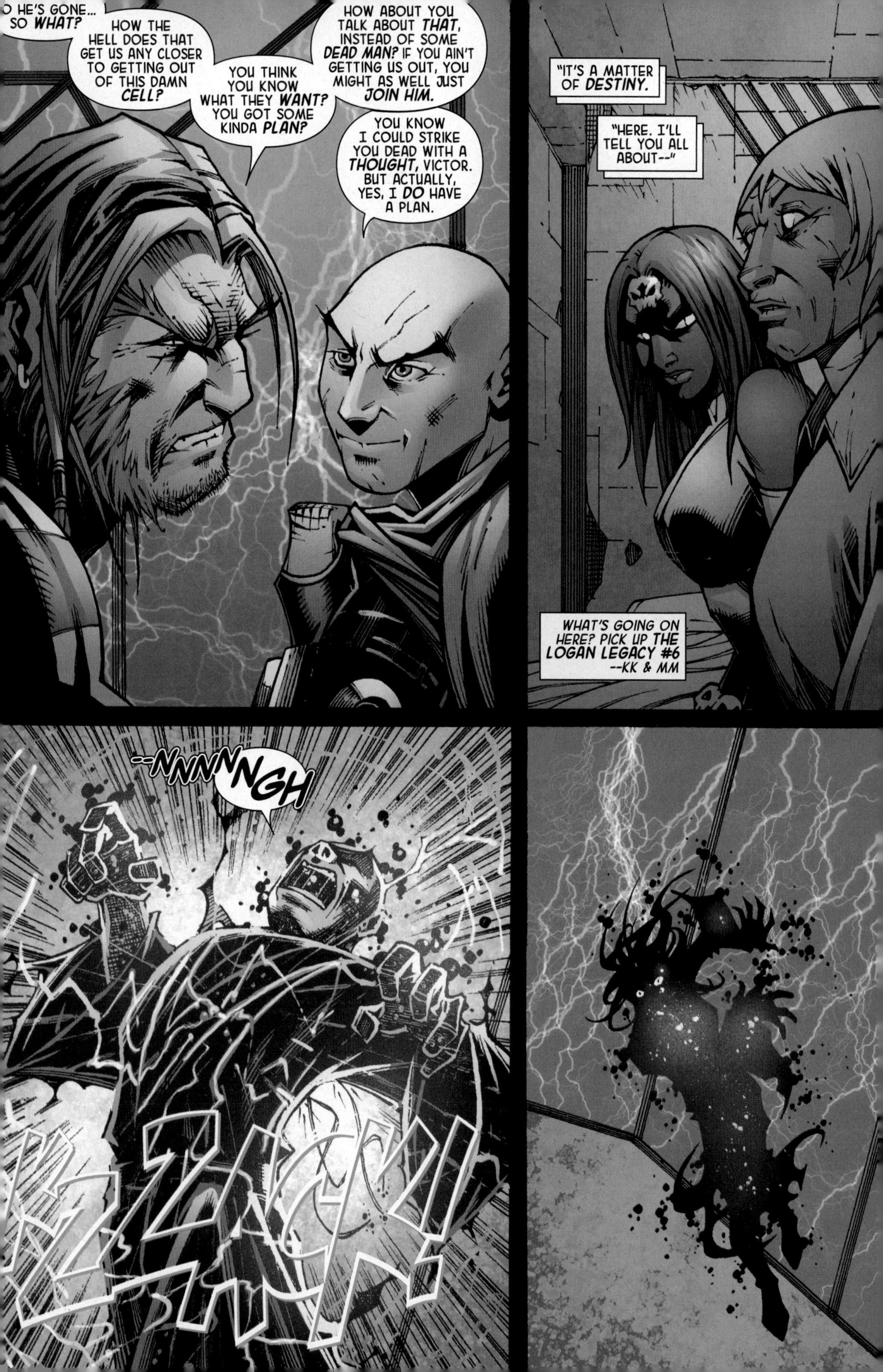

O HE'S GONE... SO WHAT?
HOW THE HELL DOES THAT GET US ANY CLOSER TO GETTING OUT OF THIS DAMN CELL?
YOU THINK YOU KNOW WHAT THEY WANT? YOU GOT SOME KINDA PLAN?
HOW ABOUT YOU TALK ABOUT THAT, INSTEAD OF SOME DEAD MAN? IF YOU AIN'T GETTING US OUT, YOU MIGHT AS WELL JUST JOIN HIM.
YOU KNOW I COULD STRIKE YOU DEAD WITH A THOUGHT, VICTOR. BUT ACTUALLY, YES, I DO HAVE A PLAN.
"IT'S A MATTER OF DESTINY.
"HERE. I'LL TELL YOU ALL ABOUT--"
WHAT'S GOING ON HERE? PICK UP THE LOGAN LEGACY #6 --KK & MM
--NNNNNGH
KZZAK!!

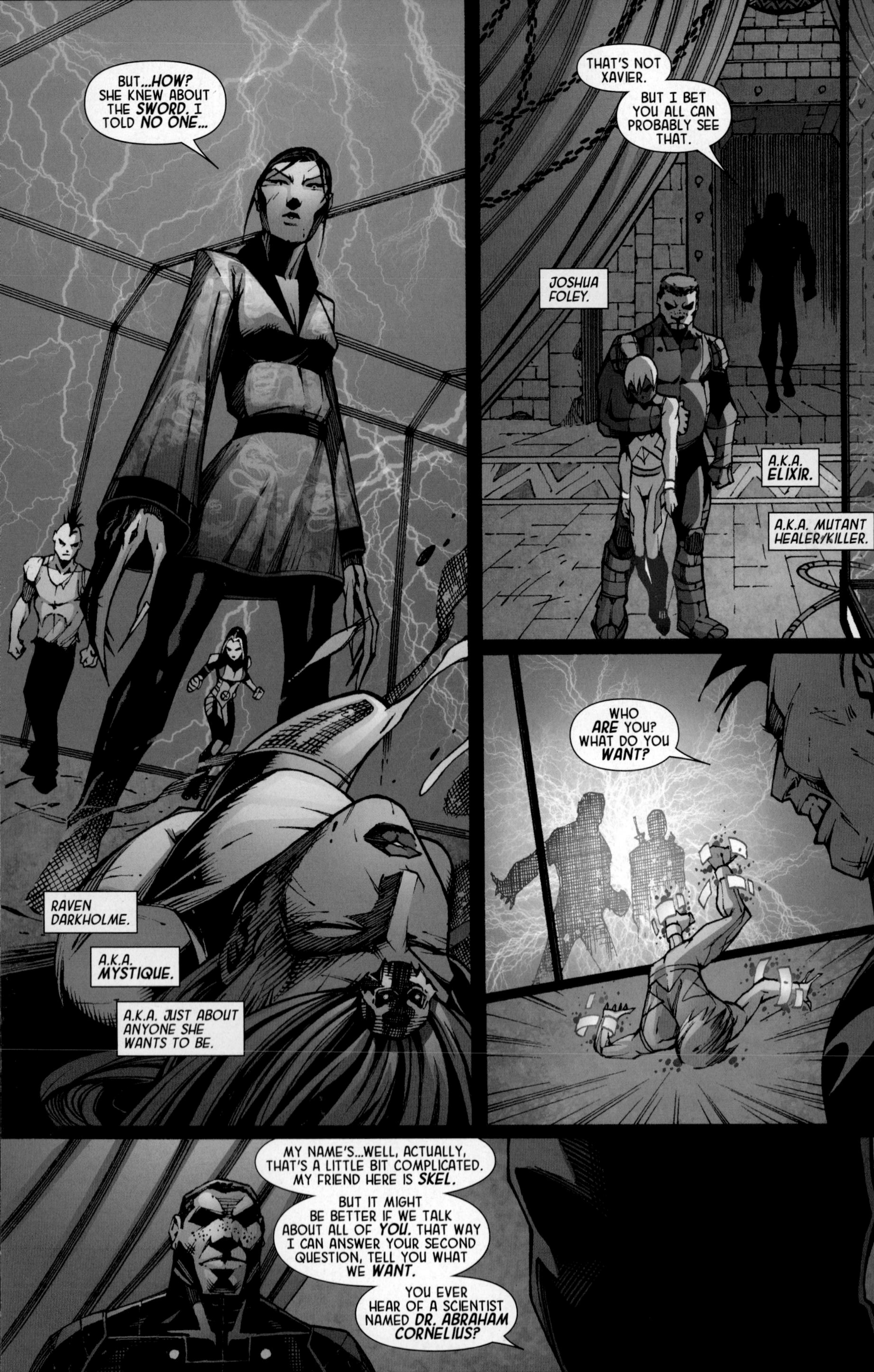
BUT...HOW? SHE KNEW ABOUT THE SWORD. I TOLD NO ONE...
RAVEN DARKHOLME.
A.K.A. MYSTIQUE.
A.K.A. JUST ABOUT ANYONE SHE WANTS TO BE.
THAT'S NOT XAVIER.
BUT I BET YOU ALL CAN PROBABLY SEE THAT.
JOSHUA FOLEY.
A.K.A. ELIXIR.
A.K.A. MUTANT HEALER/KILLER.
WHO ARE YOU? WHAT DO YOU WANT?
MY NAME'S...WELL, ACTUALLY, THAT'S A LITTLE BIT COMPLICATED. MY FRIEND HERE IS SKEL.
BUT IT MIGHT BE BETTER IF WE TALK ABOUT ALL OF YOU. THAT WAY I CAN ANSWER YOUR SECOND QUESTION, TELL YOU WHAT WE WANT.
YOU EVER HEAR OF A SCIENTIST NAMED DR. ABRAHAM CORNELIUS?

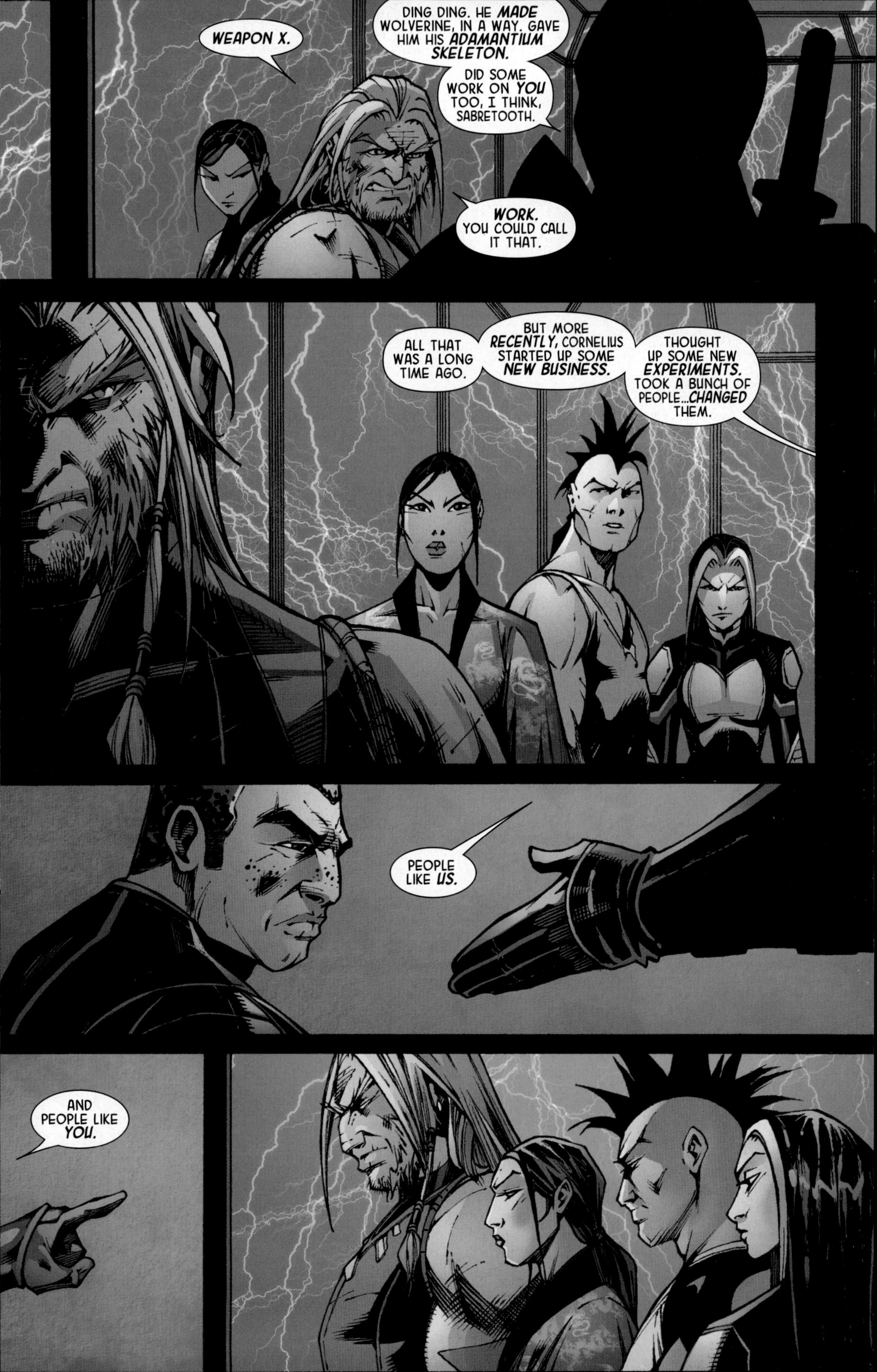
WEAPON X.
DING DING. HE MADE WOLVERINE, IN A WAY. GAVE HIM HIS ADAMANTIUM SKELETON.
DID SOME WORK ON YOU TOO, I THINK, SABRETOOTH.
WORK. YOU COULD CALL IT THAT.
ALL THAT WAS A LONG TIME AGO.
BUT MORE RECENTLY, CORNELIUS STARTED UP SOME NEW BUSINESS.
THOUGHT UP SOME NEW EXPERIMENTS. TOOK A BUNCH OF PEOPLE...CHANGED THEM.
PEOPLE LIKE US.
AND PEOPLE LIKE YOU.

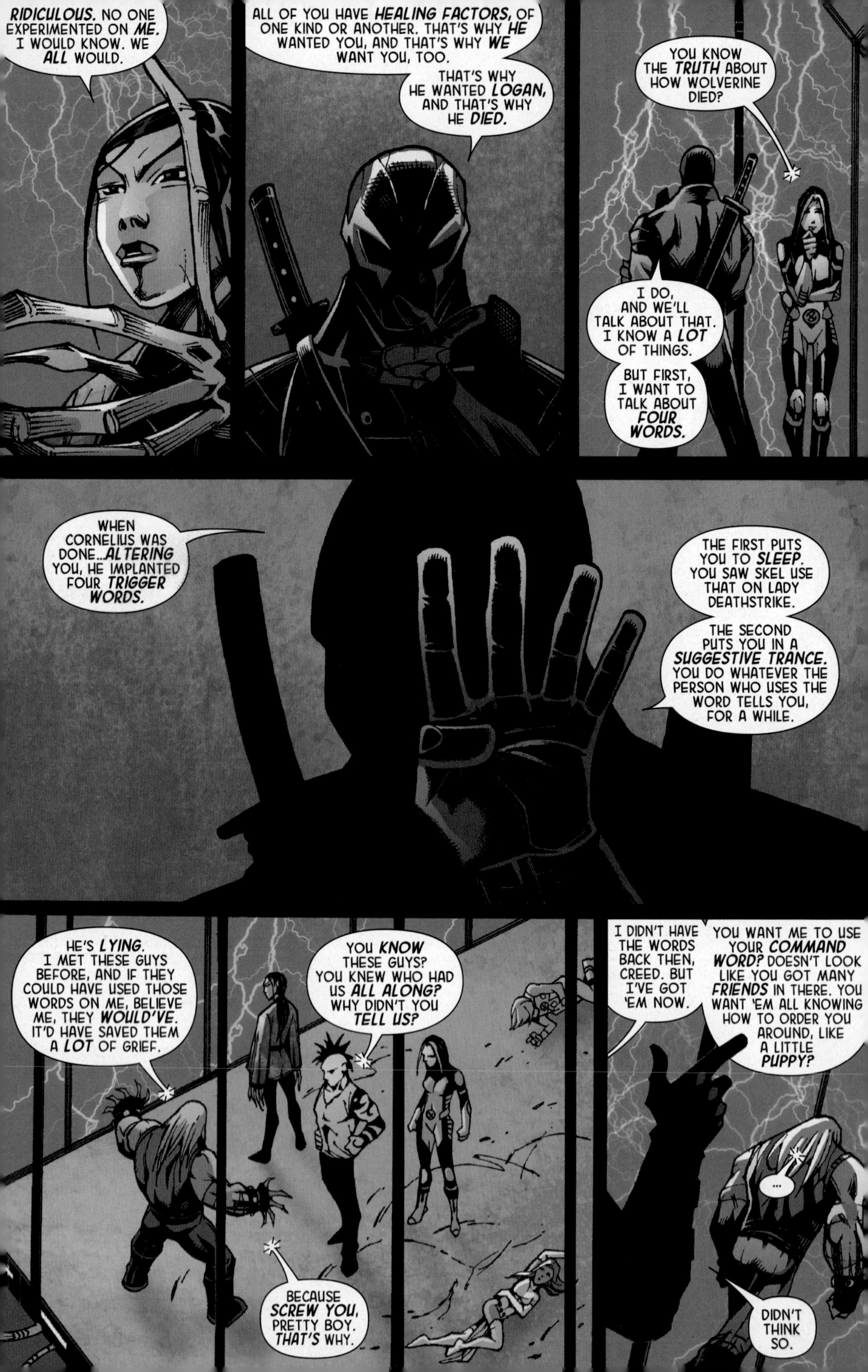
RIDICULOUS. NO ONE EXPERIMENTED ON ME. I WOULD KNOW. WE ALL WOULD.
ALL OF YOU HAVE HEALING FACTORS, OF ONE KIND OR ANOTHER. THAT'S WHY HE WANTED YOU, AND THAT'S WHY WE WANT YOU, TOO.
THAT'S WHY HE WANTED LOGAN, AND THAT'S WHY HE DIED.
YOU KNOW THE TRUTH ABOUT HOW WOLVERINE DIED?
I DO, AND WE'LL TALK ABOUT THAT. I KNOW A LOT OF THINGS.
BUT FIRST, I WANT TO TALK ABOUT FOUR WORDS.
WHEN CORNELIUS WAS DONE...ALTERING YOU, HE IMPLANTED FOUR TRIGGER WORDS.
THE FIRST PUTS YOU TO SLEEP. YOU SAW SKEL USE THAT ON LADY DEATHSTRIKE.
THE SECOND PUTS YOU IN A SUGGESTIVE TRANCE. YOU DO WHATEVER THE PERSON WHO USES THE WORD TELLS YOU, FOR A WHILE.
HE'S LYING. I MET THESE GUYS BEFORE, AND IF THEY COULD HAVE USED THOSE WORDS ON ME, BELIEVE ME, THEY WOULD'VE. IT'D HAVE SAVED THEM A LOT OF GRIEF.
YOU KNOW THESE GUYS? YOU KNEW WHO HAD US ALL ALONG? WHY DIDN'T YOU TELL US?
BECAUSE SCREW YOU, PRETTY BOY. THAT'S WHY.
I DIDN'T HAVE THE WORDS BACK THEN, CREED. BUT I'VE GOT 'EM NOW.
YOU WANT ME TO USE YOUR COMMAND WORD? DOESN'T LOOK LIKE YOU GOT MANY FRIENDS IN THERE. YOU WANT 'EM ALL KNOWING HOW TO ORDER YOU AROUND, LIKE A LITTLE PUPPY?
...
DIDN'T THINK SO.

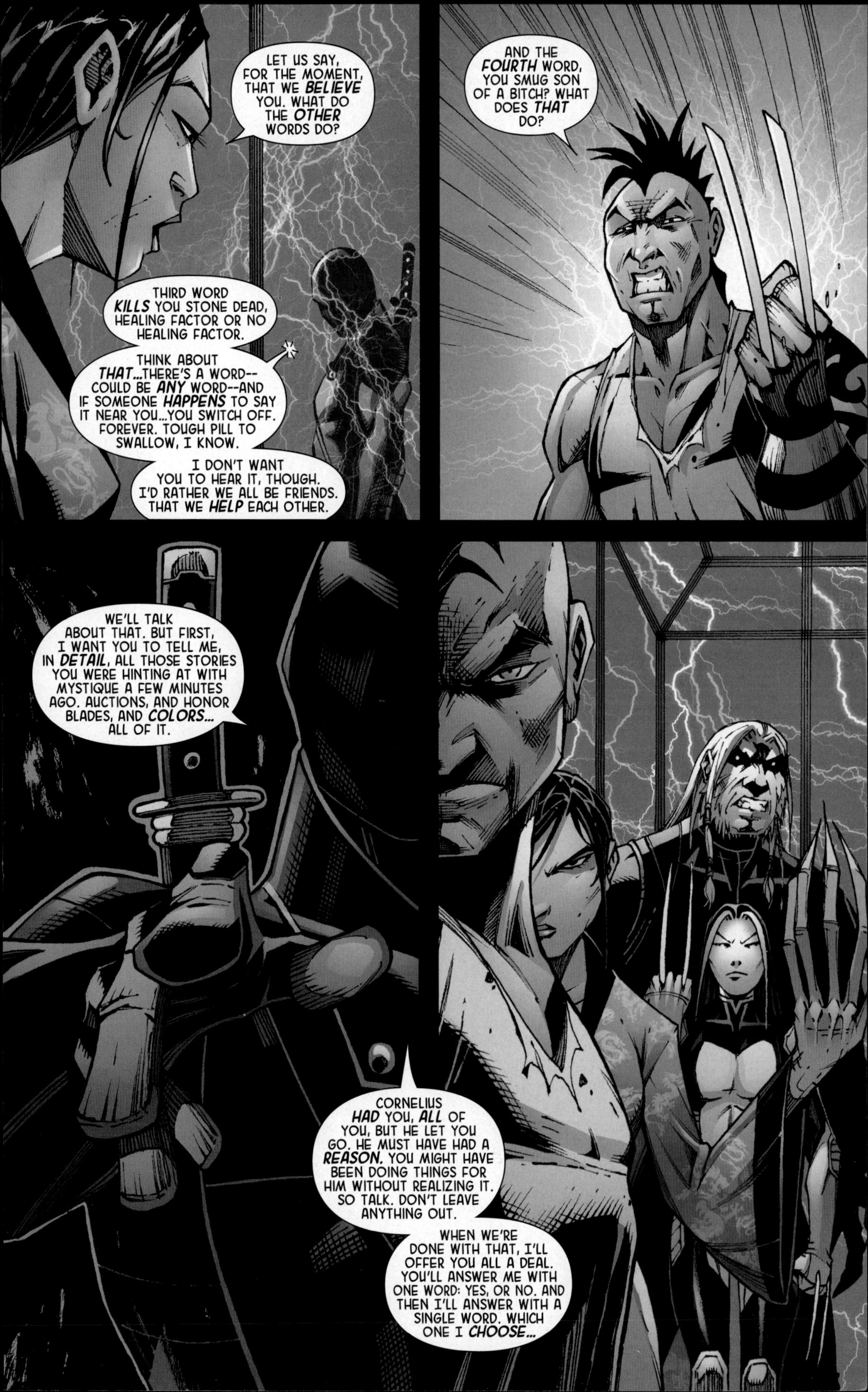
LET US SAY, FOR THE MOMENT, THAT WE BELIEVE YOU. WHAT DO THE OTHER WORDS DO?
THIRD WORD KILLS YOU STONE DEAD, HEALING FACTOR OR NO HEALING FACTOR.
THINK ABOUT THAT...THERE'S A WORD--COULD BE ANY WORD--AND IF SOMEONE HAPPENS TO SAY IT NEAR YOU...YOU SWITCH OFF. FOREVER. TOUGH PILL TO SWALLOW, I KNOW.
I DON'T WANT YOU TO HEAR IT, THOUGH. I'D RATHER WE ALL BE FRIENDS. THAT WE HELP EACH OTHER.
AND THE FOURTH WORD, YOU SMUG SON OF A BITCH? WHAT DOES THAT DO?
WE'LL TALK ABOUT THAT. BUT FIRST, I WANT YOU TO TELL ME, IN DETAIL, ALL THOSE STORIES YOU WERE HINTING AT WITH MYSTIQUE A FEW MINUTES AGO. AUCTIONS, AND HONOR BLADES, AND COLORS... ALL OF IT.
CORNELIUS HAD YOU, ALL OF YOU, BUT HE LET YOU GO. HE MUST HAVE HAD A REASON. YOU MIGHT HAVE BEEN DOING THINGS FOR HIM WITHOUT REALIZING IT. SO TALK. DON'T LEAVE ANYTHING OUT.
WHEN WE'RE DONE WITH THAT, I'LL OFFER YOU ALL A DEAL. YOU'LL ANSWER ME WITH ONE WORD: YES, OR NO. AND THEN I'LL ANSWER WITH A SINGLE WORD. WHICH ONE I CHOOSE...

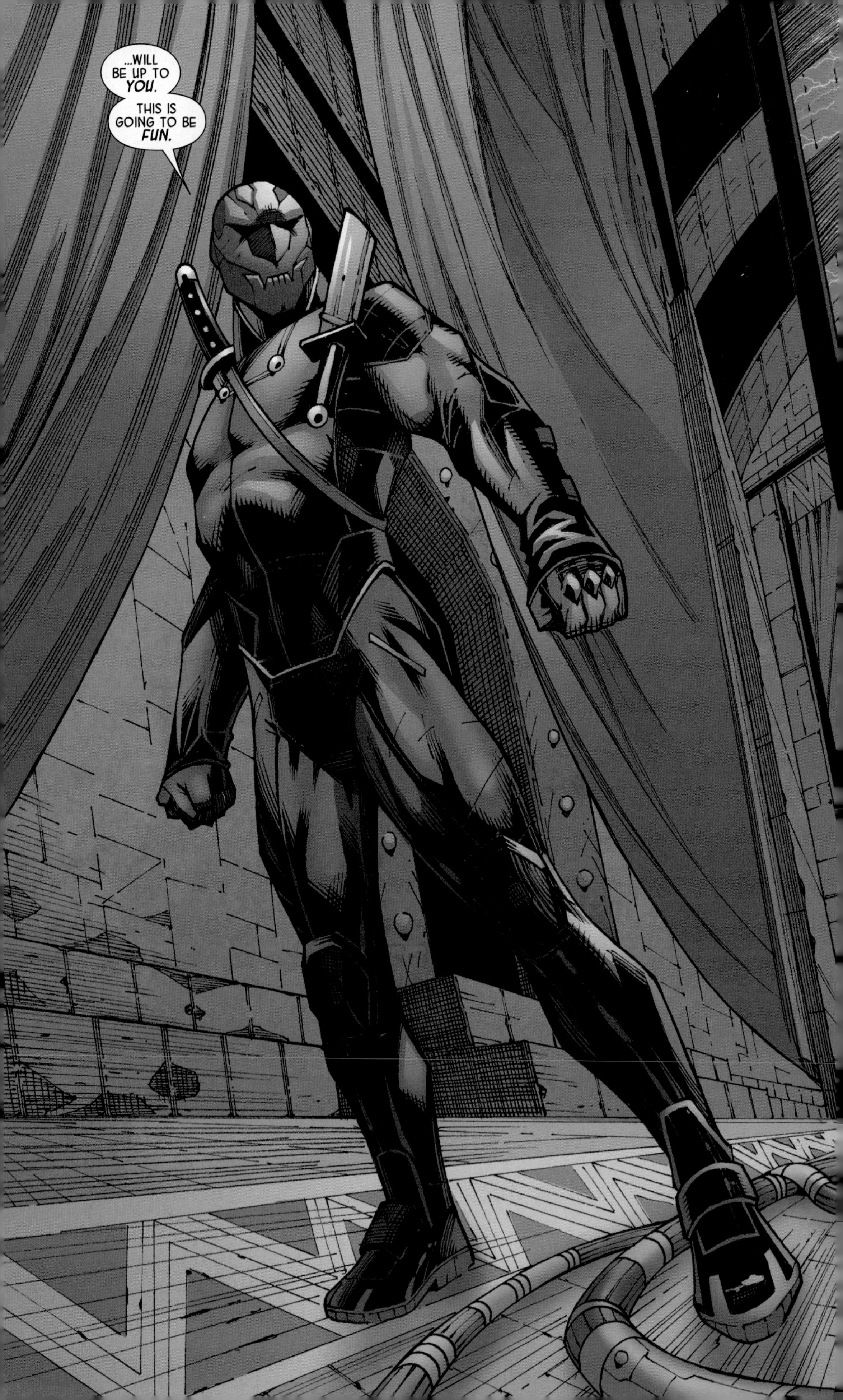
...WILL BE UP TO *YOU*.
THIS IS GOING TO BE *FUN*.

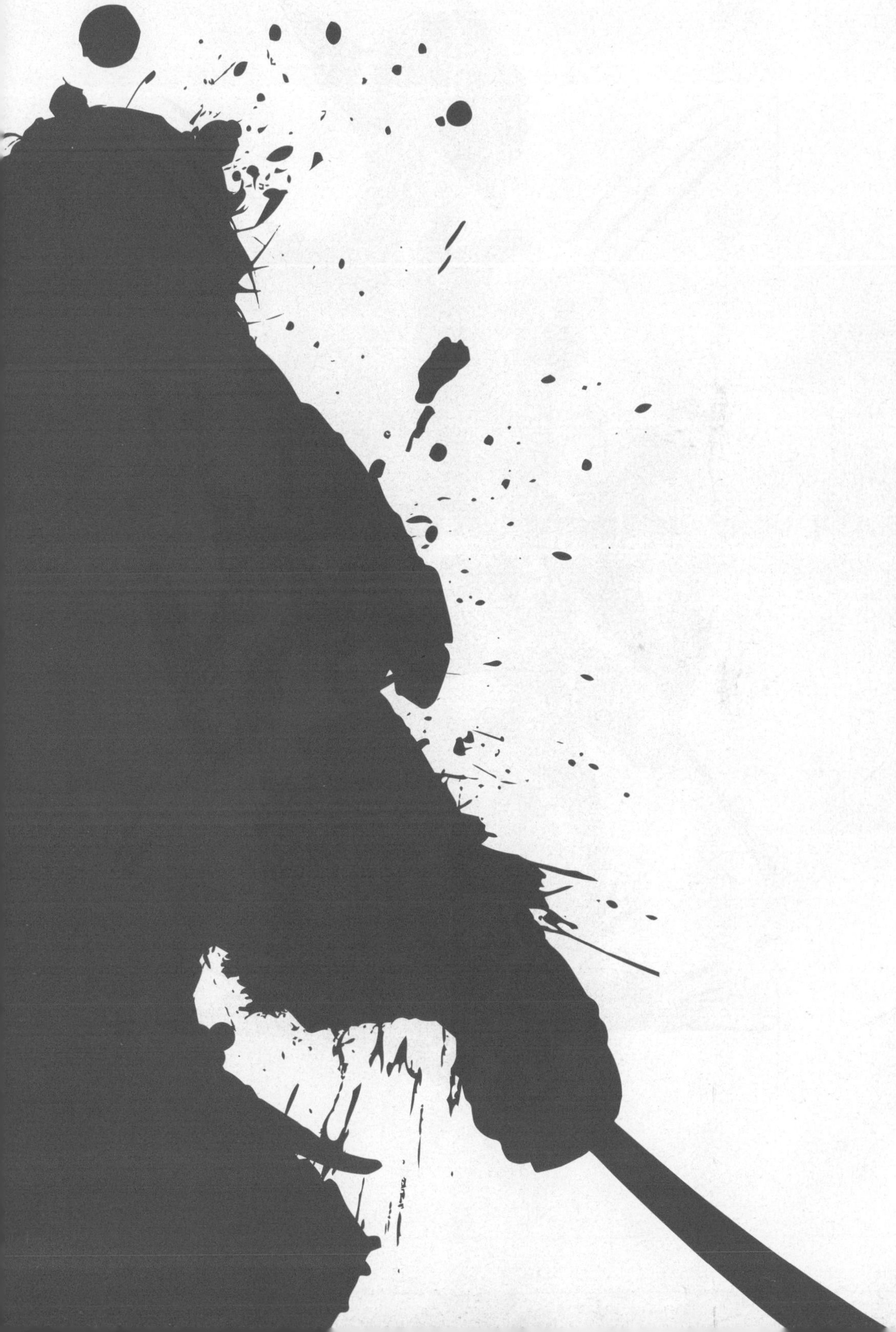

2

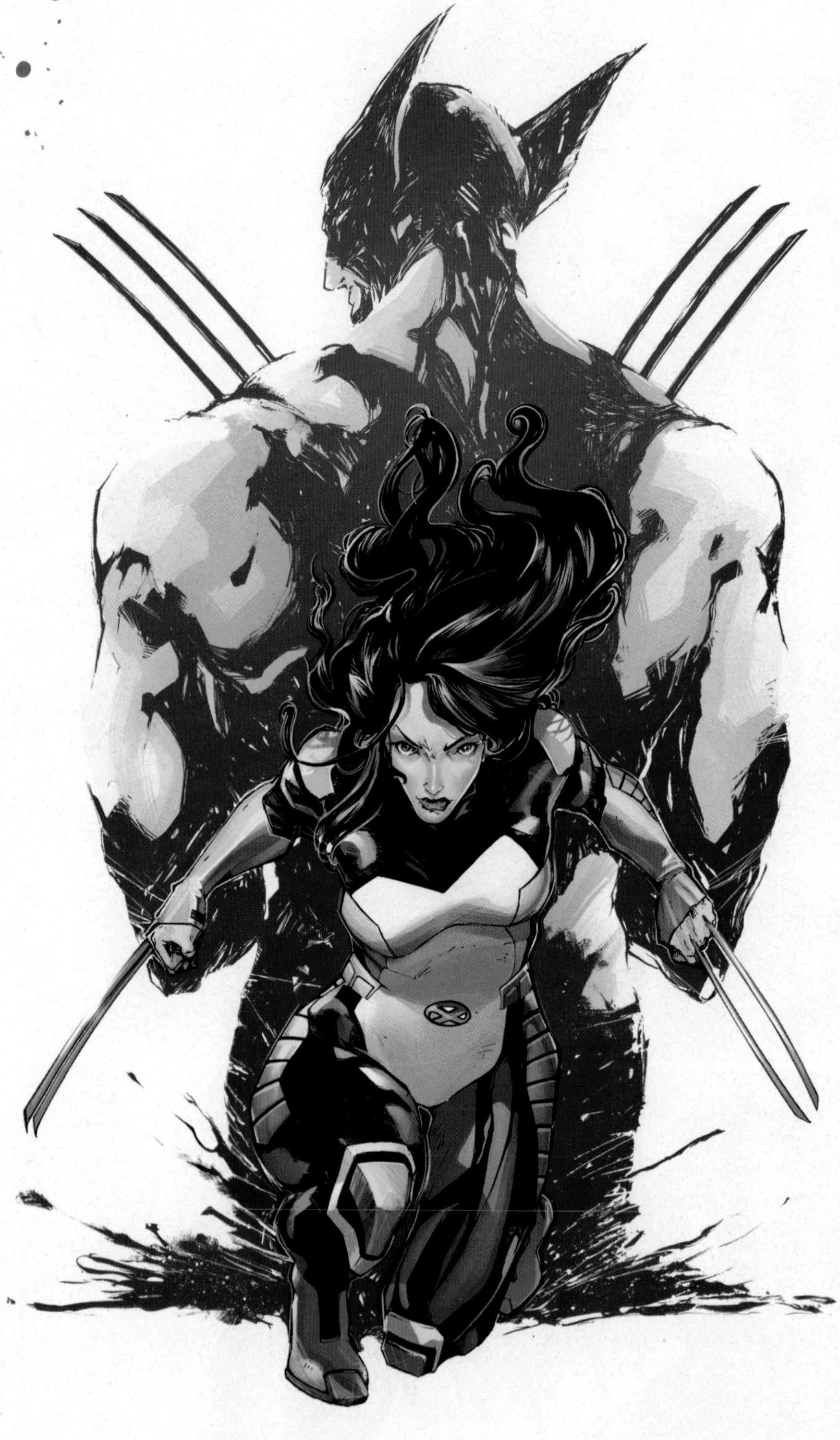

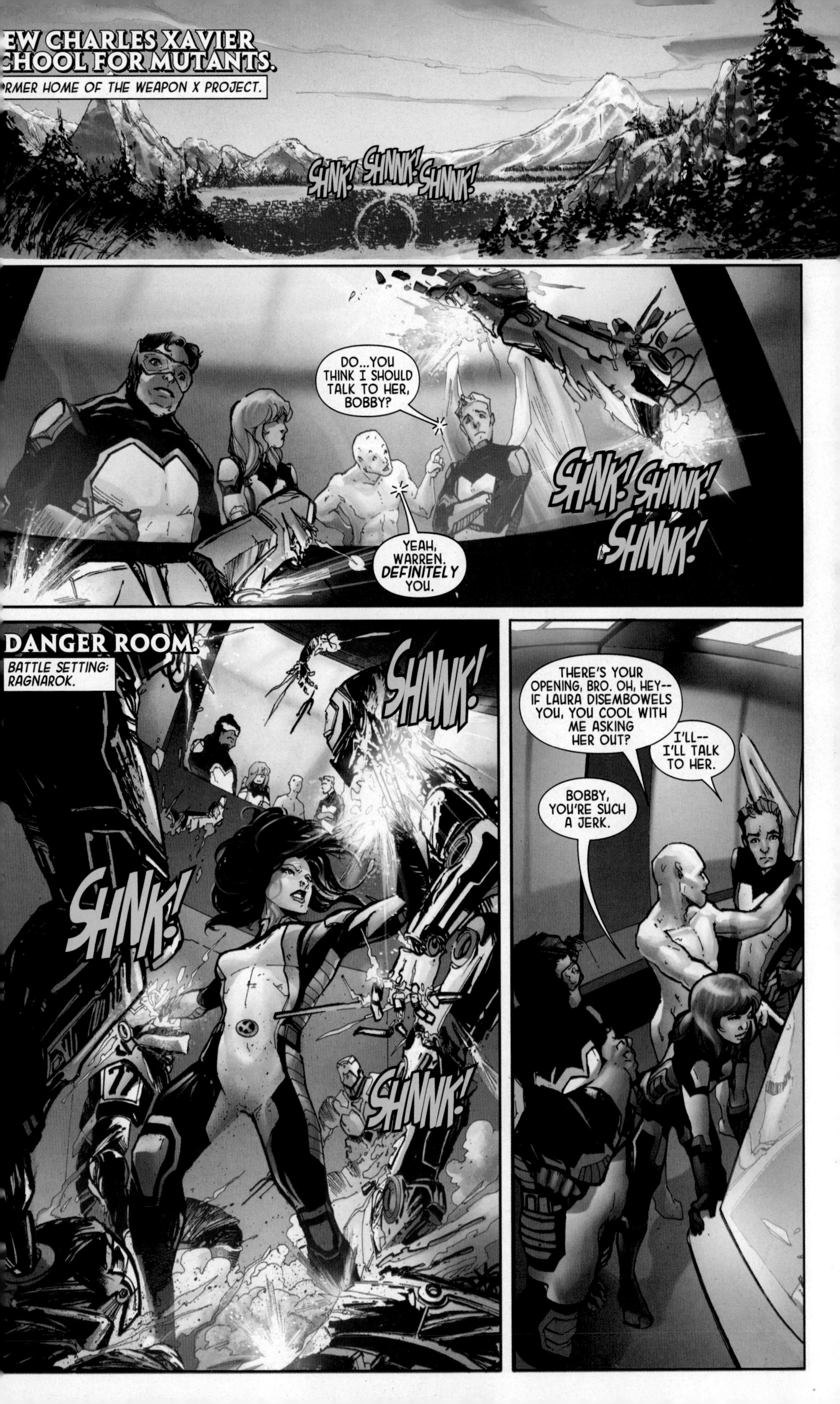

EW CHARLES XAVIER
CHOOL FOR MUTANTS.
RMER HOME OF THE WEAPON X PROJECT.
SHNK! SHNNK! SHNNK!
DO...YOU THINK I SHOULD TALK TO HER, BOBBY?
YEAH, WARREN. DEFINITELY YOU.
SHNK! SHNNK! SHNNK!
DANGER ROOM.
BATTLE SETTING: RAGNAROK.
SHNNK!
SHNK!
SHNNK!
THERE'S YOUR OPENING, BRO. OH, HEY-- IF LAURA DISEMBOWELS YOU, YOU COOL WITH ME ASKING HER OUT?
I'LL-- I'LL TALK TO HER.
BOBBY, YOU'RE SUCH A JERK.

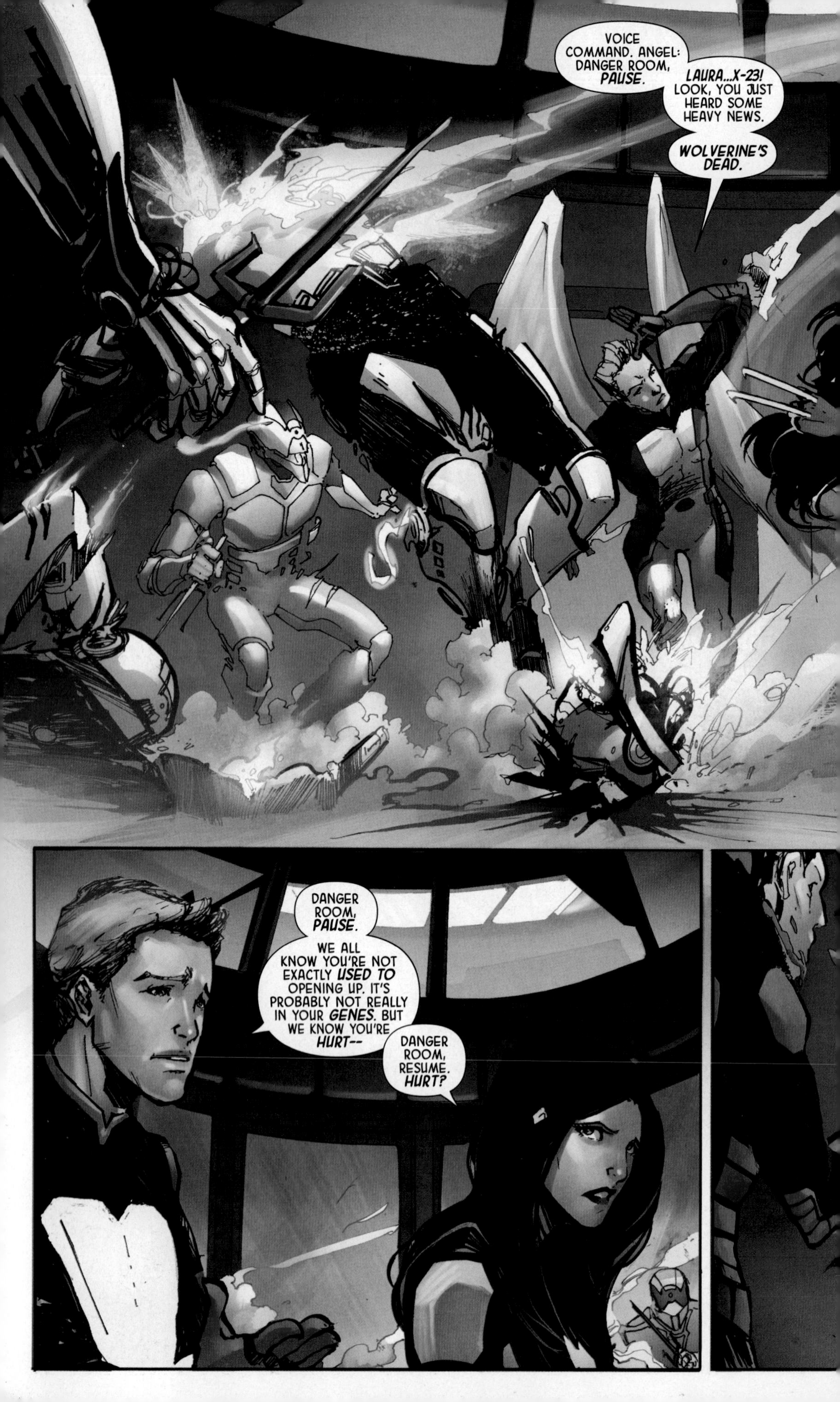
VOICE COMMAND. ANGEL: DANGER ROOM, PAUSE.
LAURA...X-23! LOOK, YOU JUST HEARD SOME HEAVY NEWS.
WOLVERINE'S DEAD.
DANGER ROOM, PAUSE.
WE ALL KNOW YOU'RE NOT EXACTLY USED TO OPENING UP. IT'S PROBABLY NOT REALLY IN YOUR GENES. BUT WE KNOW YOU'RE HURT--
DANGER ROOM, RESUME. HURT?

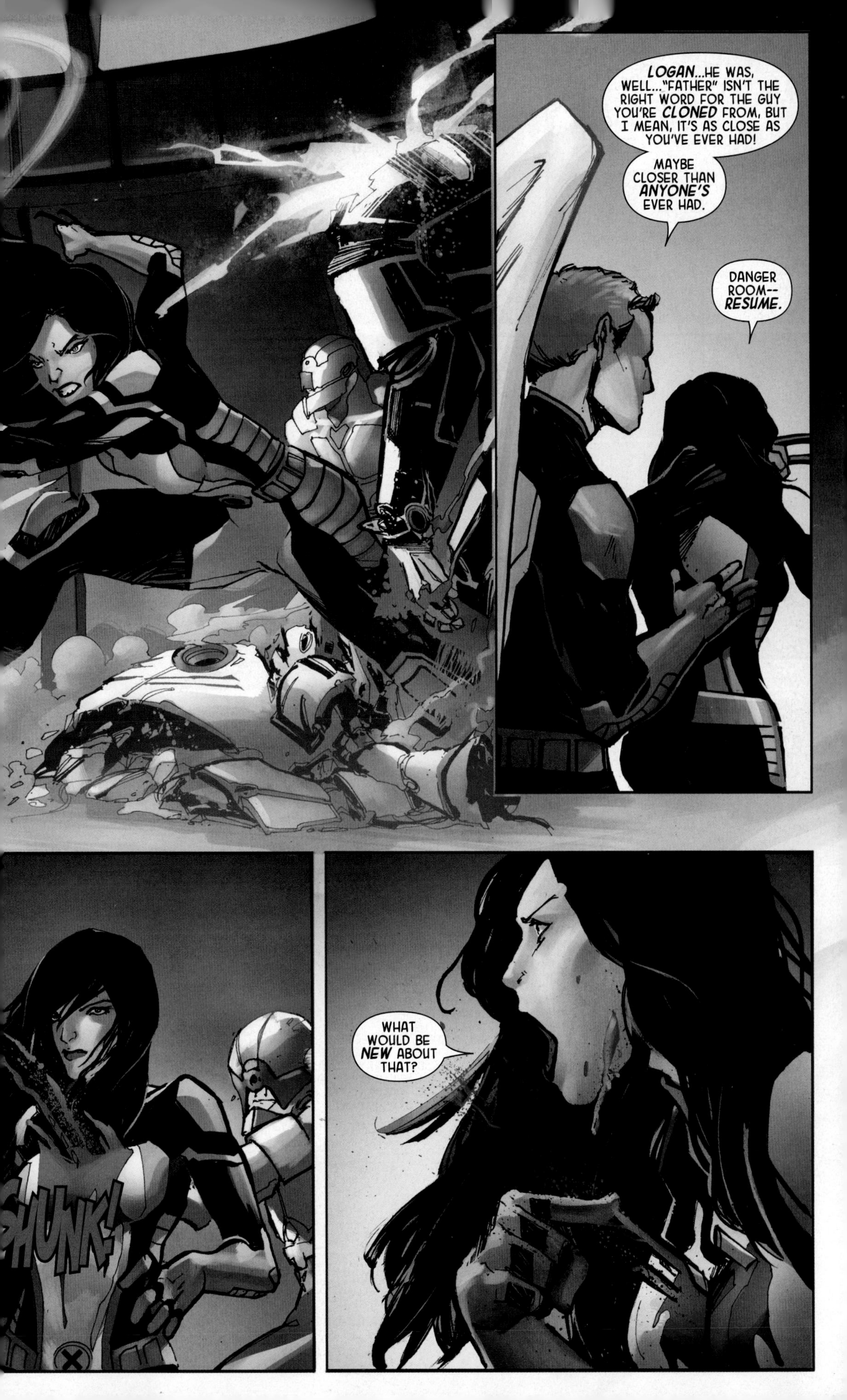
LOGAN...HE WAS, WELL..."FATHER" ISN'T THE RIGHT WORD FOR THE GUY YOU'RE CLONED FROM, BUT I MEAN, IT'S AS CLOSE AS YOU'VE EVER HAD!
MAYBE CLOSER THAN ANYONE'S EVER HAD.
DANGER ROOM-- RESUME.
SHUNK!
WHAT WOULD BE NEW ABOUT THAT?

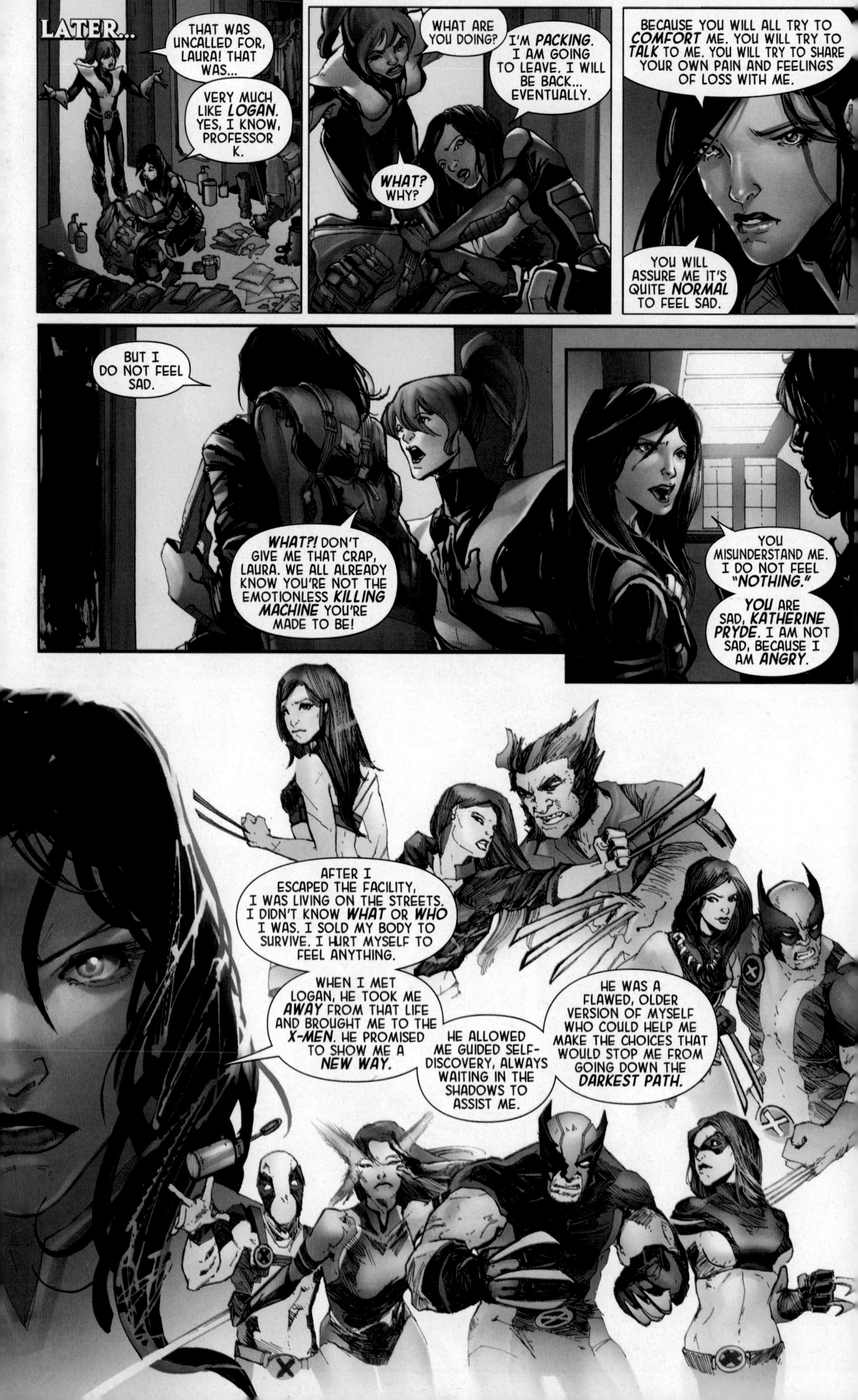
LATER...
THAT WAS UNCALLED FOR, LAURA! THAT WAS...
VERY MUCH LIKE LOGAN. YES, I KNOW, PROFESSOR K.
WHAT ARE YOU DOING?
I'M PACKING. I AM GOING TO LEAVE. I WILL BE BACK... EVENTUALLY.
WHAT? WHY?
BECAUSE YOU WILL ALL TRY TO COMFORT ME. YOU WILL TRY TO TALK TO ME. YOU WILL TRY TO SHARE YOUR OWN PAIN AND FEELINGS OF LOSS WITH ME.
YOU WILL ASSURE ME IT'S QUITE NORMAL TO FEEL SAD.
BUT I DO NOT FEEL SAD.
WHAT?! DON'T GIVE ME THAT CRAP, LAURA. WE ALL ALREADY KNOW YOU'RE NOT THE EMOTIONLESS KILLING MACHINE YOU'RE MADE TO BE!
YOU MISUNDERSTAND ME. I DO NOT FEEL "NOTHING."
YOU ARE SAD, KATHERINE PRYDE. I AM NOT SAD, BECAUSE I AM ANGRY.
AFTER I ESCAPED THE FACILITY, I WAS LIVING ON THE STREETS. I DIDN'T KNOW WHAT OR WHO I WAS. I SOLD MY BODY TO SURVIVE. I HURT MYSELF TO FEEL ANYTHING.
WHEN I MET LOGAN, HE TOOK ME AWAY FROM THAT LIFE AND BROUGHT ME TO THE X-MEN. HE PROMISED TO SHOW ME A NEW WAY.
HE ALLOWED ME GUIDED SELF-DISCOVERY, ALWAYS WAITING IN THE SHADOWS TO ASSIST ME.
HE WAS A FLAWED, OLDER VERSION OF MYSELF WHO COULD HELP ME MAKE THE CHOICES THAT WOULD STOP ME FROM GOING DOWN THE DARKEST PATH.

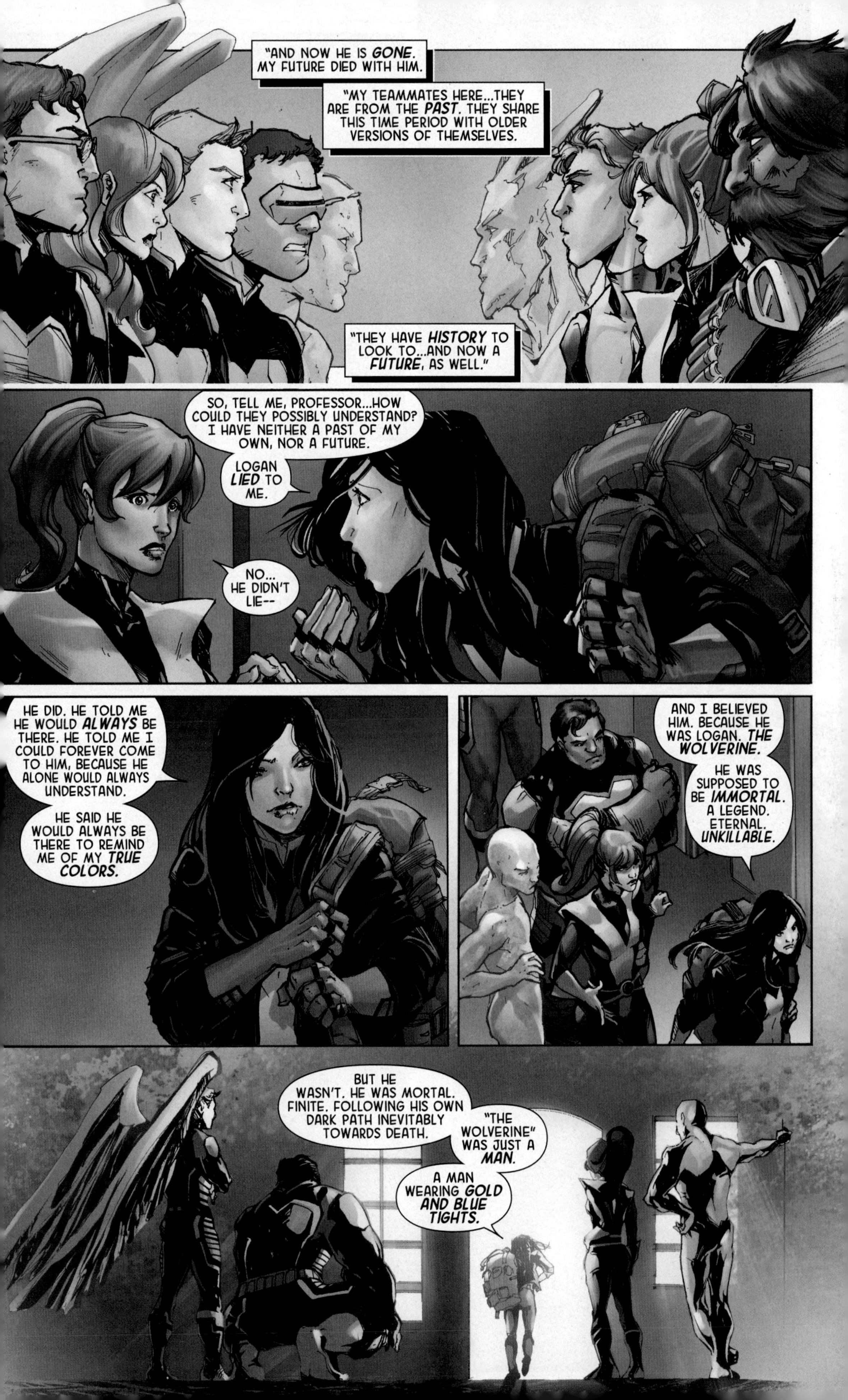
"AND NOW HE IS GONE. MY FUTURE DIED WITH HIM.
"MY TEAMMATES HERE...THEY ARE FROM THE PAST. THEY SHARE THIS TIME PERIOD WITH OLDER VERSIONS OF THEMSELVES.
"THEY HAVE HISTORY TO LOOK TO...AND NOW A FUTURE, AS WELL."
SO, TELL ME, PROFESSOR...HOW COULD THEY POSSIBLY UNDERSTAND? I HAVE NEITHER A PAST OF MY OWN, NOR A FUTURE.
LOGAN LIED TO ME.
NO... HE DIDN'T LIE--
HE DID. HE TOLD ME HE WOULD ALWAYS BE THERE. HE TOLD ME I COULD FOREVER COME TO HIM, BECAUSE HE ALONE WOULD ALWAYS UNDERSTAND.
HE SAID HE WOULD ALWAYS BE THERE TO REMIND ME OF MY TRUE COLORS.
AND I BELIEVED HIM. BECAUSE HE WAS LOGAN. THE WOLVERINE.
HE WAS SUPPOSED TO BE IMMORTAL. A LEGEND. ETERNAL. UNKILLABLE.
BUT HE WASN'T. HE WAS MORTAL. FINITE. FOLLOWING HIS OWN DARK PATH INEVITABLY TOWARDS DEATH.
"THE WOLVERINE" WAS JUST A MAN.
A MAN WEARING GOLD AND BLUE TIGHTS.

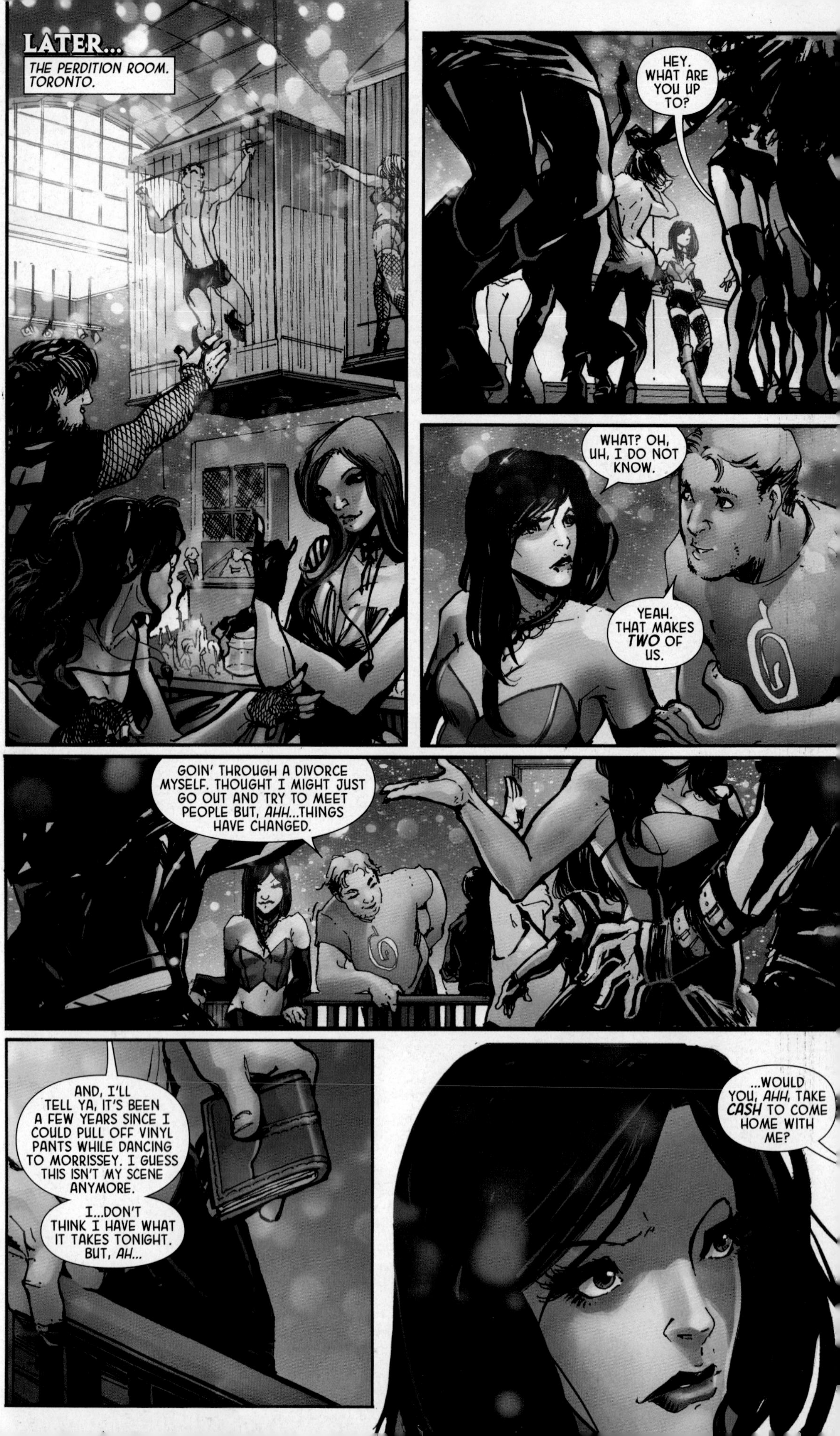
LATER...
THE PERDITION ROOM. TORONTO.
HEY. WHAT ARE YOU UP TO?
WHAT? OH, UH, I DO NOT KNOW.
YEAH. THAT MAKES TWO OF US.
GOIN' THROUGH A DIVORCE MYSELF. THOUGHT I MIGHT JUST GO OUT AND TRY TO MEET PEOPLE BUT, AHH...THINGS HAVE CHANGED.
AND, I'LL TELL YA, IT'S BEEN A FEW YEARS SINCE I COULD PULL OFF VINYL PANTS WHILE DANCING TO MORRISSEY. I GUESS THIS ISN'T MY SCENE ANYMORE.
I...DON'T THINK I HAVE WHAT IT TAKES TONIGHT. BUT, AH...
...WOULD YOU, AHH, TAKE CASH TO COME HOME WITH ME?

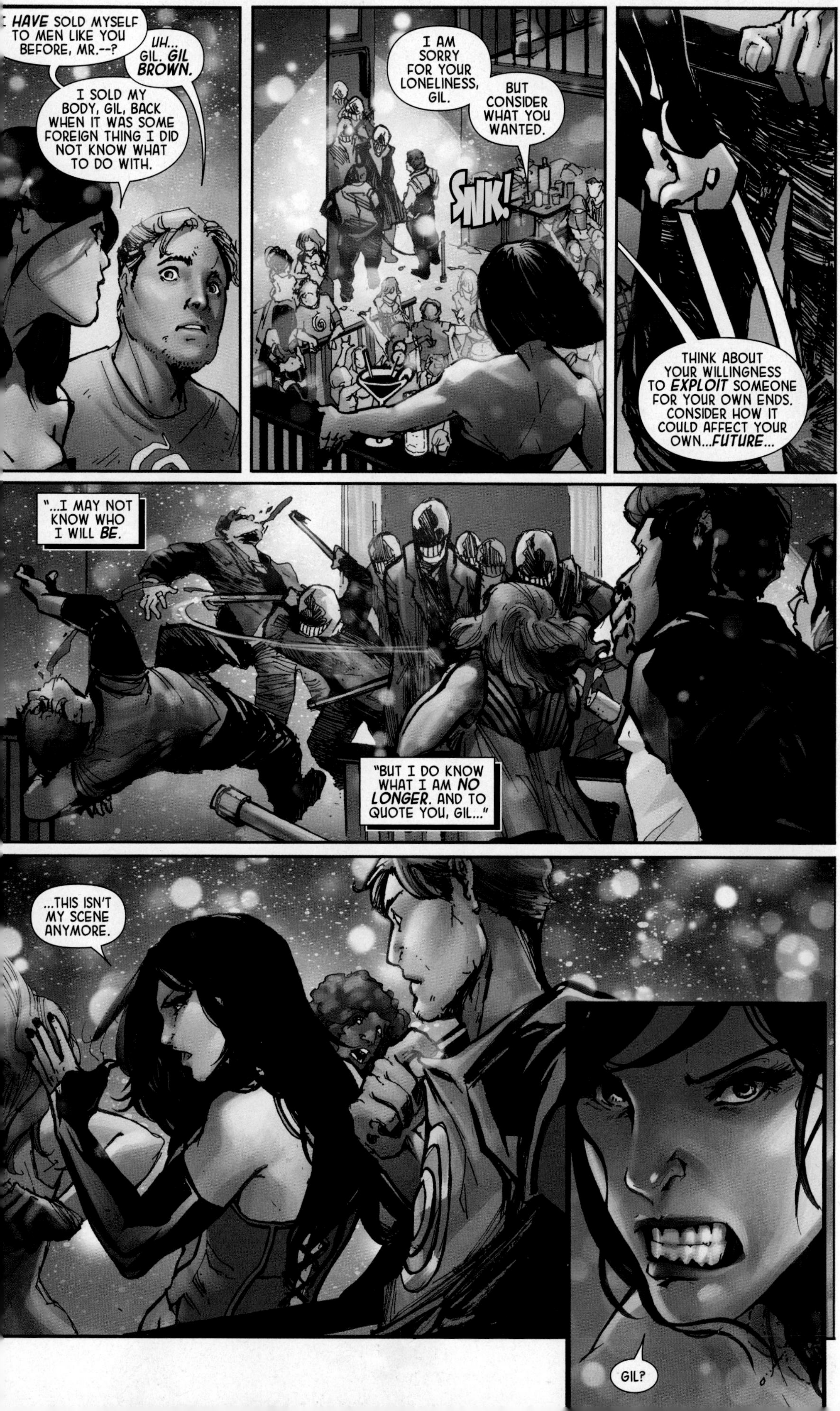
I HAVE SOLD MYSELF TO MEN LIKE YOU BEFORE, MR.--?
UH... GIL. GIL BROWN.
I SOLD MY BODY, GIL, BACK WHEN IT WAS SOME FOREIGN THING I DID NOT KNOW WHAT TO DO WITH.
I AM SORRY FOR YOUR LONELINESS, GIL.
BUT CONSIDER WHAT YOU WANTED.
SNK!
THINK ABOUT YOUR WILLINGNESS TO EXPLOIT SOMEONE FOR YOUR OWN ENDS. CONSIDER HOW IT COULD AFFECT YOUR OWN...FUTURE...
"...I MAY NOT KNOW WHO I WILL BE.
"BUT I DO KNOW WHAT I AM NO LONGER. AND TO QUOTE YOU, GIL..."
...THIS ISN'T MY SCENE ANYMORE.
GIL?

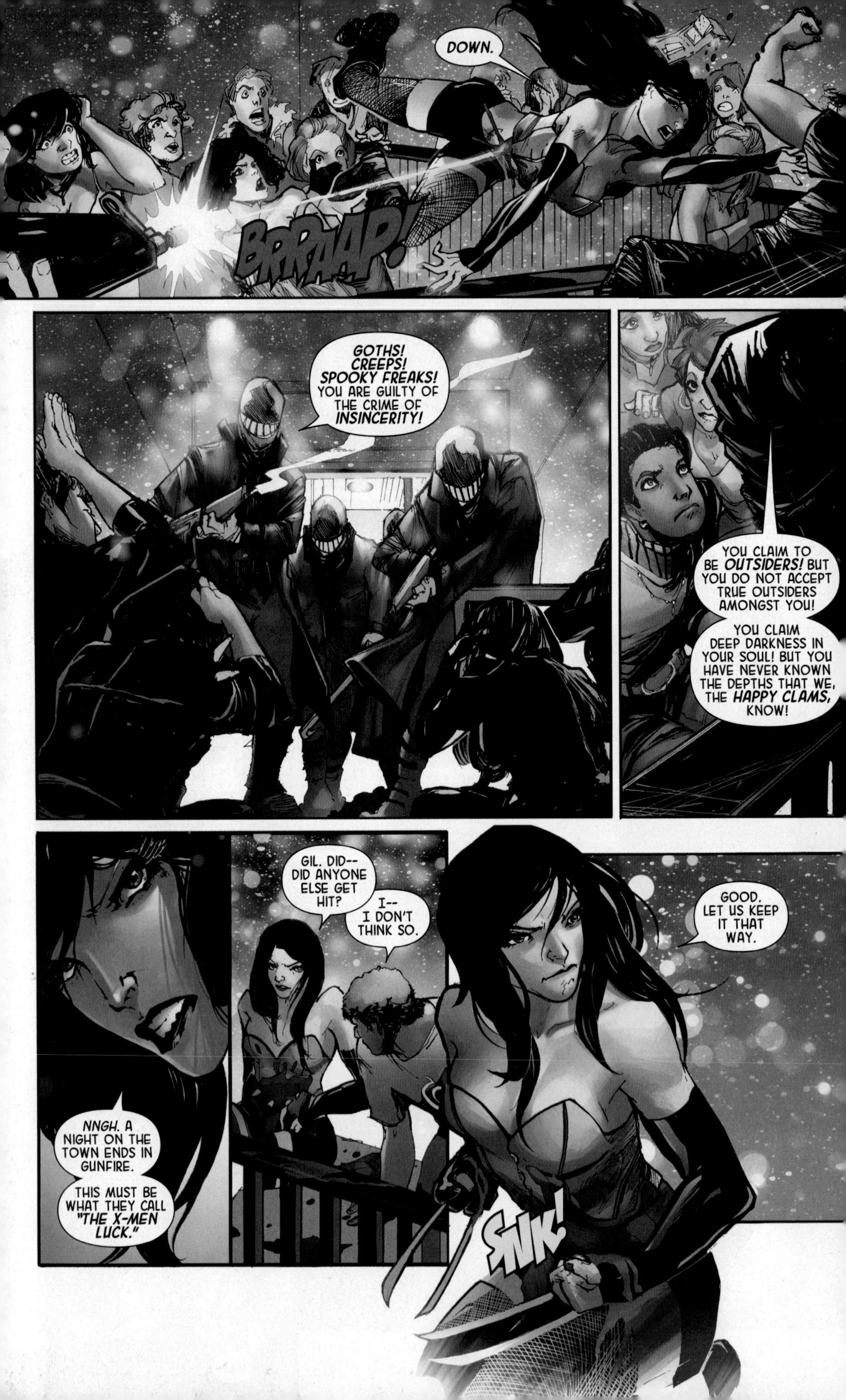
DOWN.
BRRAAP!
GOTHS! CREEPS! SPOOKY FREAKS! YOU ARE GUILTY OF THE CRIME OF INSINCERITY!
YOU CLAIM TO BE OUTSIDERS! BUT YOU DO NOT ACCEPT TRUE OUTSIDERS AMONGST YOU!
YOU CLAIM DEEP DARKNESS IN YOUR SOUL! BUT YOU HAVE NEVER KNOWN THE DEPTHS THAT WE, THE HAPPY CLAMS, KNOW!
NNGH. A NIGHT ON THE TOWN ENDS IN GUNFIRE.
THIS MUST BE WHAT THEY CALL "THE X-MEN LUCK."
GIL. DID-- DID ANYONE ELSE GET HIT?
I-- I DON'T THINK SO.
GOOD. LET US KEEP IT THAT WAY.
SNIK!

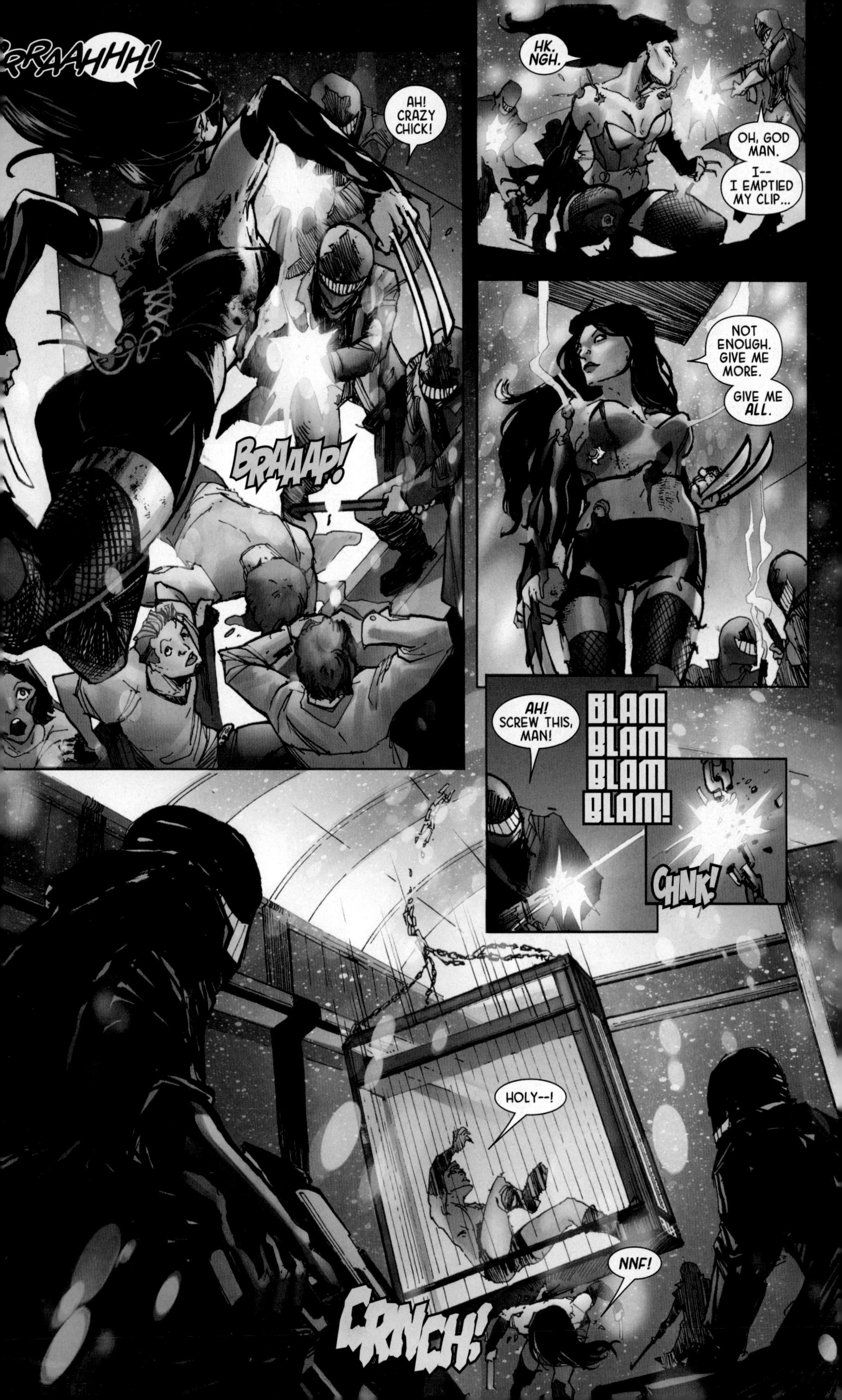
RRAAHHH!
AH! CRAZY CHICK!
BRAAAP!
HK. NGH.
OH, GOD MAN.
I-- I EMPTIED MY CLIP...
NOT ENOUGH. GIVE ME MORE.
GIVE ME ALL.
AH! SCREW THIS, MAN!
BLAM BLAM BLAM BLAM!
CHNK!
HOLY--!
NNF!
CRNCH!

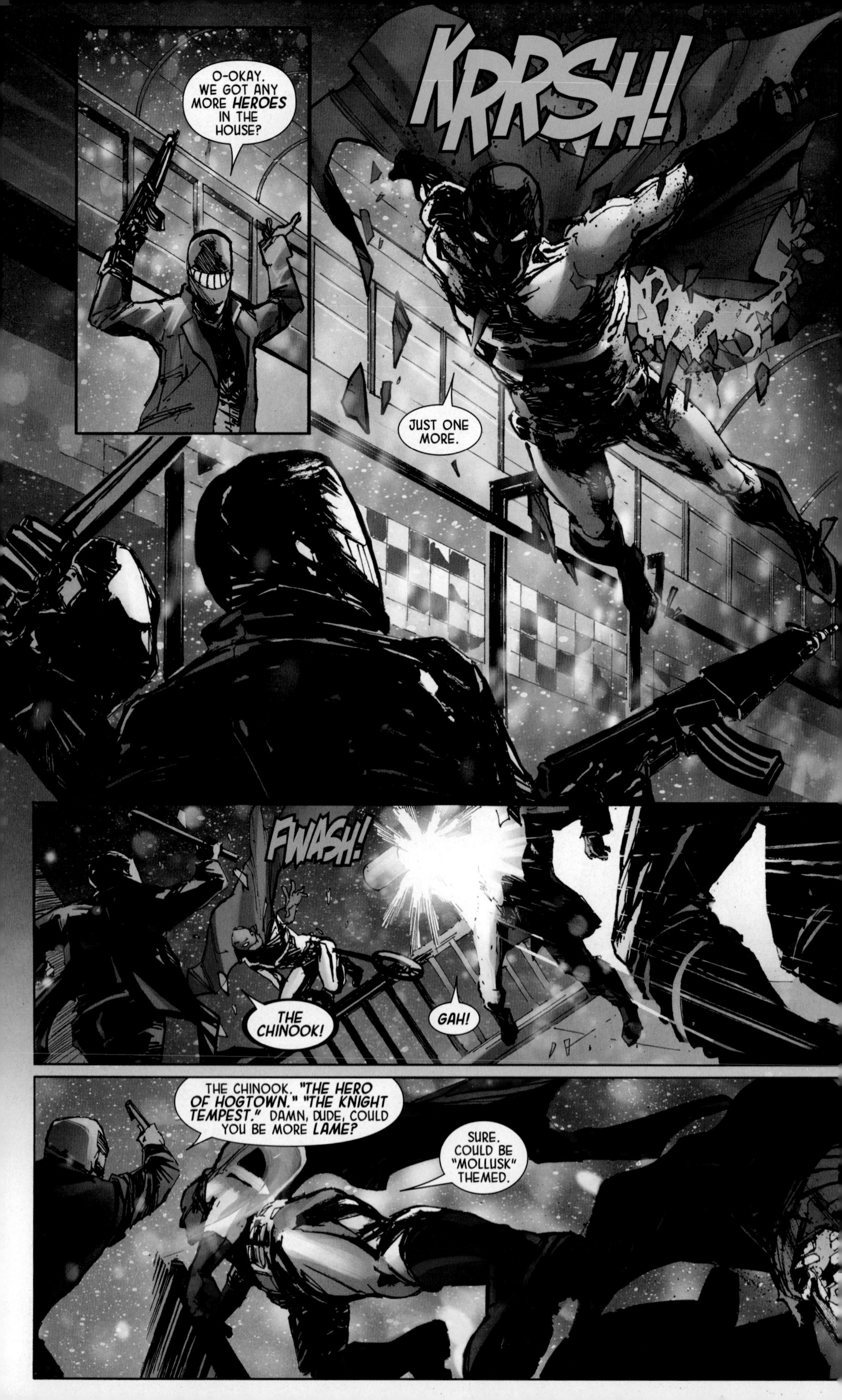
O-OKAY. WE GOT ANY MORE HEROES IN THE HOUSE?
KRRSH!
JUST ONE MORE.
FWASH!
THE CHINOOK!
GAH!
THE CHINOOK. "THE HERO OF HOGTOWN." "THE KNIGHT TEMPEST." DAMN, DUDE, COULD YOU BE MORE LAME?
SURE. COULD BE "MOLLUSK" THEMED.

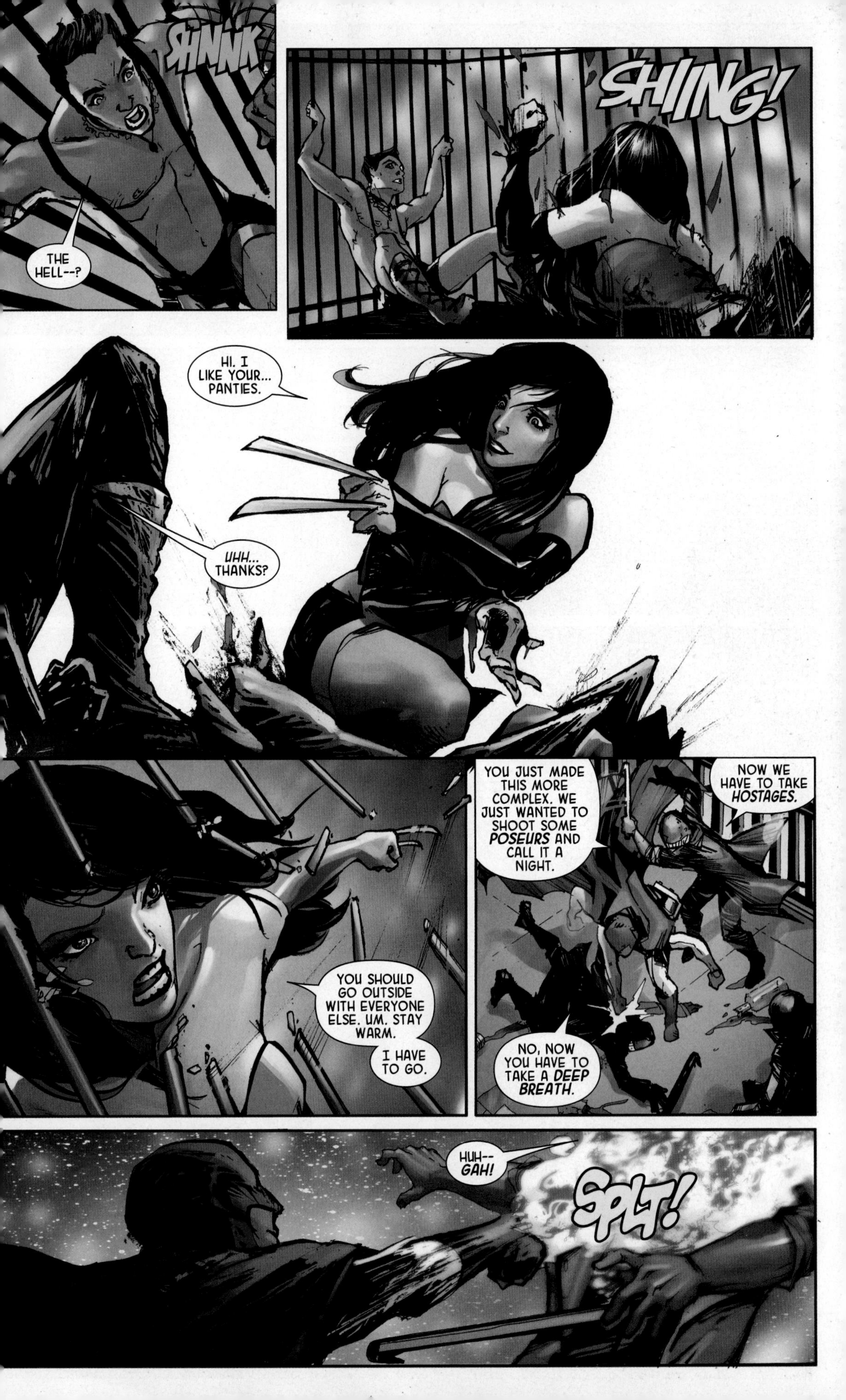
SHNNK
THE HELL--?
SHIING!
HI. I LIKE YOUR... PANTIES.
UHH... THANKS?
YOU SHOULD GO OUTSIDE WITH EVERYONE ELSE. UM. STAY WARM.
I HAVE TO GO.
YOU JUST MADE THIS MORE COMPLEX. WE JUST WANTED TO SHOOT SOME POSEURS AND CALL IT A NIGHT.
NOW WE HAVE TO TAKE HOSTAGES.
NO, NOW YOU HAVE TO TAKE A DEEP BREATH.
HUH-- GAH!
SPLT!

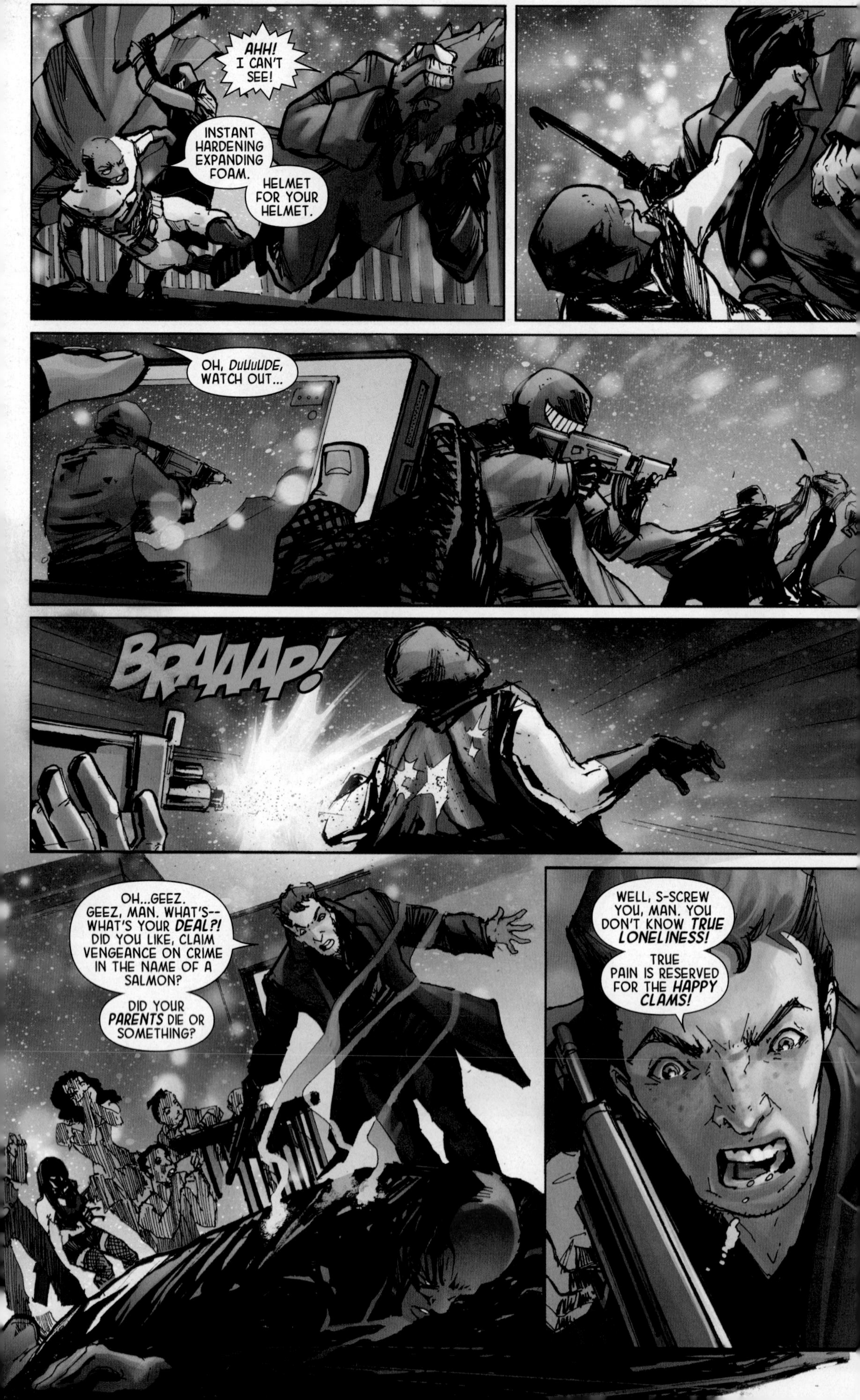
AHH! I CAN'T SEE!
INSTANT HARDENING EXPANDING FOAM.
HELMET FOR YOUR HELMET.
OH, DUUUUDE, WATCH OUT...
BRAAAP!
OH...GEEZ. GEEZ, MAN. WHAT'S-- WHAT'S YOUR DEAL?! DID YOU LIKE, CLAIM VENGEANCE ON CRIME IN THE NAME OF A SALMON?
DID YOUR PARENTS DIE OR SOMETHING?
WELL, S-SCREW YOU, MAN. YOU DON'T KNOW TRUE LONELINESS!
TRUE PAIN IS RESERVED FOR THE HAPPY CLAMS!

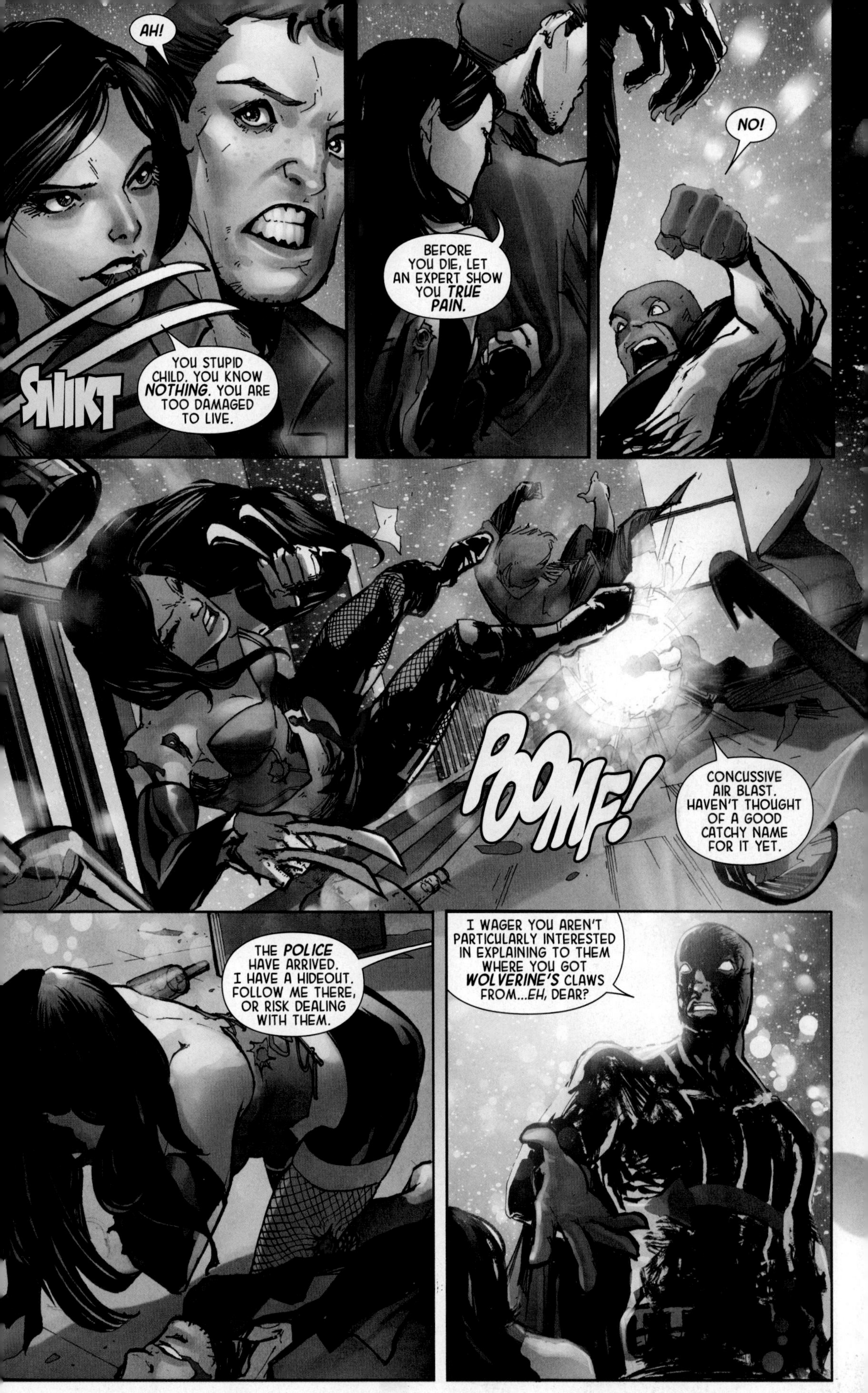
AH!
SNIKT
YOU STUPID CHILD. YOU KNOW NOTHING. YOU ARE TOO DAMAGED TO LIVE.
BEFORE YOU DIE, LET AN EXPERT SHOW YOU TRUE PAIN.
NO!
POOMF!
CONCUSSIVE AIR BLAST. HAVEN'T THOUGHT OF A GOOD CATCHY NAME FOR IT YET.
THE POLICE HAVE ARRIVED. I HAVE A HIDEOUT. FOLLOW ME THERE, OR RISK DEALING WITH THEM.
I WAGER YOU AREN'T PARTICULARLY INTERESTED IN EXPLAINING TO THEM WHERE YOU GOT WOLVERINE'S CLAWS FROM...EH, DEAR?

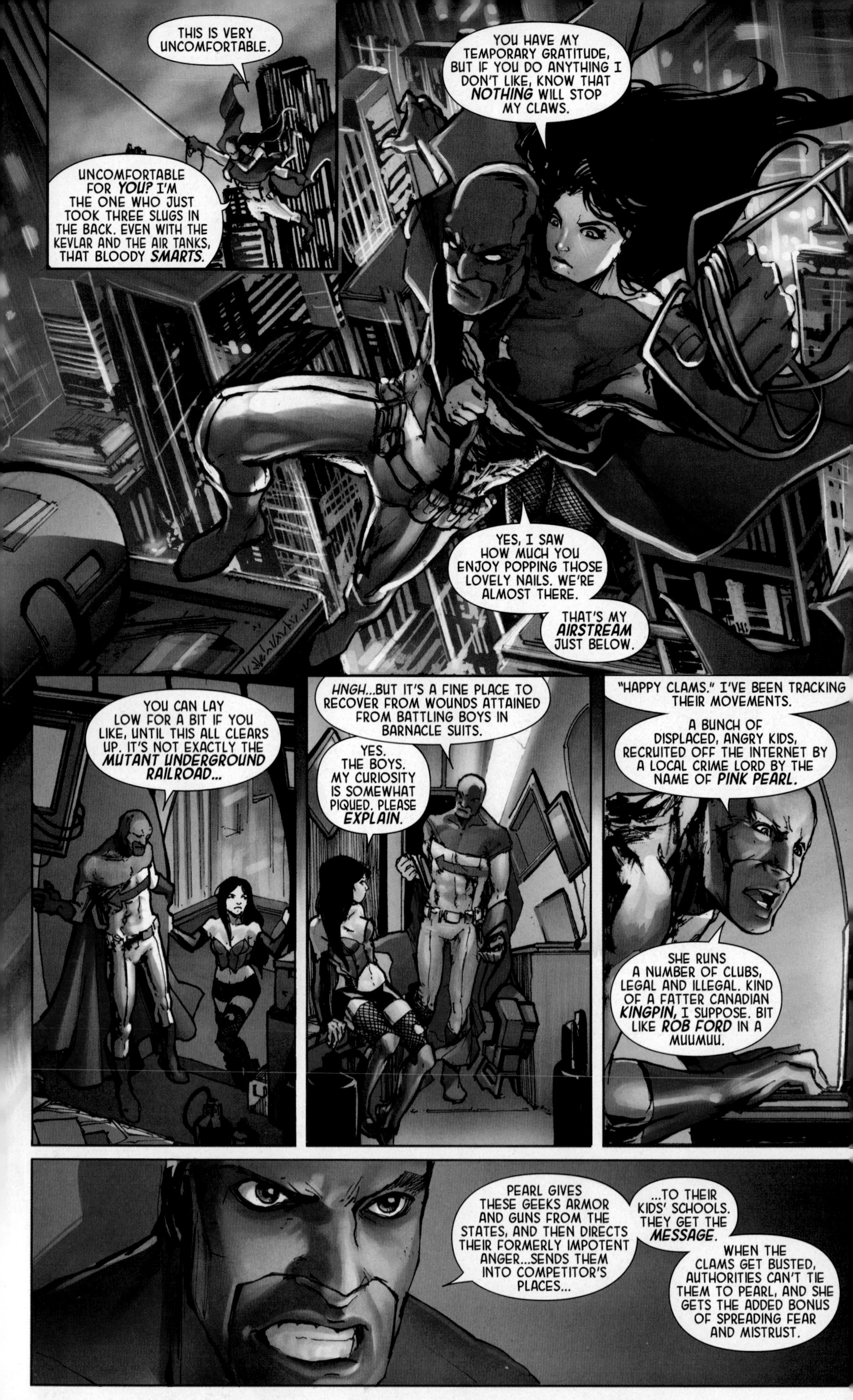
THIS IS VERY UNCOMFORTABLE.
UNCOMFORTABLE FOR YOU? I'M THE ONE WHO JUST TOOK THREE SLUGS IN THE BACK. EVEN WITH THE KEVLAR AND THE AIR TANKS, THAT BLOODY SMARTS.
YOU HAVE MY TEMPORARY GRATITUDE, BUT IF YOU DO ANYTHING I DON'T LIKE, KNOW THAT NOTHING WILL STOP MY CLAWS.
YES, I SAW HOW MUCH YOU ENJOY POPPING THOSE LOVELY NAILS. WE'RE ALMOST THERE.
THAT'S MY AIRSTREAM JUST BELOW.
YOU CAN LAY LOW FOR A BIT IF YOU LIKE, UNTIL THIS ALL CLEARS UP. IT'S NOT EXACTLY THE MUTANT UNDERGROUND RAILROAD...
HNGH...BUT IT'S A FINE PLACE TO RECOVER FROM WOUNDS ATTAINED FROM BATTLING BOYS IN BARNACLE SUITS.
YES. THE BOYS. MY CURIOSITY IS SOMEWHAT PIQUED. PLEASE EXPLAIN.
"HAPPY CLAMS." I'VE BEEN TRACKING THEIR MOVEMENTS.
A BUNCH OF DISPLACED, ANGRY KIDS, RECRUITED OFF THE INTERNET BY A LOCAL CRIME LORD BY THE NAME OF PINK PEARL.
SHE RUNS A NUMBER OF CLUBS, LEGAL AND ILLEGAL. KIND OF A FATTER CANADIAN KINGPIN, I SUPPOSE. BIT LIKE ROB FORD IN A MUUMUU.
PEARL GIVES THESE GEEKS ARMOR AND GUNS FROM THE STATES, AND THEN DIRECTS THEIR FORMERLY IMPOTENT ANGER...SENDS THEM INTO COMPETITOR'S PLACES...
...TO THEIR KIDS' SCHOOLS. THEY GET THE MESSAGE.
WHEN THE CLAMS GET BUSTED, AUTHORITIES CAN'T TIE THEM TO PEARL, AND SHE GETS THE ADDED BONUS OF SPREADING FEAR AND MISTRUST.

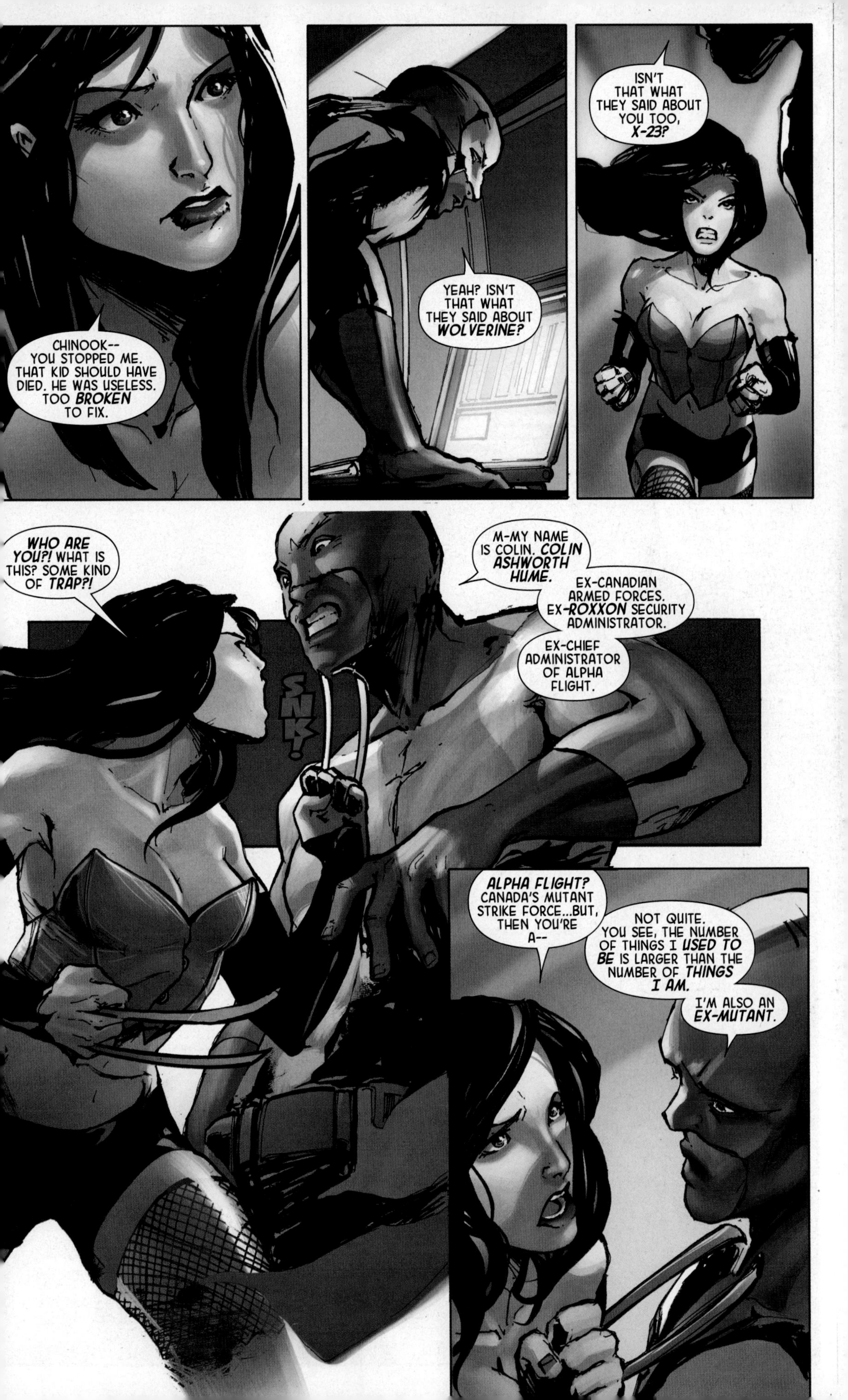

CHINOOK-- YOU STOPPED ME. THAT KID SHOULD HAVE DIED. HE WAS USELESS. TOO **BROKEN** TO FIX.
YEAH? ISN'T THAT WHAT THEY SAID ABOUT **WOLVERINE?**
ISN'T THAT WHAT THEY SAID ABOUT YOU TOO, **X-23?**
WHO ARE YOU?! WHAT IS THIS? SOME KIND OF **TRAP?!**
SNK!
M-MY NAME IS COLIN. **COLIN ASHWORTH HUME.**
EX-CANADIAN ARMED FORCES. EX-**ROXXON** SECURITY ADMINISTRATOR.
EX-CHIEF ADMINISTRATOR OF ALPHA FLIGHT.
ALPHA FLIGHT? CANADA'S MUTANT STRIKE FORCE...BUT, THEN YOU'RE A--
NOT QUITE. YOU SEE, THE NUMBER OF THINGS I **USED TO BE** IS LARGER THAN THE NUMBER OF **THINGS I AM.**
I'M ALSO AN **EX-MUTANT.**

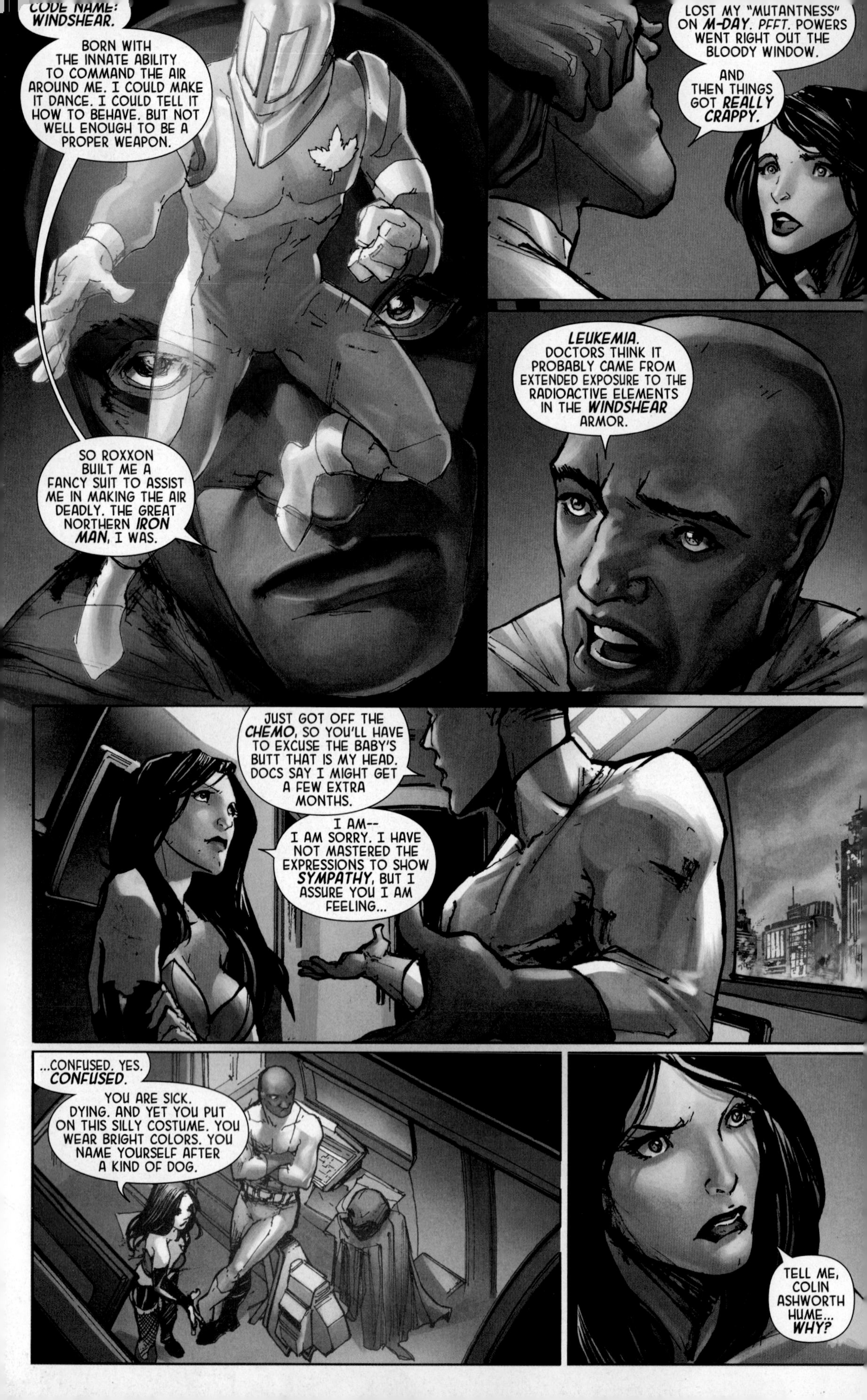
CODE NAME: WINDSHEAR.
BORN WITH THE INNATE ABILITY TO COMMAND THE AIR AROUND ME. I COULD MAKE IT DANCE. I COULD TELL IT HOW TO BEHAVE. BUT NOT WELL ENOUGH TO BE A PROPER WEAPON.
SO ROXXON BUILT ME A FANCY SUIT TO ASSIST ME IN MAKING THE AIR DEADLY. THE GREAT NORTHERN IRON MAN, I WAS.
LOST MY "MUTANTNESS" ON M-DAY. PFFT. POWERS WENT RIGHT OUT THE BLOODY WINDOW.
AND THEN THINGS GOT REALLY CRAPPY.
LEUKEMIA. DOCTORS THINK IT PROBABLY CAME FROM EXTENDED EXPOSURE TO THE RADIOACTIVE ELEMENTS IN THE WINDSHEAR ARMOR.
JUST GOT OFF THE CHEMO, SO YOU'LL HAVE TO EXCUSE THE BABY'S BUTT THAT IS MY HEAD. DOCS SAY I MIGHT GET A FEW EXTRA MONTHS.
I AM-- I AM SORRY. I HAVE NOT MASTERED THE EXPRESSIONS TO SHOW SYMPATHY, BUT I ASSURE YOU I AM FEELING...
...CONFUSED. YES. CONFUSED.
YOU ARE SICK. DYING. AND YET YOU PUT ON THIS SILLY COSTUME. YOU WEAR BRIGHT COLORS. YOU NAME YOURSELF AFTER A KIND OF DOG.
TELL ME, COLIN ASHWORTH HUME... WHY?

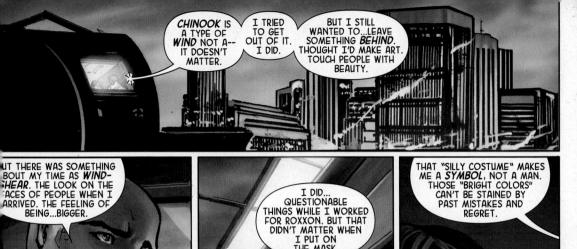

CHINOOK IS A TYPE OF *WIND* NOT A-- IT DOESN'T MATTER.

I TRIED TO GET OUT OF IT. I DID.

BUT I STILL WANTED TO...LEAVE SOMETHING *BEHIND.* THOUGHT I'D MAKE ART. TOUCH PEOPLE WITH BEAUTY.

UT THERE WAS SOMETHING BOUT MY TIME AS *WIND-SHEAR.* THE LOOK ON THE FACES OF PEOPLE WHEN I ARRIVED. THE FEELING OF BEING...BIGGER.

I DID... QUESTIONABLE THINGS WHILE I WORKED FOR ROXXON. BUT THAT DIDN'T MATTER WHEN I PUT ON THE MASK.

THAT "SILLY COSTUME" MAKES ME A *SYMBOL,* NOT A MAN. THOSE "BRIGHT COLORS" CAN'T BE STAINED BY PAST MISTAKES AND REGRET.

HELL YEAH, MAN. THESE'LL DO THE TRICK.

BAM! BAM! CRITICAL HIT, BEE-YOTCH!

QUIT SWINGING IT AROUND YOU IDIOT. THIS ISN'T A DAMN *VIDEO GAME.*

"THOSE COLORS ARE A SYMBOL, X-23, FOR THE MOST UNCOMPLICATED, MOST UNTAINTED *ELEMENTS* OF WHAT TRULY LIES IN OUR *SOULS.*"

NOW, THE YANKS ARE GIVING ME A PRETTY CRAP DEAL ON THE BORDER TRADE. HOW DO YOU BOYS FEEL ABOUT HITTING UP A COLLEGE? LOTS OF POSEURS THERE, *EH?*

"IN AN AGE OF MISTRUST AND DIVISIVENESS, WE NEED A FEW THINGS THAT ARE JUST BLOODY SIMPLE AND *PURE.*"

DAMN IT, SOMEONE FIND WHERE THAT *DRAFT* IS COMING FROM...

THAT'S NO DRAFT, PEARL...

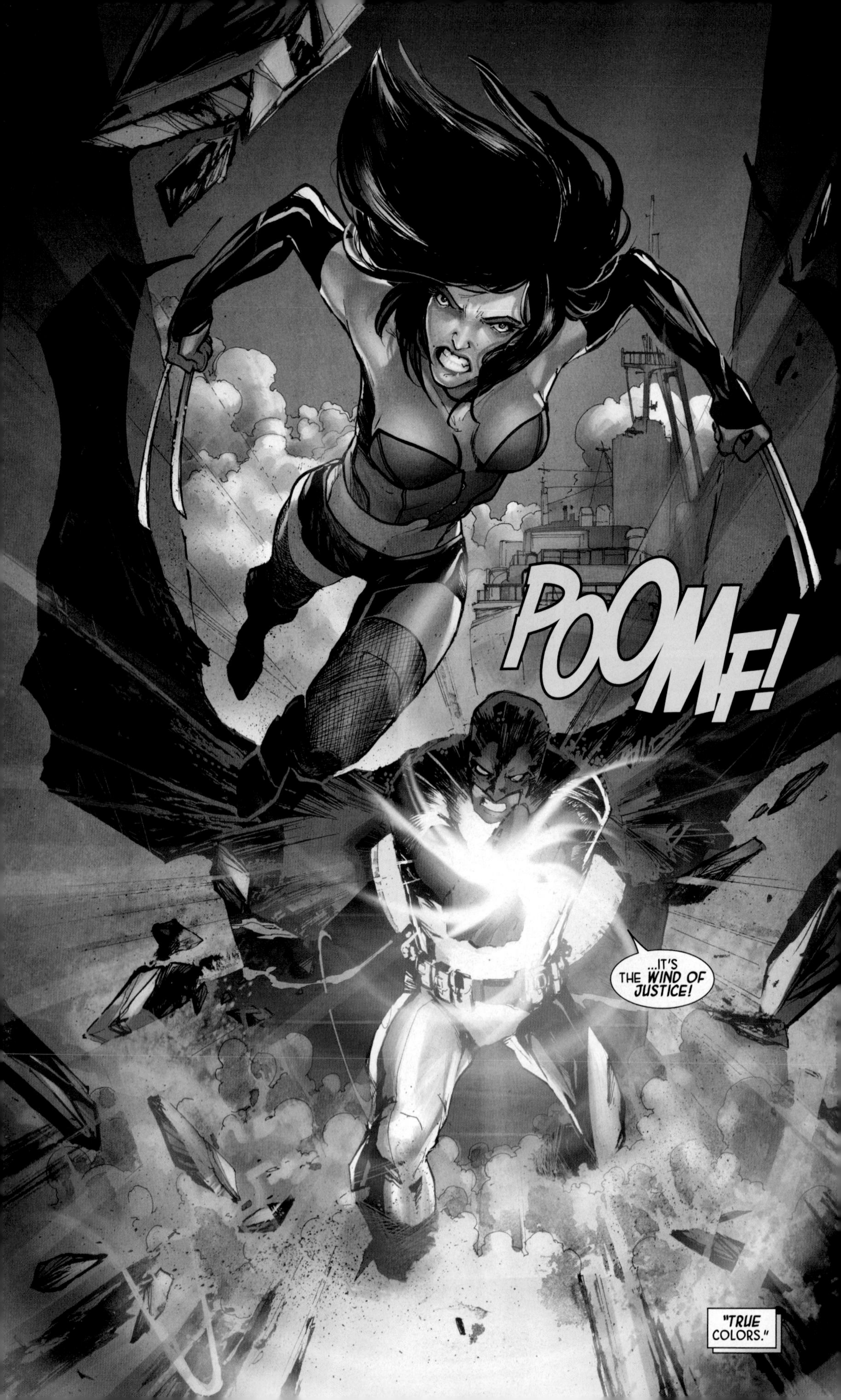
POOMF!
...IT'S THE WIND OF JUSTICE!
"TRUE COLORS."

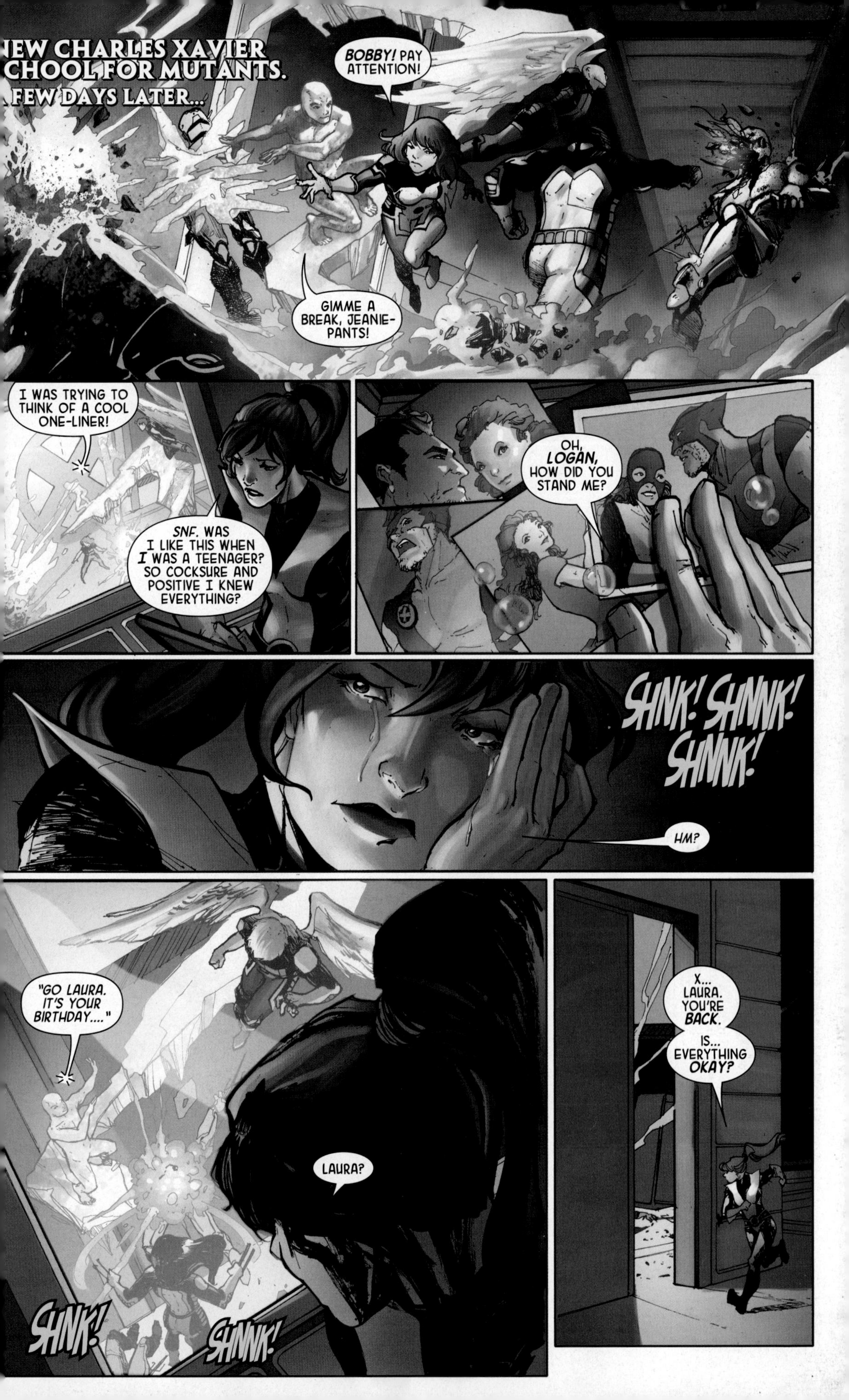
IEW CHARLES XAVIER
CHOOL FOR MUTANTS.
FEW DAYS LATER...
BOBBY! PAY ATTENTION!
GIMME A BREAK, JEANIE-PANTS!
I WAS TRYING TO THINK OF A COOL ONE-LINER!
SNF. WAS I LIKE THIS WHEN I WAS A TEENAGER? SO COCKSURE AND POSITIVE I KNEW EVERYTHING?
OH, LOGAN, HOW DID YOU STAND ME?
SHNK! SHNNK! SHNNK!
HM?
"GO LAURA. IT'S YOUR BIRTHDAY...."
LAURA?
SHNK!
SHNNK!
X... LAURA. YOU'RE BACK.
IS... EVERYTHING OKAY?

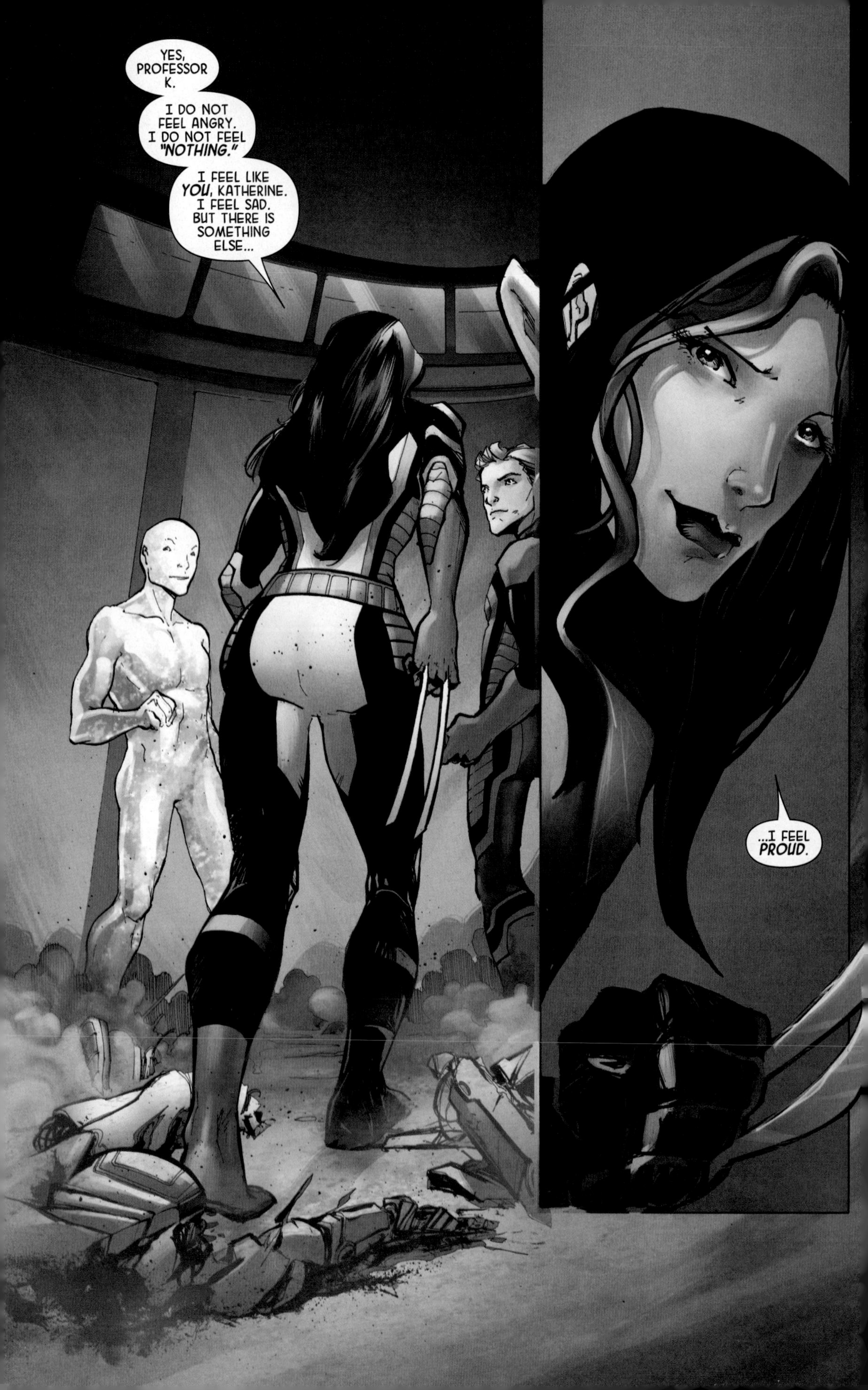
YES, PROFESSOR K.
I DO NOT FEEL ANGRY. I DO NOT FEEL ***"NOTHING."***
I FEEL LIKE ***YOU***, KATHERINE. I FEEL SAD. BUT THERE IS SOMETHING ELSE...
...I FEEL ***PROUD***.

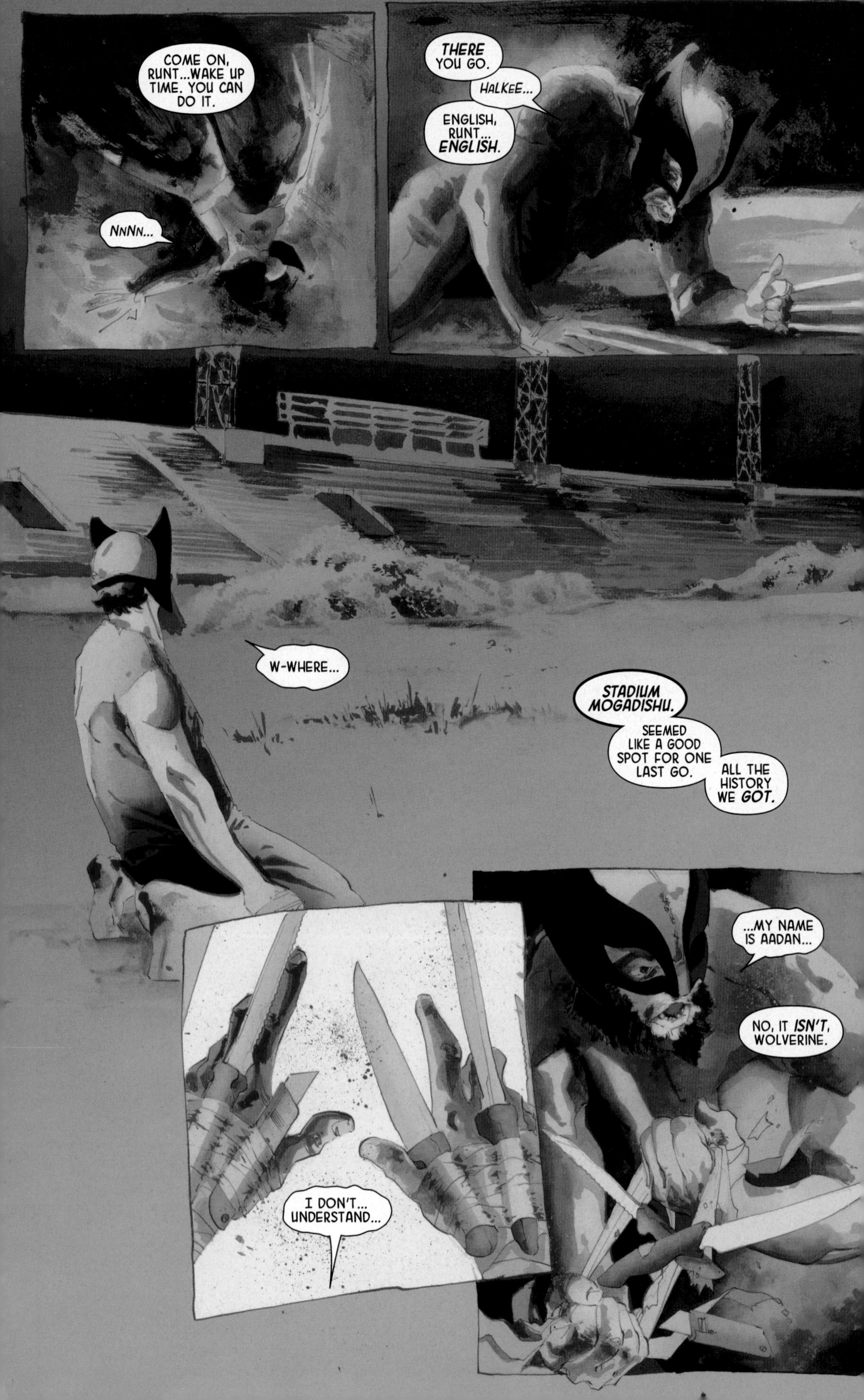

COME ON, RUNT...WAKE UP TIME. YOU CAN DO IT.
NNNN...
THERE YOU GO.
HALKEE...
ENGLISH, RUNT... ENGLISH.
W-WHERE...
STADIUM MOGADISHU.
SEEMED LIKE A GOOD SPOT FOR ONE LAST GO.
ALL THE HISTORY WE GOT.
I DON'T... UNDERSTAND...
...MY NAME IS AADAN...
NO, IT ISN'T, WOLVERINE.

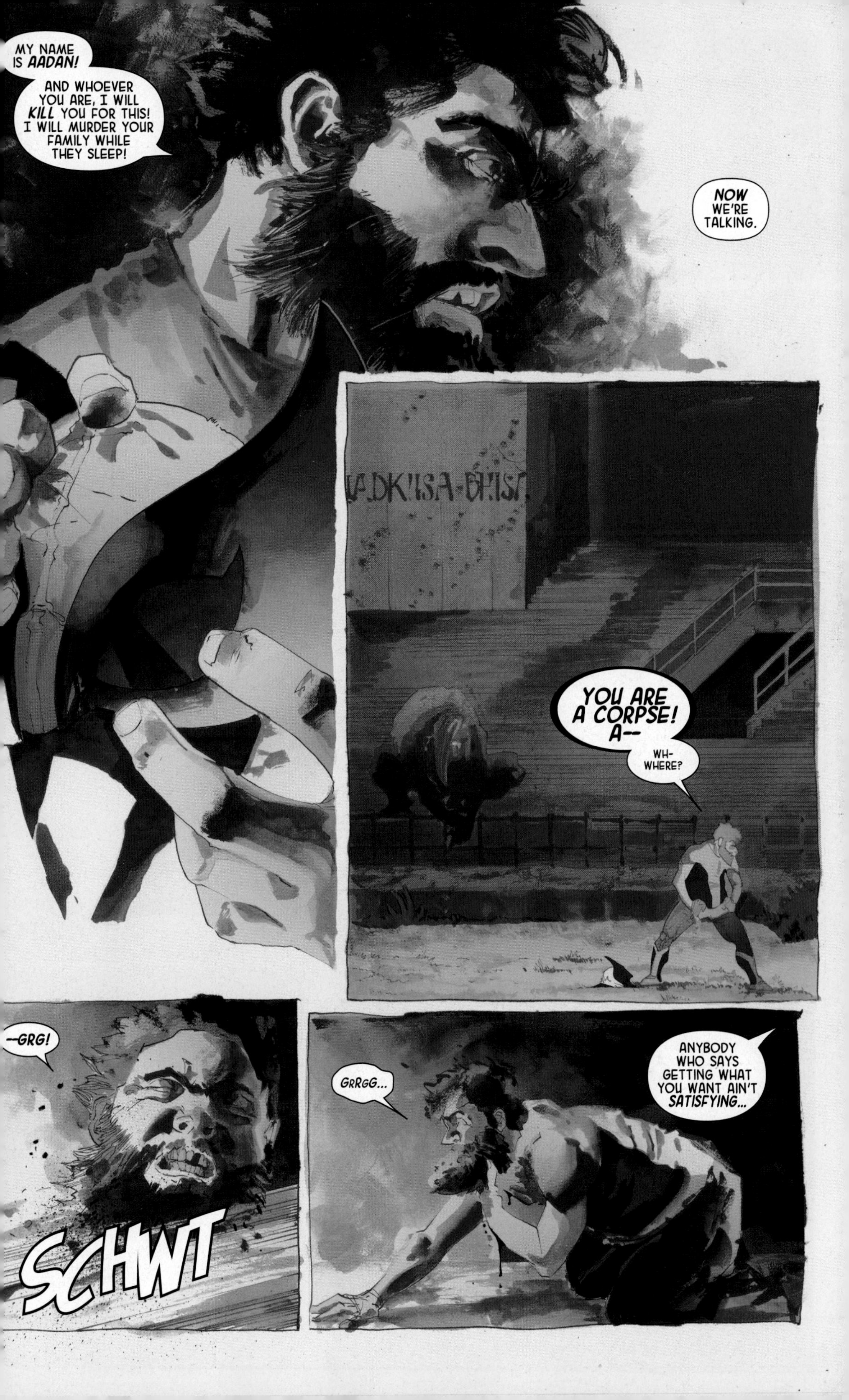
MY NAME IS AADAN!
AND WHOEVER YOU ARE, I WILL KILL YOU FOR THIS! I WILL MURDER YOUR FAMILY WHILE THEY SLEEP!
NOW WE'RE TALKING.
YOU ARE A CORPSE! A--
WH- WHERE?
--GRG!
SCHWT
GRRGG...
ANYBODY WHO SAYS GETTING WHAT YOU WANT AIN'T SATISFYING...

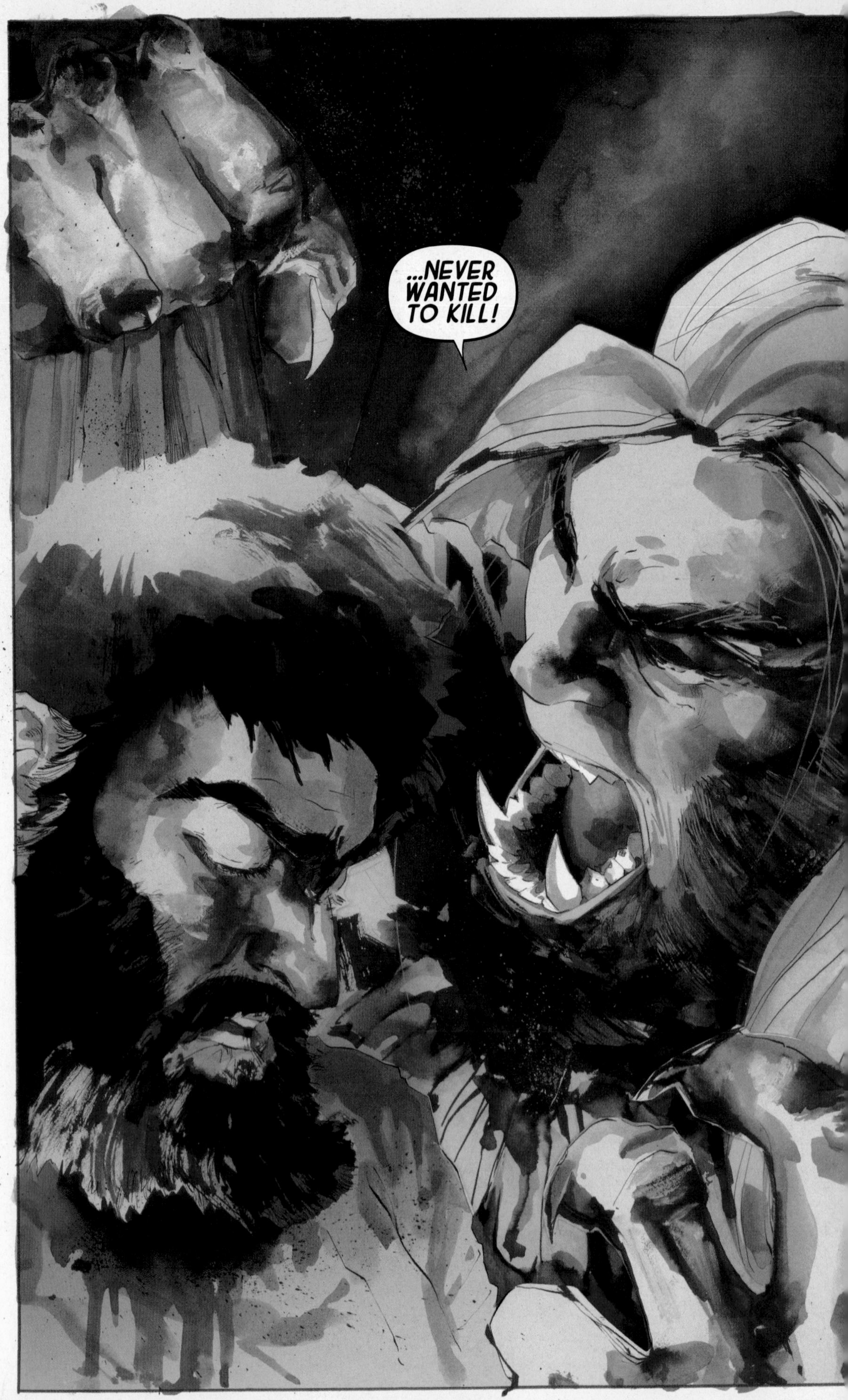
...NEVER WANTED TO KILL!

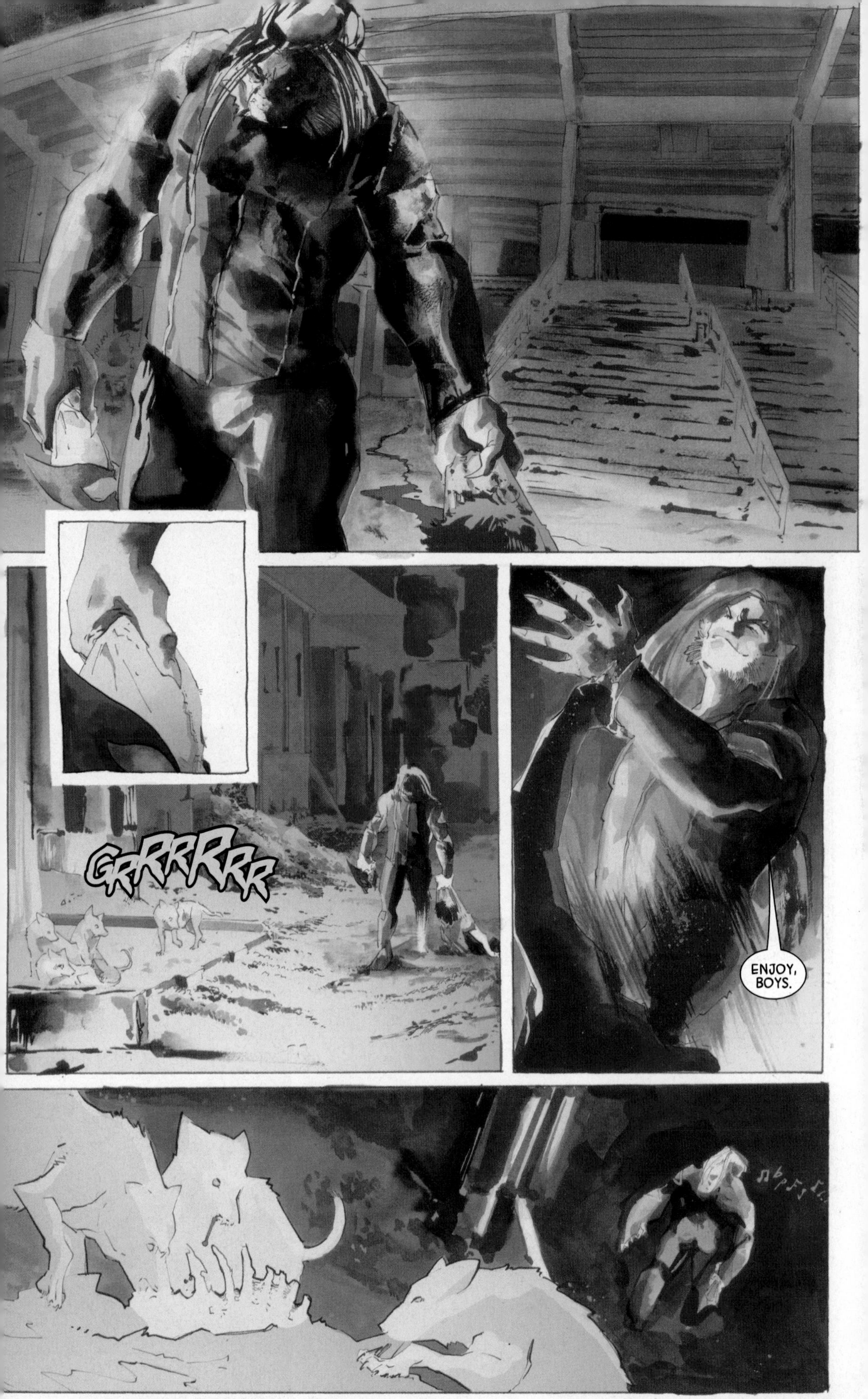
GRRRRRR
ENJOY, BOYS.

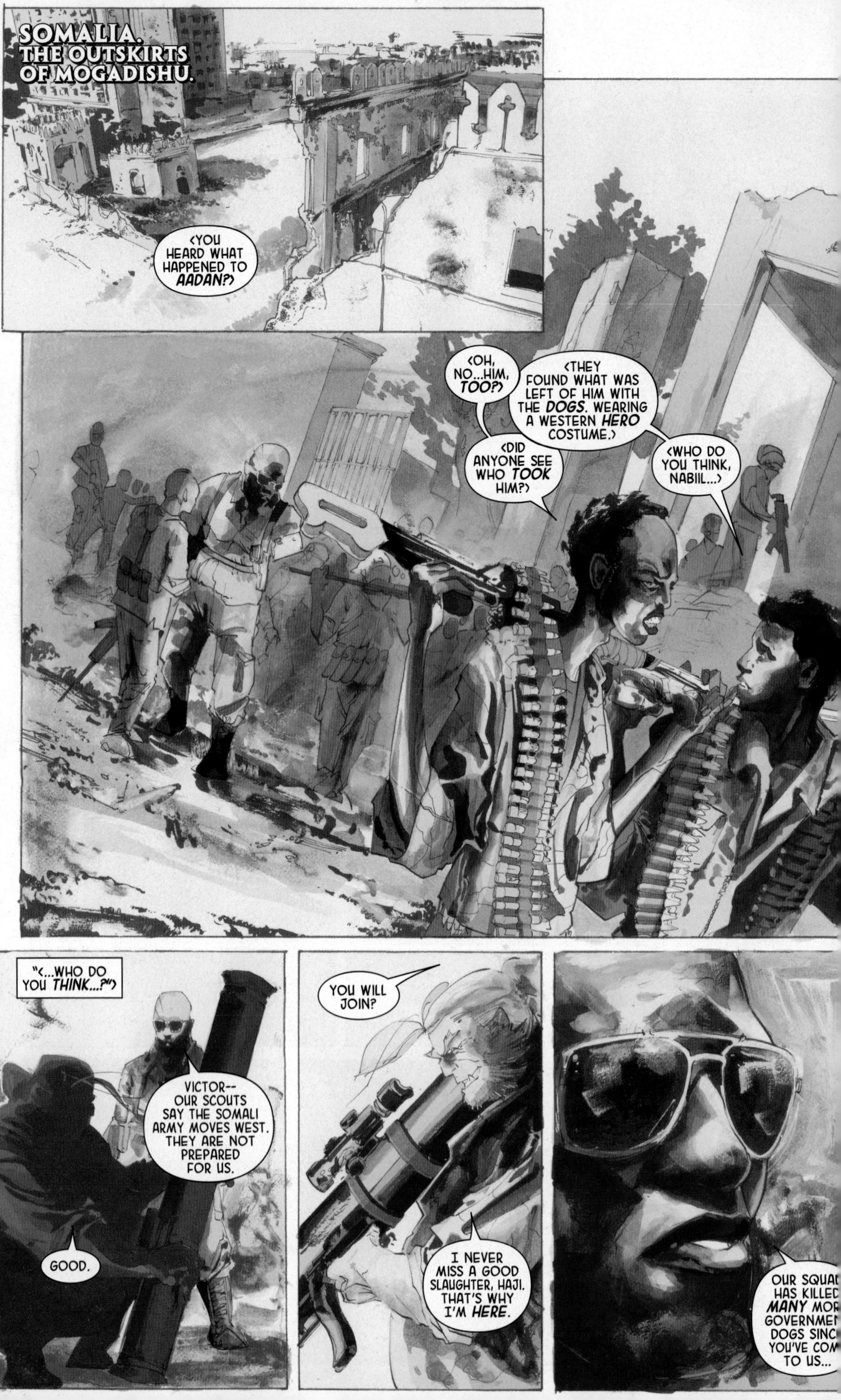
SOMALIA. THE OUTSKIRTS OF MOGADISHU.
<YOU HEARD WHAT HAPPENED TO AADAN?>
<OH, NO...HIM, TOO?>
<THEY FOUND WHAT WAS LEFT OF HIM WITH THE DOGS. WEARING A WESTERN HERO COSTUME.>
<DID ANYONE SEE WHO TOOK HIM?>
<WHO DO YOU THINK, NABIIL...>
"<...WHO DO YOU THINK...?">
VICTOR-- OUR SCOUTS SAY THE SOMALI ARMY MOVES WEST. THEY ARE NOT PREPARED FOR US.
GOOD.
YOU WILL JOIN?
I NEVER MISS A GOOD SLAUGHTER, HAJI. THAT'S WHY I'M HERE.
OUR SQUA HAS KILLED MANY MOR GOVERNMEN DOGS SINC YOU'VE COM TO US...

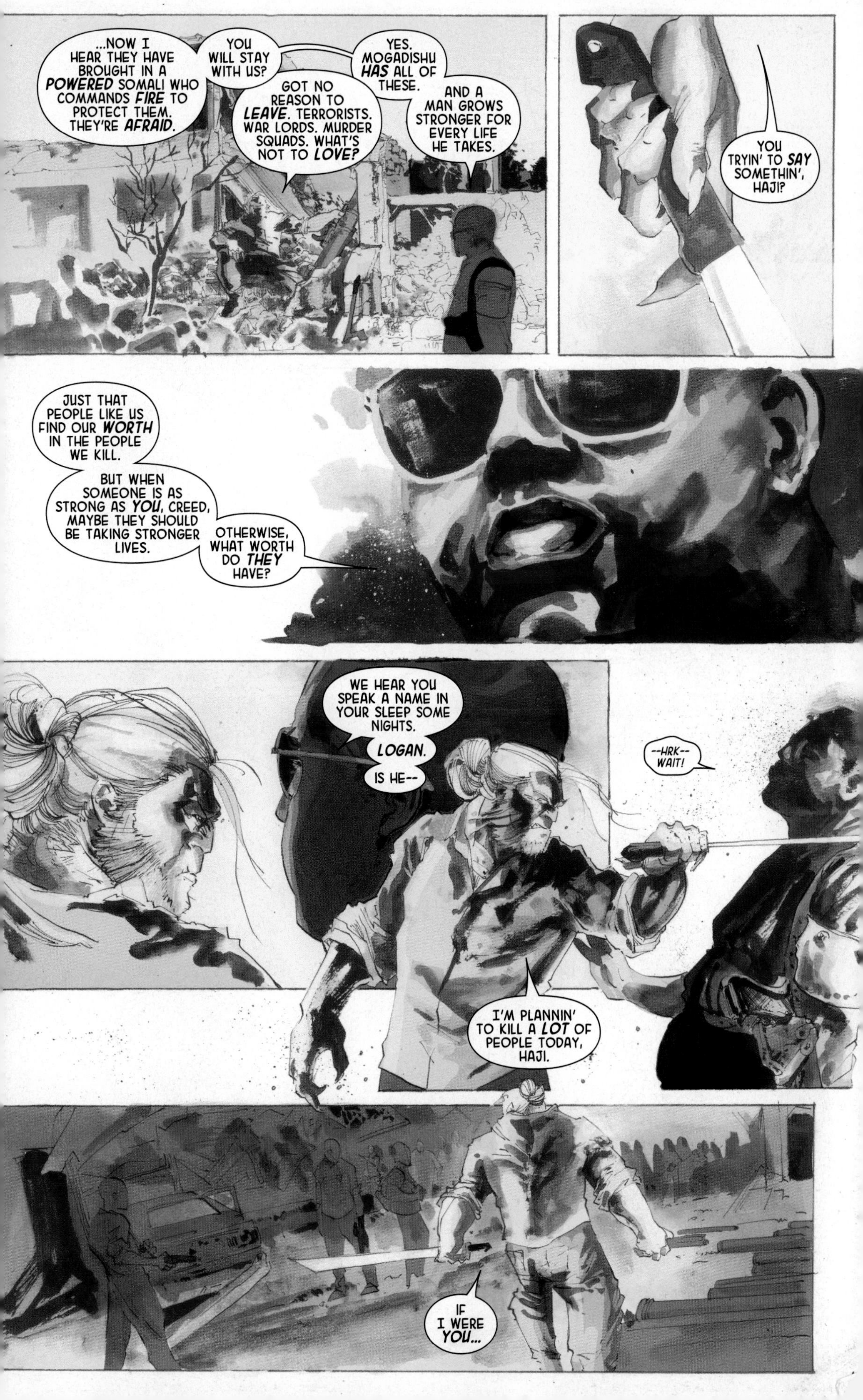

...NOW I HEAR THEY HAVE BROUGHT IN A POWERED SOMALI WHO COMMANDS FIRE TO PROTECT THEM. THEY'RE AFRAID.
YOU WILL STAY WITH US?
GOT NO REASON TO LEAVE. TERRORISTS. WAR LORDS. MURDER SQUADS. WHAT'S NOT TO LOVE?
YES. MOGADISHU HAS ALL OF THESE.
AND A MAN GROWS STRONGER FOR EVERY LIFE HE TAKES.
YOU TRYIN' TO SAY SOMETHIN', HAJI?
JUST THAT PEOPLE LIKE US FIND OUR WORTH IN THE PEOPLE WE KILL.
BUT WHEN SOMEONE IS AS STRONG AS YOU, CREED, MAYBE THEY SHOULD BE TAKING STRONGER LIVES.
OTHERWISE, WHAT WORTH DO THEY HAVE?
WE HEAR YOU SPEAK A NAME IN YOUR SLEEP SOME NIGHTS.
LOGAN.
IS HE--
--HRK-- WAIT!
I'M PLANNIN' TO KILL A LOT OF PEOPLE TODAY, HAJI.
IF I WERE YOU...

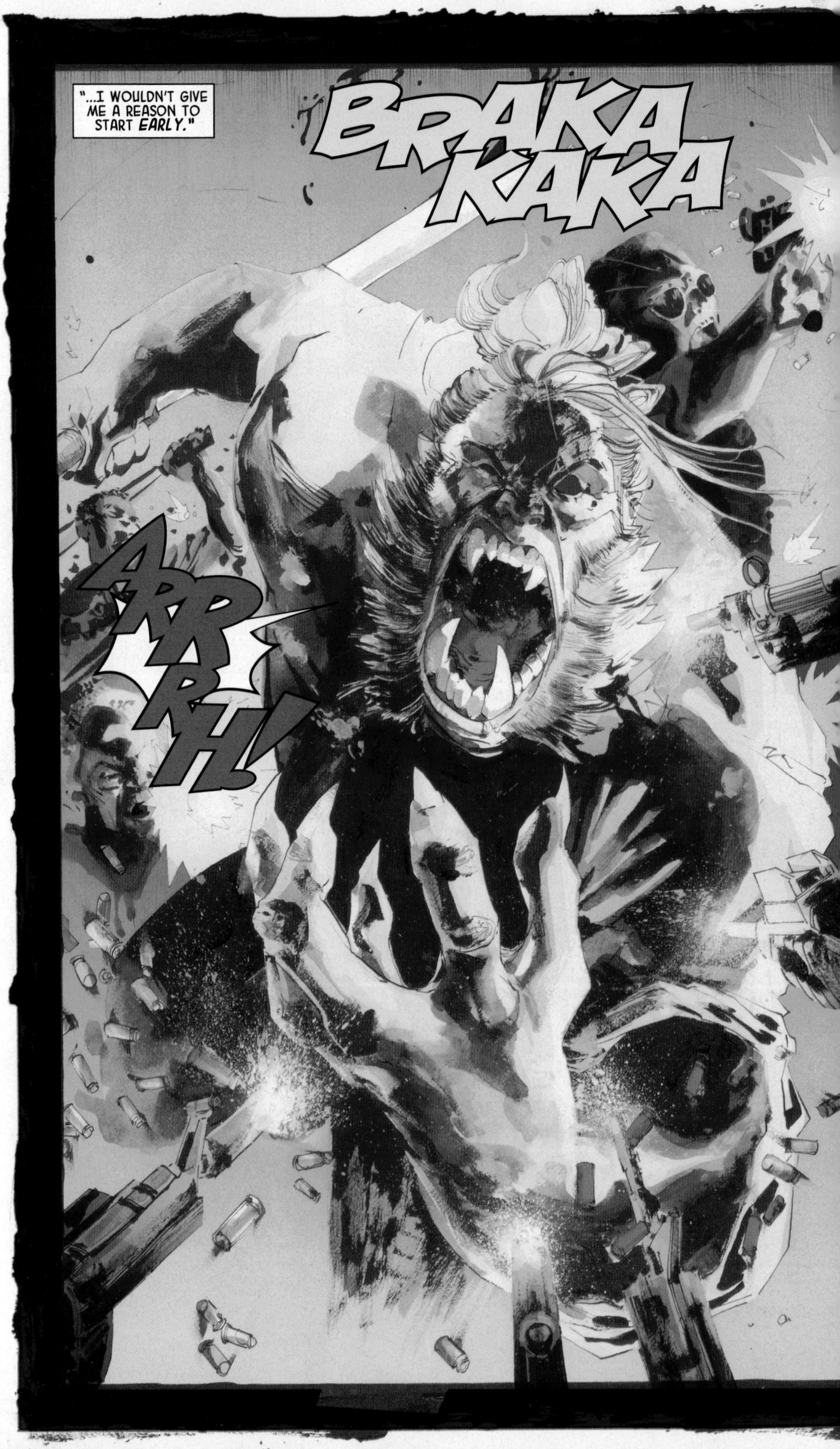
"...I WOULDN'T GIVE ME A REASON TO START EARLY."
BRAKA KAKA
ARRRH!

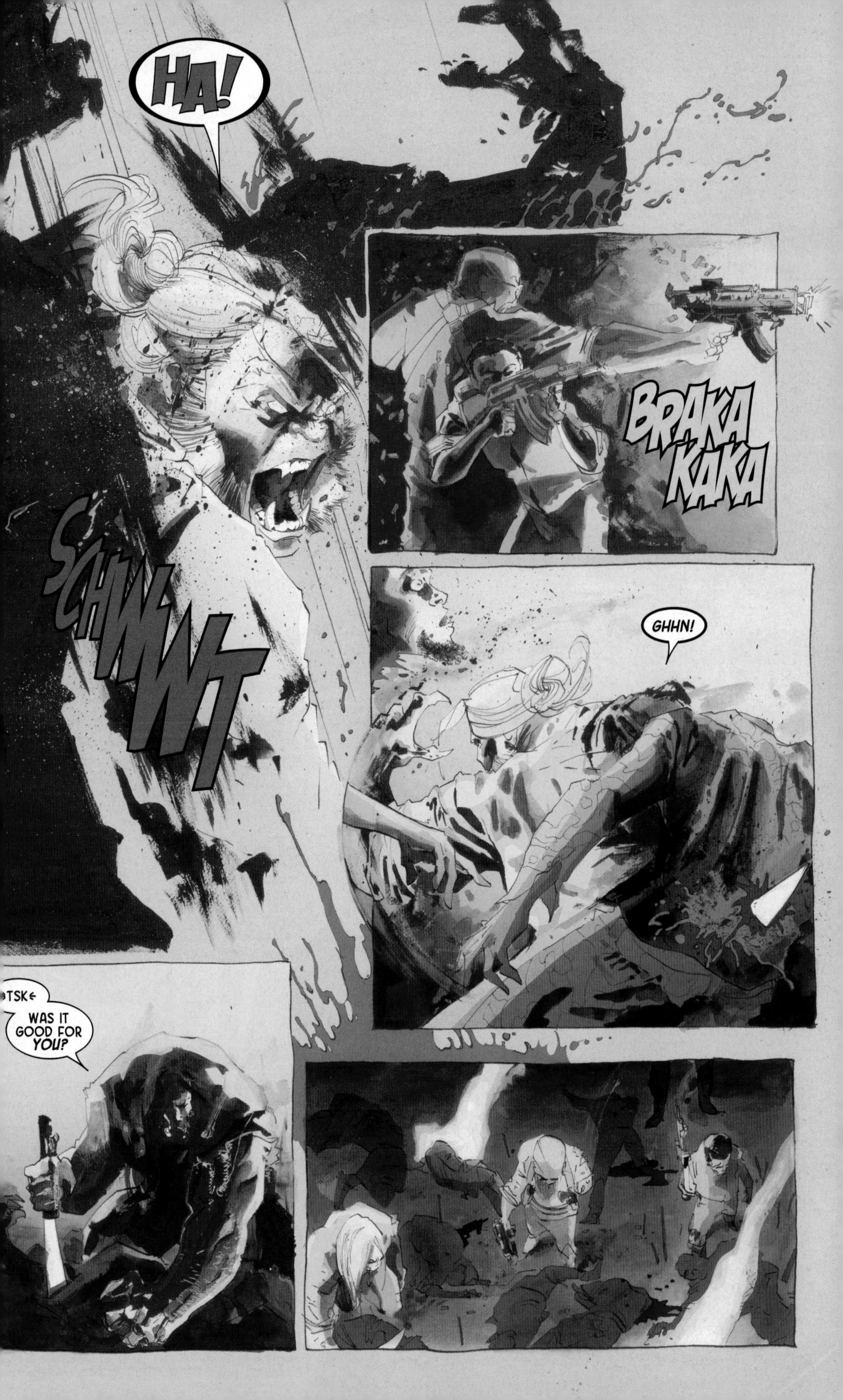
HA!
BRAKA KAKA
SCHWWT
GHHN!
»TSK«
WAS IT GOOD FOR YOU?

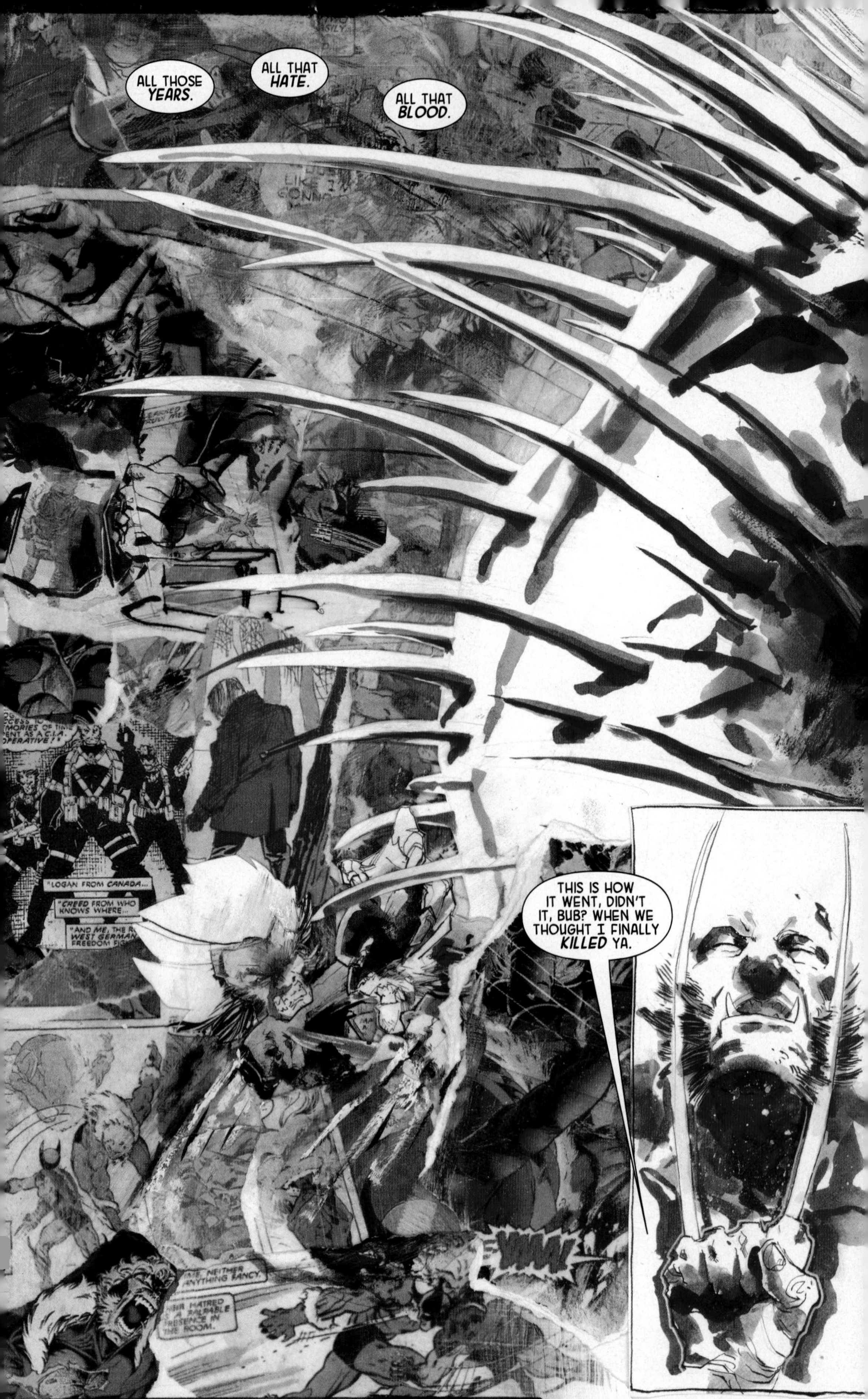
ALL THOSE YEARS.
ALL THAT HATE.
ALL THAT BLOOD.
"LOGAN FROM CANADA...
"CREED FROM WHO KNOWS WHERE...
THIS IS HOW IT WENT, DIDN'T IT, BUB? WHEN WE THOUGHT I FINALLY KILLED YA.

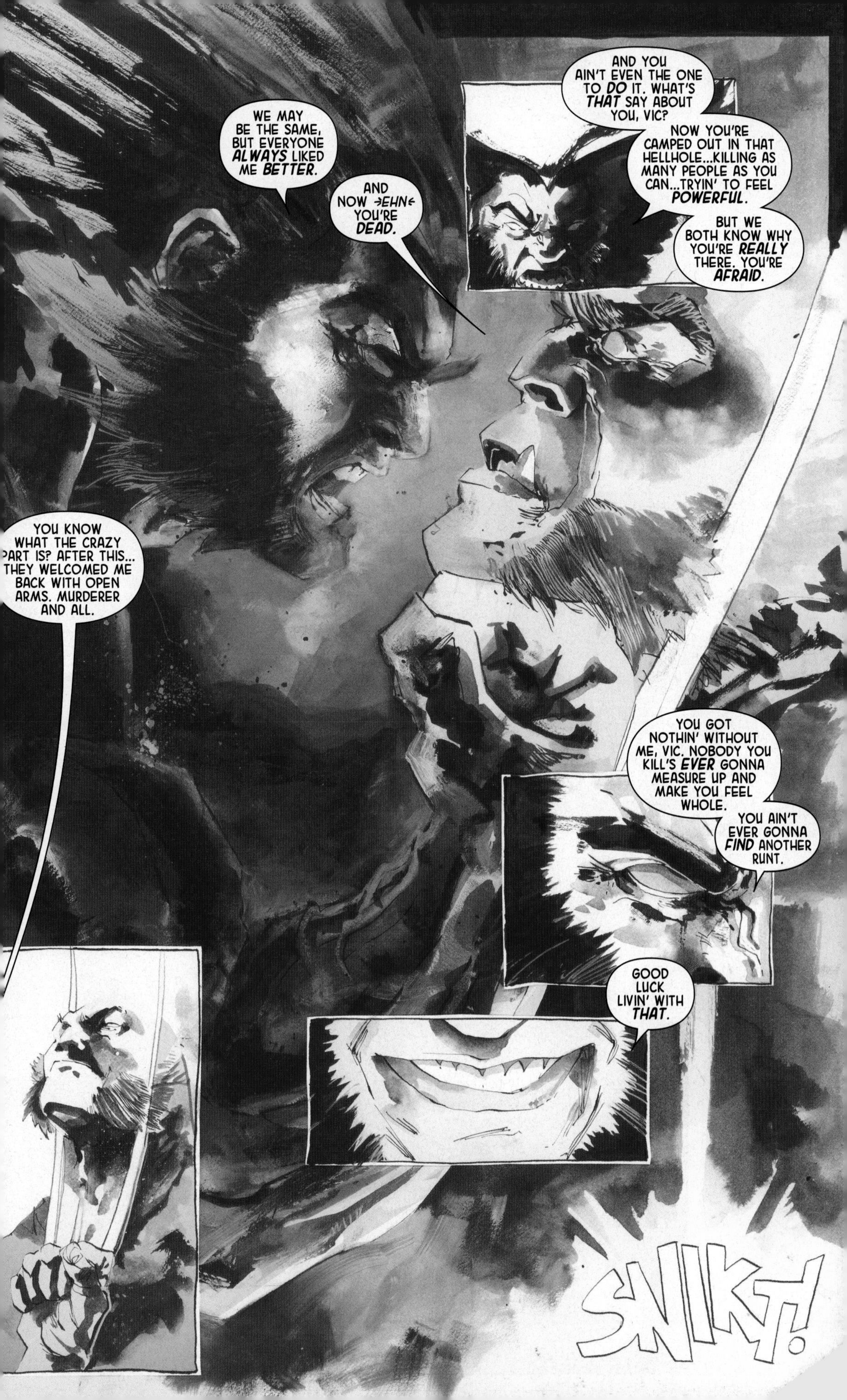

WE MAY BE THE SAME, BUT EVERYONE ALWAYS LIKED ME BETTER.
AND NOW →EHN← YOU'RE DEAD.
AND YOU AIN'T EVEN THE ONE TO DO IT. WHAT'S THAT SAY ABOUT YOU, VIC?
NOW YOU'RE CAMPED OUT IN THAT HELLHOLE...KILLING AS MANY PEOPLE AS YOU CAN...TRYIN' TO FEEL POWERFUL.
BUT WE BOTH KNOW WHY YOU'RE REALLY THERE. YOU'RE AFRAID.
YOU KNOW WHAT THE CRAZY PART IS? AFTER THIS... THEY WELCOMED ME BACK WITH OPEN ARMS. MURDERER AND ALL.
YOU GOT NOTHIN' WITHOUT ME, VIC. NOBODY YOU KILL'S EVER GONNA MEASURE UP AND MAKE YOU FEEL WHOLE.
YOU AIN'T EVER GONNA FIND ANOTHER RUNT.
GOOD LUCK LIVIN' WITH THAT.
SNIKT!

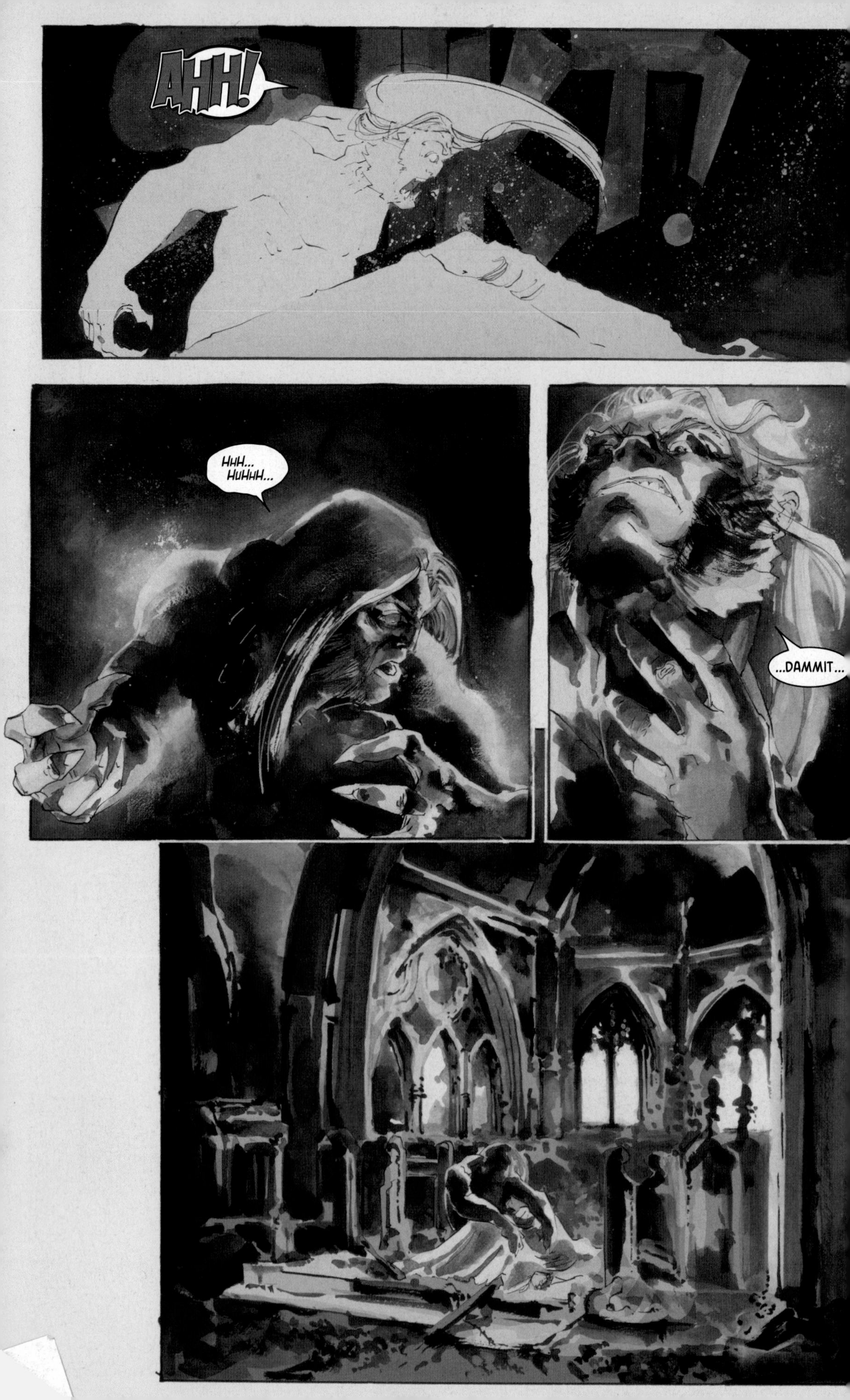
AHH!
HHH... HUHHH...
...DAMMIT...

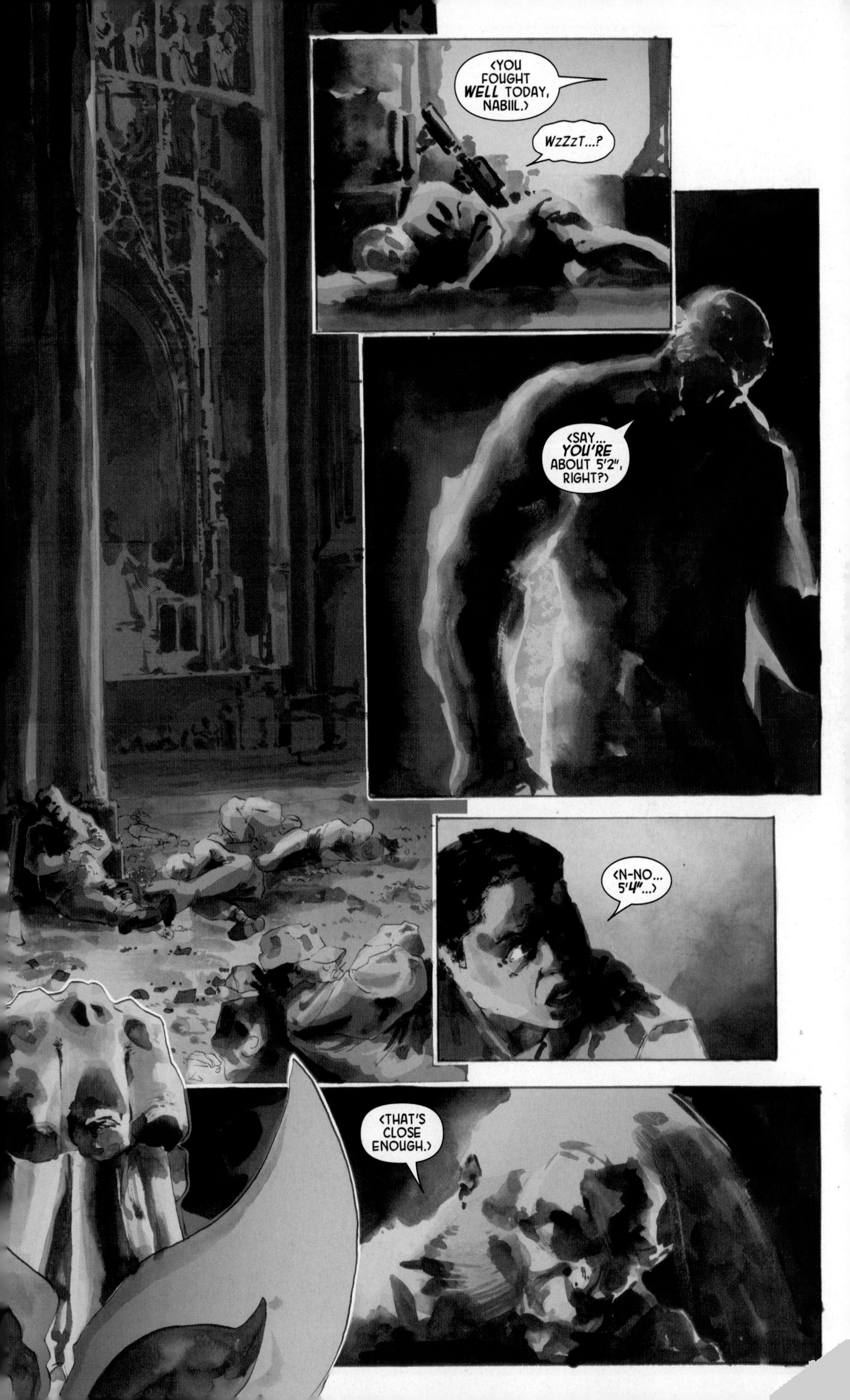

<YOU FOUGHT WELL TODAY, NABIIL.>
WzZzT...?
<SAY... YOU'RE ABOUT 5'2", RIGHT?>
<N-NO... 5'4"...>
<THAT'S CLOSE ENOUGH.>

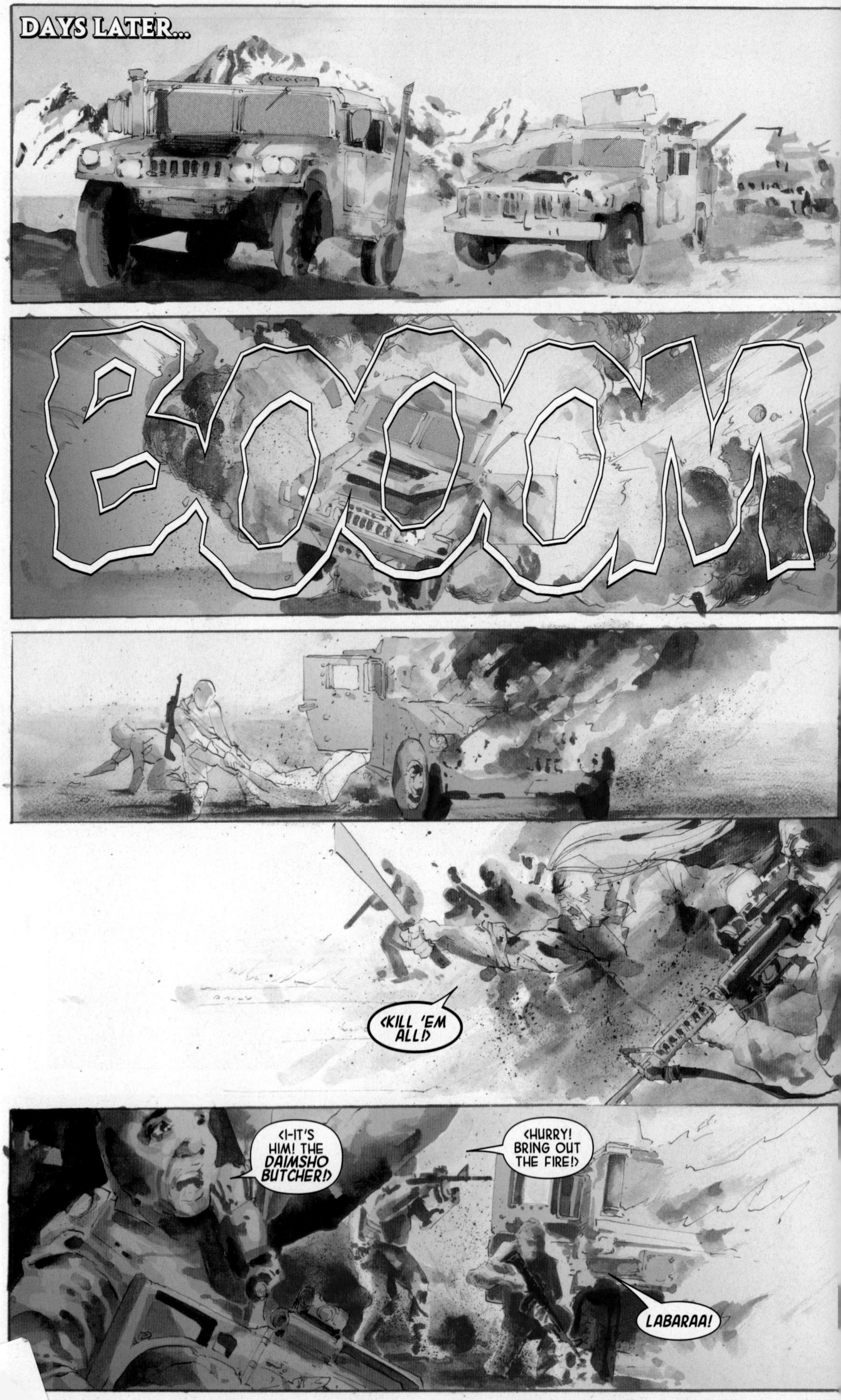
DAYS LATER...
BOOOM
<KILL 'EM ALL!>
<I-IT'S HIM! THE DAIMSHO BUTCHER!>
<HURRY! BRING OUT THE FIRE!>
LABARAA!

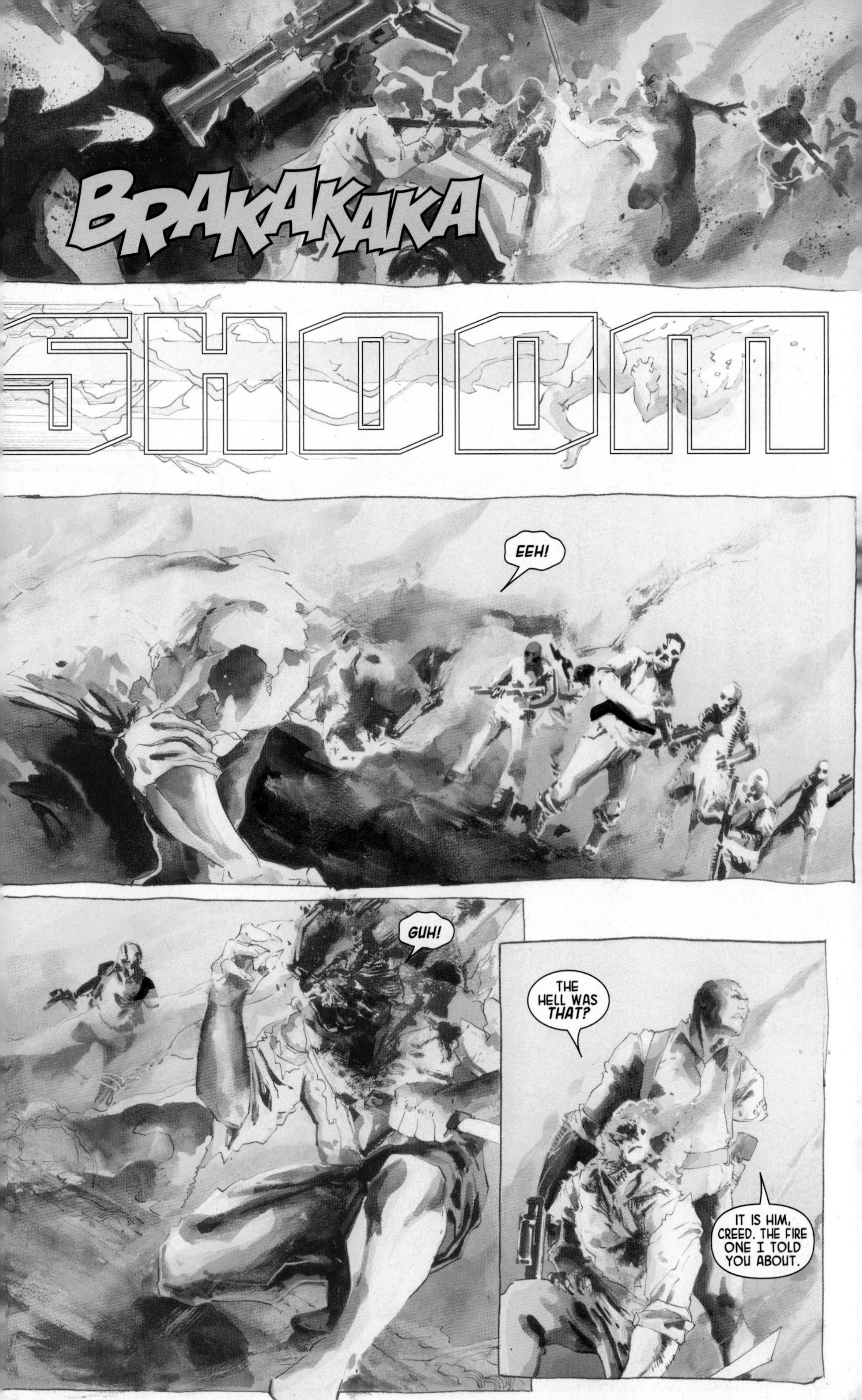
BRAKAKAKA
SHOOM
EEH!
GUH!
THE HELL WAS THAT?
IT IS HIM, CREED. THE FIRE ONE I TOLD YOU ABOUT.

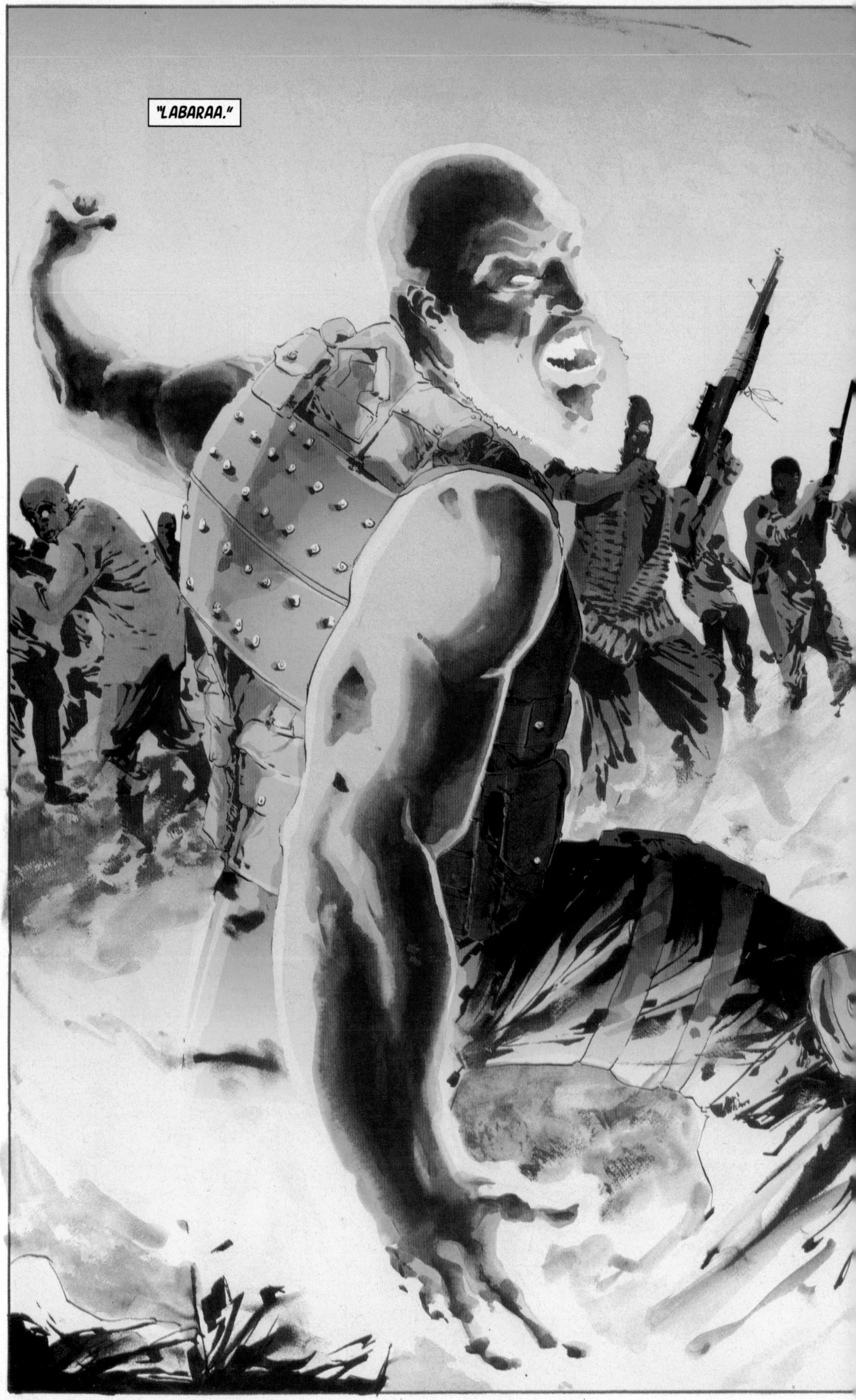
"LABARAA."

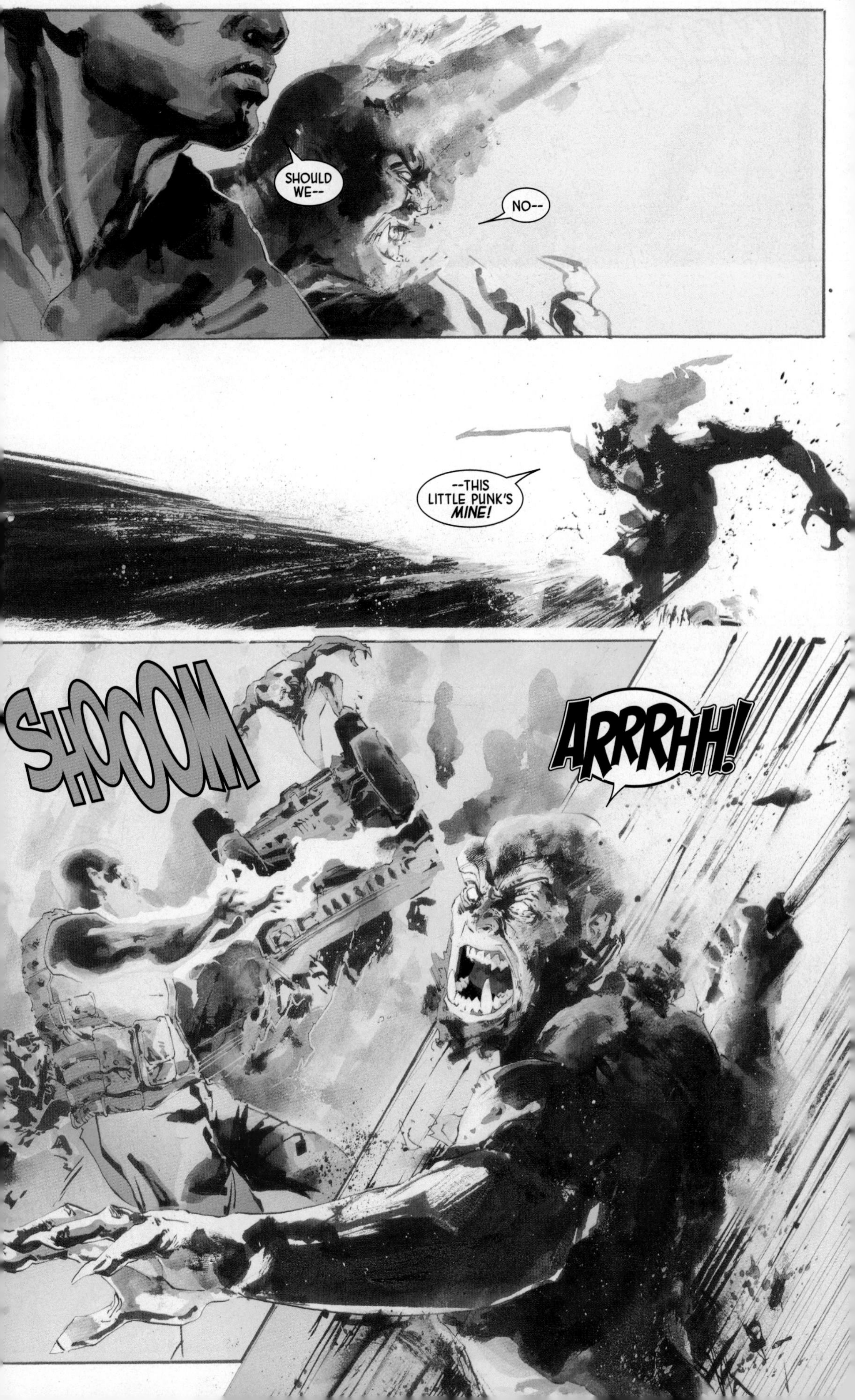

SHOULD WE--
NO--
--THIS LITTLE PUNK'S *MINE!*
SHOOOM
ARRRHH!

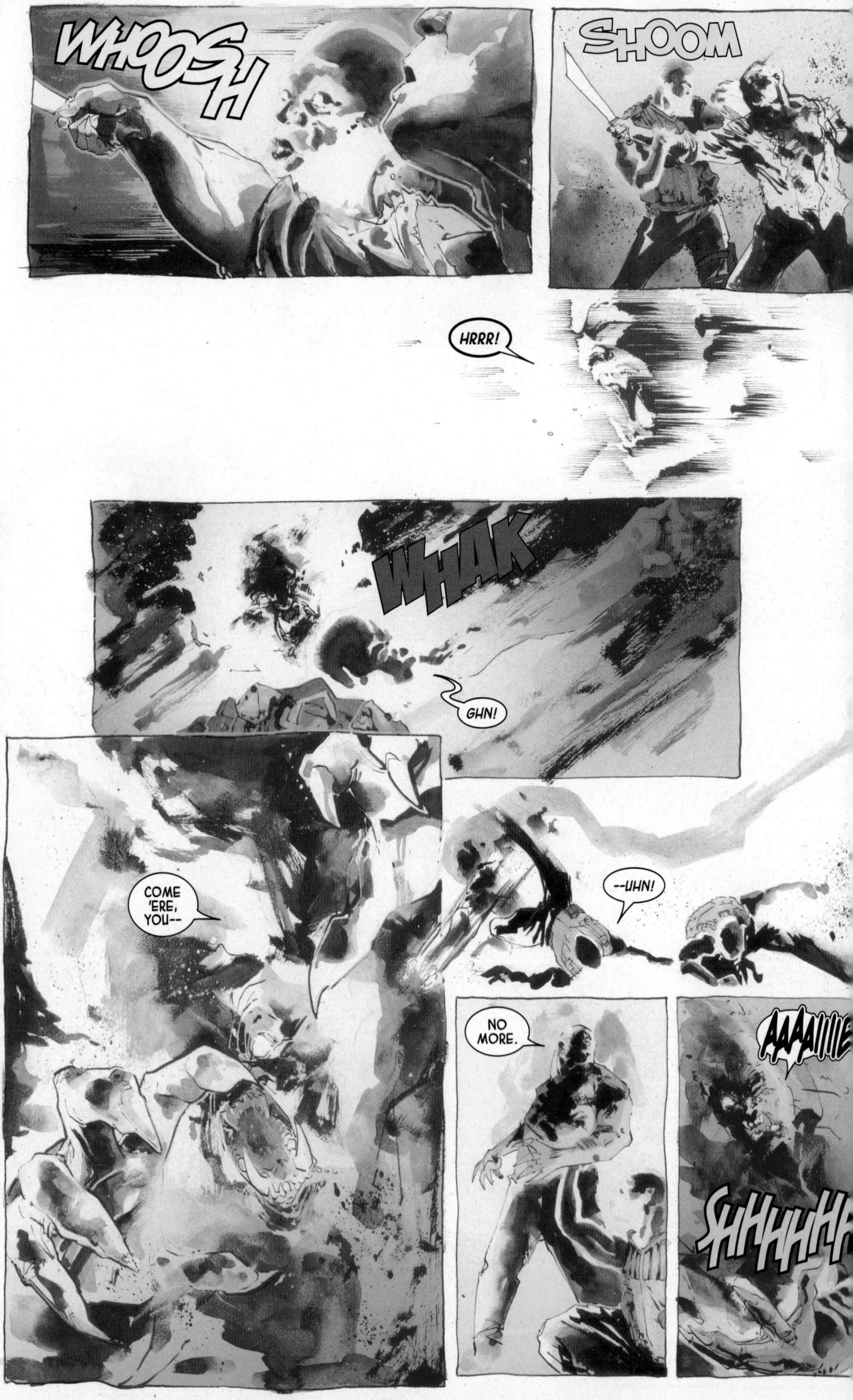
WHOOSH
SHOOM
HRRR!
WHAK
GHN!
COME 'ERE, YOU--
--UHN!
NO MORE.
AAAIIIIE
SHHHHH

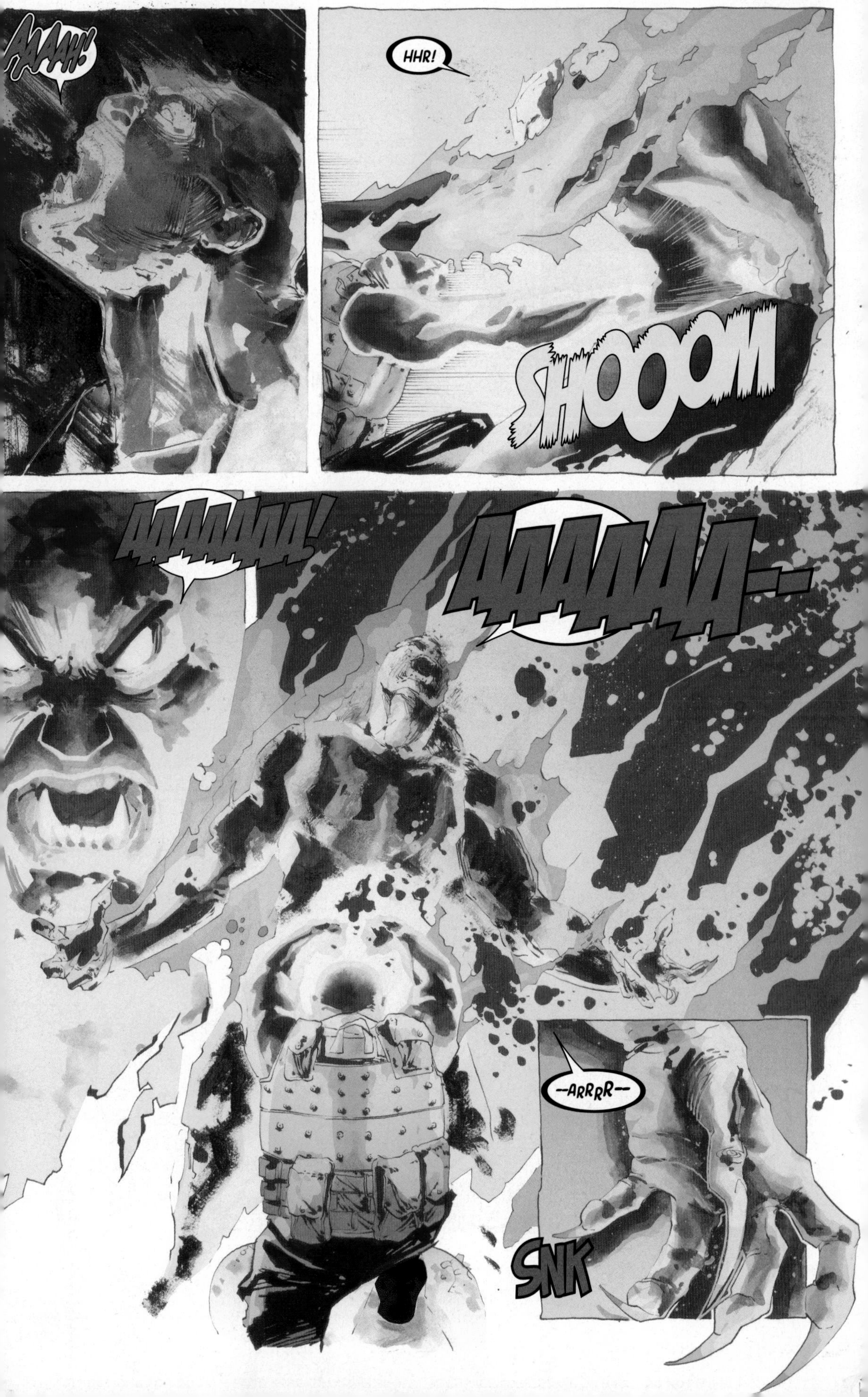
AAAAH!
HHR!
SHOOOM
AAAAAAA!
AAAAAA--
--ARRRR--
SNK

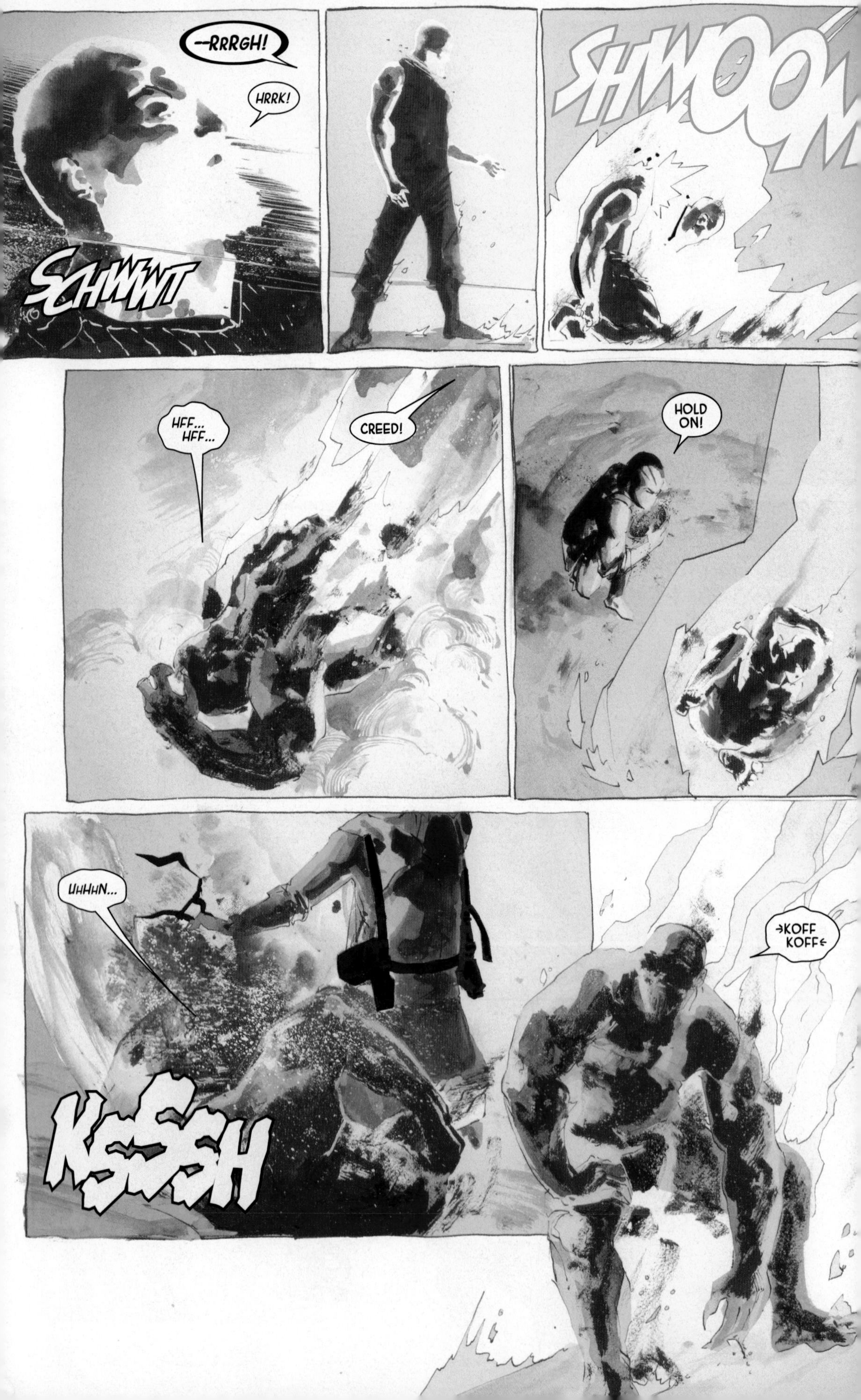

–RRRGH!
HRRK!
SCHWWT
SHWOOM
HFF... HFF...
CREED!
HOLD ON!
UHHHN...
KSSSH
KOFF KOFF

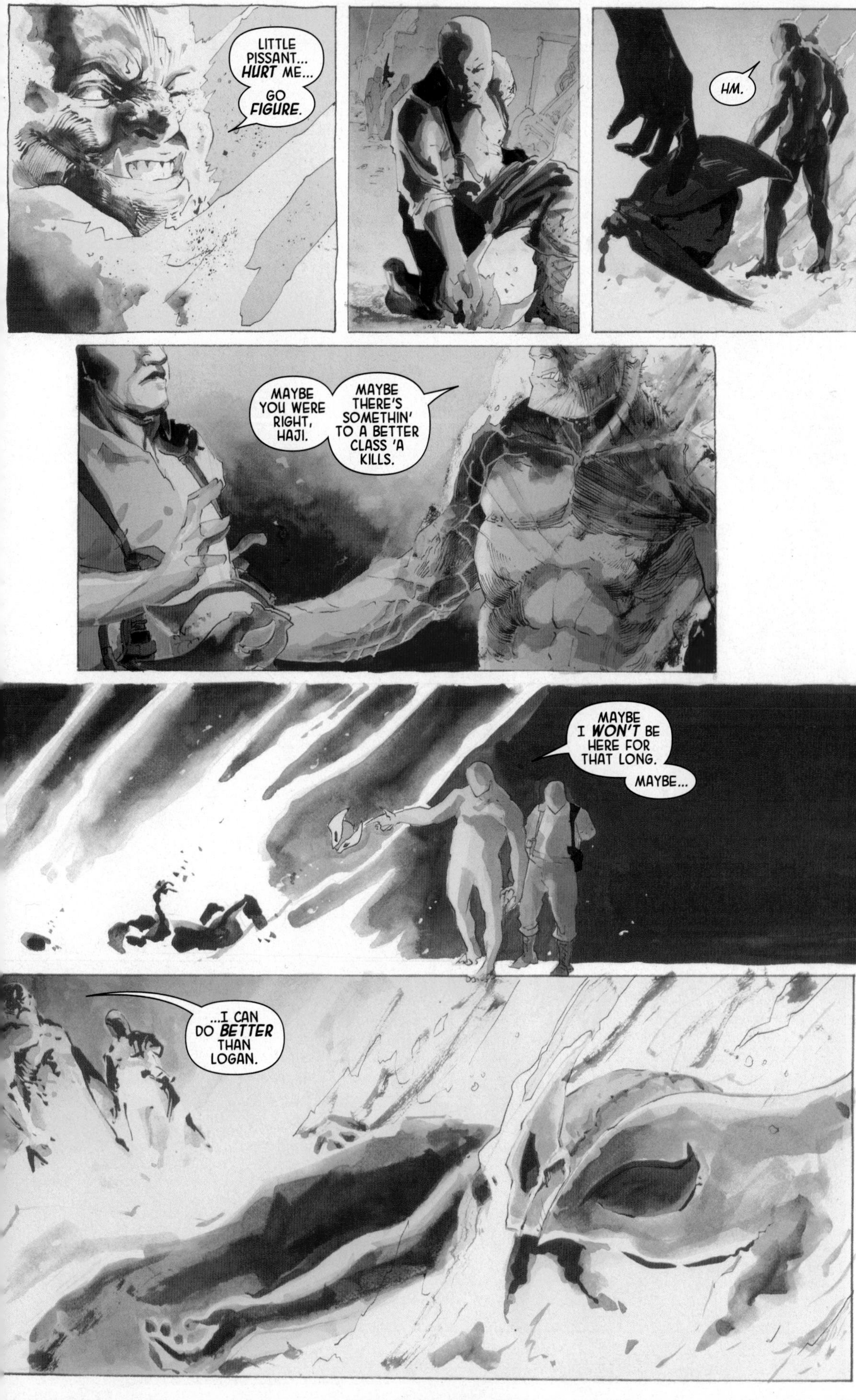
LITTLE PISSANT... HURT ME... GO FIGURE.
HM.
MAYBE YOU WERE RIGHT, HAJI.
MAYBE THERE'S SOMETHIN' TO A BETTER CLASS 'A KILLS.
MAYBE I WON'T BE HERE FOR THAT LONG.
MAYBE...
...I CAN DO BETTER THAN LOGAN.

4

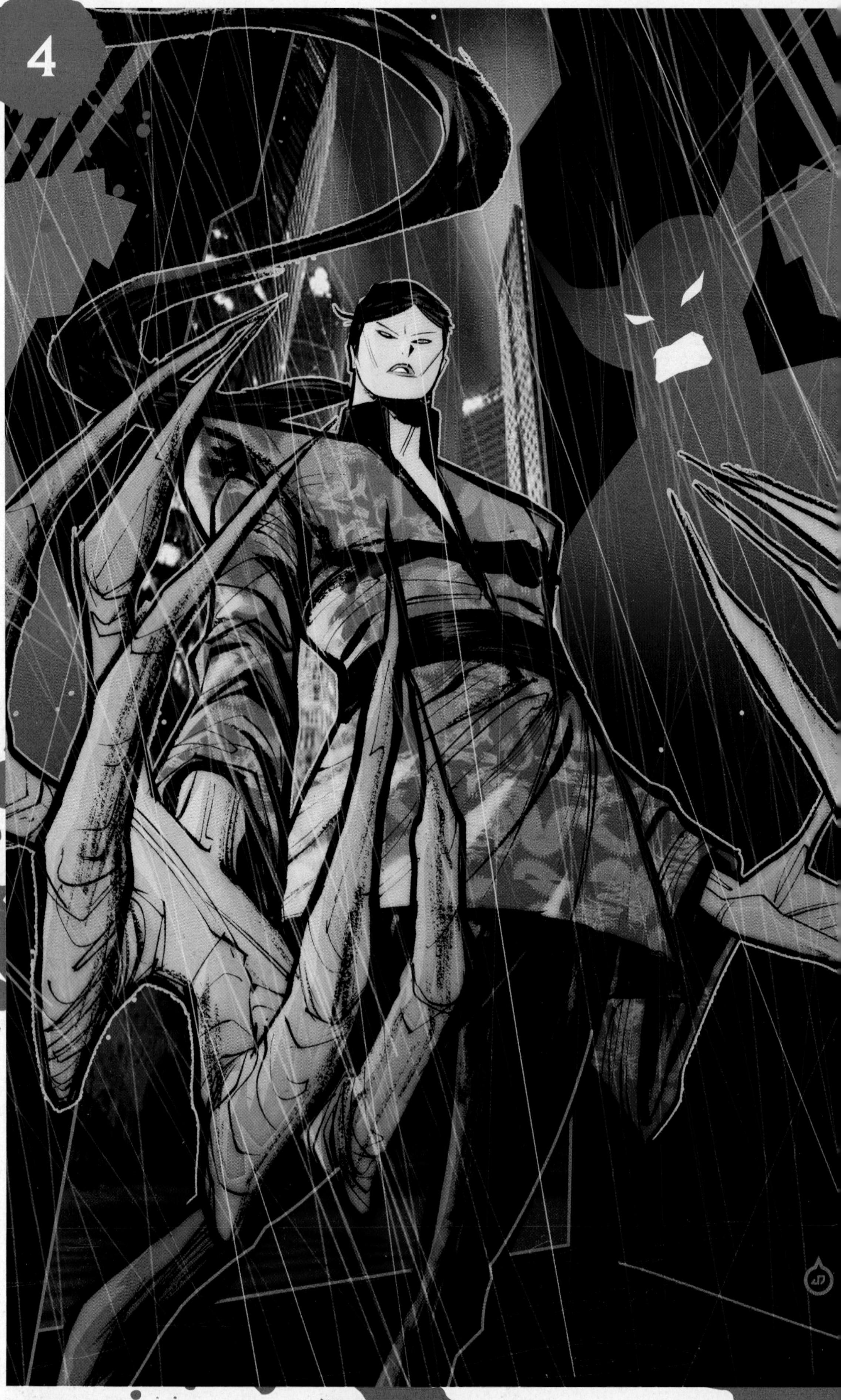

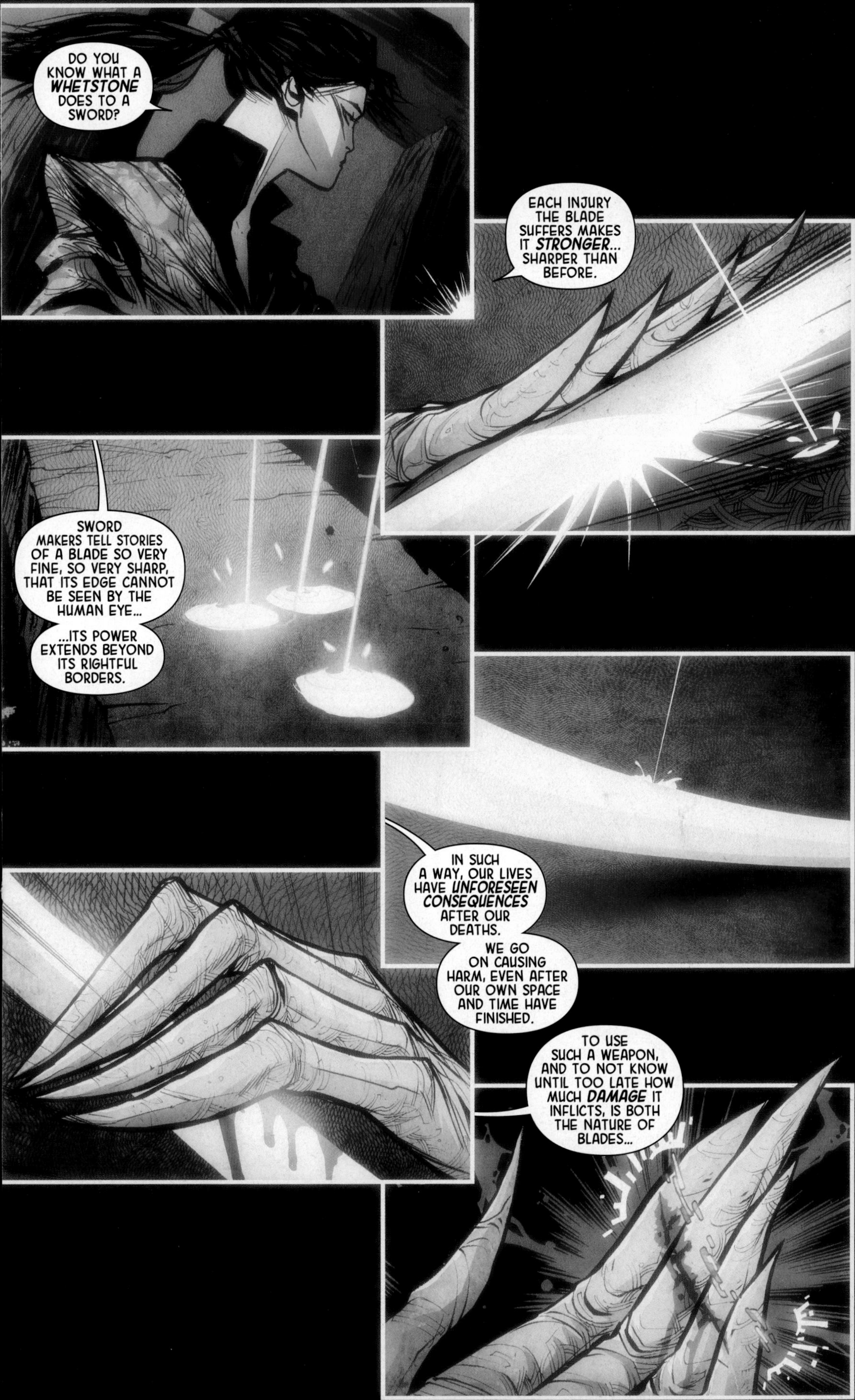
DO YOU KNOW WHAT A WHETSTONE DOES TO A SWORD?
EACH INJURY THE BLADE SUFFERS MAKES IT STRONGER... SHARPER THAN BEFORE.
SWORD MAKERS TELL STORIES OF A BLADE SO VERY FINE, SO VERY SHARP, THAT ITS EDGE CANNOT BE SEEN BY THE HUMAN EYE...
...ITS POWER EXTENDS BEYOND ITS RIGHTFUL BORDERS.
IN SUCH A WAY, OUR LIVES HAVE UNFORESEEN CONSEQUENCES AFTER OUR DEATHS.
WE GO ON CAUSING HARM, EVEN AFTER OUR OWN SPACE AND TIME HAVE FINISHED.
TO USE SUCH A WEAPON, AND TO NOT KNOW UNTIL TOO LATE HOW MUCH DAMAGE IT INFLICTS, IS BOTH THE NATURE OF BLADES...

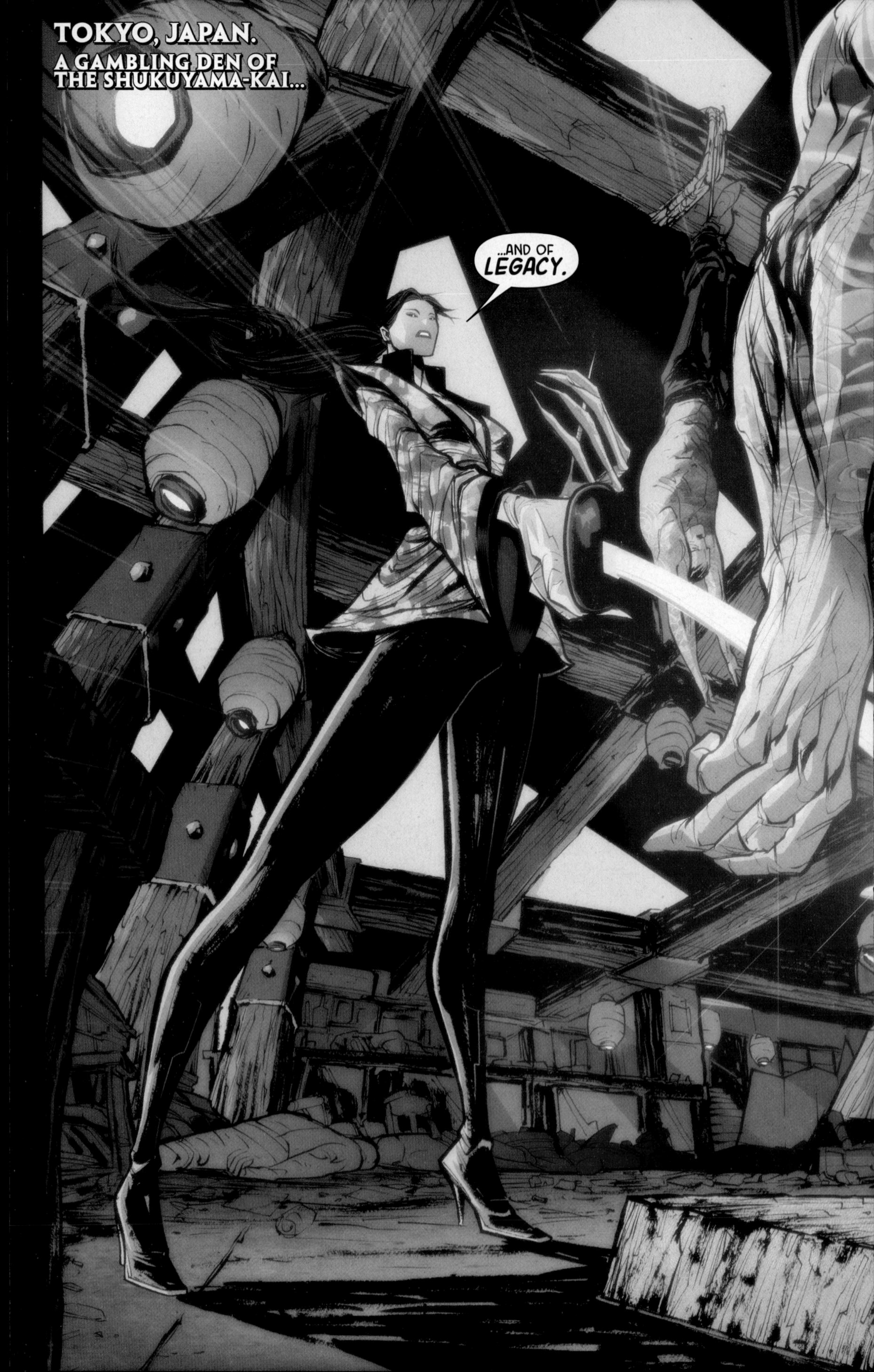
TOKYO, JAPAN.
A GAMBLING DEN OF THE SHUKUYAMA-KAI...
...AND OF LEGACY.

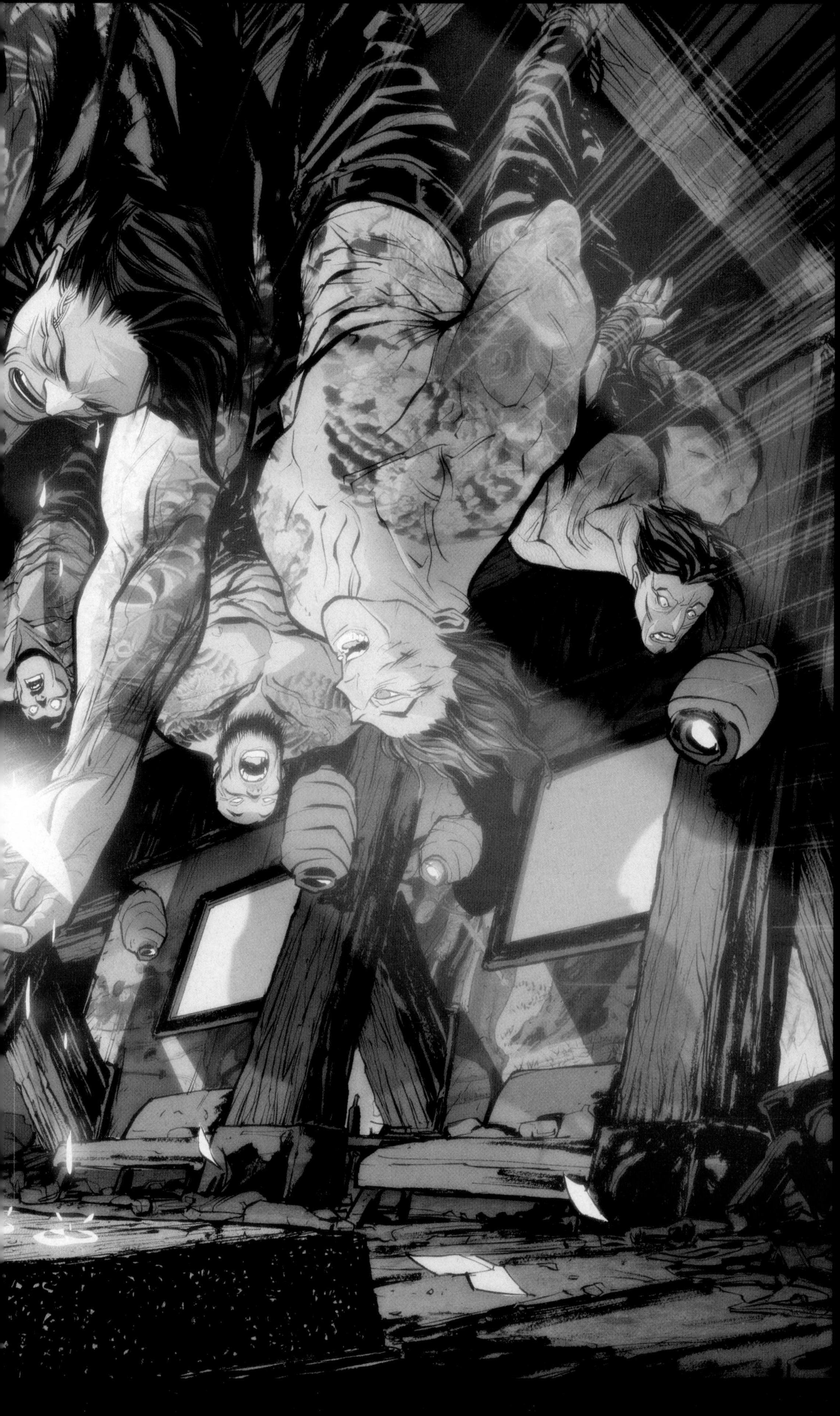

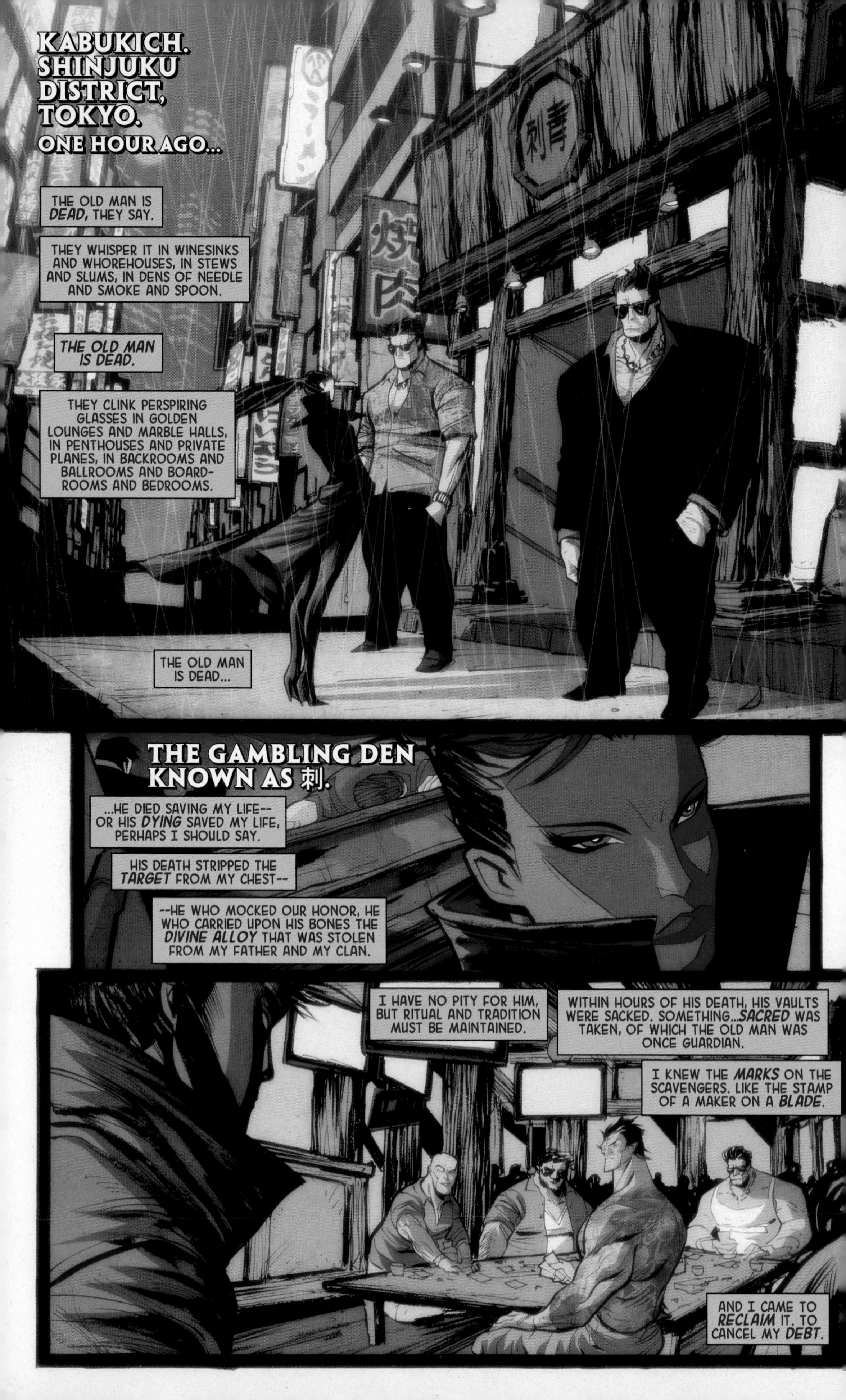
KABUKICH. SHINJUKU DISTRICT, TOKYO.
ONE HOUR AGO...
THE OLD MAN IS DEAD, THEY SAY.
THEY WHISPER IT IN WINESINKS AND WHOREHOUSES, IN STEWS AND SLUMS, IN DENS OF NEEDLE AND SMOKE AND SPOON.
THE OLD MAN IS DEAD.
THEY CLINK PERSPIRING GLASSES IN GOLDEN LOUNGES AND MARBLE HALLS, IN PENTHOUSES AND PRIVATE PLANES, IN BACKROOMS AND BALLROOMS AND BOARD-ROOMS AND BEDROOMS.
THE OLD MAN IS DEAD...
THE GAMBLING DEN KNOWN AS 刺.
...HE DIED SAVING MY LIFE-- OR HIS DYING SAVED MY LIFE, PERHAPS I SHOULD SAY.
HIS DEATH STRIPPED THE TARGET FROM MY CHEST--
--HE WHO MOCKED OUR HONOR, HE WHO CARRIED UPON HIS BONES THE DIVINE ALLOY THAT WAS STOLEN FROM MY FATHER AND MY CLAN.
I HAVE NO PITY FOR HIM, BUT RITUAL AND TRADITION MUST BE MAINTAINED.
WITHIN HOURS OF HIS DEATH, HIS VAULTS WERE SACKED. SOMETHING...SACRED WAS TAKEN, OF WHICH THE OLD MAN WAS ONCE GUARDIAN.
I KNEW THE MARKS ON THE SCAVENGERS. LIKE THE STAMP OF A MAKER ON A BLADE.
AND I CAME TO RECLAIM IT. TO CANCEL MY DEBT.

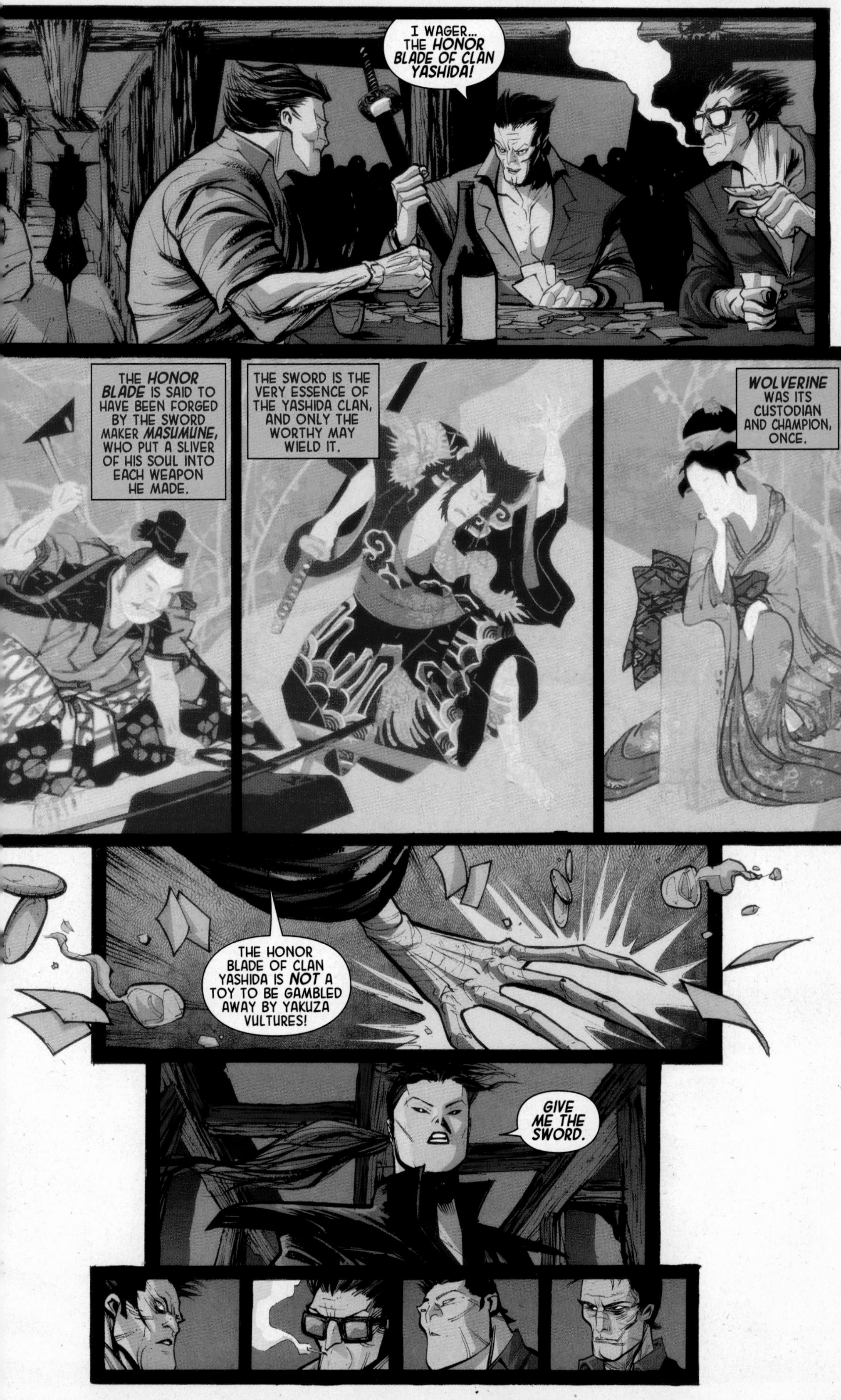
I WAGER... THE HONOR BLADE OF CLAN YASHIDA!
THE HONOR BLADE IS SAID TO HAVE BEEN FORGED BY THE SWORD MAKER MASUMUNE, WHO PUT A SLIVER OF HIS SOUL INTO EACH WEAPON HE MADE.
THE SWORD IS THE VERY ESSENCE OF THE YASHIDA CLAN, AND ONLY THE WORTHY MAY WIELD IT.
WOLVERINE WAS ITS CUSTODIAN AND CHAMPION, ONCE.
THE HONOR BLADE OF CLAN YASHIDA IS NOT A TOY TO BE GAMBLED AWAY BY YAKUZA VULTURES!
GIVE ME THE SWORD.

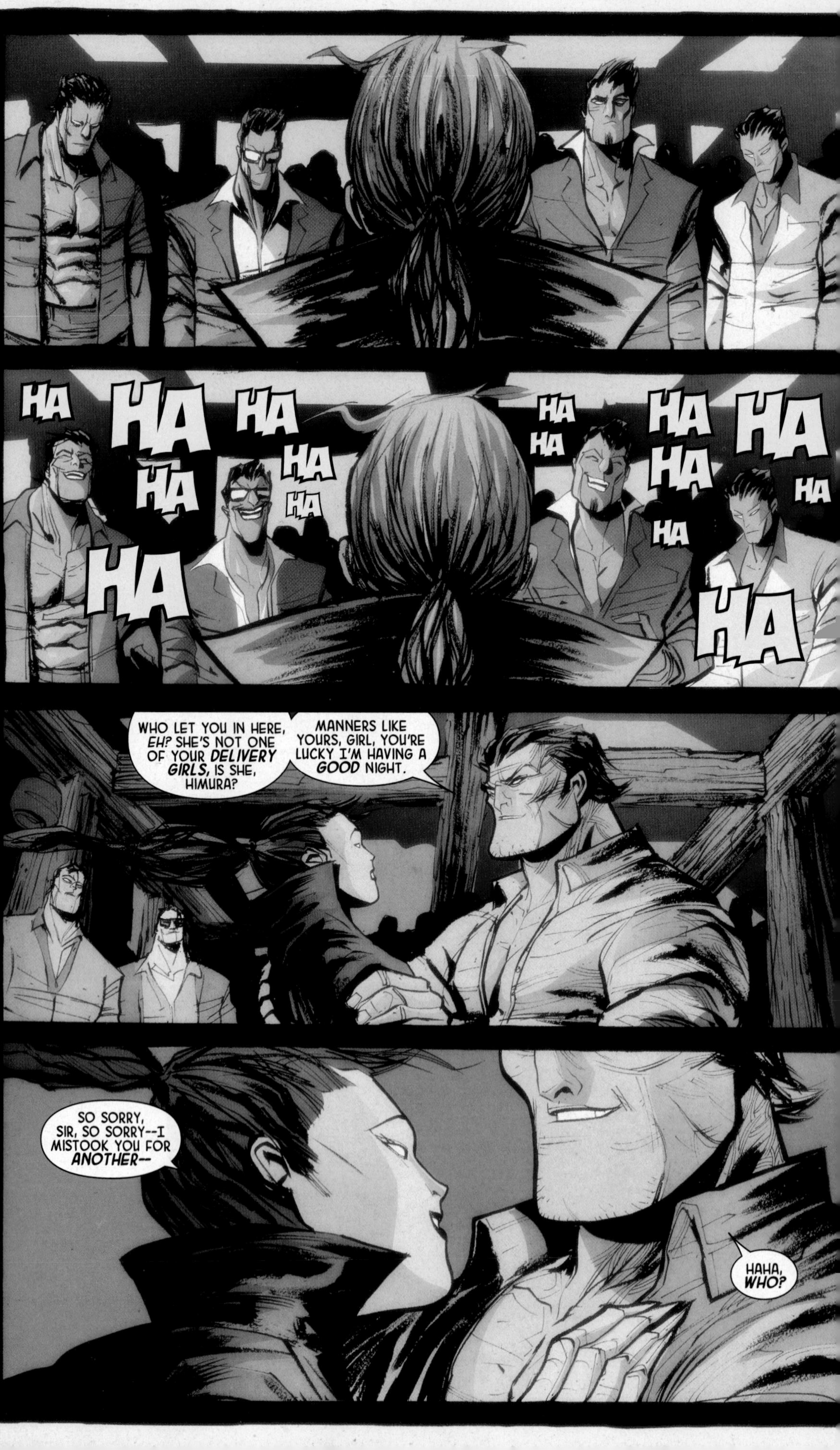
HA HA HA HA HA HA HA HA HA HA HA HA HA HA HA HA
WHO LET YOU IN HERE, EH? SHE'S NOT ONE OF YOUR DELIVERY GIRLS, IS SHE, HIMURA?
MANNERS LIKE YOURS, GIRL, YOU'RE LUCKY I'M HAVING A GOOD NIGHT.
SO SORRY, SIR, SO SORRY--I MISTOOK YOU FOR ANOTHER--
HAHA, WHO?

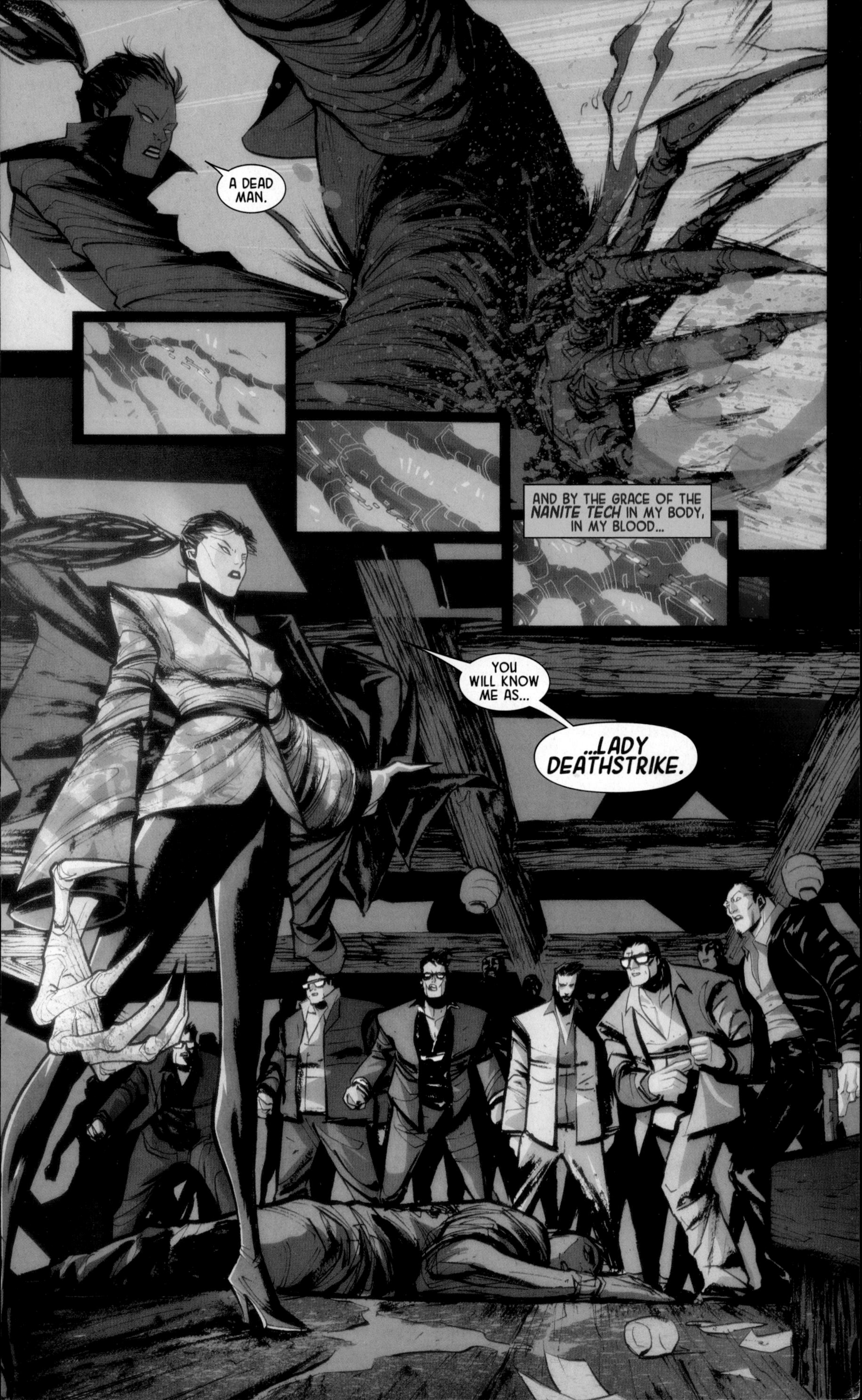
A DEAD MAN.
AND BY THE GRACE OF THE *NANITE TECH* IN MY BODY, IN MY BLOOD...
YOU WILL KNOW ME AS...
...LADY DEATHSTRIKE.

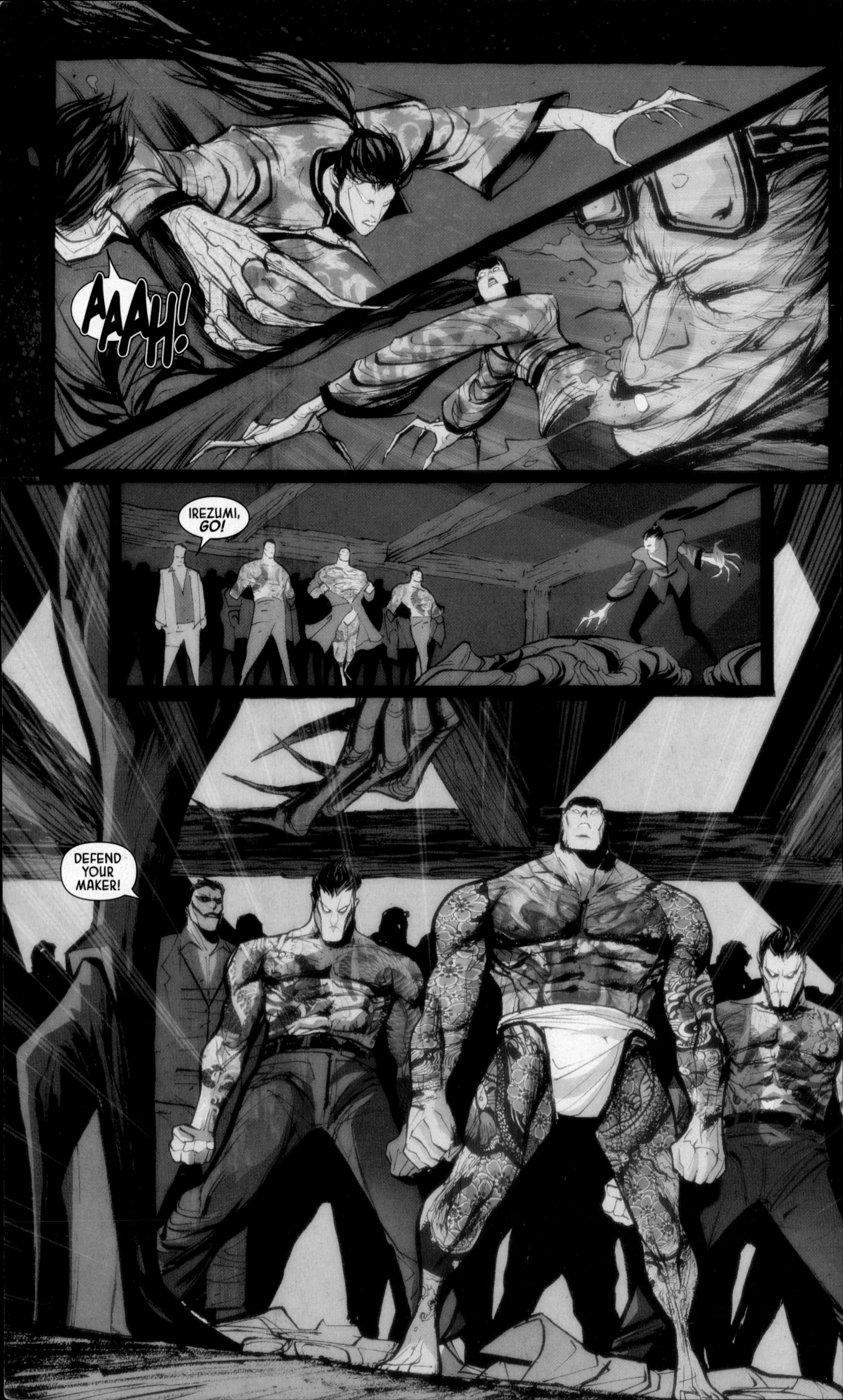
AAAH!
IREZUMI, GO!
DEFEND YOUR MAKER!

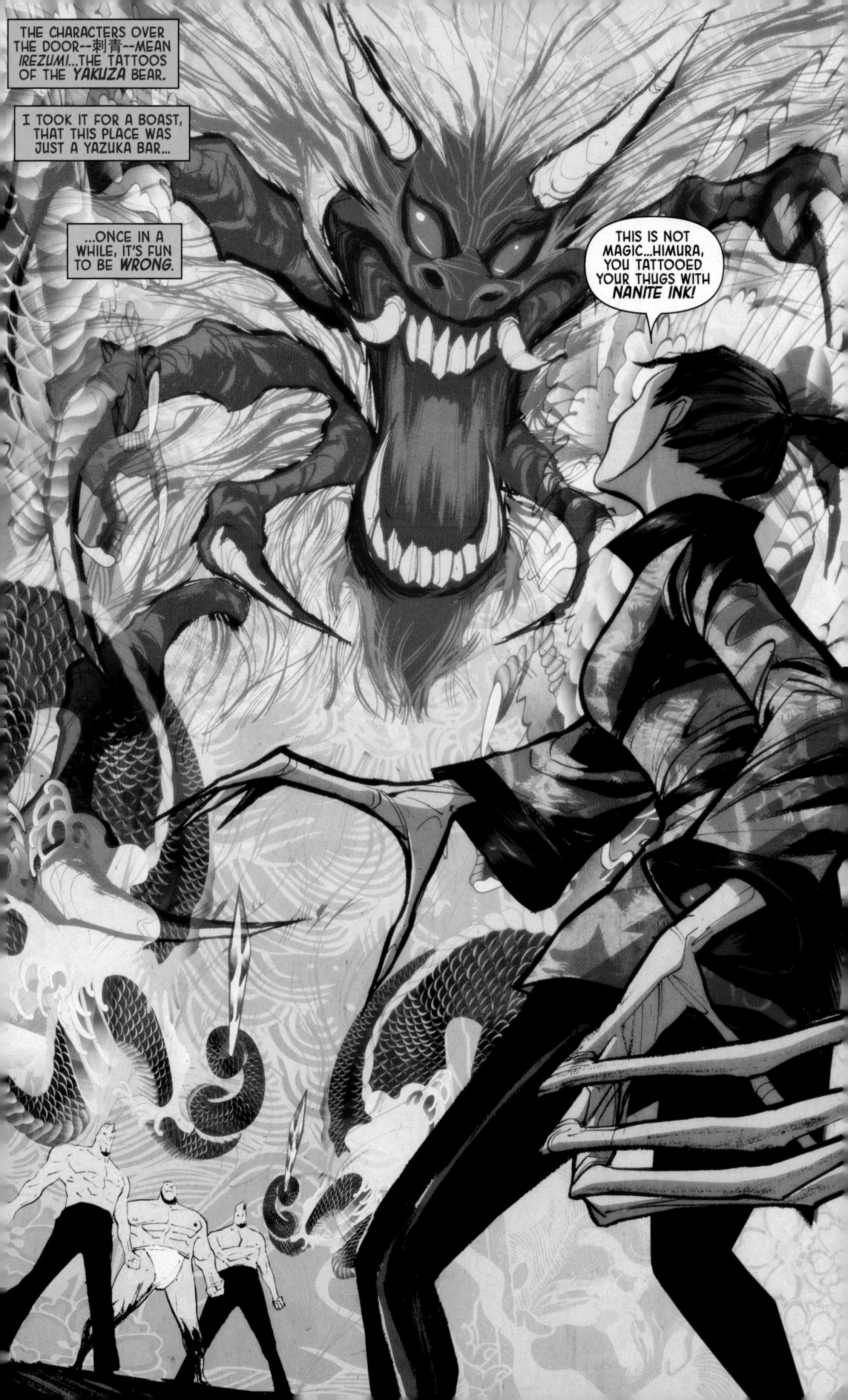
THE CHARACTERS OVER THE DOOR--刺青--MEAN *IREZUMI*...THE TATTOOS OF THE ***YAKUZA*** BEAR.
I TOOK IT FOR A BOAST, THAT THIS PLACE WAS JUST A YAZUKA BAR...
...ONCE IN A WHILE, IT'S FUN TO BE ***WRONG***.
THIS IS NOT MAGIC...HIMURA, YOU TATTOOED YOUR THUGS WITH ***NANITE INK!***

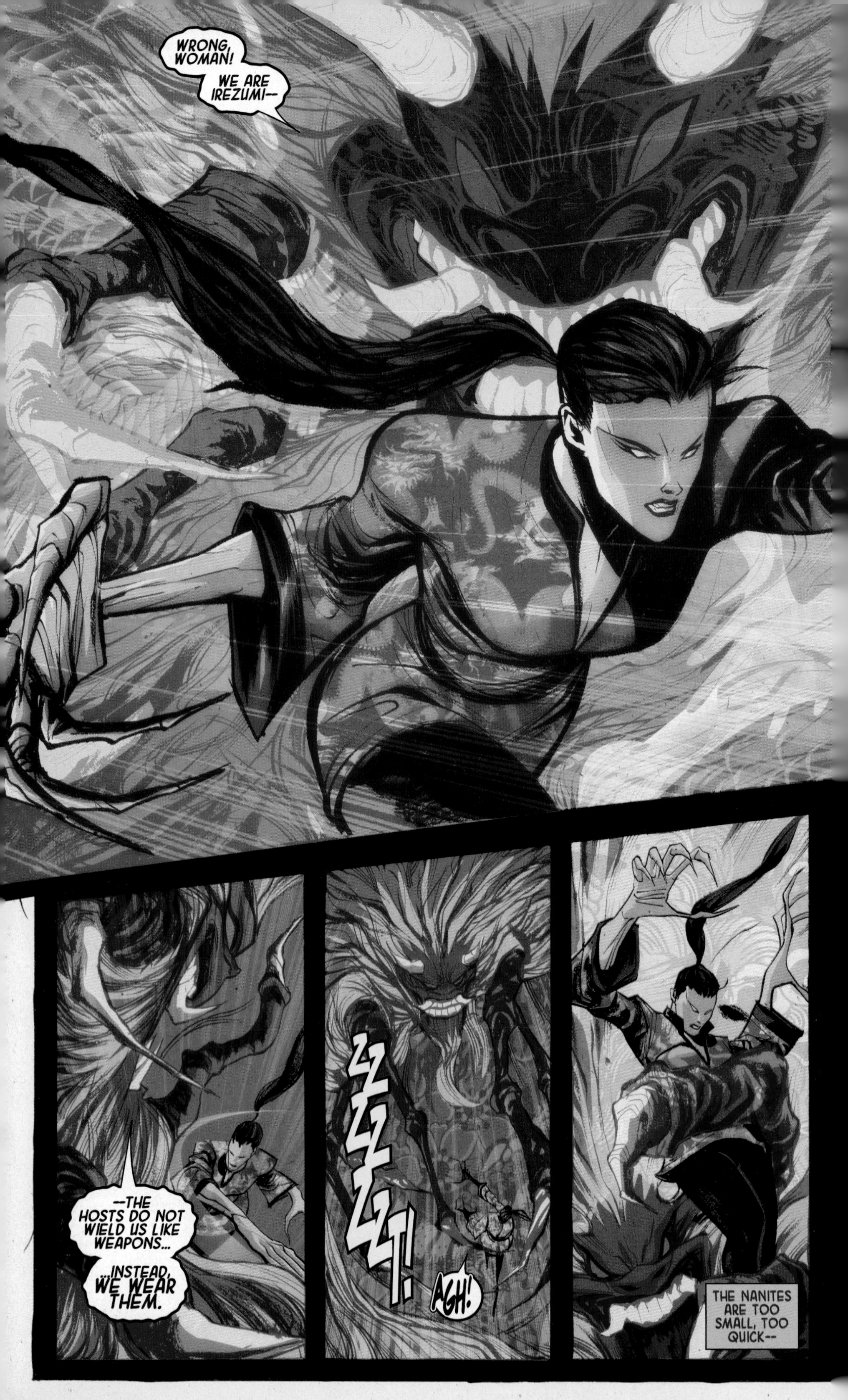
WRONG, WOMAN!
WE ARE IREZUMI--
--THE HOSTS DO NOT WIELD US LIKE WEAPONS...
...INSTEAD, WE WEAR THEM.
ZZZZZZT!
AGH!
THE NANITES ARE TOO SMALL, TOO QUICK--

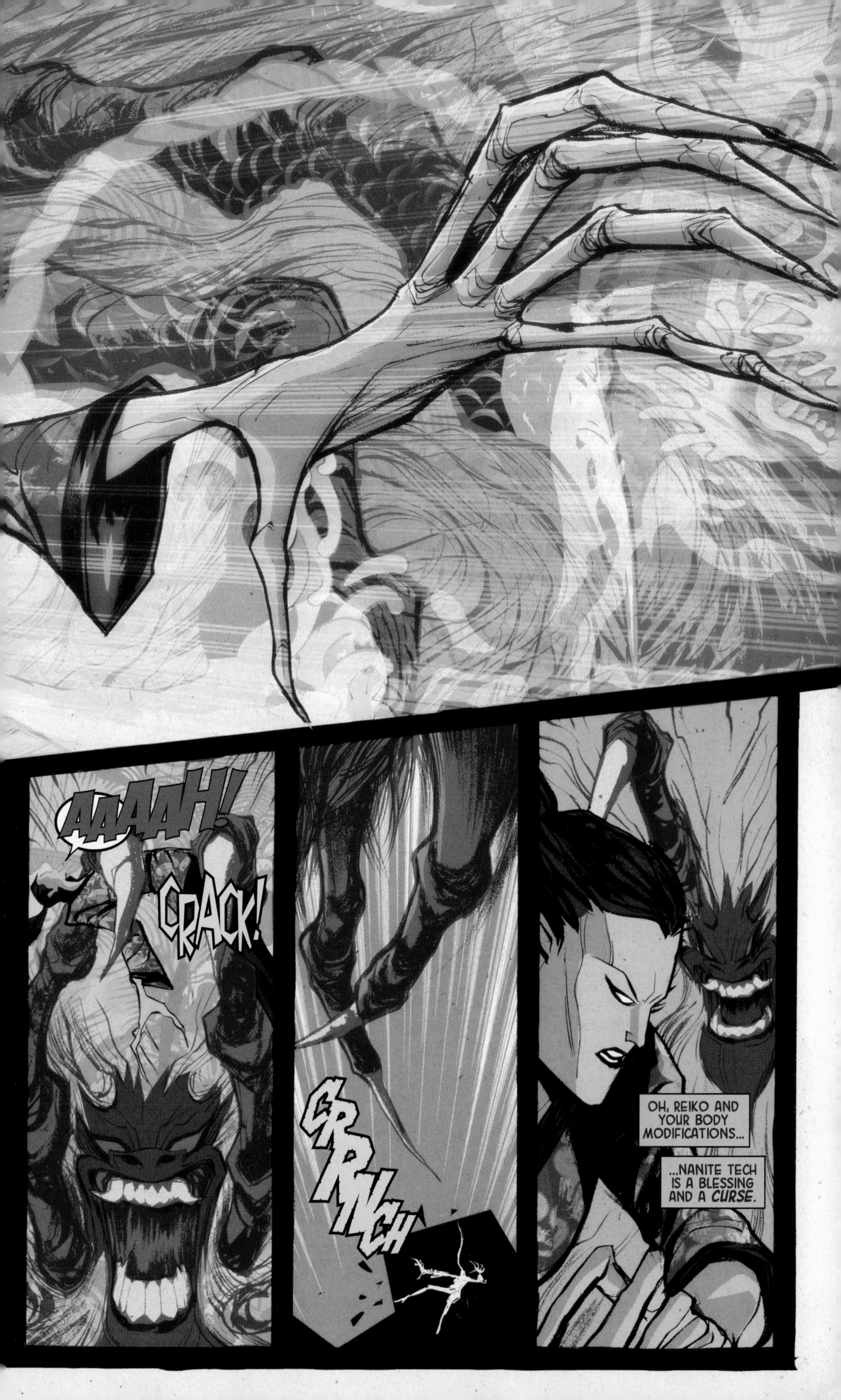

AAAAH!
CRACK!
CRRNCH
OH, REIKO AND YOUR BODY MODIFICATIONS...
...NANITE TECH IS A BLESSING AND A CURSE.

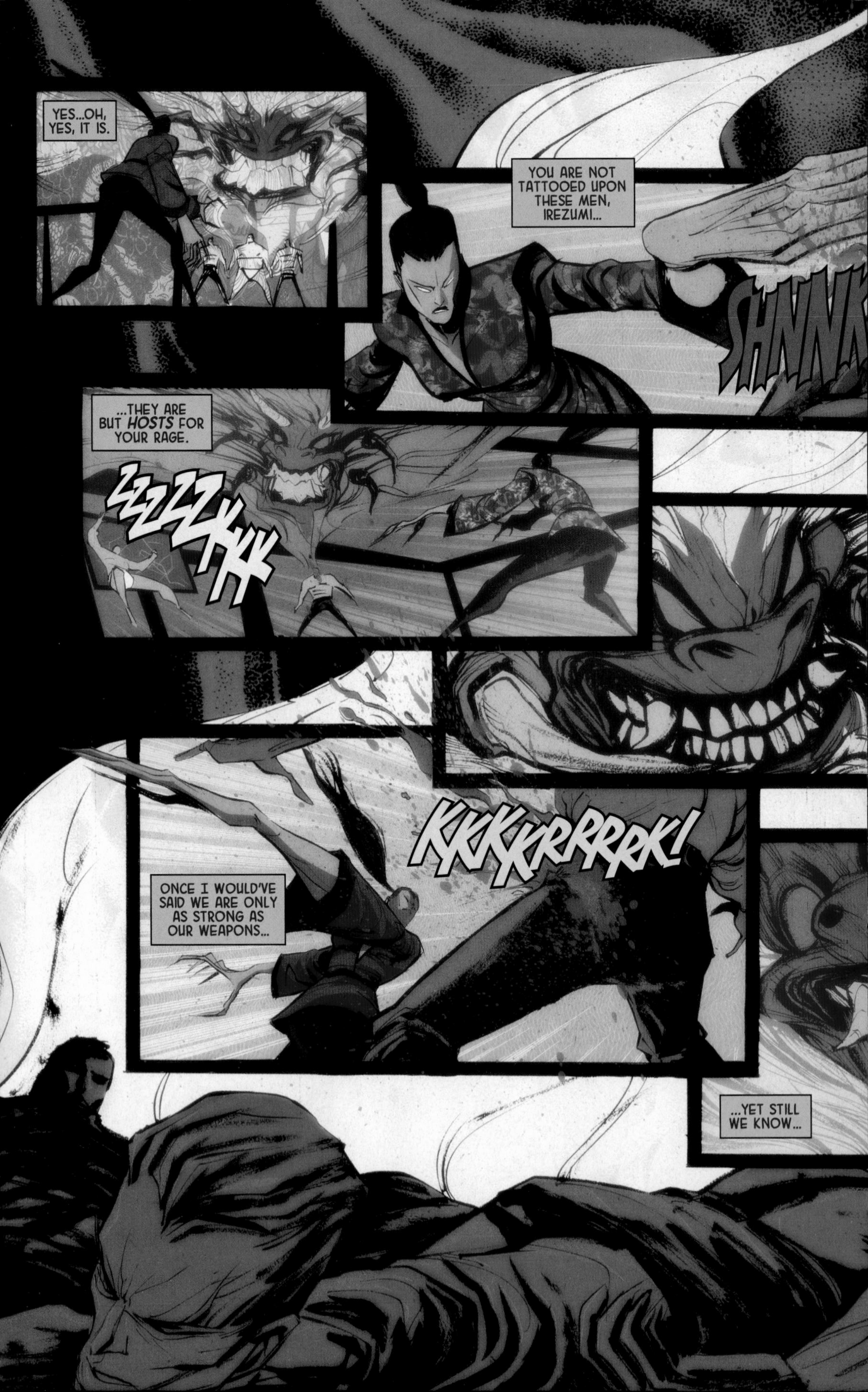

YES...OH, YES, IT IS.
YOU ARE NOT TATTOOED UPON THESE MEN, IREZUMI...
SHNNK
...THEY ARE BUT HOSTS FOR YOUR RAGE.
ZZZZZKKK
KKKKKRRRRRK!
ONCE I WOULD'VE SAID WE ARE ONLY AS STRONG AS OUR WEAPONS...
...YET STILL WE KNOW...

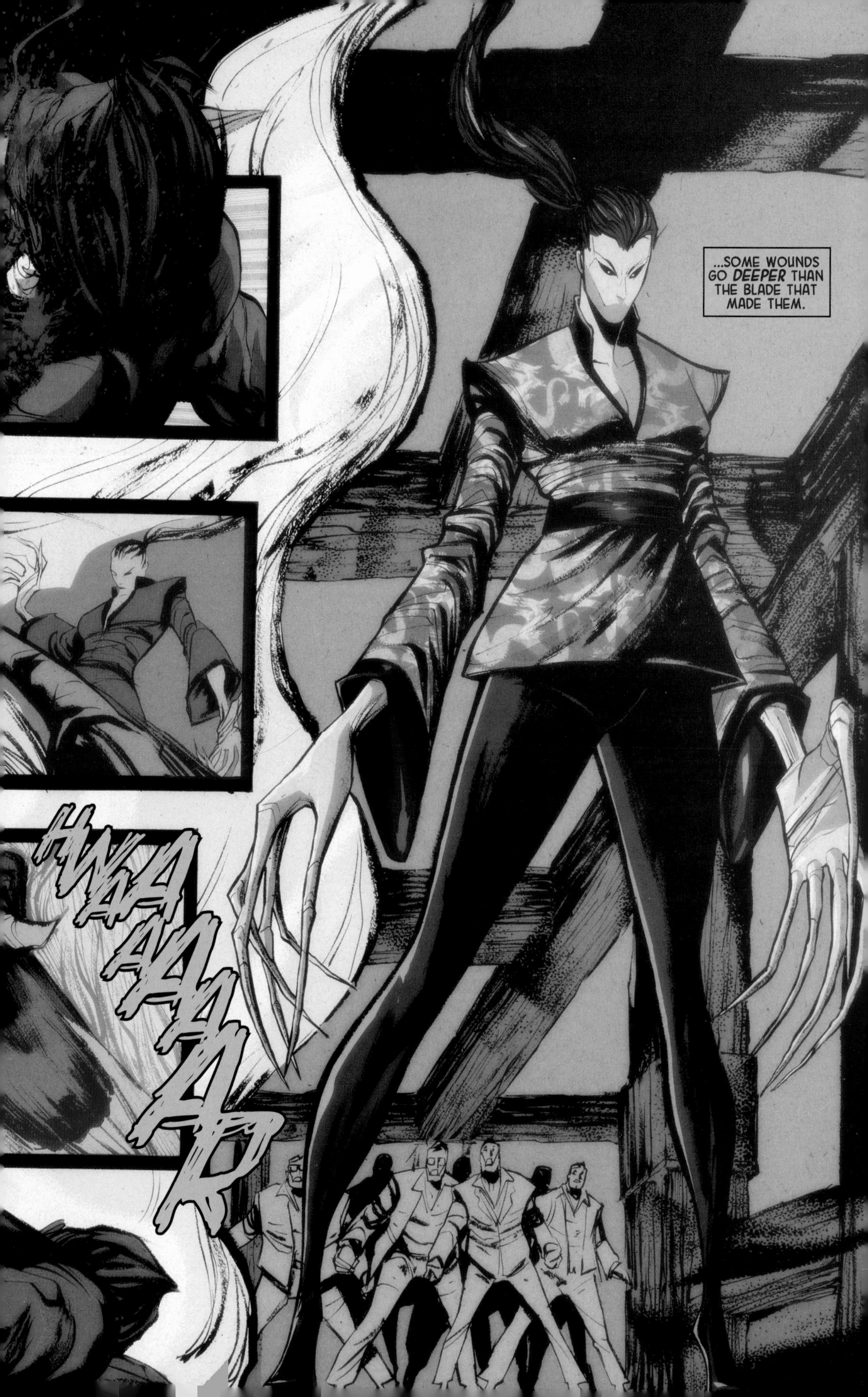
...SOME WOUNDS GO DEEPER THAN THE BLADE THAT MADE THEM.
HWAAAAAAR

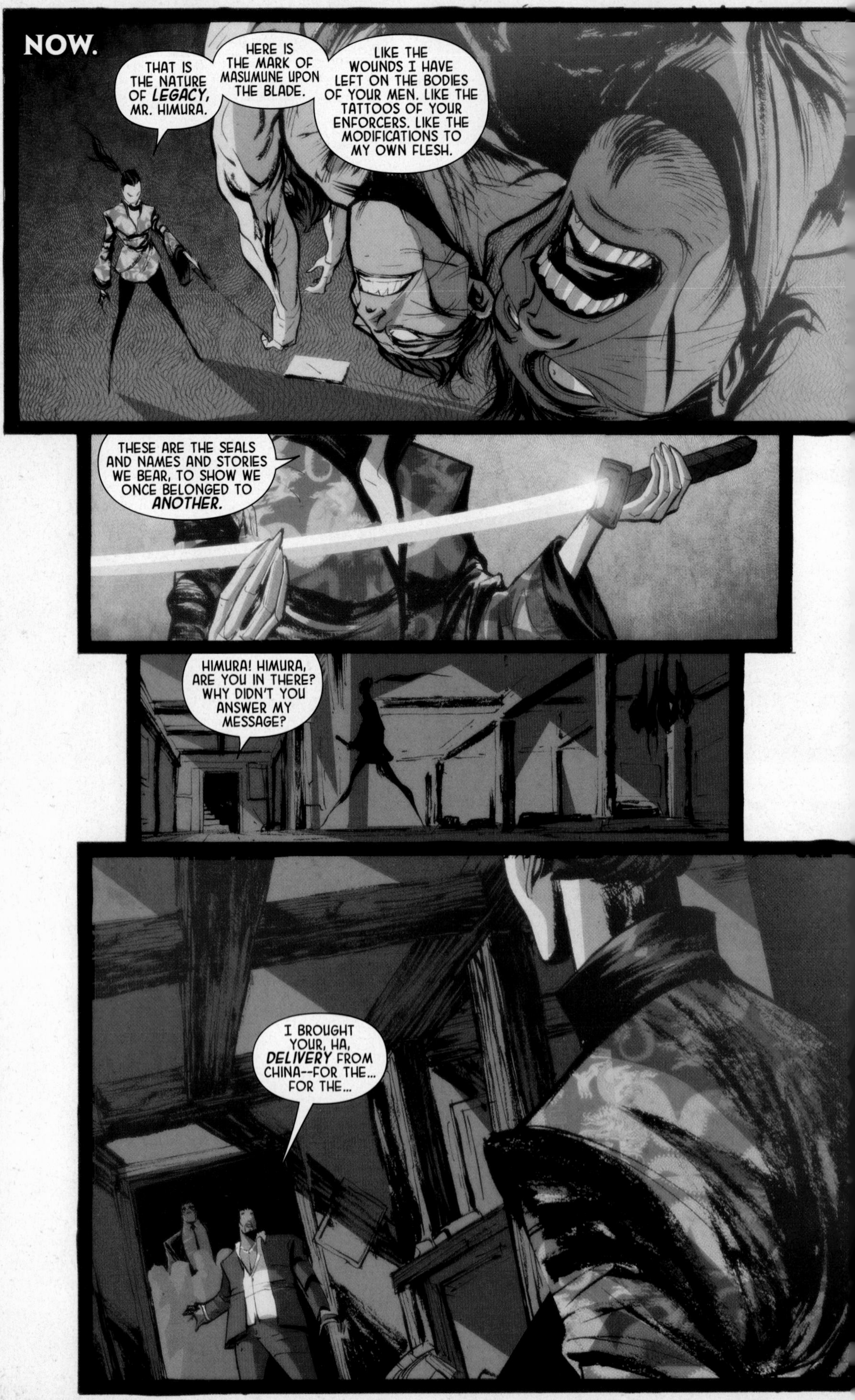
NOW.
THAT IS THE NATURE OF LEGACY, MR. HIMURA.
HERE IS THE MARK OF MASUMUNE UPON THE BLADE.
LIKE THE WOUNDS I HAVE LEFT ON THE BODIES OF YOUR MEN. LIKE THE TATTOOS OF YOUR ENFORCERS. LIKE THE MODIFICATIONS TO MY OWN FLESH.
THESE ARE THE SEALS AND NAMES AND STORIES WE BEAR, TO SHOW WE ONCE BELONGED TO ANOTHER.
HIMURA! HIMURA, ARE YOU IN THERE? WHY DIDN'T YOU ANSWER MY MESSAGE?
I BROUGHT YOUR, HA, DELIVERY FROM CHINA--FOR THE... FOR THE...

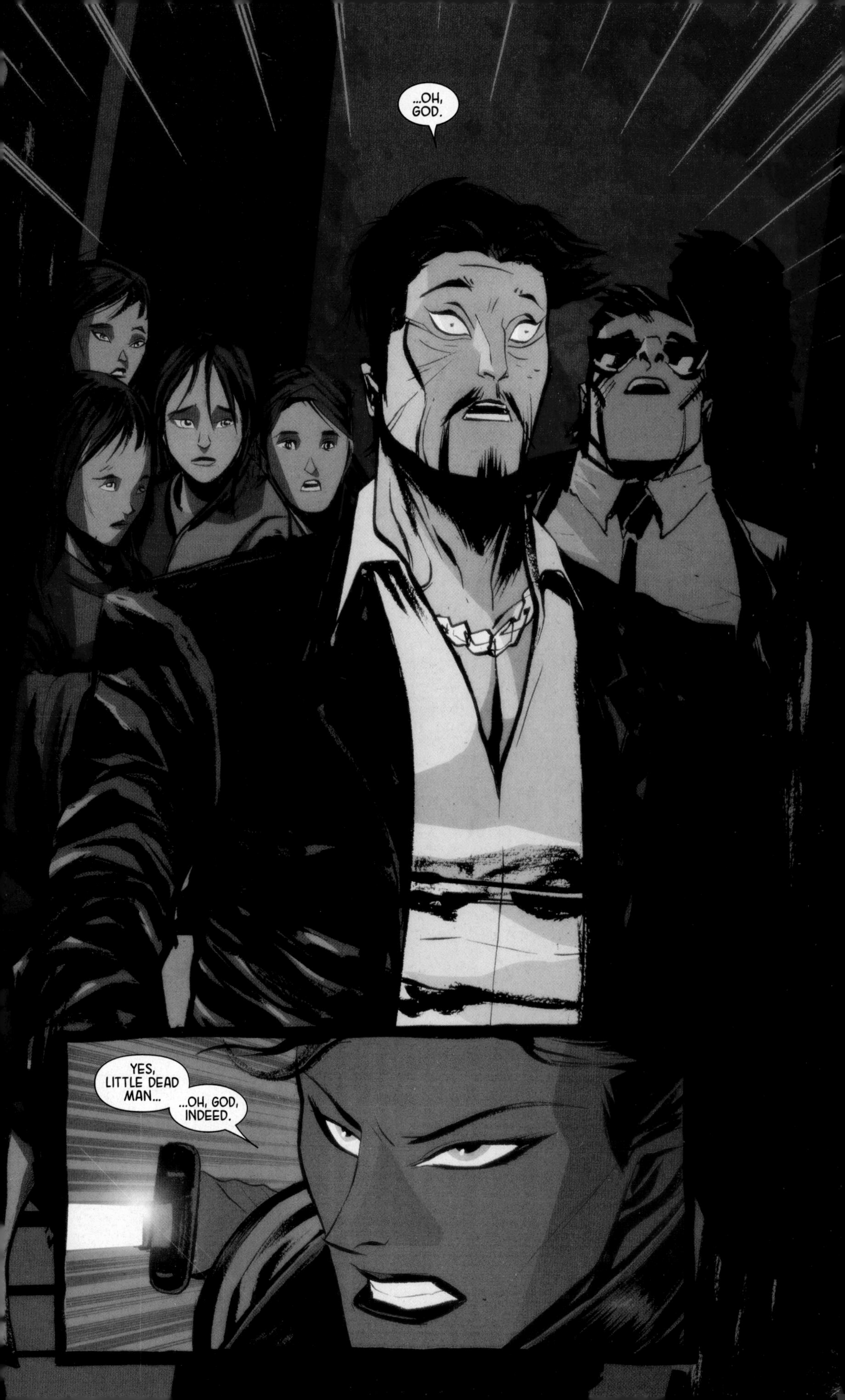
...OH, GOD.
YES, LITTLE DEAD MAN...
...OH, GOD, INDEED.

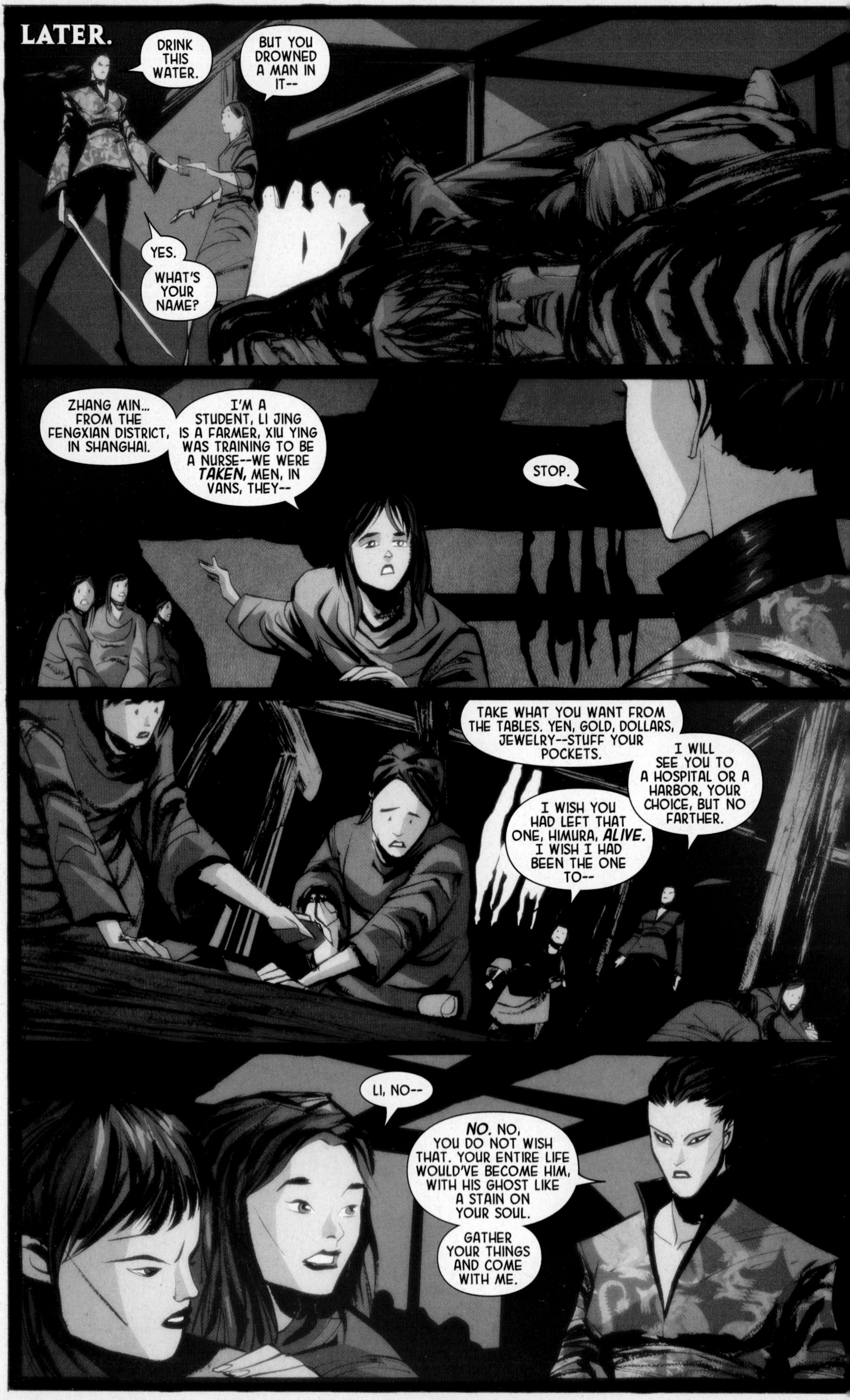
LATER.
DRINK THIS WATER.
BUT YOU DROWNED A MAN IN IT--
YES.
WHAT'S YOUR NAME?
ZHANG MIN... FROM THE FENGXIAN DISTRICT, IN SHANGHAI.
I'M A STUDENT, LI JING IS A FARMER, XIU YING WAS TRAINING TO BE A NURSE--WE WERE TAKEN, MEN, IN VANS, THEY--
STOP.
TAKE WHAT YOU WANT FROM THE TABLES. YEN, GOLD, DOLLARS, JEWELRY--STUFF YOUR POCKETS.
I WILL SEE YOU TO A HOSPITAL OR A HARBOR, YOUR CHOICE, BUT NO FARTHER.
I WISH YOU HAD LEFT THAT ONE, HIMURA, ALIVE. I WISH I HAD BEEN THE ONE TO--
LI, NO--
NO. NO, YOU DO NOT WISH THAT. YOUR ENTIRE LIFE WOULD'VE BECOME HIM, WITH HIS GHOST LIKE A STAIN ON YOUR SOUL.
GATHER YOUR THINGS AND COME WITH ME.

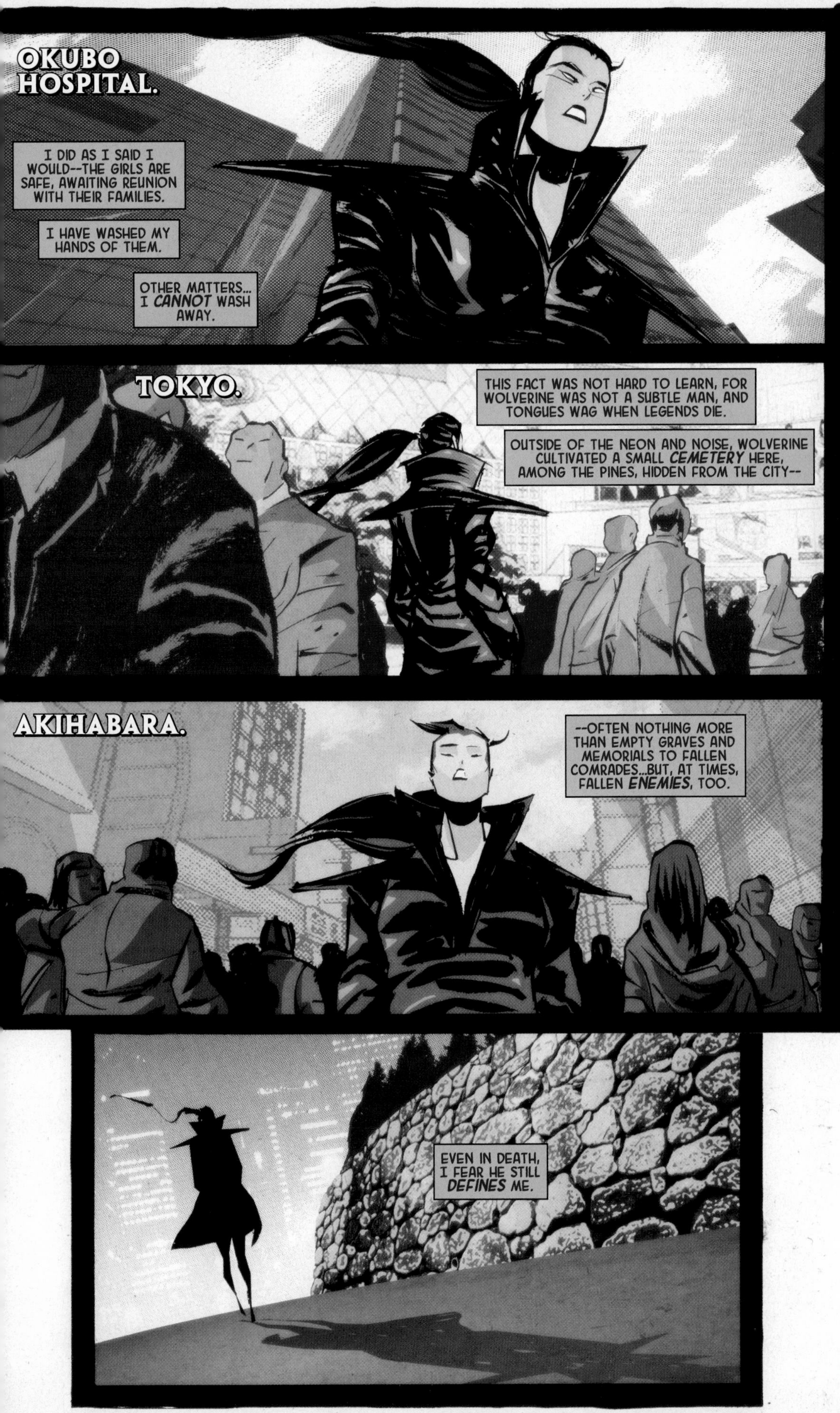
OKUBO HOSPITAL.
I DID AS I SAID I WOULD--THE GIRLS ARE SAFE, AWAITING REUNION WITH THEIR FAMILIES.
I HAVE WASHED MY HANDS OF THEM.
OTHER MATTERS... I CANNOT WASH AWAY.
TOKYO.
THIS FACT WAS NOT HARD TO LEARN, FOR WOLVERINE WAS NOT A SUBTLE MAN, AND TONGUES WAG WHEN LEGENDS DIE.
OUTSIDE OF THE NEON AND NOISE, WOLVERINE CULTIVATED A SMALL CEMETERY HERE, AMONG THE PINES, HIDDEN FROM THE CITY--
AKIHABARA.
--OFTEN NOTHING MORE THAN EMPTY GRAVES AND MEMORIALS TO FALLEN COMRADES...BUT, AT TIMES, FALLEN ENEMIES, TOO.
EVEN IN DEATH, I FEAR HE STILL DEFINES ME.

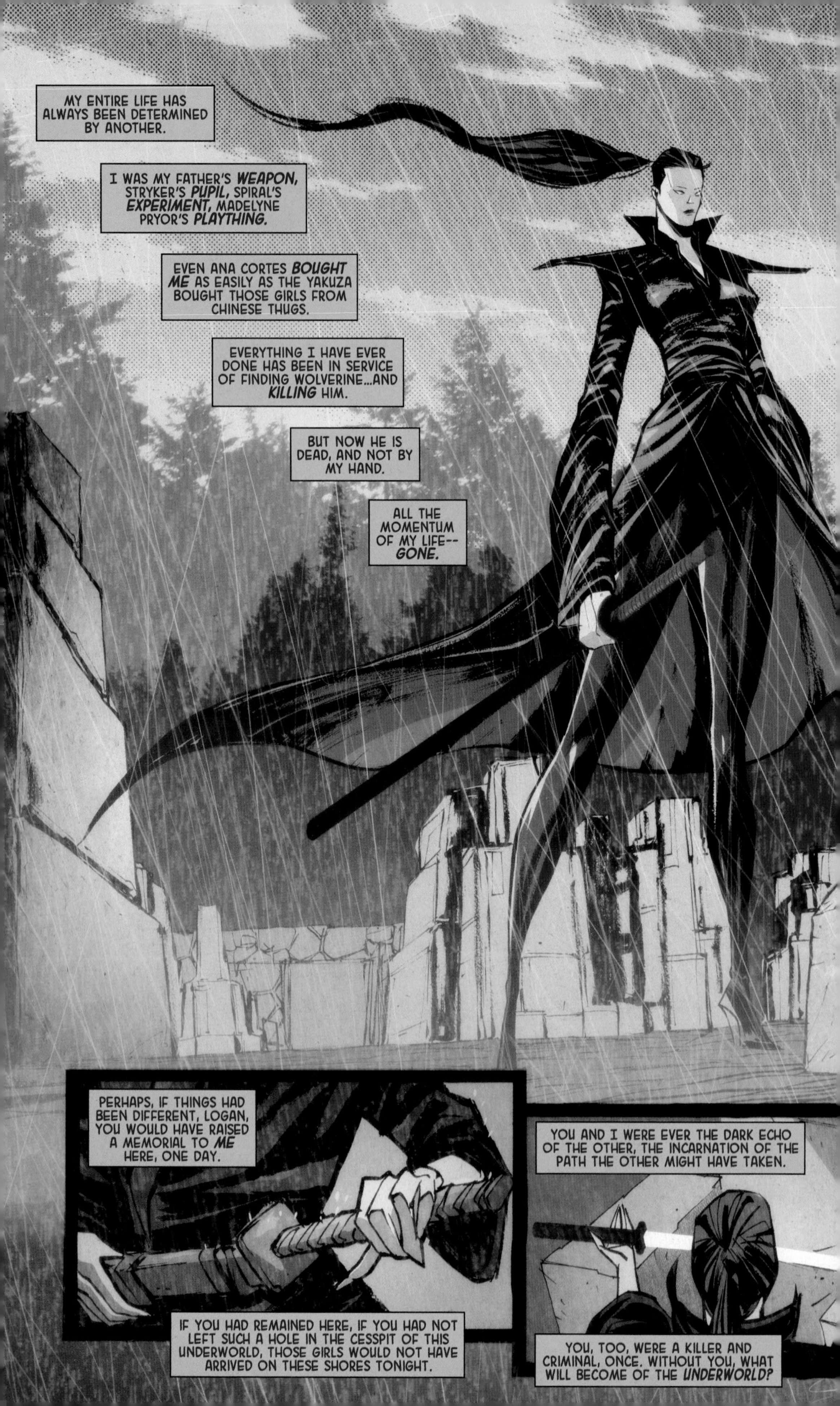
MY ENTIRE LIFE HAS ALWAYS BEEN DETERMINED BY ANOTHER.
I WAS MY FATHER'S *WEAPON*, STRYKER'S *PUPIL*, SPIRAL'S *EXPERIMENT*, MADELYNE PRYOR'S *PLAYTHING*.
EVEN ANA CORTES *BOUGHT ME* AS EASILY AS THE YAKUZA BOUGHT THOSE GIRLS FROM CHINESE THUGS.
EVERYTHING I HAVE EVER DONE HAS BEEN IN SERVICE OF FINDING WOLVERINE...AND *KILLING* HIM.
BUT NOW HE IS DEAD, AND NOT BY MY HAND.
ALL THE MOMENTUM OF MY LIFE-- *GONE.*
PERHAPS, IF THINGS HAD BEEN DIFFERENT, LOGAN, YOU WOULD HAVE RAISED A MEMORIAL TO *ME* HERE, ONE DAY.
IF YOU HAD REMAINED HERE, IF YOU HAD NOT LEFT SUCH A HOLE IN THE CESSPIT OF THIS UNDERWORLD, THOSE GIRLS WOULD NOT HAVE ARRIVED ON THESE SHORES TONIGHT.
YOU AND I WERE EVER THE DARK ECHO OF THE OTHER, THE INCARNATION OF THE PATH THE OTHER MIGHT HAVE TAKEN.
YOU, TOO, WERE A KILLER AND CRIMINAL, ONCE. WITHOUT YOU, WHAT WILL BECOME OF THE *UNDERWORLD?*

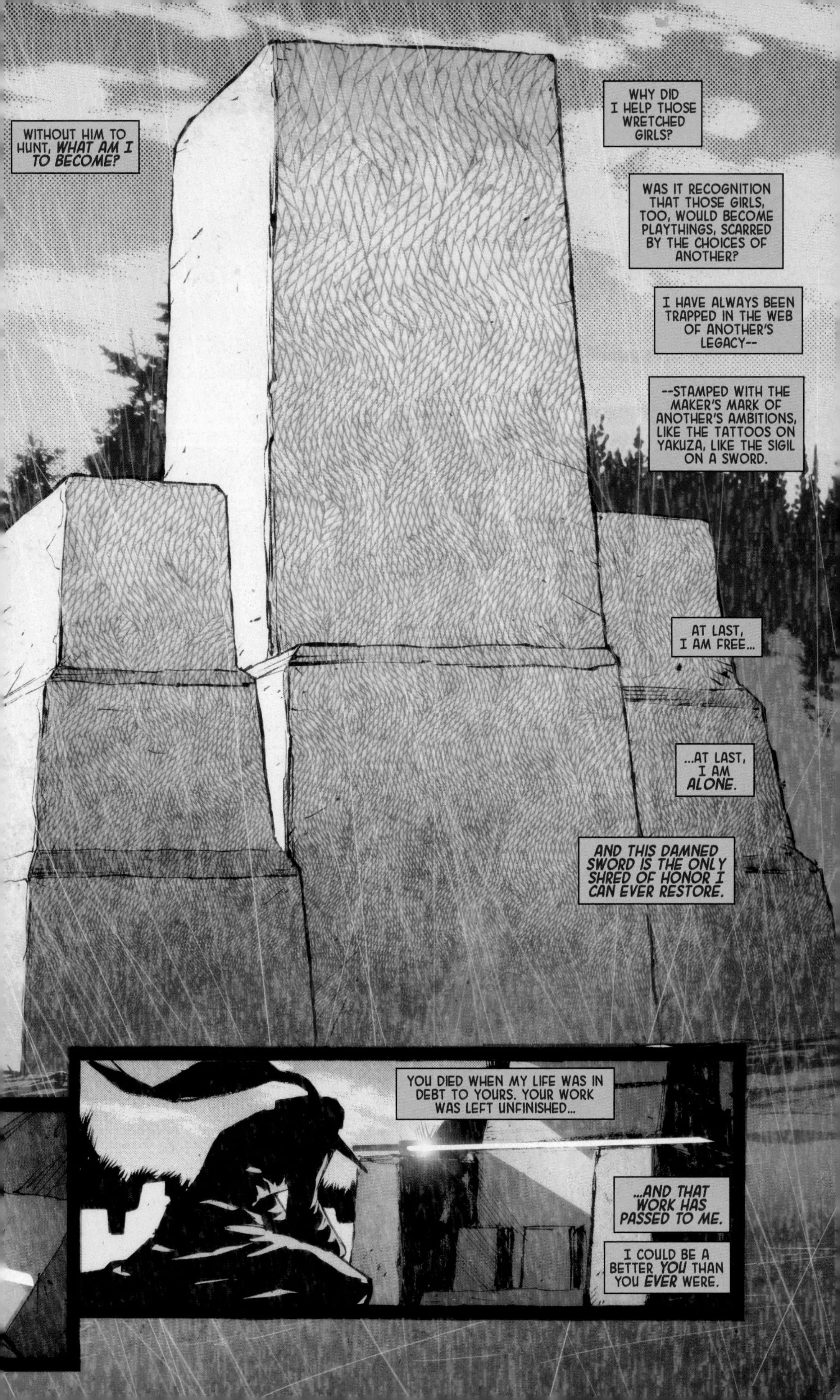

WITHOUT HIM TO HUNT, WHAT AM I TO BECOME?
WHY DID I HELP THOSE WRETCHED GIRLS?
WAS IT RECOGNITION THAT THOSE GIRLS, TOO, WOULD BECOME PLAYTHINGS, SCARRED BY THE CHOICES OF ANOTHER?
I HAVE ALWAYS BEEN TRAPPED IN THE WEB OF ANOTHER'S LEGACY--
--STAMPED WITH THE MAKER'S MARK OF ANOTHER'S AMBITIONS, LIKE THE TATTOOS ON YAKUZA, LIKE THE SIGIL ON A SWORD.
AT LAST, I AM FREE...
...AT LAST, I AM ALONE.
AND THIS DAMNED SWORD IS THE ONLY SHRED OF HONOR I CAN EVER RESTORE.
YOU DIED WHEN MY LIFE WAS IN DEBT TO YOURS. YOUR WORK WAS LEFT UNFINISHED...
...AND THAT WORK HAS PASSED TO ME.
I COULD BE A BETTER YOU THAN YOU EVER WERE.

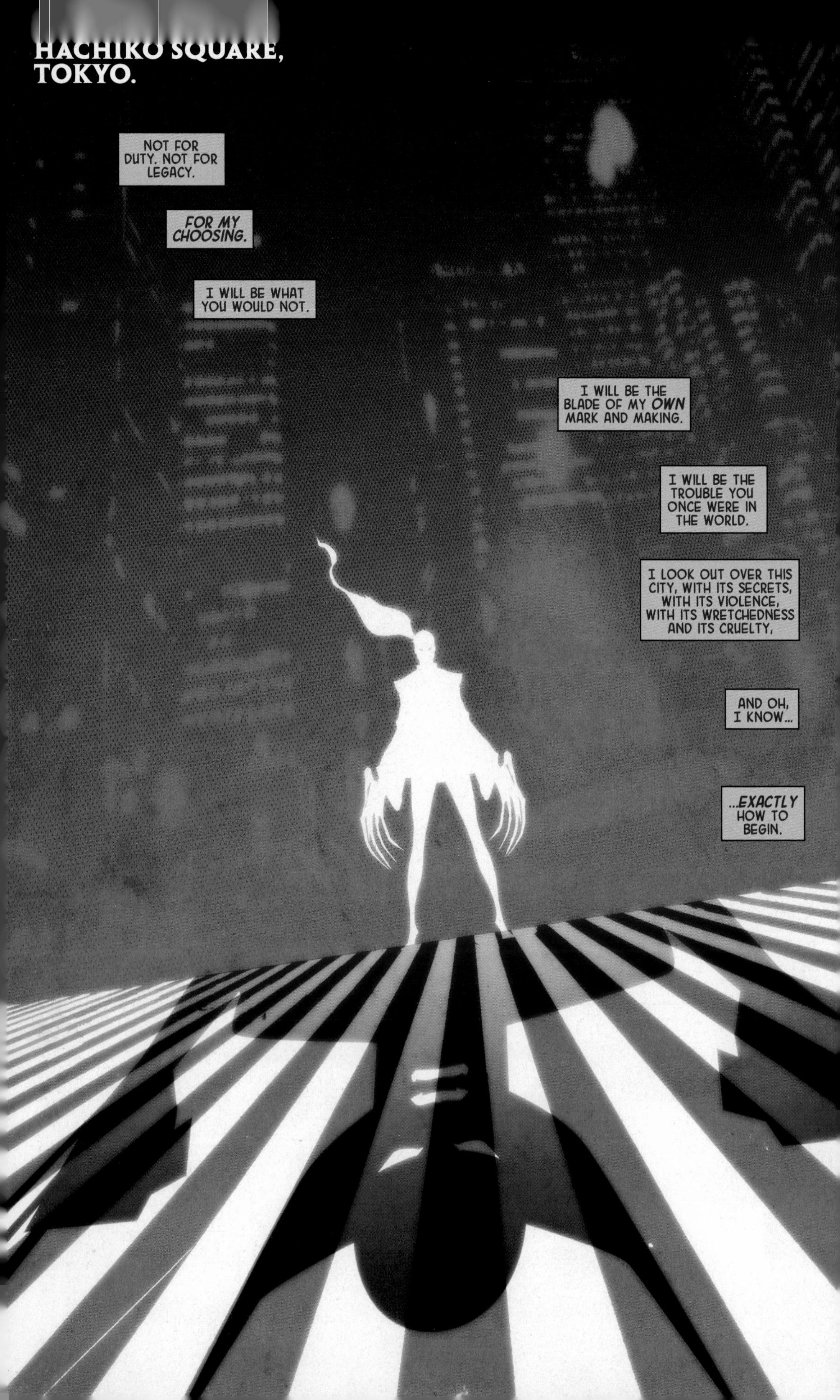
HACHIKO SQUARE, TOKYO.
NOT FOR DUTY. NOT FOR LEGACY.
FOR MY CHOOSING.
I WILL BE WHAT YOU WOULD NOT.
I WILL BE THE BLADE OF MY OWN MARK AND MAKING.
I WILL BE THE TROUBLE YOU ONCE WERE IN THE WORLD.
I LOOK OUT OVER THIS CITY, WITH ITS SECRETS, WITH ITS VIOLENCE, WITH ITS WRETCHEDNESS AND ITS CRUELTY,
AND OH, I KNOW...
...EXACTLY HOW TO BEGIN.

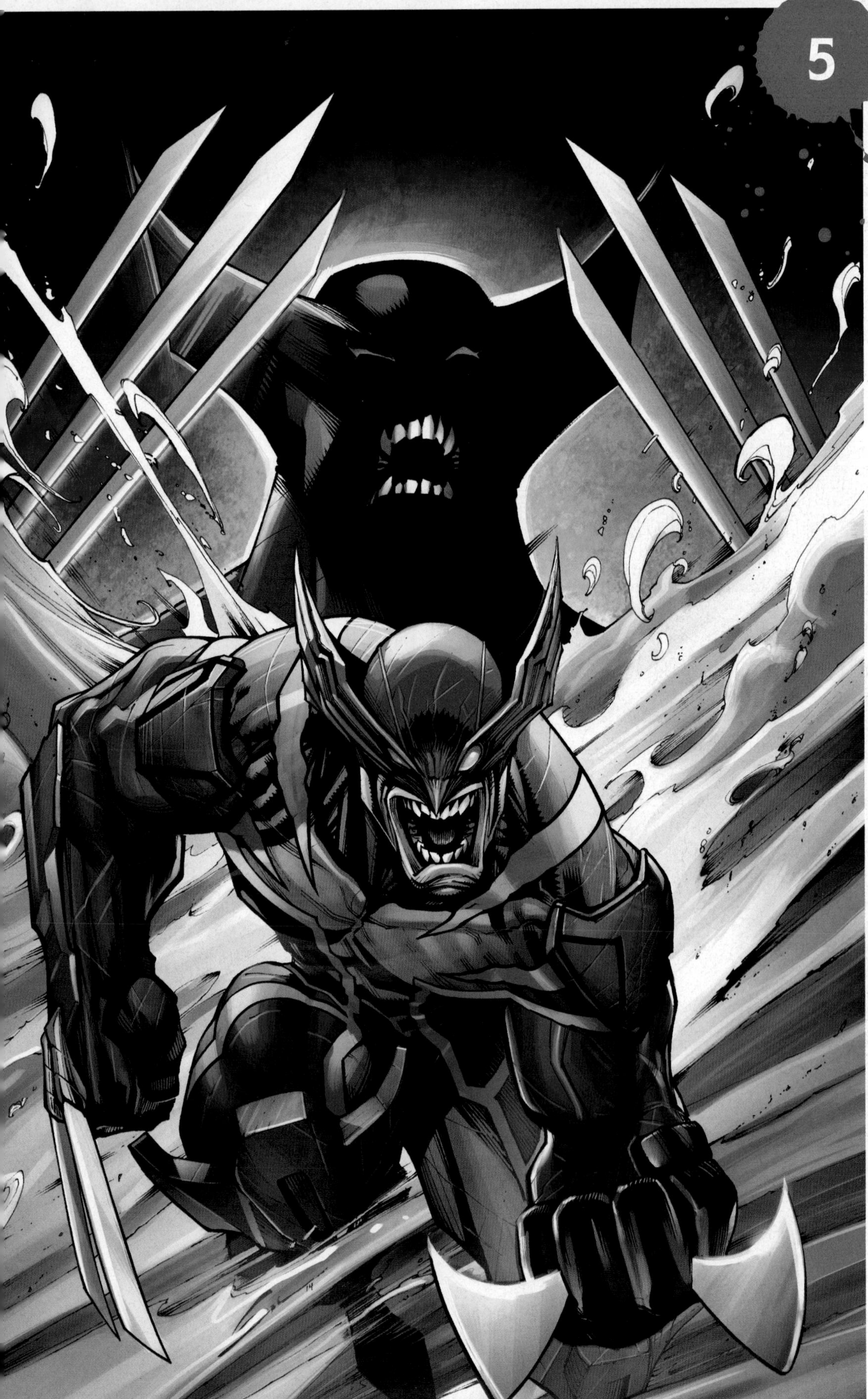
5

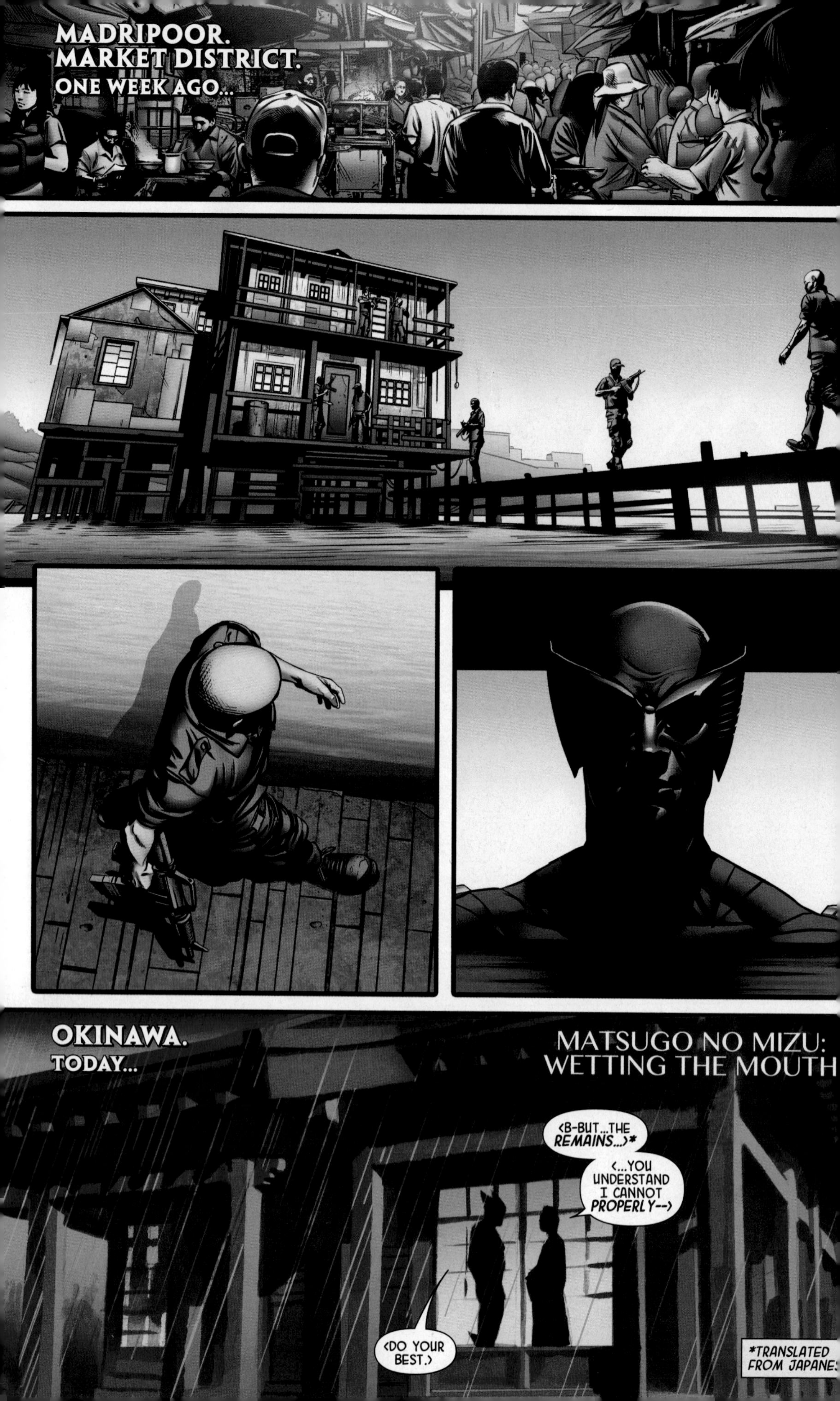
MADRIPOOR.
MARKET DISTRICT.
ONE WEEK AGO...
OKINAWA.
TODAY...
MATSUGO NO MIZU:
WETTING THE MOUTH
<B-BUT...THE REMAINS...>*
<...YOU UNDERSTAND I CANNOT PROPERLY-->
<DO YOUR BEST.>
*TRANSLATED FROM JAPANESE.

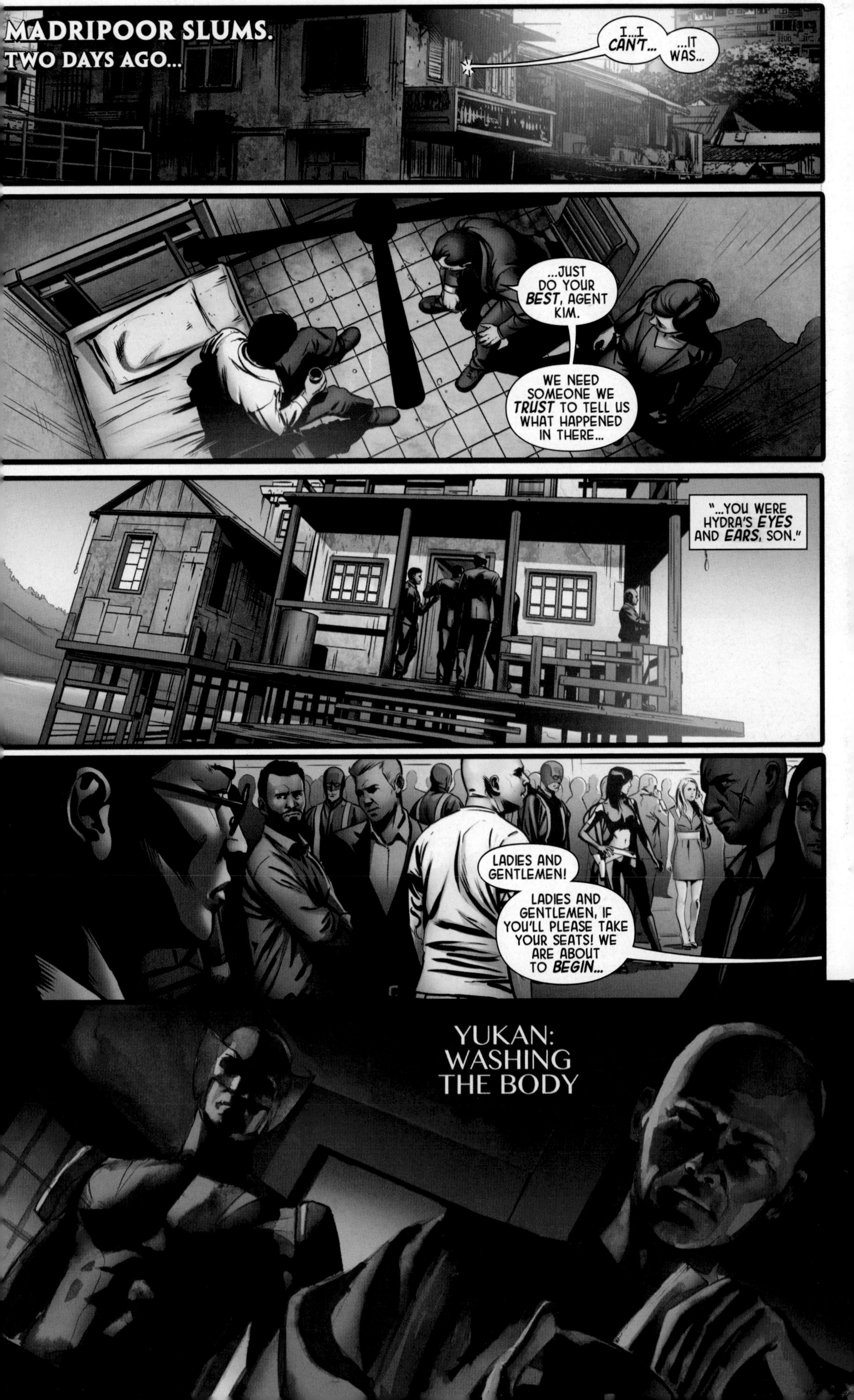
MADRIPOOR SLUMS.
TWO DAYS AGO...
I...I CAN'T...
...IT WAS...
...JUST DO YOUR BEST, AGENT KIM.
WE NEED SOMEONE WE TRUST TO TELL US WHAT HAPPENED IN THERE...
"...YOU WERE HYDRA'S EYES AND EARS, SON."
LADIES AND GENTLEMEN!
LADIES AND GENTLEMEN, IF YOU'LL PLEASE TAKE YOUR SEATS! WE ARE ABOUT TO BEGIN...
YUKAN: WASHING THE BODY

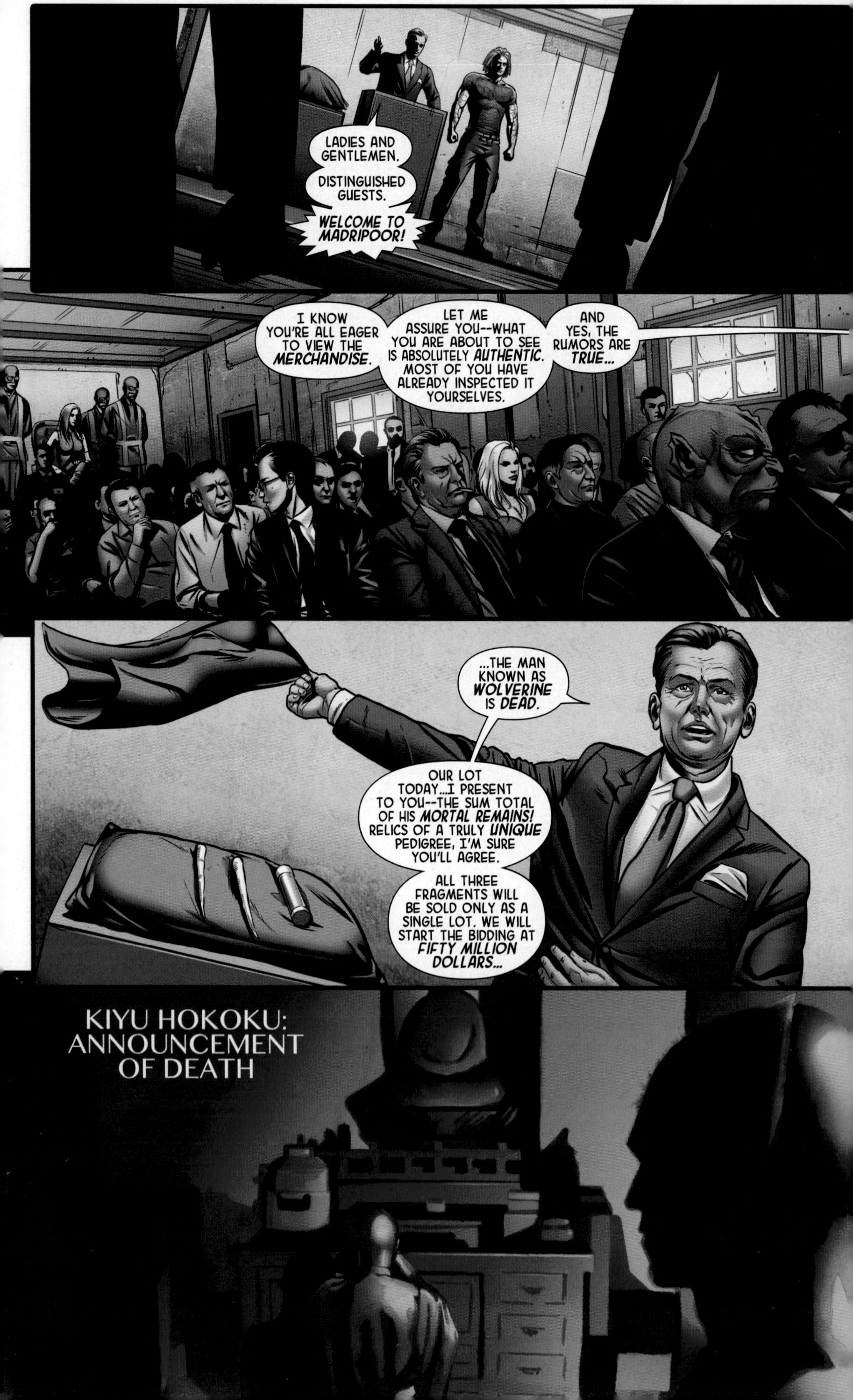
LADIES AND GENTLEMEN.
DISTINGUISHED GUESTS.
WELCOME TO MADRIPOOR!
I KNOW YOU'RE ALL EAGER TO VIEW THE MERCHANDISE.
LET ME ASSURE YOU--WHAT YOU ARE ABOUT TO SEE IS ABSOLUTELY AUTHENTIC. MOST OF YOU HAVE ALREADY INSPECTED IT YOURSELVES.
AND YES, THE RUMORS ARE TRUE...
...THE MAN KNOWN AS WOLVERINE IS DEAD.
OUR LOT TODAY...I PRESENT TO YOU--THE SUM TOTAL OF HIS MORTAL REMAINS! RELICS OF A TRULY UNIQUE PEDIGREE, I'M SURE YOU'LL AGREE.
ALL THREE FRAGMENTS WILL BE SOLD ONLY AS A SINGLE LOT. WE WILL START THE BIDDING AT FIFTY MILLION DOLLARS...
KIYU HOKOKU: ANNOUNCEMENT OF DEATH

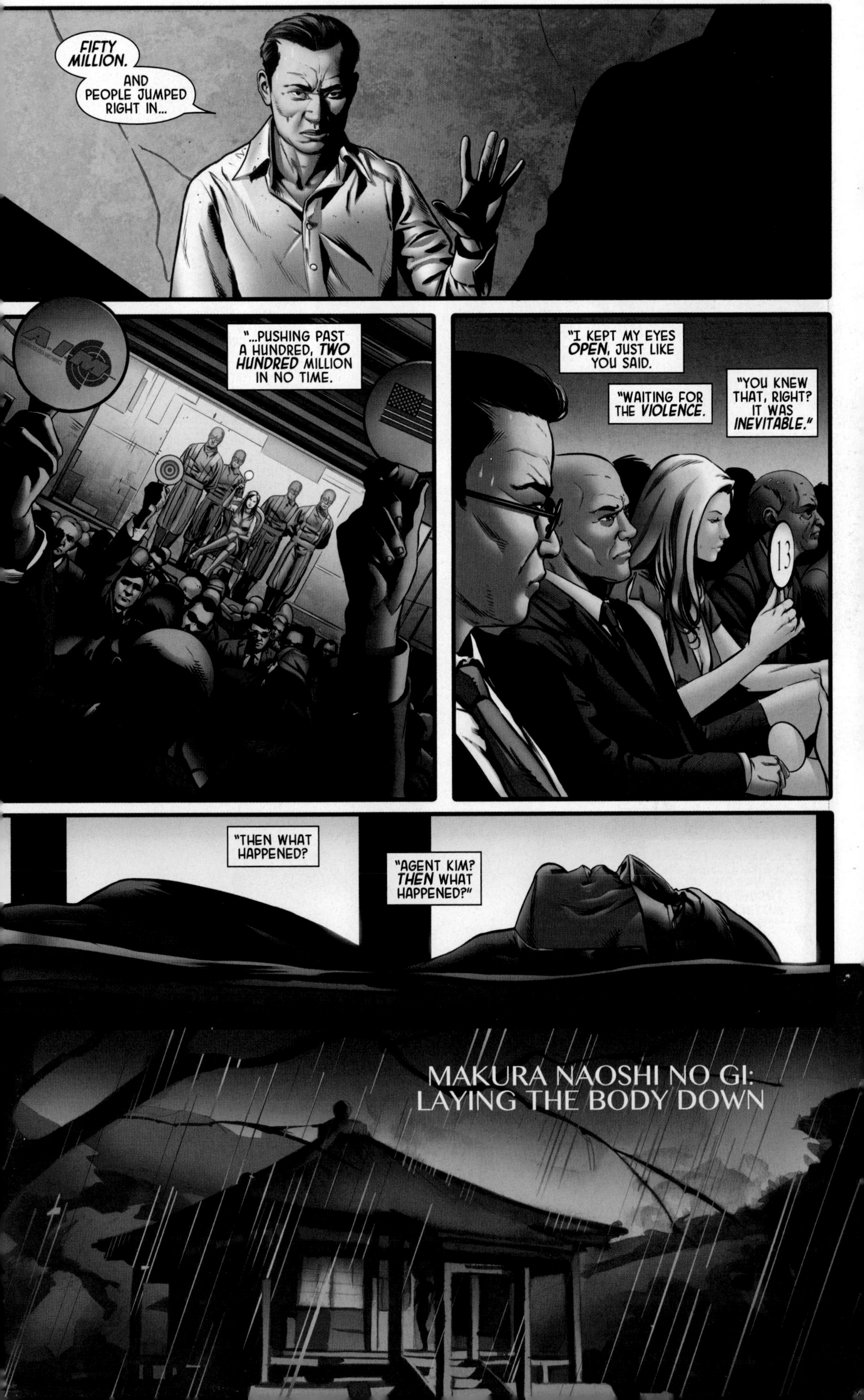
FIFTY MILLION.
AND PEOPLE JUMPED RIGHT IN...
"...PUSHING PAST A HUNDRED, TWO HUNDRED MILLION IN NO TIME.
"I KEPT MY EYES OPEN, JUST LIKE YOU SAID.
"WAITING FOR THE VIOLENCE.
"YOU KNEW THAT, RIGHT? IT WAS INEVITABLE."
13
"THEN WHAT HAPPENED?
"AGENT KIM? THEN WHAT HAPPENED?"
MAKURA NAOSHI NO GI: LAYING THE BODY DOWN

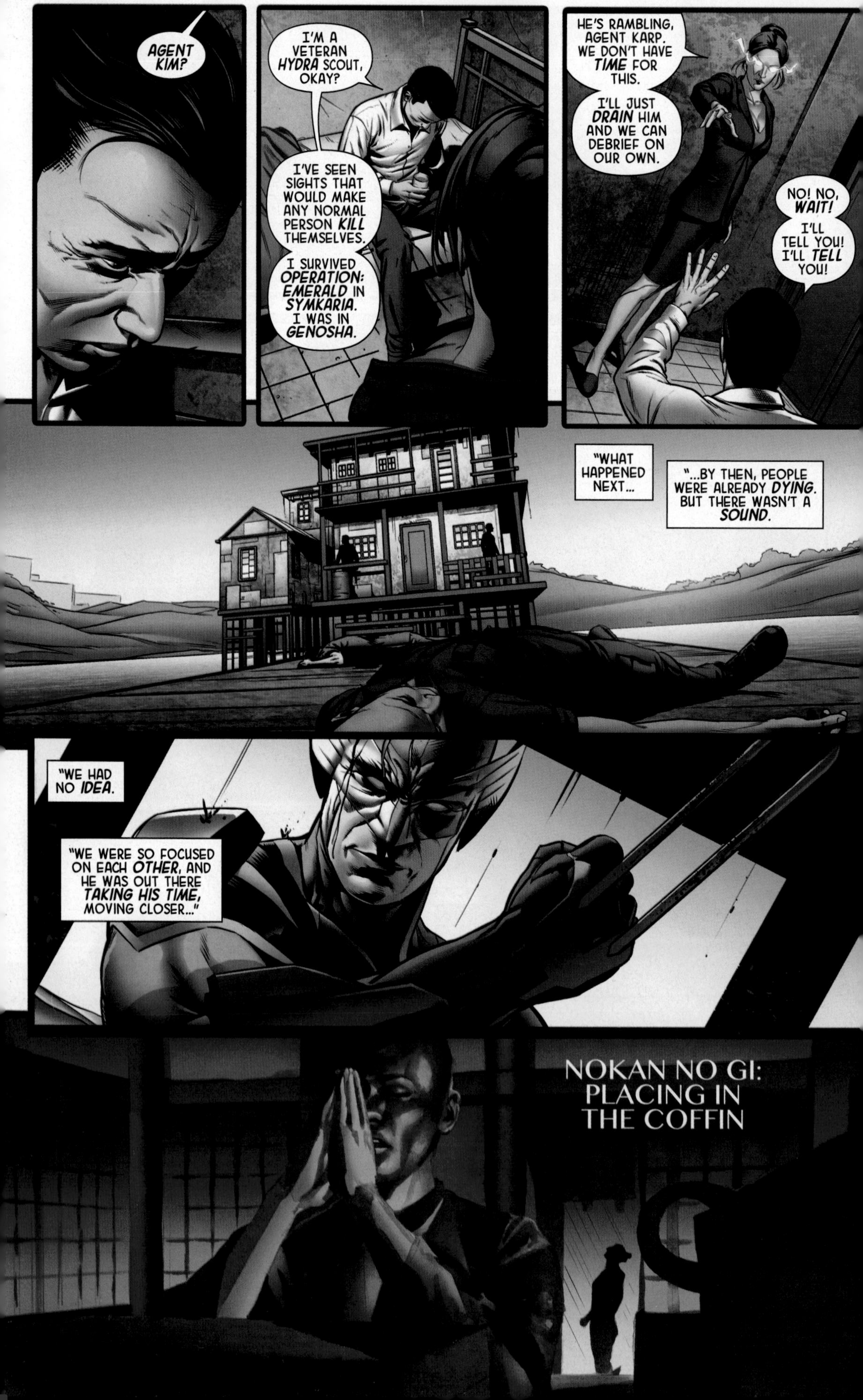
AGENT KIM?
I'M A VETERAN HYDRA SCOUT, OKAY?
I'VE SEEN SIGHTS THAT WOULD MAKE ANY NORMAL PERSON KILL THEMSELVES.
I SURVIVED OPERATION: EMERALD IN SYMKARIA. I WAS IN GENOSHA.
HE'S RAMBLING, AGENT KARP. WE DON'T HAVE TIME FOR THIS.
I'LL JUST DRAIN HIM AND WE CAN DEBRIEF ON OUR OWN.
NO! NO, WAIT!
I'LL TELL YOU! I'LL TELL YOU!
"WHAT HAPPENED NEXT...
"...BY THEN, PEOPLE WERE ALREADY DYING. BUT THERE WASN'T A SOUND.
"WE HAD NO IDEA.
"WE WERE SO FOCUSED ON EACH OTHER, AND HE WAS OUT THERE TAKING HIS TIME, MOVING CLOSER..."
NOKAN NO GI: PLACING IN THE COFFIN

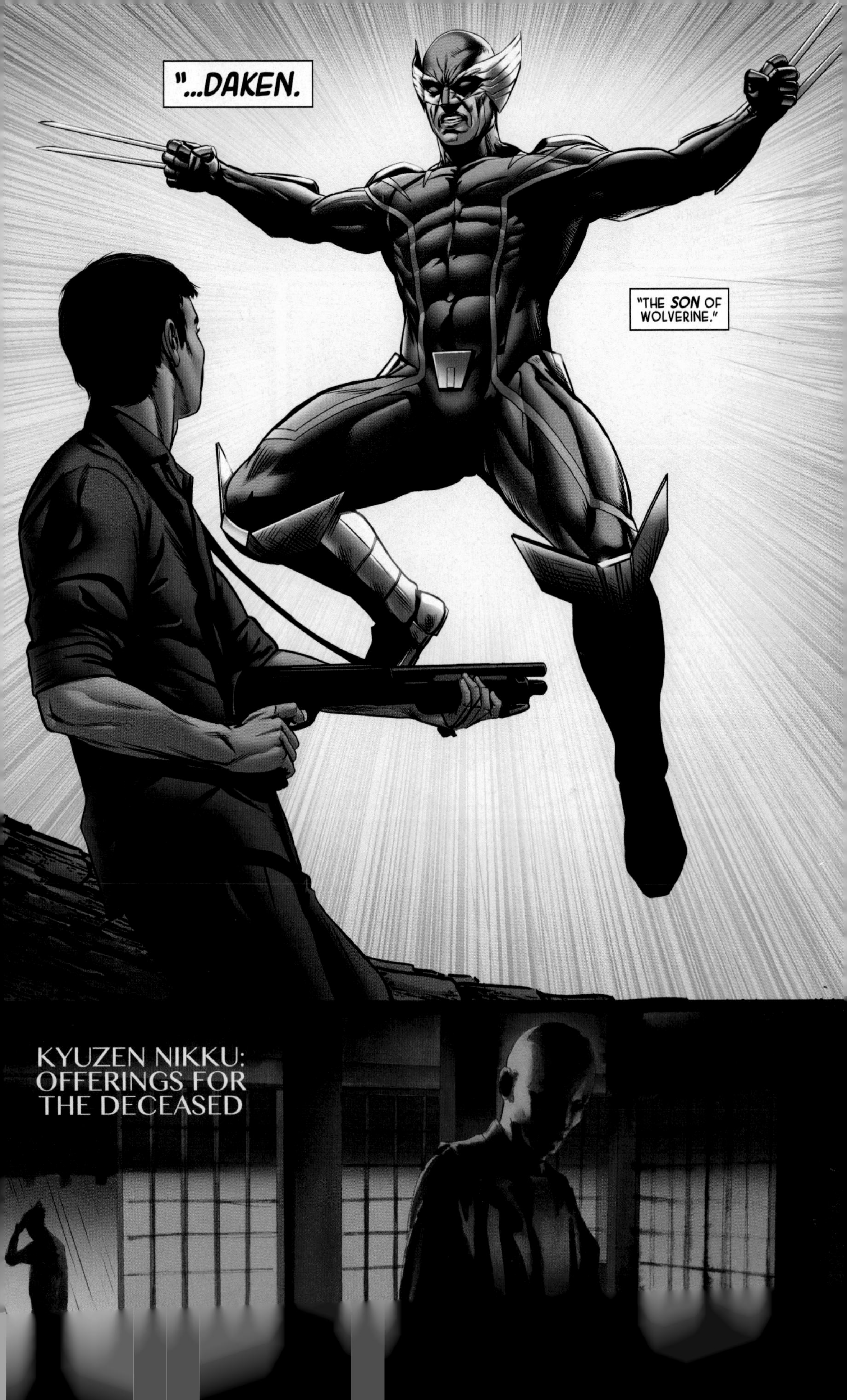
"...DAKEN.
"THE SON OF WOLVERINE."
KYUZEN NIKKU: OFFERINGS FOR THE DECEASED

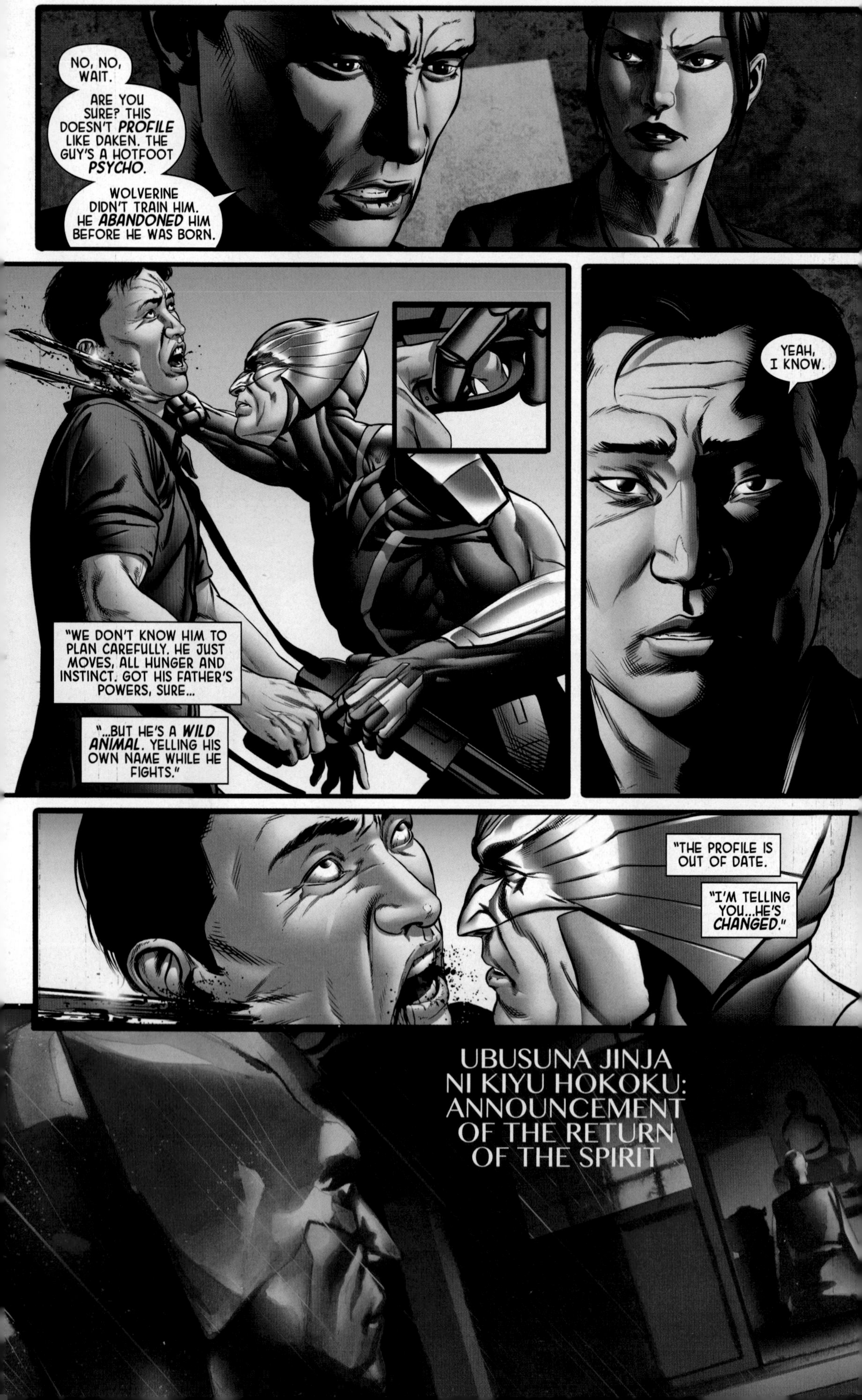
NO, NO, WAIT.
ARE YOU SURE? THIS DOESN'T PROFILE LIKE DAKEN. THE GUY'S A HOTFOOT PSYCHO.
WOLVERINE DIDN'T TRAIN HIM. HE ABANDONED HIM BEFORE HE WAS BORN.
"WE DON'T KNOW HIM TO PLAN CAREFULLY. HE JUST MOVES, ALL HUNGER AND INSTINCT. GOT HIS FATHER'S POWERS, SURE...
"...BUT HE'S A WILD ANIMAL. YELLING HIS OWN NAME WHILE HE FIGHTS."
YEAH, I KNOW.
"THE PROFILE IS OUT OF DATE.
"I'M TELLING YOU...HE'S CHANGED."
UBUSUNA JINJA NI KIYU HOKOKU: ANNOUNCEMENT OF THE RETURN OF THE SPIRIT

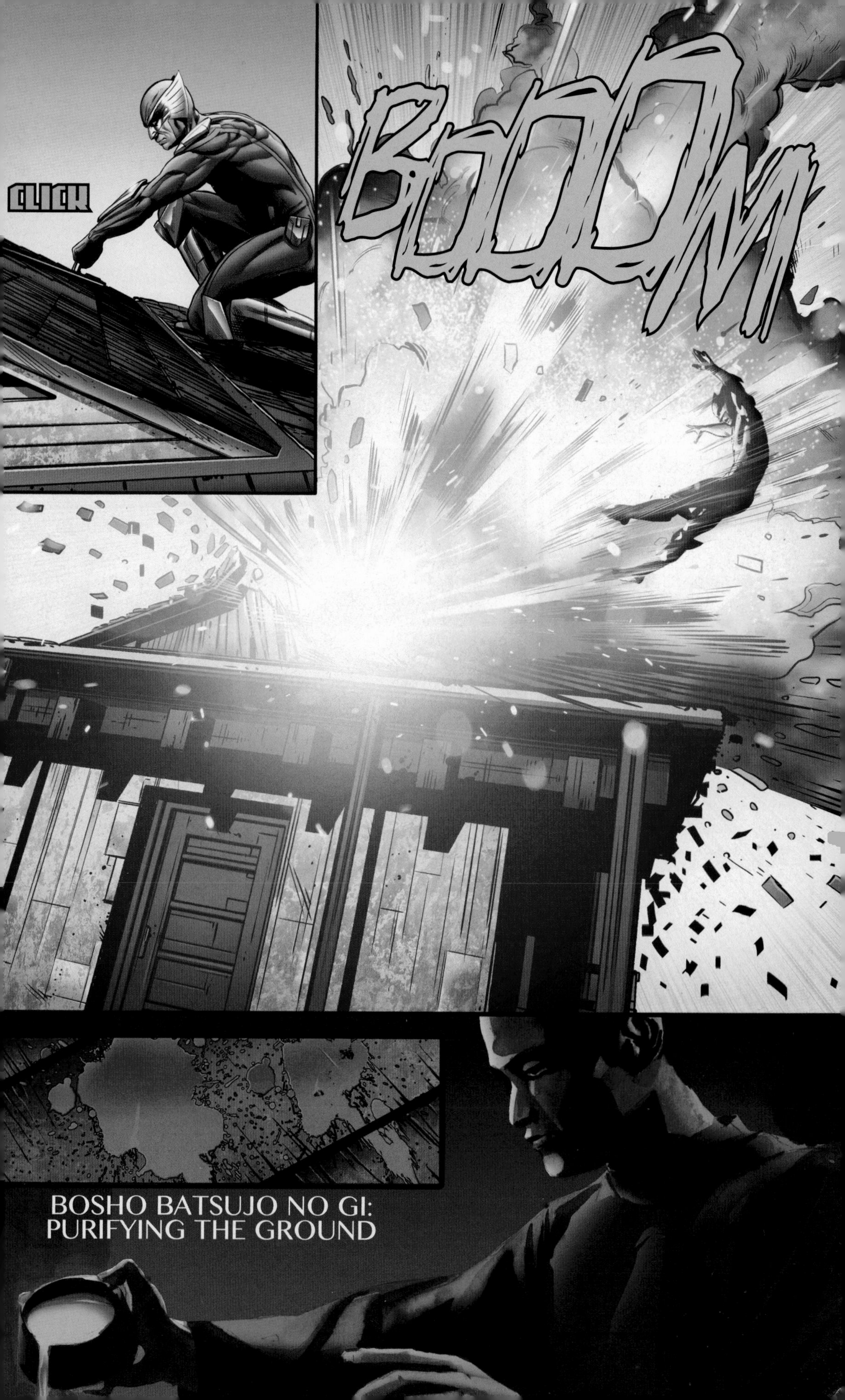
CLICK
BOOOM
BOSHO BATSUJO NO GI:
PURIFYING THE GROUND

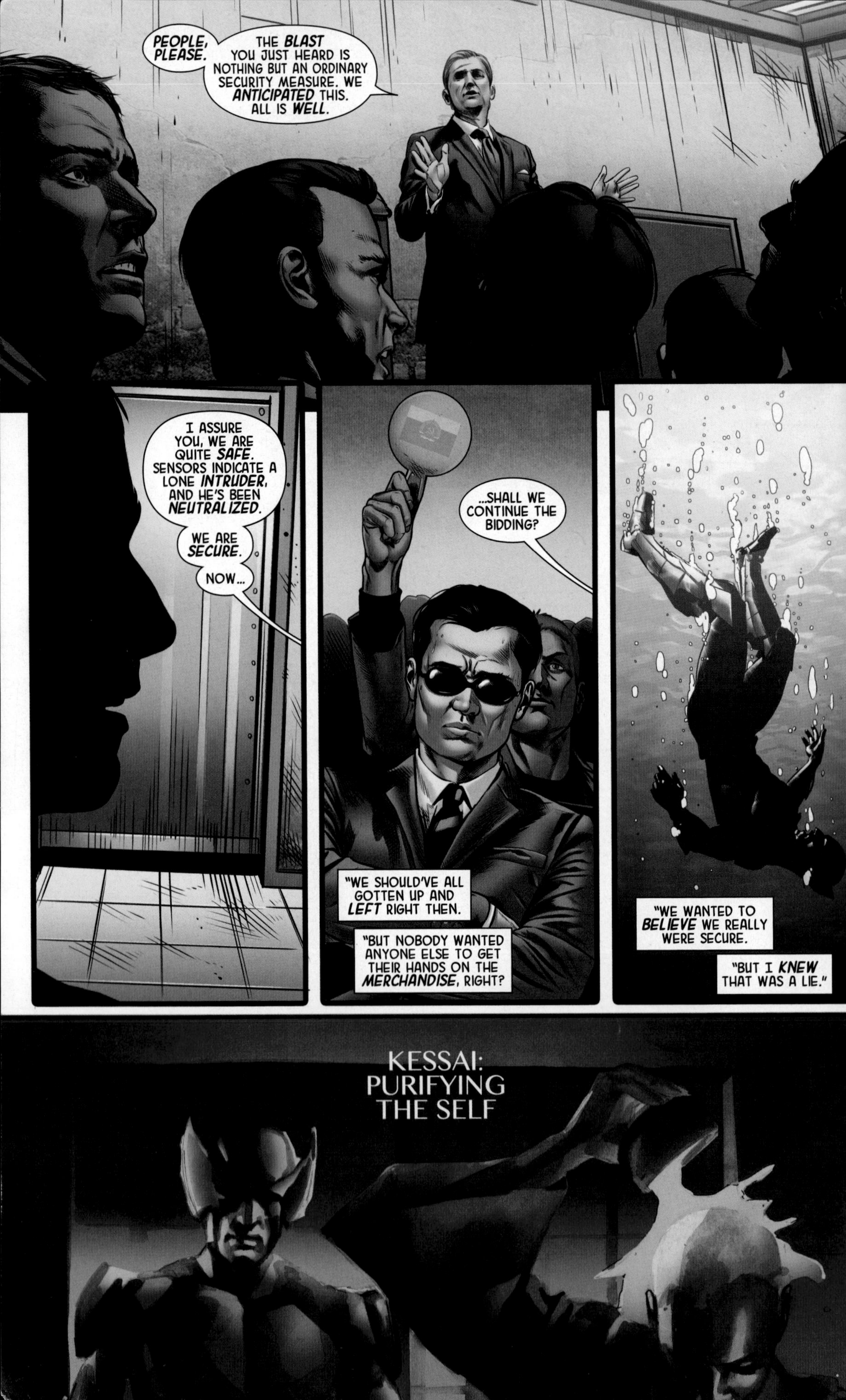
PEOPLE, PLEASE.
THE BLAST YOU JUST HEARD IS NOTHING BUT AN ORDINARY SECURITY MEASURE. WE ANTICIPATED THIS. ALL IS WELL.
I ASSURE YOU, WE ARE QUITE SAFE. SENSORS INDICATE A LONE INTRUDER, AND HE'S BEEN NEUTRALIZED.
WE ARE SECURE.
NOW...
...SHALL WE CONTINUE THE BIDDING?
"WE SHOULD'VE ALL GOTTEN UP AND LEFT RIGHT THEN.
"BUT NOBODY WANTED ANYONE ELSE TO GET THEIR HANDS ON THE MERCHANDISE, RIGHT?
"WE WANTED TO BELIEVE WE REALLY WERE SECURE.
"BUT I KNEW THAT WAS A LIE."
KESSAI: PURIFYING THE SELF

THREE HUNDRED! *THREE-HUNDRED MILLION* OVER THERE, SIR.

DO WE HAVE THREE-HUNDRED AND TWENTY?

HNN.

SOO-- SOMETHING'S STILL OUT THERE.

SOO, *REPORT.*

THREE HUNDRED AND TWENTY, YES, MA'AM!

THREE HUNDRED AND TWENTY, DO WE HAVE THREE-FORTY?

SOO, *REPORT!*

THREE HUNDRED AND FORTY MILLION.

THAT WAS AIM'S BID. THE *LAST* BID ANYONE HAD A CHANCE TO MAKE...

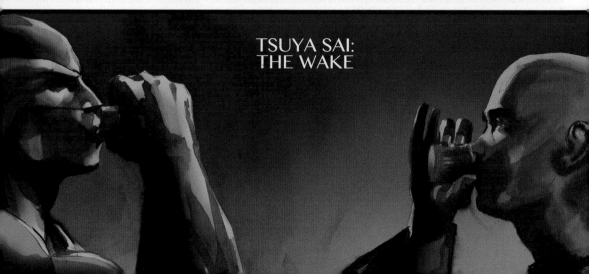

TSUYA SAI:
THE WAKE

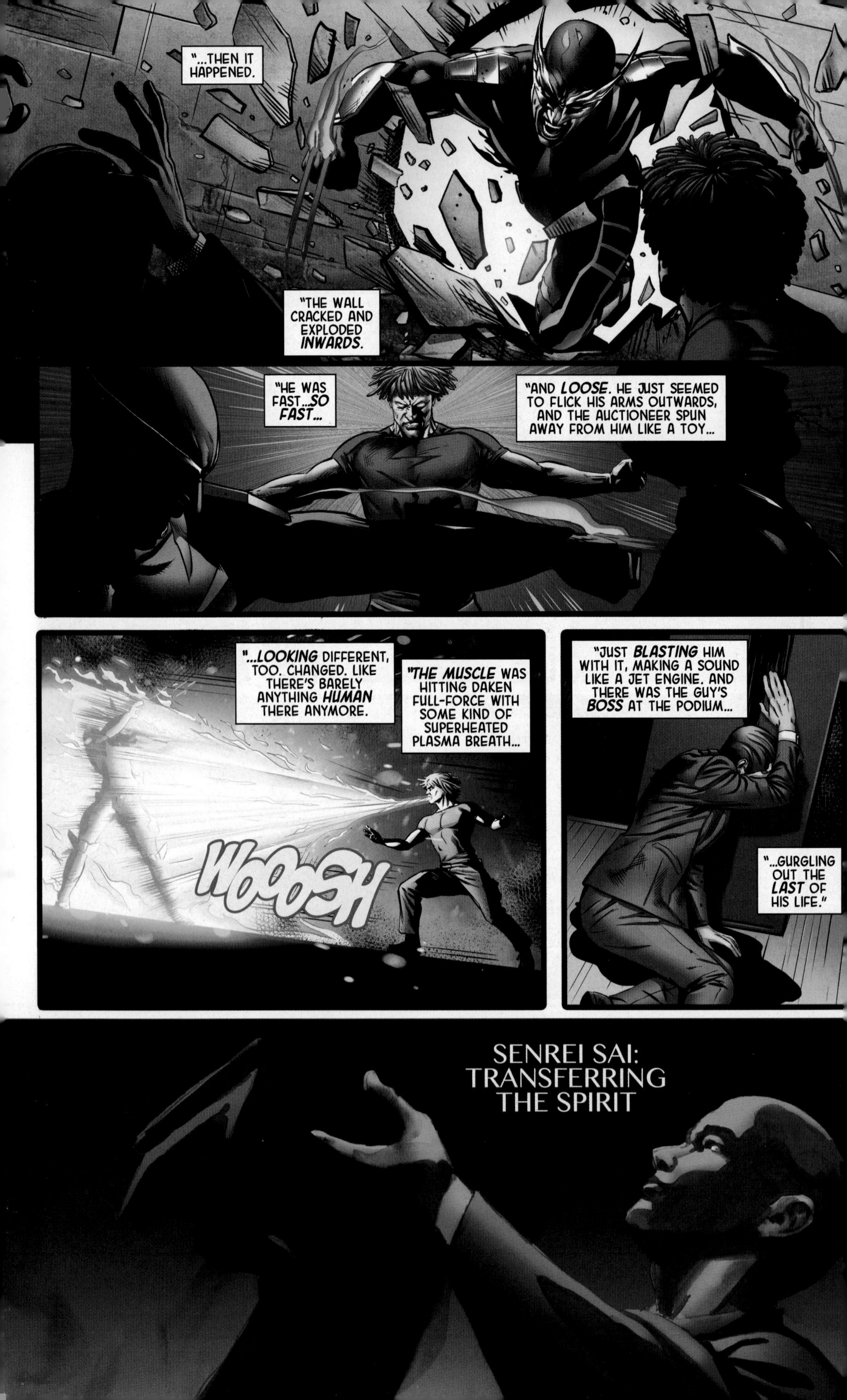
"...THEN IT HAPPENED.
"THE WALL CRACKED AND EXPLODED INWARDS.
"HE WAS FAST...SO FAST...
"AND LOOSE. HE JUST SEEMED TO FLICK HIS ARMS OUTWARDS, AND THE AUCTIONEER SPUN AWAY FROM HIM LIKE A TOY...
"...LOOKING DIFFERENT, TOO. CHANGED. LIKE THERE'S BARELY ANYTHING HUMAN THERE ANYMORE.
"THE MUSCLE WAS HITTING DAKEN FULL-FORCE WITH SOME KIND OF SUPERHEATED PLASMA BREATH...
WOOOSH
"JUST BLASTING HIM WITH IT, MAKING A SOUND LIKE A JET ENGINE. AND THERE WAS THE GUY'S BOSS AT THE PODIUM...
"...GURGLING OUT THE LAST OF HIS LIFE."
SENREI SAI: TRANSFERRING THE SPIRIT

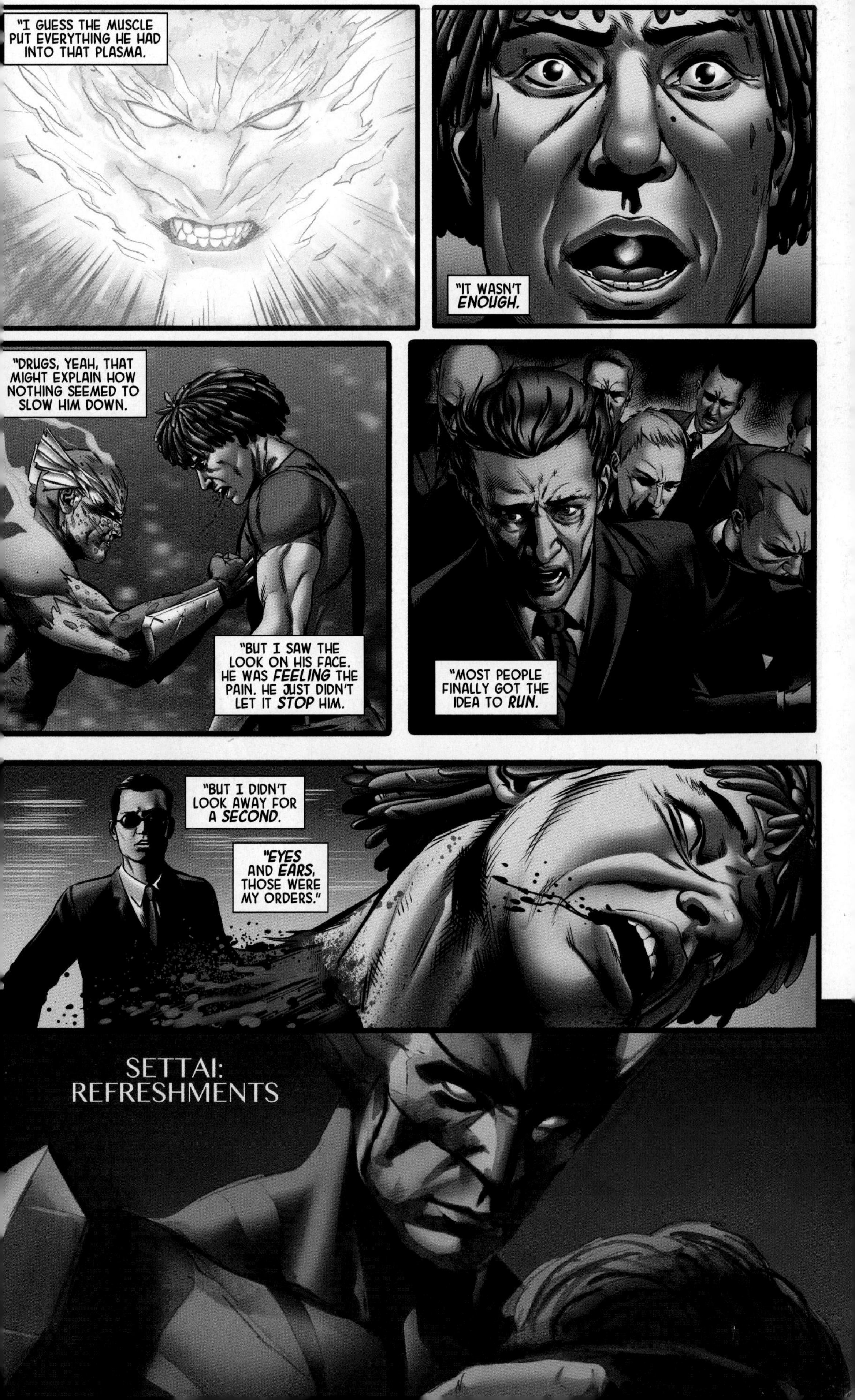
"I GUESS THE MUSCLE PUT EVERYTHING HE HAD INTO THAT PLASMA.
"IT WASN'T ENOUGH.
"DRUGS, YEAH, THAT MIGHT EXPLAIN HOW NOTHING SEEMED TO SLOW HIM DOWN.
"BUT I SAW THE LOOK ON HIS FACE. HE WAS FEELING THE PAIN. HE JUST DIDN'T LET IT STOP HIM.
"MOST PEOPLE FINALLY GOT THE IDEA TO RUN.
"BUT I DIDN'T LOOK AWAY FOR A SECOND.
"EYES AND EARS, THOSE WERE MY ORDERS."
SETTAI: REFRESHMENTS

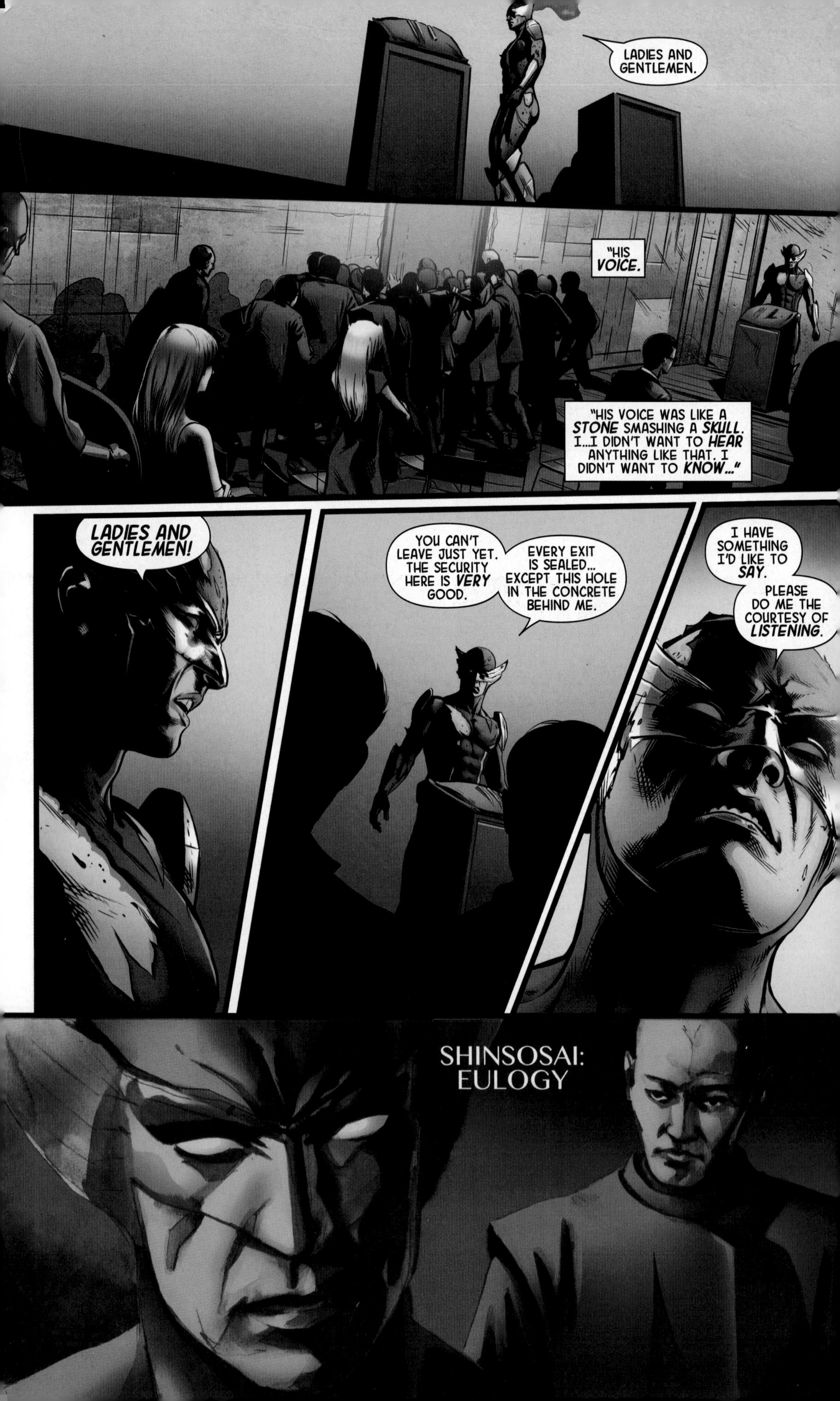
LADIES AND GENTLEMEN.
"HIS VOICE.
"HIS VOICE WAS LIKE A STONE SMASHING A SKULL. I...I DIDN'T WANT TO HEAR ANYTHING LIKE THAT. I DIDN'T WANT TO KNOW..."
LADIES AND GENTLEMEN!
YOU CAN'T LEAVE JUST YET. THE SECURITY HERE IS VERY GOOD.
EVERY EXIT IS SEALED... EXCEPT THIS HOLE IN THE CONCRETE BEHIND ME.
I HAVE SOMETHING I'D LIKE TO SAY.
PLEASE DO ME THE COURTESY OF LISTENING.
SHINSOSAI: EULOGY

TELL US WHAT HE SAID, AGENT KIM.

EXACTLY AS HE SAID IT. EVERY WORD.

THESE ARTIFACTS ARE MY FATHER'S REMAINS. *MY FATHER'S.*

I KNOW YOU WANT WHAT'S LEFT OF HIM. TO STUDY, OR TO PUT TO *OTHER* USES. TO WORSHIP. TO REVILE. TO *REVIVE.*

I DON'T CARE WHICH.

YOU SHALL NOT HAVE THEM.

YOU HAVE *NO RIGHT* TO THEM.

FROM THIS MOMENT FORWARD, LET IT BE KNOWN--

ANYONE WHO MAKES ANY MOVE... *ANY MOVE* AT ALL, WITH INTENT TO BUY, SELL, TRADE, OR REPLICATE ANY *PIECE* OF THE WOLVERINE...

...THAT PERSON WILL DIE UNFULFILLED.

PAINFULLY.

SUDDENLY.

BY *MY* HAND.

ON *MY* HONOR.

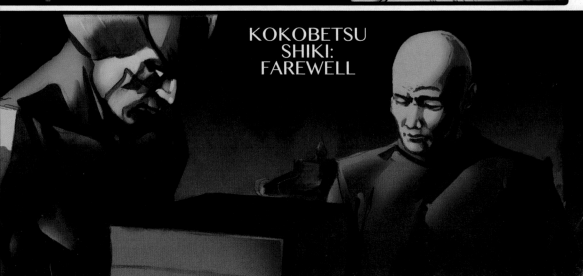

KOKOBETSU SHIKI: FAREWELL

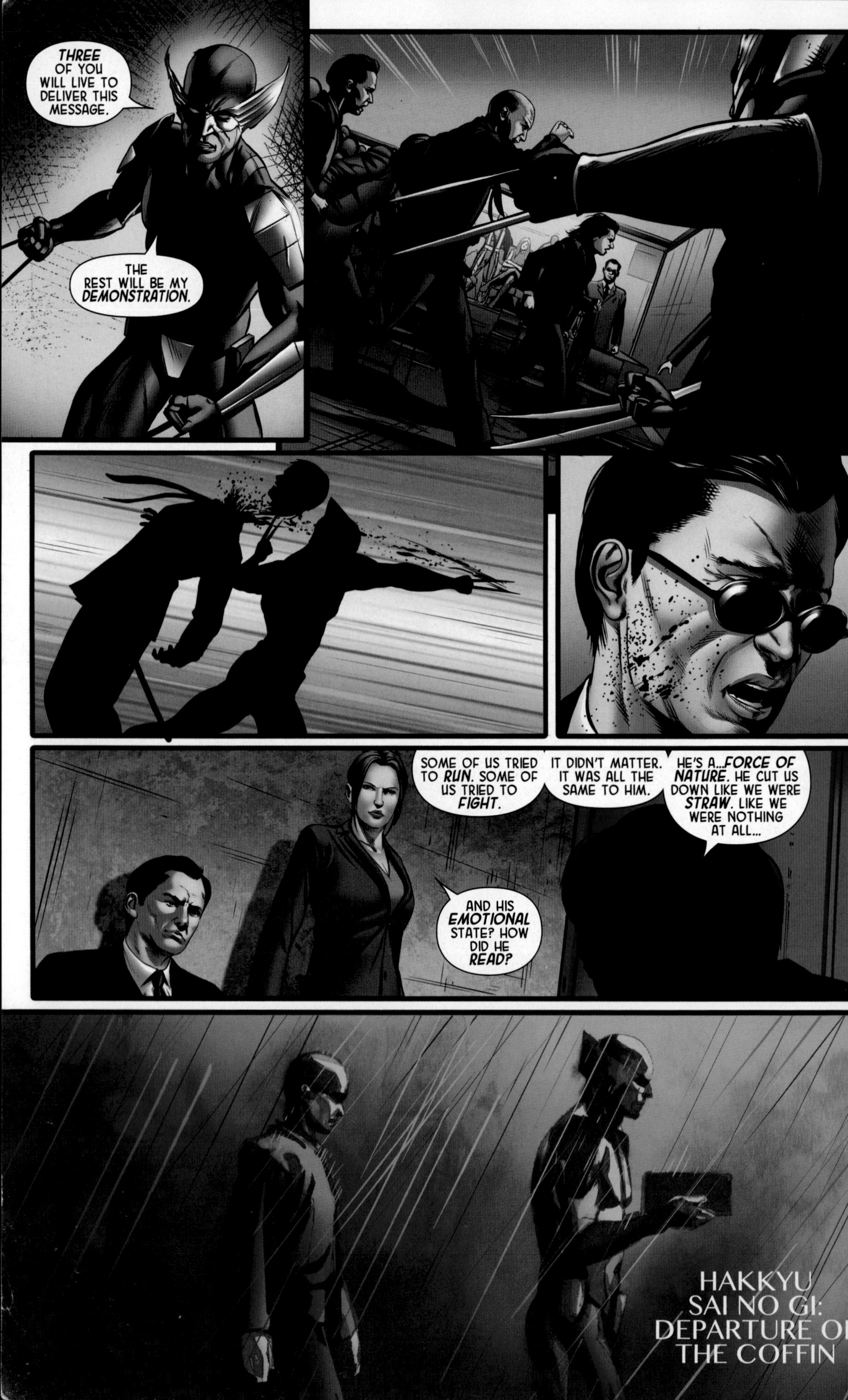
THREE OF YOU WILL LIVE TO DELIVER THIS MESSAGE.
THE REST WILL BE MY DEMONSTRATION.
SOME OF US TRIED TO RUN. SOME OF US TRIED TO FIGHT.
IT DIDN'T MATTER. IT WAS ALL THE SAME TO HIM.
HE'S A...FORCE OF NATURE. HE CUT US DOWN LIKE WE WERE STRAW. LIKE WE WERE NOTHING AT ALL...
AND HIS EMOTIONAL STATE? HOW DID HE READ?
HAKKYU SAI NO GI: DEPARTURE OF THE COFFIN

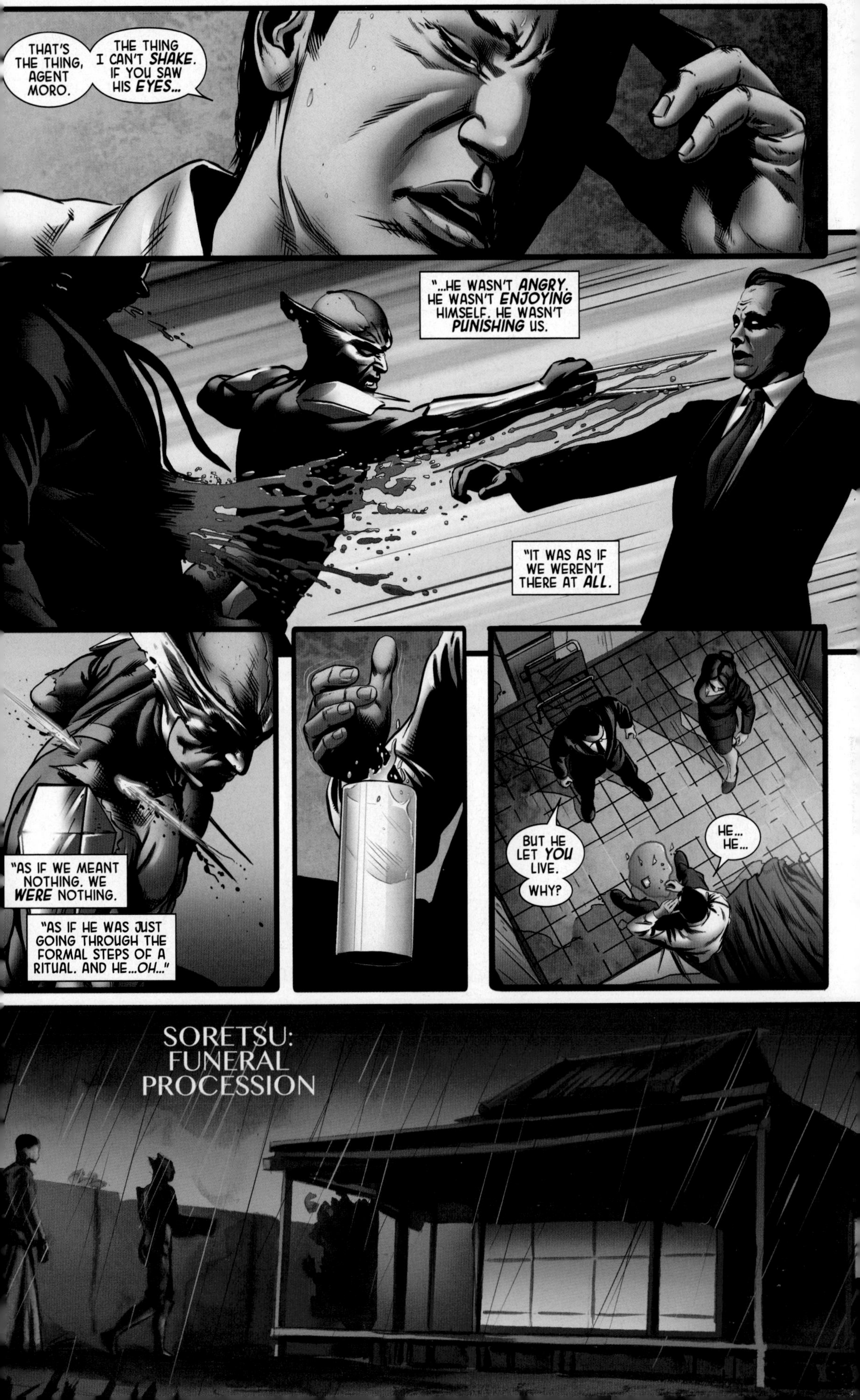
THAT'S THE THING, AGENT MORO.
THE THING I CAN'T SHAKE. IF YOU SAW HIS EYES...
"...HE WASN'T ANGRY. HE WASN'T ENJOYING HIMSELF. HE WASN'T PUNISHING US.
"IT WAS AS IF WE WEREN'T THERE AT ALL.
"AS IF WE MEANT NOTHING. WE WERE NOTHING.
"AS IF HE WAS JUST GOING THROUGH THE FORMAL STEPS OF A RITUAL. AND HE...OH..."
BUT HE LET YOU LIVE.
WHY?
HE... HE...
SORETSU: FUNERAL PROCESSION

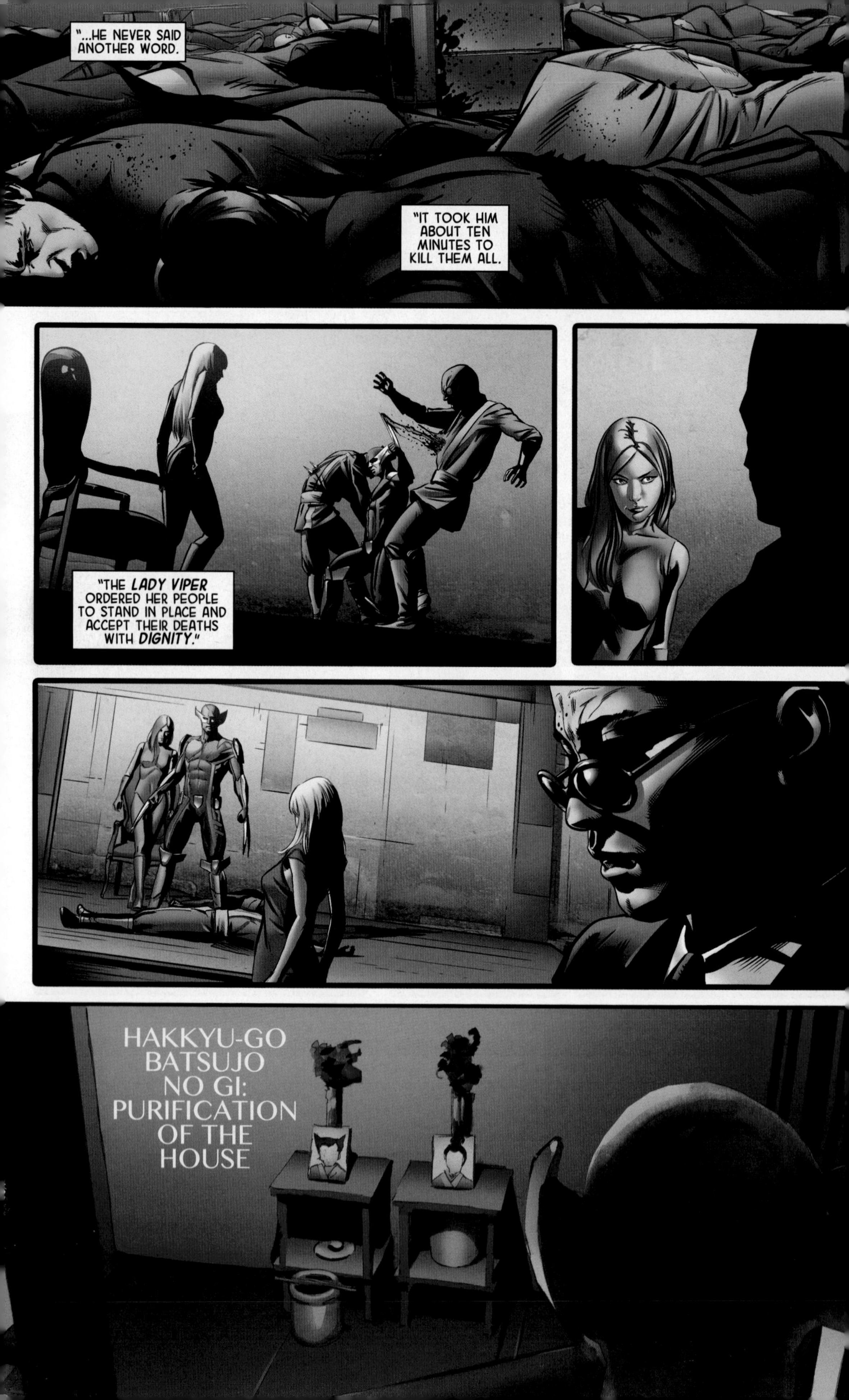
"...HE NEVER SAID ANOTHER WORD.
"IT TOOK HIM ABOUT TEN MINUTES TO KILL THEM ALL.
"THE LADY VIPER ORDERED HER PEOPLE TO STAND IN PLACE AND ACCEPT THEIR DEATHS WITH DIGNITY."
HAKKYU-GO BATSUJO NO GI: PURIFICATION OF THE HOUSE

YOU KNEW.

DAKEN. YOU KNEW WHO I WAS.

YOU DIDN'T HAVE TO DO *ANY* OF THIS. I COULD'VE WON THE AUCTION.

I WOULD'VE HIDDEN IT ALL AWAY. I WOULD'VE GIVEN HIM A PROPER--

VIPER. MYSTIQUE.

LEAVE.

NOW.

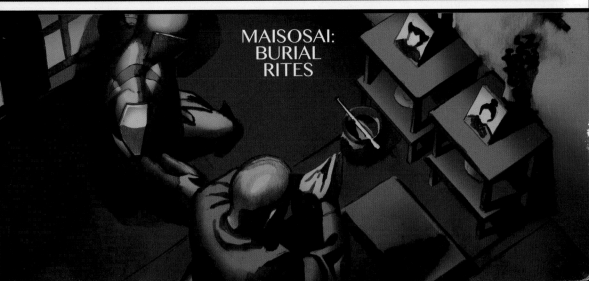

MAISOSAI: BURIAL RITES

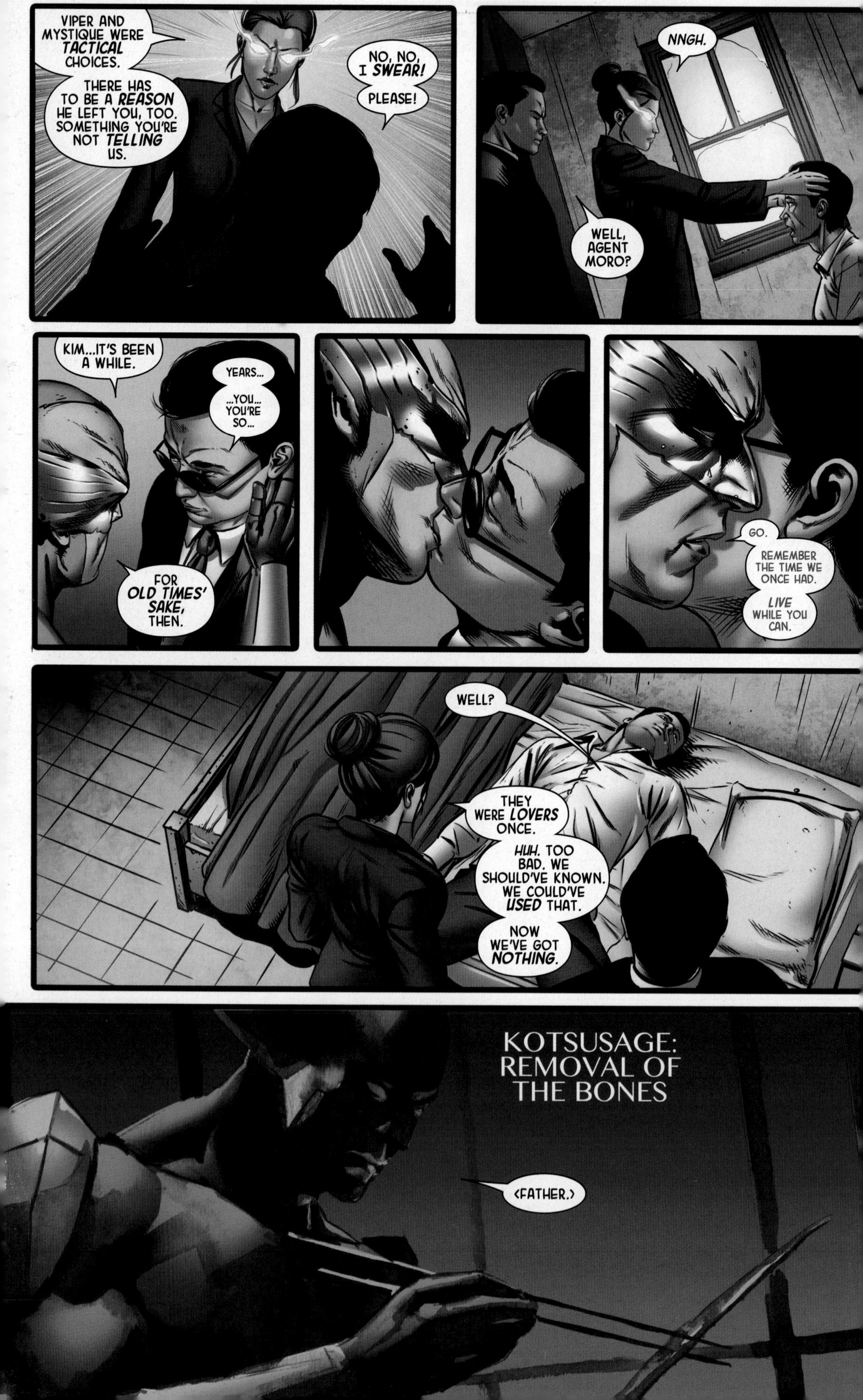
VIPER AND MYSTIQUE WERE TACTICAL CHOICES.
THERE HAS TO BE A REASON HE LEFT YOU, TOO. SOMETHING YOU'RE NOT TELLING US.
NO, NO, I SWEAR!
PLEASE!
NNGH.
WELL, AGENT MORO?
KIM...IT'S BEEN A WHILE.
YEARS...
...YOU... YOU'RE SO...
FOR OLD TIMES' SAKE, THEN.
GO.
REMEMBER THE TIME WE ONCE HAD.
LIVE WHILE YOU CAN.
WELL?
THEY WERE LOVERS ONCE.
HUH. TOO BAD. WE SHOULD'VE KNOWN. WE COULD'VE USED THAT.
NOW WE'VE GOT NOTHING.
KOTSUSAGE: REMOVAL OF THE BONES
<FATHER.>

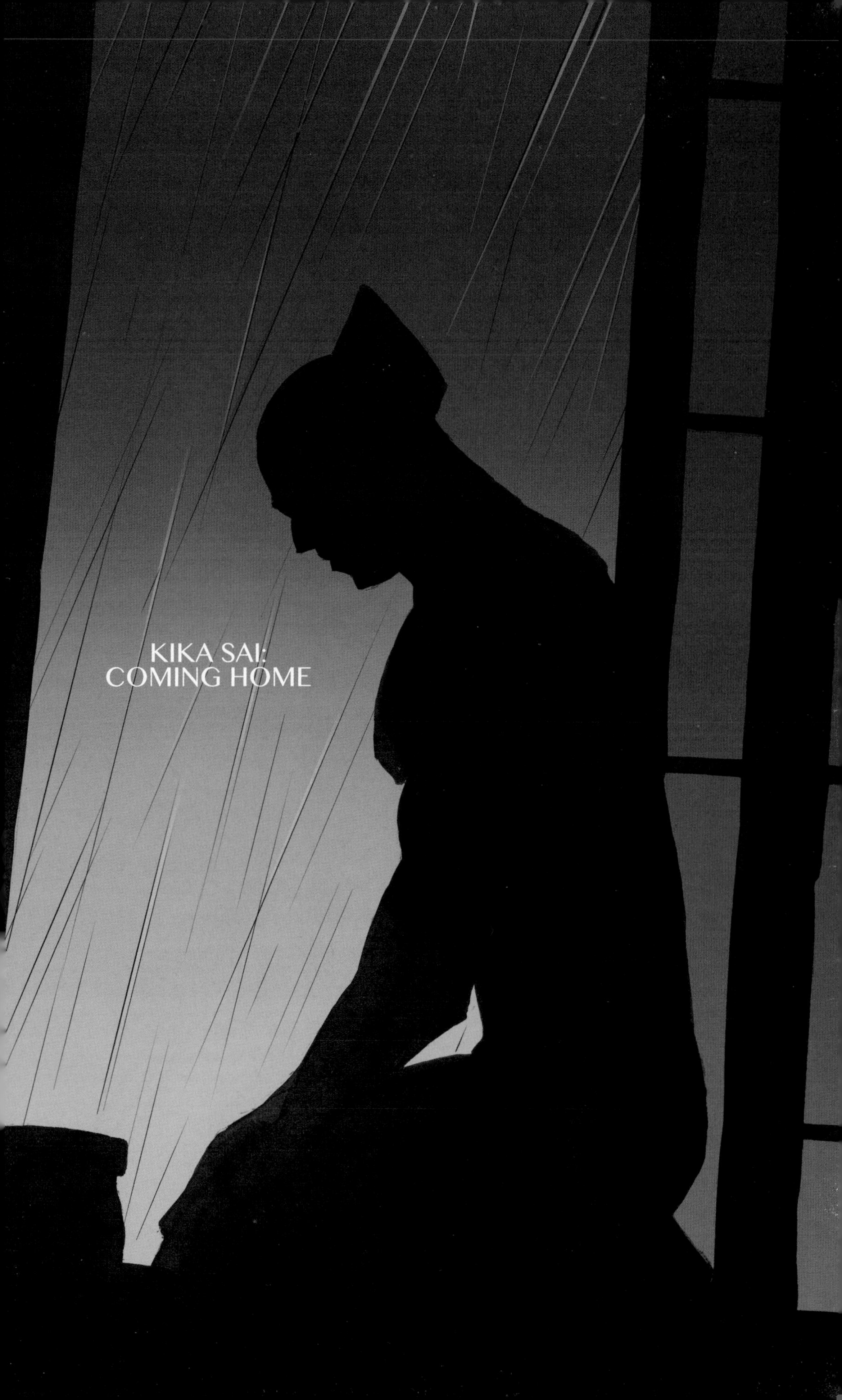
KIKA SAI:
COMING HOME

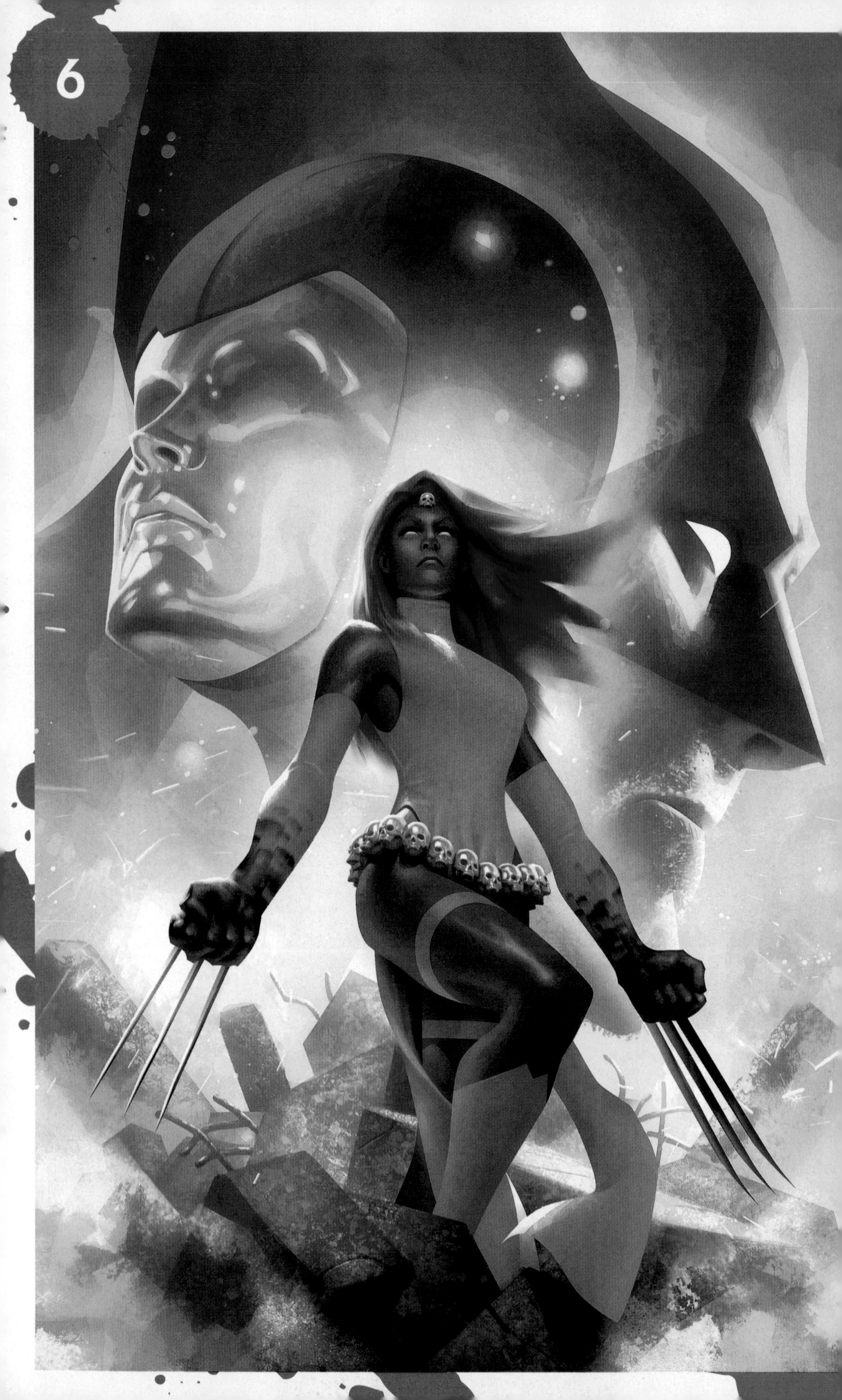
6

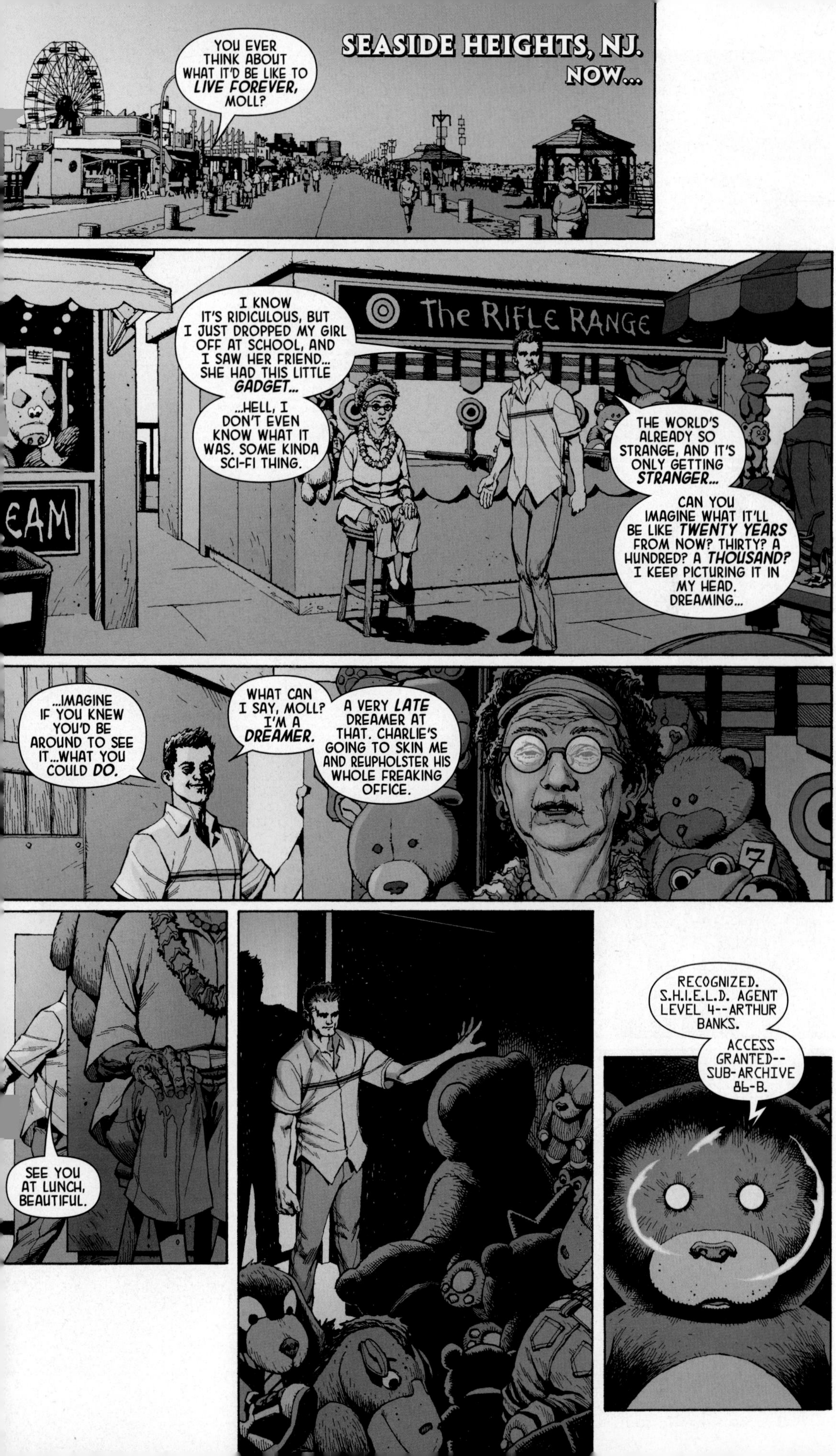
SEASIDE HEIGHTS, NJ.
NOW...
YOU EVER THINK ABOUT WHAT IT'D BE LIKE TO LIVE FOREVER, MOLL?
The RIFLE RANGE
I KNOW IT'S RIDICULOUS, BUT I JUST DROPPED MY GIRL OFF AT SCHOOL, AND I SAW HER FRIEND... SHE HAD THIS LITTLE GADGET...
...HELL, I DON'T EVEN KNOW WHAT IT WAS. SOME KINDA SCI-FI THING.
THE WORLD'S ALREADY SO STRANGE, AND IT'S ONLY GETTING STRANGER...
CAN YOU IMAGINE WHAT IT'LL BE LIKE TWENTY YEARS FROM NOW? THIRTY? A HUNDRED? A THOUSAND? I KEEP PICTURING IT IN MY HEAD. DREAMING...
EAM
...IMAGINE IF YOU KNEW YOU'D BE AROUND TO SEE IT...WHAT YOU COULD DO.
WHAT CAN I SAY, MOLL? I'M A DREAMER.
A VERY LATE DREAMER AT THAT. CHARLIE'S GOING TO SKIN ME AND REUPHOLSTER HIS WHOLE FREAKING OFFICE.
SEE YOU AT LUNCH, BEAUTIFUL.
RECOGNIZED. S.H.I.E.L.D. AGENT LEVEL 4--ARTHUR BANKS.
ACCESS GRANTED-- SUB-ARCHIVE 86-B.

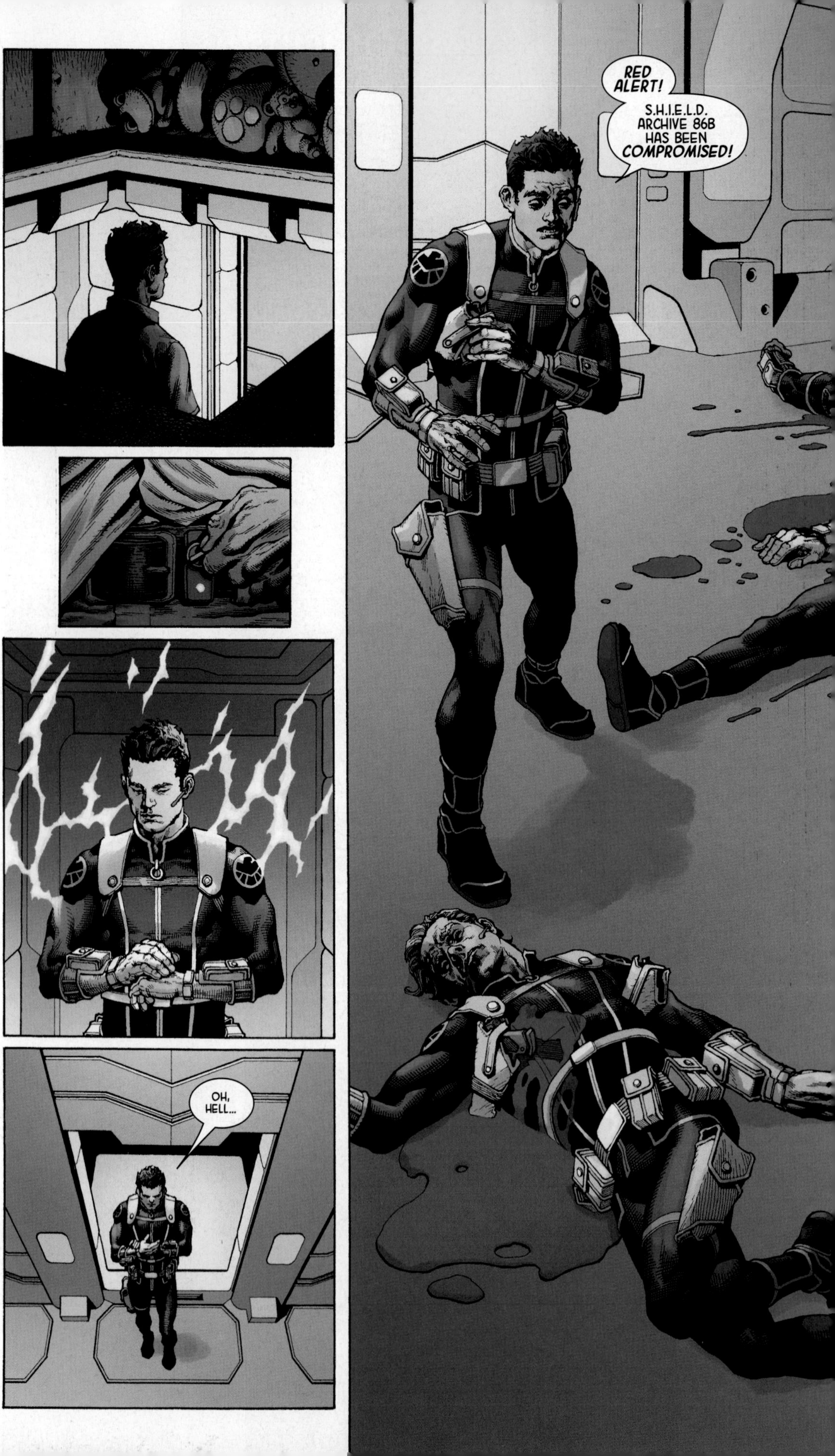
RED ALERT!
S.H.I.E.L.D. ARCHIVE 86B HAS BEEN COMPROMISED!
OH, HELL...

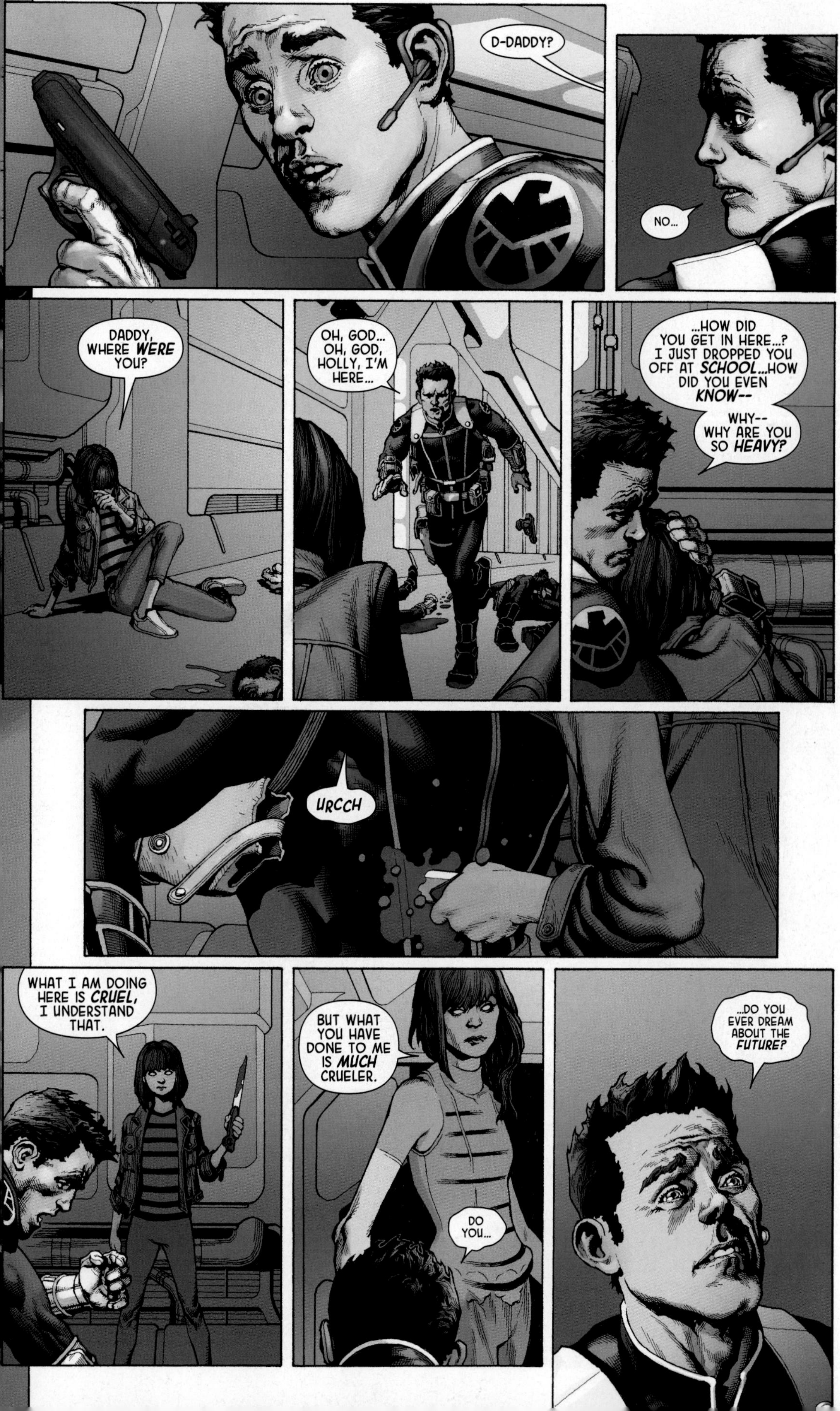
D-DADDY?
NO...
DADDY, WHERE WERE YOU?
OH, GOD... OH, GOD, HOLLY, I'M HERE...
...HOW DID YOU GET IN HERE...? I JUST DROPPED YOU OFF AT SCHOOL...HOW DID YOU EVEN KNOW--
WHY-- WHY ARE YOU SO HEAVY?
URCCH
WHAT I AM DOING HERE IS CRUEL, I UNDERSTAND THAT.
BUT WHAT YOU HAVE DONE TO ME IS MUCH CRUELER.
DO YOU...
...DO YOU EVER DREAM ABOUT THE FUTURE?

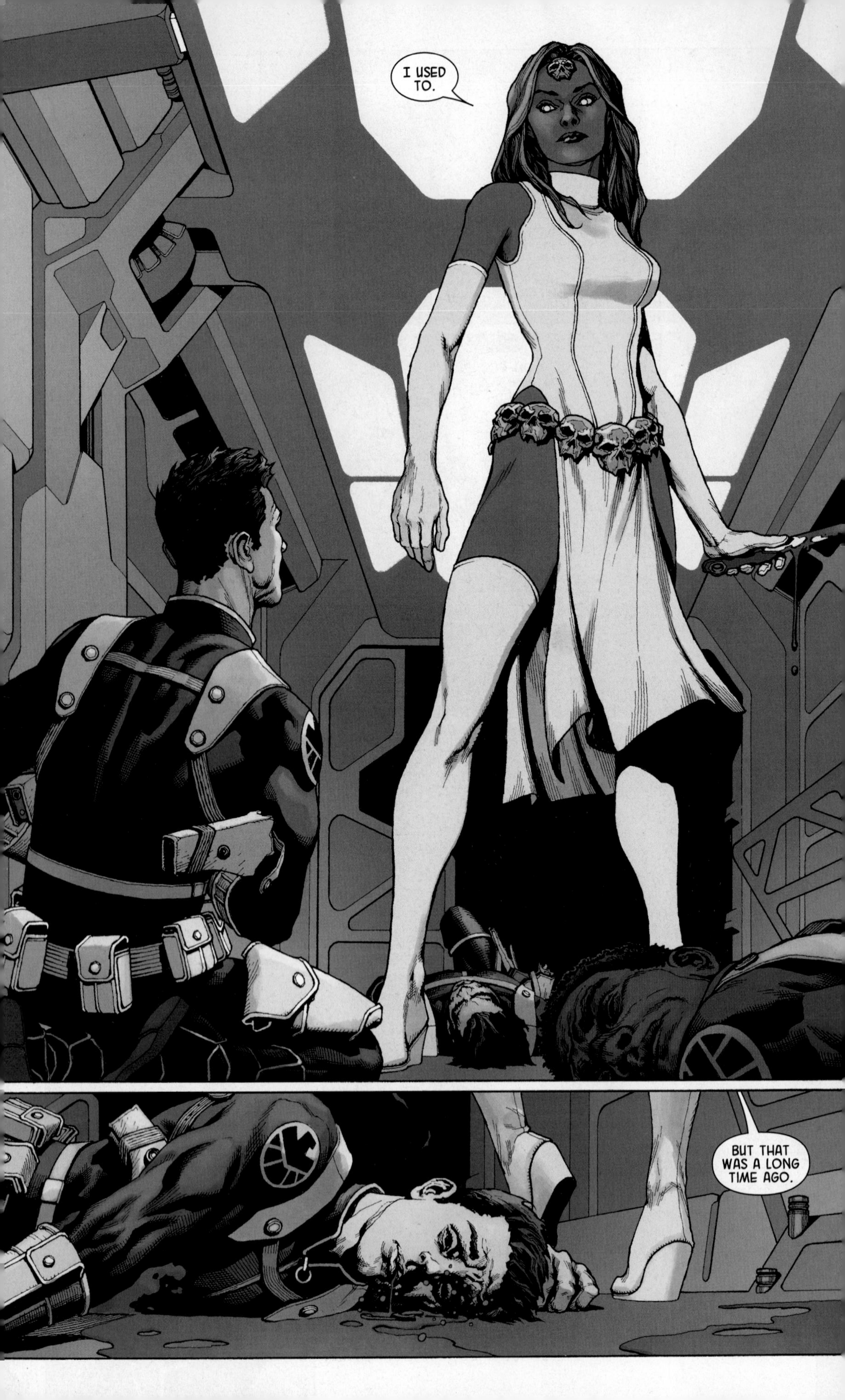
I USED TO.
BUT THAT WAS A LONG TIME AGO.

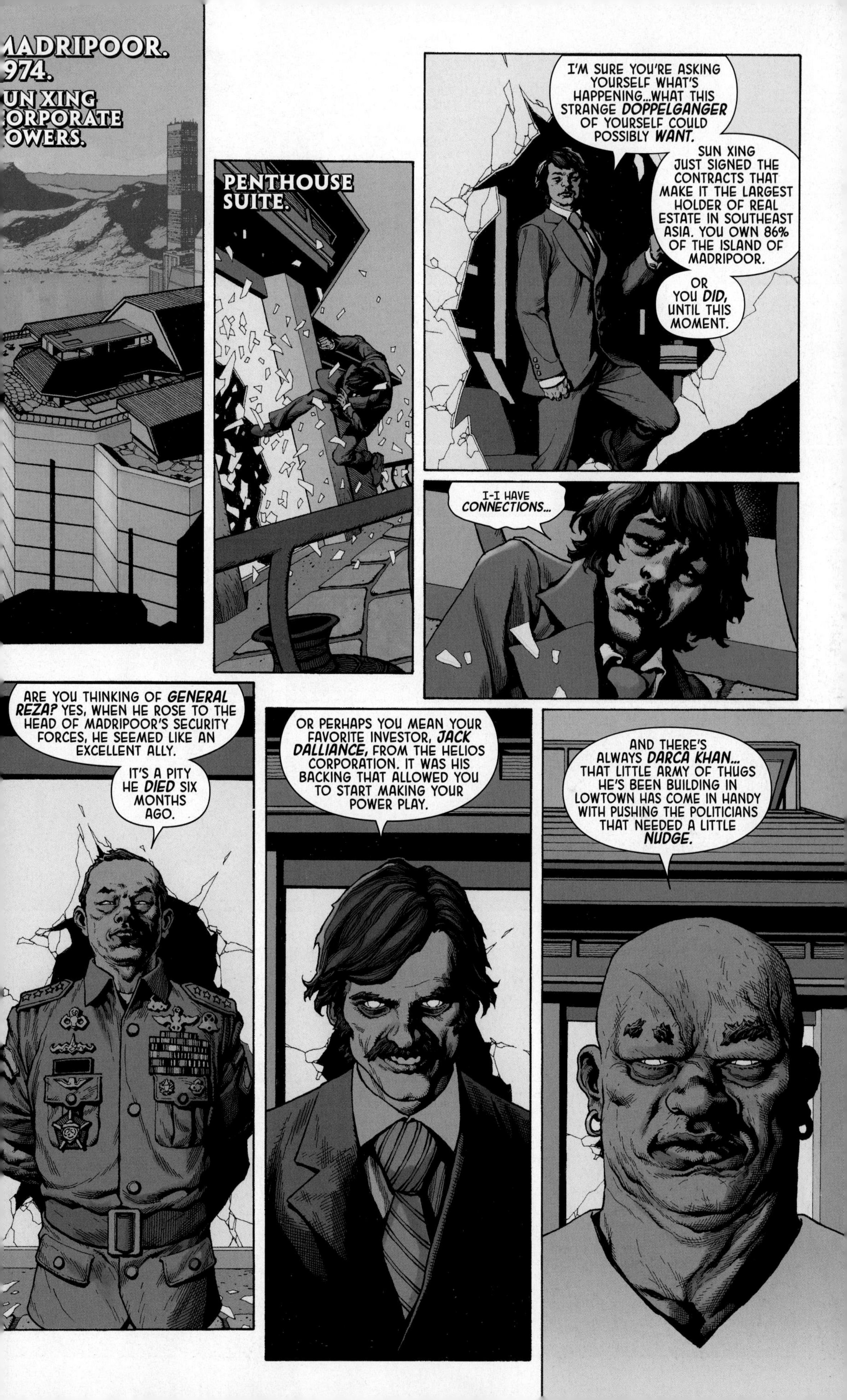

MADRIPOOR.
974.
UN XING
ORPORATE
OWERS.
PENTHOUSE SUITE.
I'M SURE YOU'RE ASKING YOURSELF WHAT'S HAPPENING...WHAT THIS STRANGE DOPPELGANGER OF YOURSELF COULD POSSIBLY WANT.
SUN XING JUST SIGNED THE CONTRACTS THAT MAKE IT THE LARGEST HOLDER OF REAL ESTATE IN SOUTHEAST ASIA. YOU OWN 86% OF THE ISLAND OF MADRIPOOR.
OR YOU DID, UNTIL THIS MOMENT.
I-I HAVE CONNECTIONS...
ARE YOU THINKING OF GENERAL REZA? YES, WHEN HE ROSE TO THE HEAD OF MADRIPOOR'S SECURITY FORCES, HE SEEMED LIKE AN EXCELLENT ALLY.
IT'S A PITY HE DIED SIX MONTHS AGO.
OR PERHAPS YOU MEAN YOUR FAVORITE INVESTOR, JACK DALLIANCE, FROM THE HELIOS CORPORATION. IT WAS HIS BACKING THAT ALLOWED YOU TO START MAKING YOUR POWER PLAY.
AND THERE'S ALWAYS DARCA KHAN... THAT LITTLE ARMY OF THUGS HE'S BEEN BUILDING IN LOWTOWN HAS COME IN HANDY WITH PUSHING THE POLITICIANS THAT NEEDED A LITTLE NUDGE.

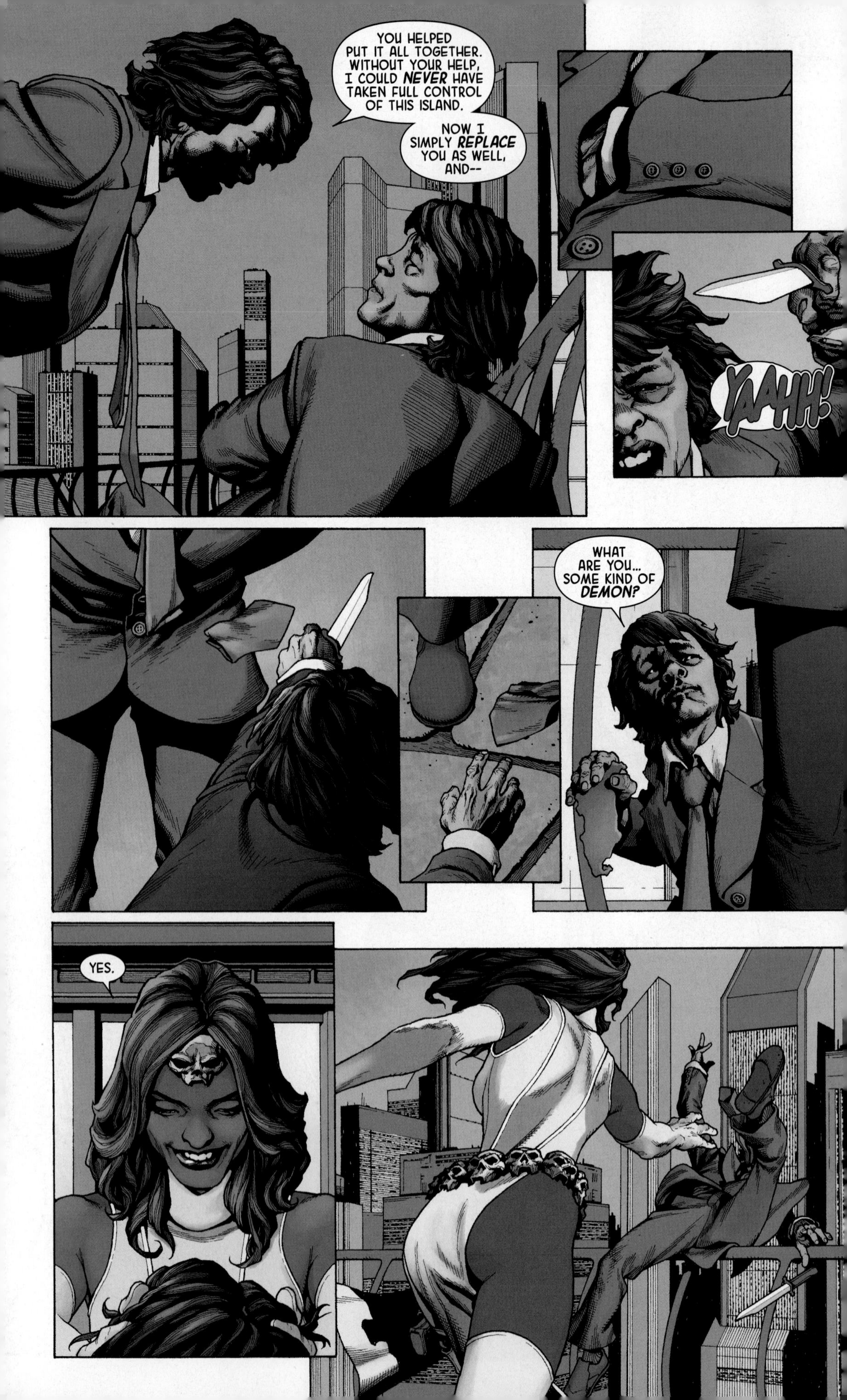
YOU HELPED PUT IT ALL TOGETHER. WITHOUT YOUR HELP, I COULD NEVER HAVE TAKEN FULL CONTROL OF THIS ISLAND.
NOW I SIMPLY REPLACE YOU AS WELL, AND--
YAAHH!
WHAT ARE YOU... SOME KIND OF DEMON?
YES.

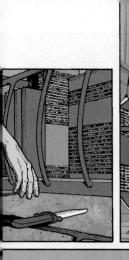

MUST YOU ALWAYS PLAY SO ROUGH WITH YOUR TOYS?

I'VE BEEN PRACTICING THAT CATCH IN MY MIND FOR *THREE HOURS*, BUT I NEVER EXPECTED THE KNIFE I GAVE YOU FOR CHRISTMAS.

WHAP

HOW ELSE AM I SUPPOSED TO *IMPRESS* YOU, IRENE? YOU CAN SEE SO MUCH OF THE FUTURE. IT'S IMPORTANT I STAY A *LITTLE* SPONTANEOUS.

IT'S *OURS*, ISN'T IT? FINALLY... AFTER ALL THIS TIME, THE PIECES ARE IN PLACE TO START BUILDING THE FUTURE WE'VE WANTED FOR YEARS.

AND NO SIGN OF THE *BRUTE*.

SORRY, KID.

YOU MUSTA BEEN LOOKING IN THE WRONG CORNERS.

BEEN A WHILE, RAVEN.

HOW DID YOU--

I'VE GOT MY WAYS. DOESN'T MATTER. YOU'VE BEEN UP TO *TROUBLE*, HAVEN'T YOU?

DON'T ANSWER. I KNOW YOU HAVE.

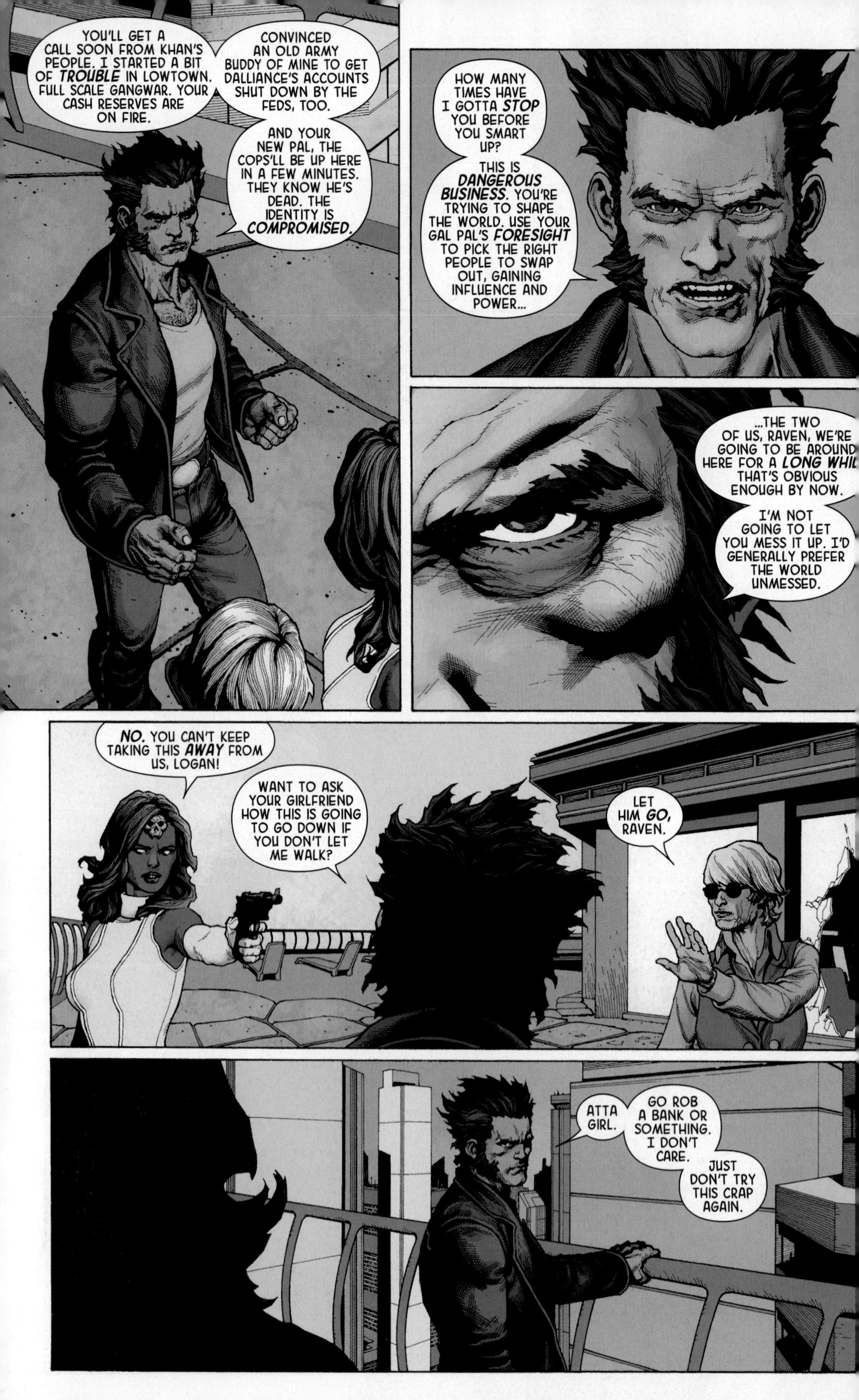
YOU'LL GET A CALL SOON FROM KHAN'S PEOPLE. I STARTED A BIT OF TROUBLE IN LOWTOWN. FULL SCALE GANGWAR. YOUR CASH RESERVES ARE ON FIRE.
CONVINCED AN OLD ARMY BUDDY OF MINE TO GET DALLIANCE'S ACCOUNTS SHUT DOWN BY THE FEDS, TOO.
AND YOUR NEW PAL, THE COPS'LL BE UP HERE IN A FEW MINUTES. THEY KNOW HE'S DEAD. THE IDENTITY IS COMPROMISED.
HOW MANY TIMES HAVE I GOTTA STOP YOU BEFORE YOU SMART UP?
THIS IS DANGEROUS BUSINESS. YOU'RE TRYING TO SHAPE THE WORLD. USE YOUR GAL PAL'S FORESIGHT TO PICK THE RIGHT PEOPLE TO SWAP OUT, GAINING INFLUENCE AND POWER...
...THE TWO OF US, RAVEN, WE'RE GOING TO BE AROUND HERE FOR A LONG WHIL THAT'S OBVIOUS ENOUGH BY NOW.
I'M NOT GOING TO LET YOU MESS IT UP. I'D GENERALLY PREFER THE WORLD UNMESSED.
NO. YOU CAN'T KEEP TAKING THIS AWAY FROM US, LOGAN!
WANT TO ASK YOUR GIRLFRIEND HOW THIS IS GOING TO GO DOWN IF YOU DON'T LET ME WALK?
LET HIM GO, RAVEN.
ATTA GIRL.
GO ROB A BANK OR SOMETHING. I DON'T CARE.
JUST DON'T TRY THIS CRAP AGAIN.

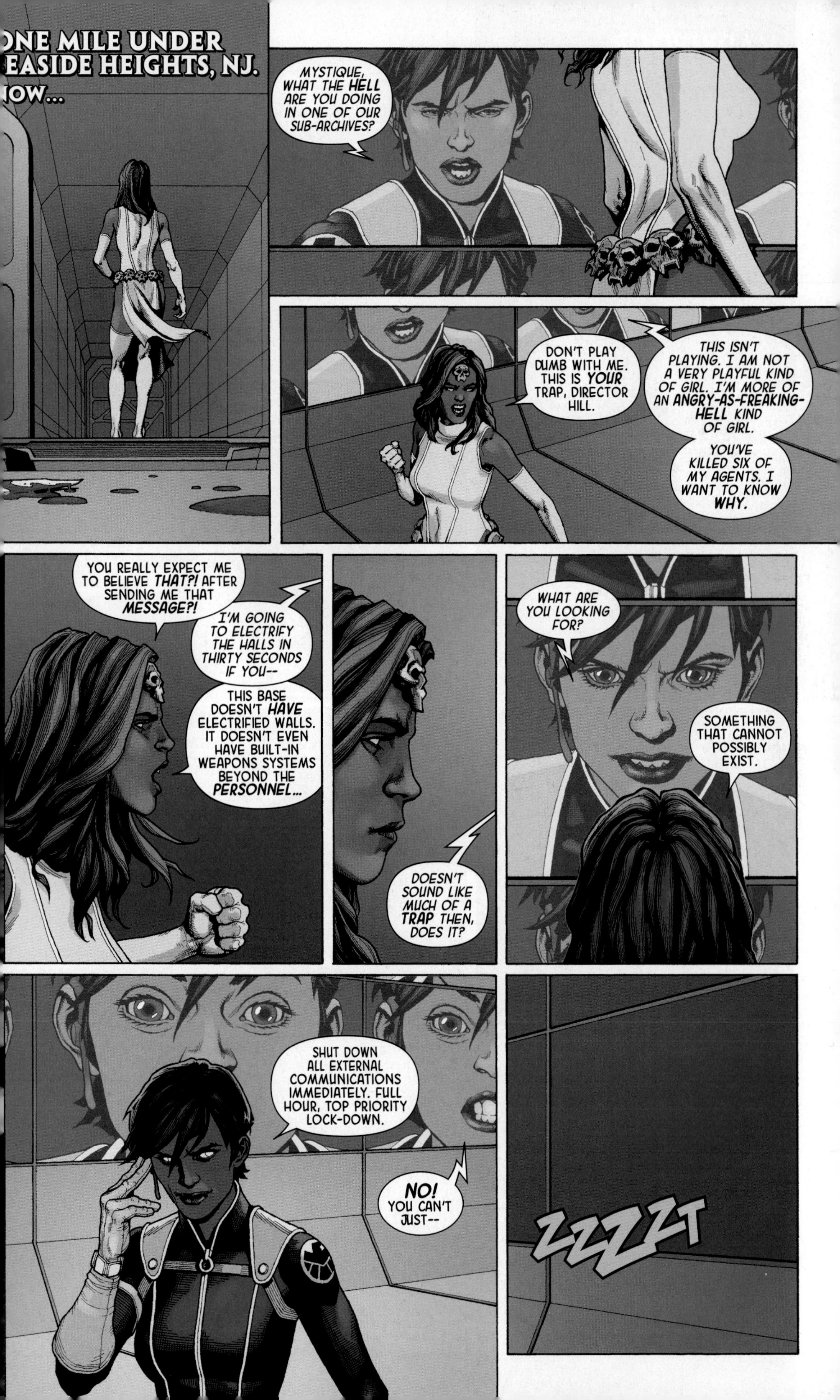
ONE MILE UNDER SEASIDE HEIGHTS, NJ. NOW...
MYSTIQUE, WHAT THE HELL ARE YOU DOING IN ONE OF OUR SUB-ARCHIVES?
DON'T PLAY DUMB WITH ME. THIS IS YOUR TRAP, DIRECTOR HILL.
THIS ISN'T PLAYING. I AM NOT A VERY PLAYFUL KIND OF GIRL. I'M MORE OF AN ANGRY-AS-FREAKING-HELL KIND OF GIRL.
YOU'VE KILLED SIX OF MY AGENTS. I WANT TO KNOW WHY.
YOU REALLY EXPECT ME TO BELIEVE THAT?! AFTER SENDING ME THAT MESSAGE?!
I'M GOING TO ELECTRIFY THE HALLS IN THIRTY SECONDS IF YOU--
THIS BASE DOESN'T HAVE ELECTRIFIED WALLS. IT DOESN'T EVEN HAVE BUILT-IN WEAPONS SYSTEMS BEYOND THE PERSONNEL...
DOESN'T SOUND LIKE MUCH OF A TRAP THEN, DOES IT?
WHAT ARE YOU LOOKING FOR?
SOMETHING THAT CANNOT POSSIBLY EXIST.
SHUT DOWN ALL EXTERNAL COMMUNICATIONS IMMEDIATELY. FULL HOUR, TOP PRIORITY LOCK-DOWN.
NO! YOU CAN'T JUST--
ZZZZZT

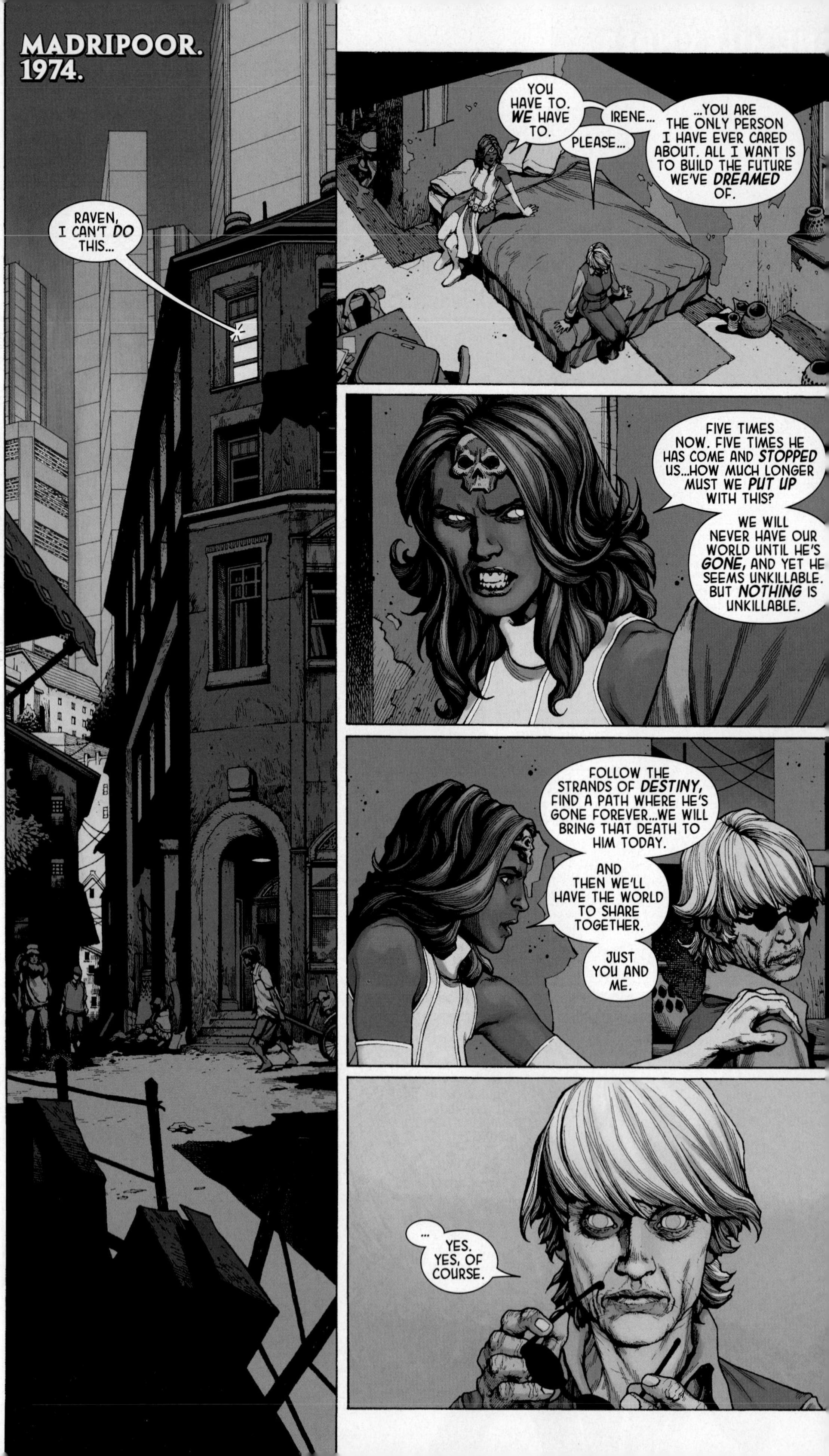
MADRIPOOR. 1974.
RAVEN, I CAN'T DO THIS...
YOU HAVE TO. WE HAVE TO.
IRENE...
PLEASE...
...YOU ARE THE ONLY PERSON I HAVE EVER CARED ABOUT. ALL I WANT IS TO BUILD THE FUTURE WE'VE DREAMED OF.
FIVE TIMES NOW. FIVE TIMES HE HAS COME AND STOPPED US...HOW MUCH LONGER MUST WE PUT UP WITH THIS?
WE WILL NEVER HAVE OUR WORLD UNTIL HE'S GONE, AND YET HE SEEMS UNKILLABLE. BUT NOTHING IS UNKILLABLE.
FOLLOW THE STRANDS OF DESTINY, FIND A PATH WHERE HE'S GONE FOREVER...WE WILL BRING THAT DEATH TO HIM TODAY.
AND THEN WE'LL HAVE THE WORLD TO SHARE TOGETHER.
JUST YOU AND ME.
... YES. YES, OF COURSE.

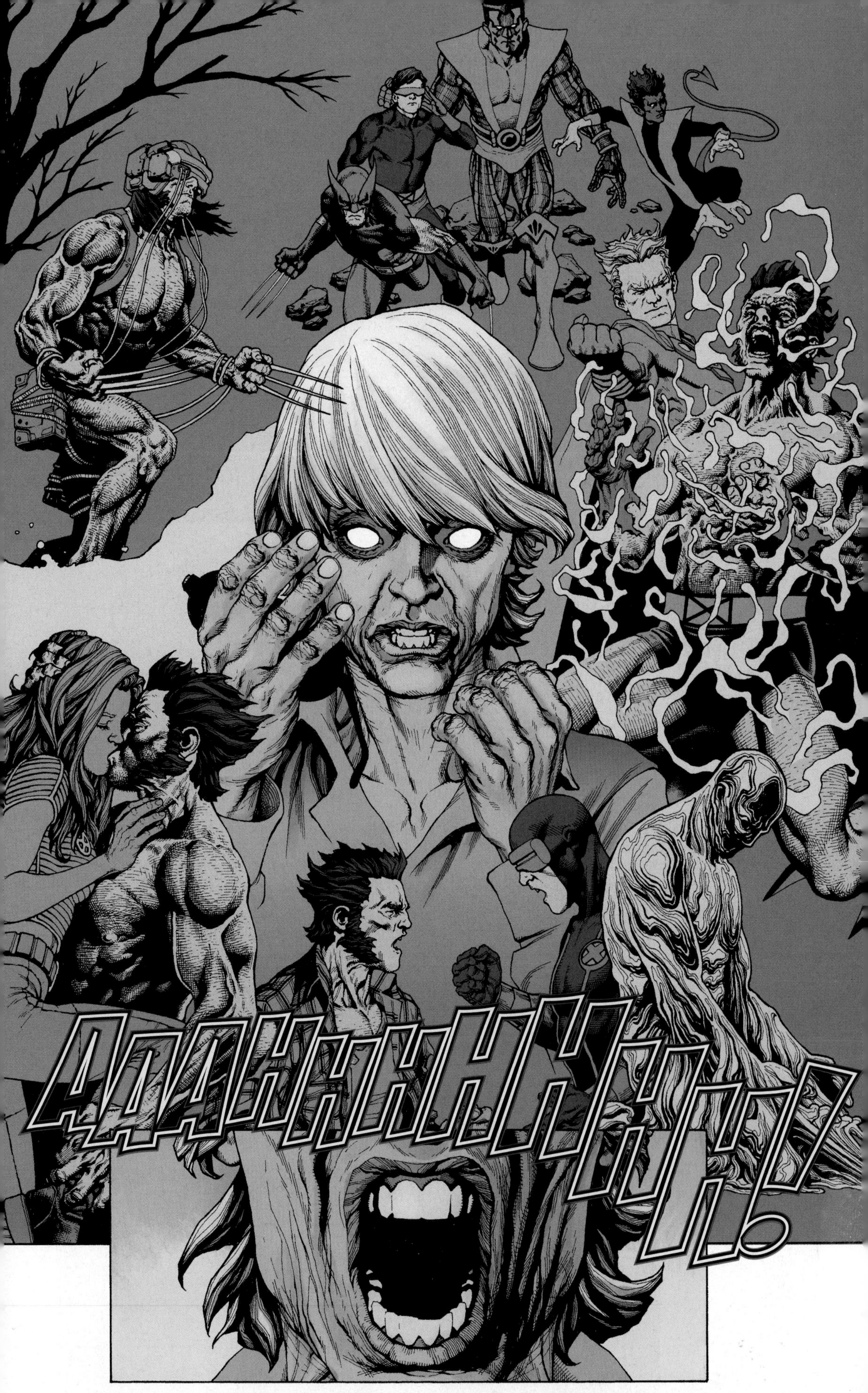
AAAHHHHHHHH!!

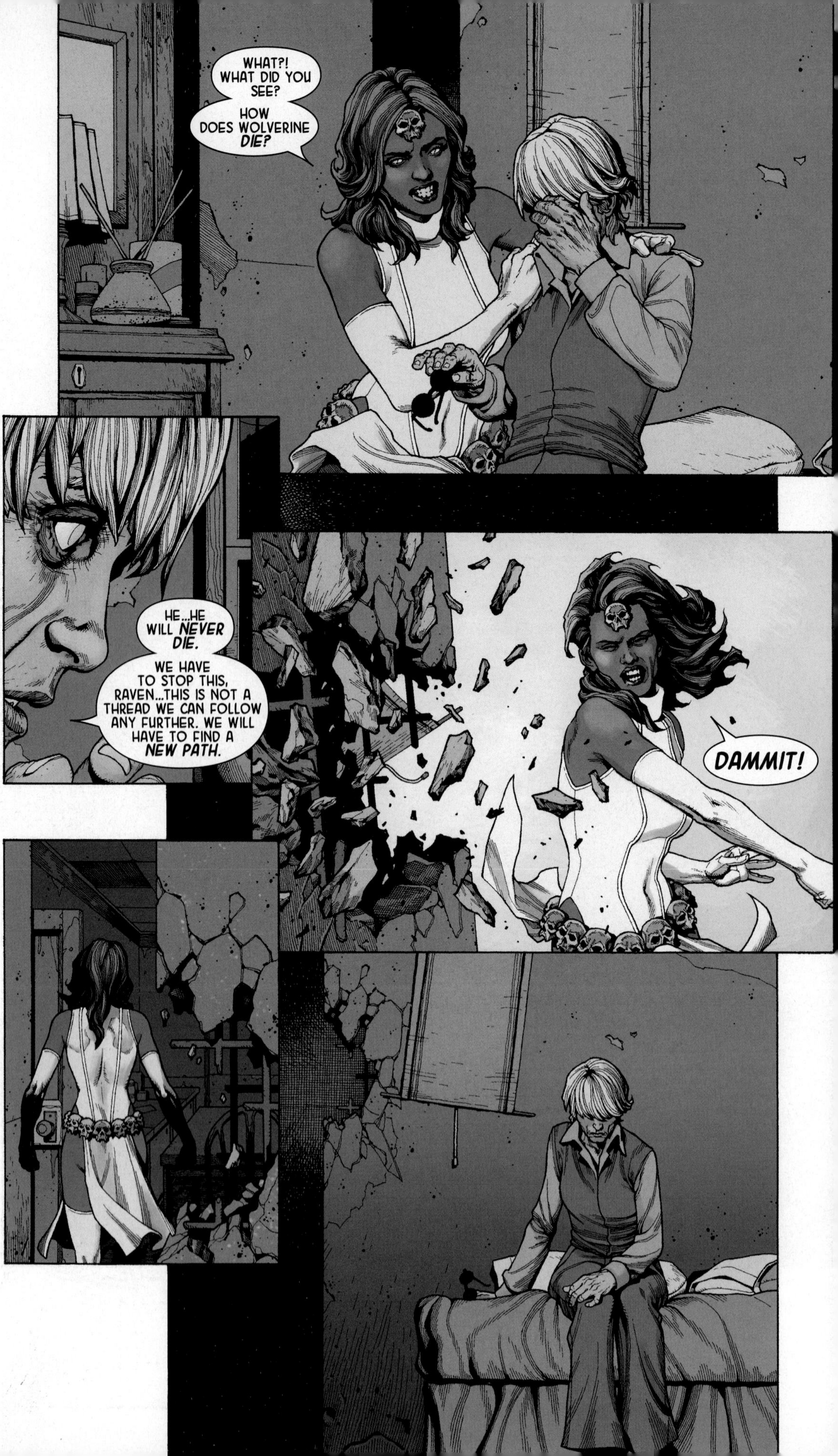
WHAT?! WHAT DID YOU SEE?
HOW DOES WOLVERINE DIE?
HE...HE WILL NEVER DIE.
WE HAVE TO STOP THIS, RAVEN...THIS IS NOT A THREAD WE CAN FOLLOW ANY FURTHER. WE WILL HAVE TO FIND A NEW PATH.
DAMMIT!

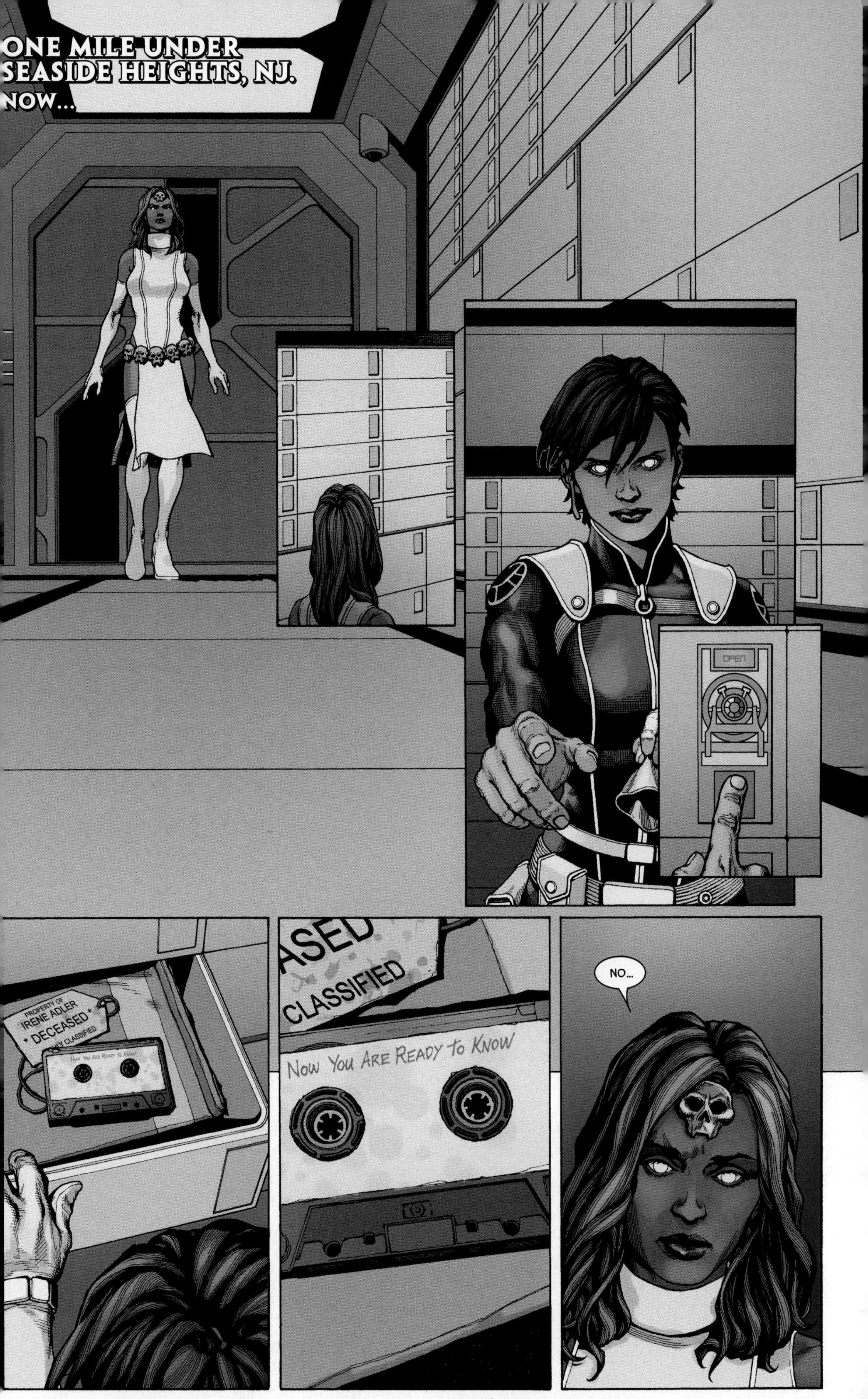
ONE MILE UNDER SEASIDE HEIGHTS, NJ.
NOW...
OPEN
PROPERTY OF IRENE ADLER * DECEASED * CLASSIFIED
Now You Are Ready to Know
ASED
CLASSIFIED
Now You Are Ready to Know
NO...

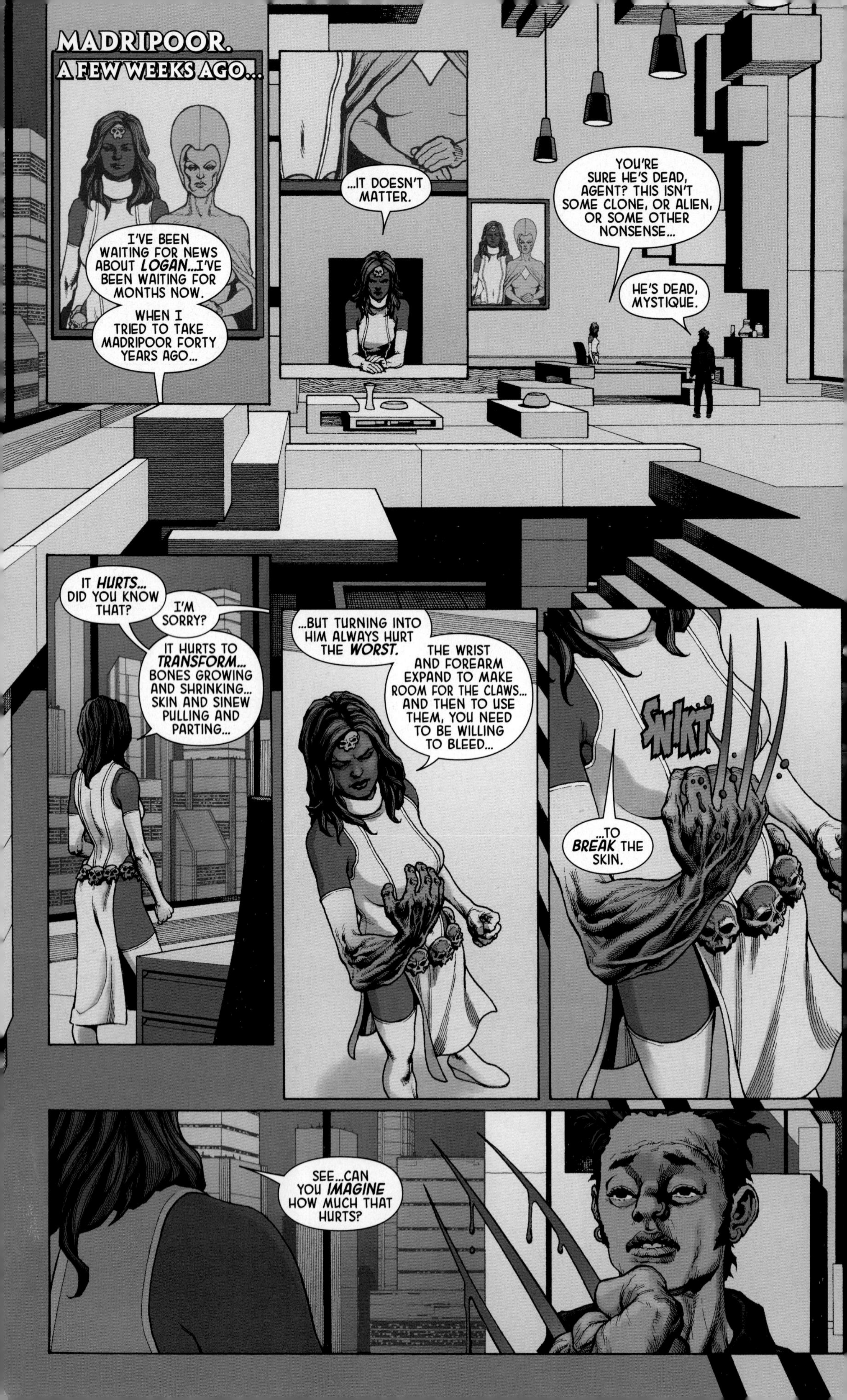
MADRIPOOR.
A FEW WEEKS AGO...
I'VE BEEN WAITING FOR NEWS ABOUT LOGAN...I'VE BEEN WAITING FOR MONTHS NOW.
WHEN I TRIED TO TAKE MADRIPOOR FORTY YEARS AGO...
...IT DOESN'T MATTER.
YOU'RE SURE HE'S DEAD, AGENT? THIS ISN'T SOME CLONE, OR ALIEN, OR SOME OTHER NONSENSE...
HE'S DEAD, MYSTIQUE.
IT HURTS... DID YOU KNOW THAT?
I'M SORRY?
IT HURTS TO TRANSFORM... BONES GROWING AND SHRINKING... SKIN AND SINEW PULLING AND PARTING...
...BUT TURNING INTO HIM ALWAYS HURT THE WORST.
THE WRIST AND FOREARM EXPAND TO MAKE ROOM FOR THE CLAWS... AND THEN TO USE THEM, YOU NEED TO BE WILLING TO BLEED...
SNIKT
...TO BREAK THE SKIN.
SEE...CAN YOU IMAGINE HOW MUCH THAT HURTS?

THERE'S... THERE'S ONE MORE THING.

WHAT *IS* THIS?

THE CARD ARRIVED *SECONDS* AFTER WE GOT THE INTELLIGENCE ON THE WOLVERINE.

Raven
My dear, I'm sorry. It is time for you to know the truth.
SHIELD Sub-Archive 86B
Irene Adler

YOU KNOW HOW I SAID IT HURTS... HURTS TO GROW THE CLAWS? THAT'S WHY I NEVER GO A STEP FORWARD...

...TO EXTEND THE BONES BEYOND HUMAN PHYSIOLOGY.

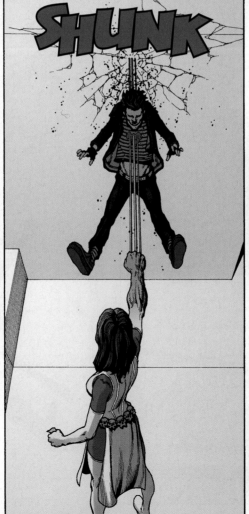

SHUNK

IT *HURTS* TOO MUCH.

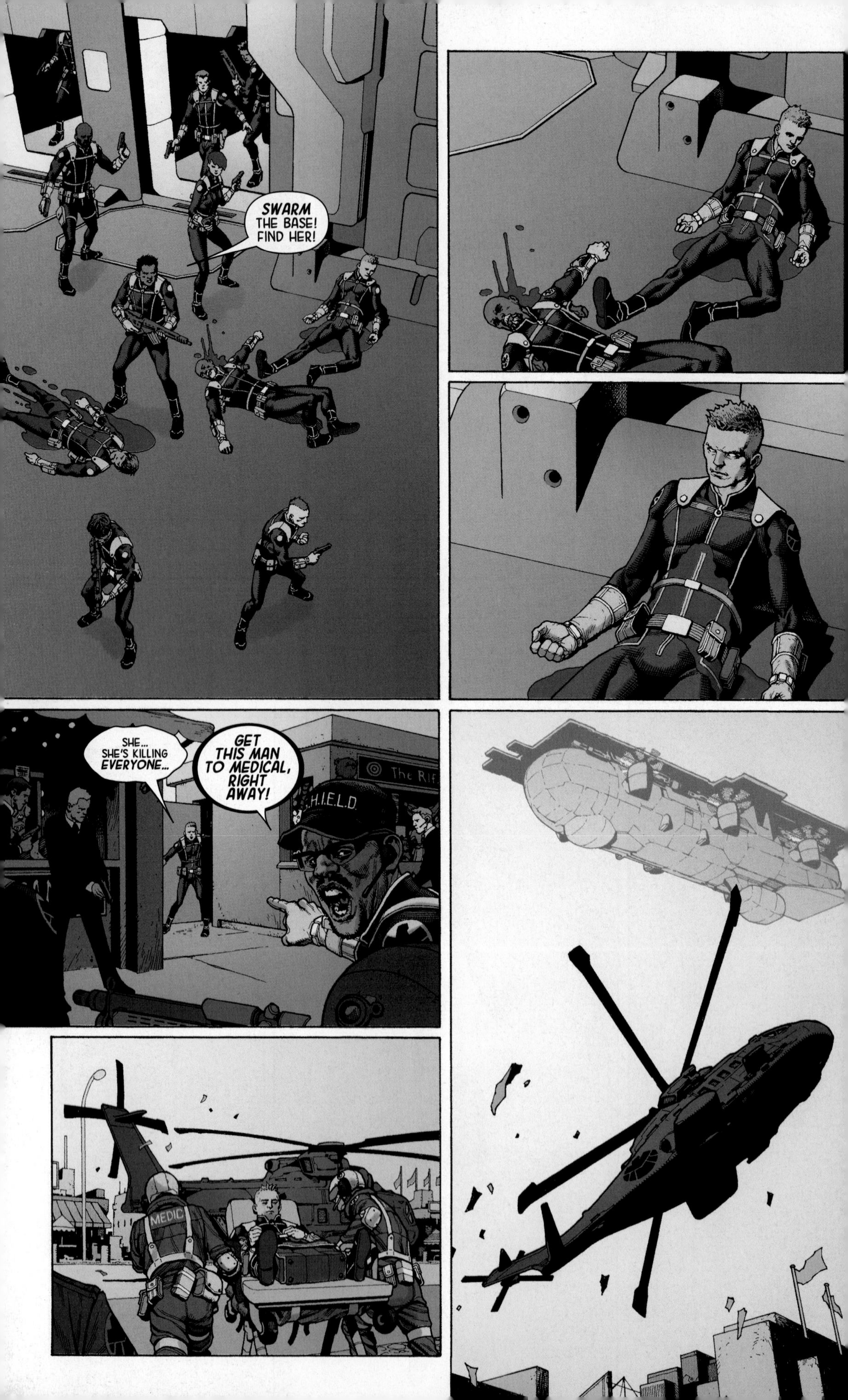
SWARM THE BASE! FIND HER!
SHE... SHE'S KILLING EVERYONE...
GET THIS MAN TO MEDICAL, RIGHT AWAY!
S.H.I.E.L.D.
MEDIC

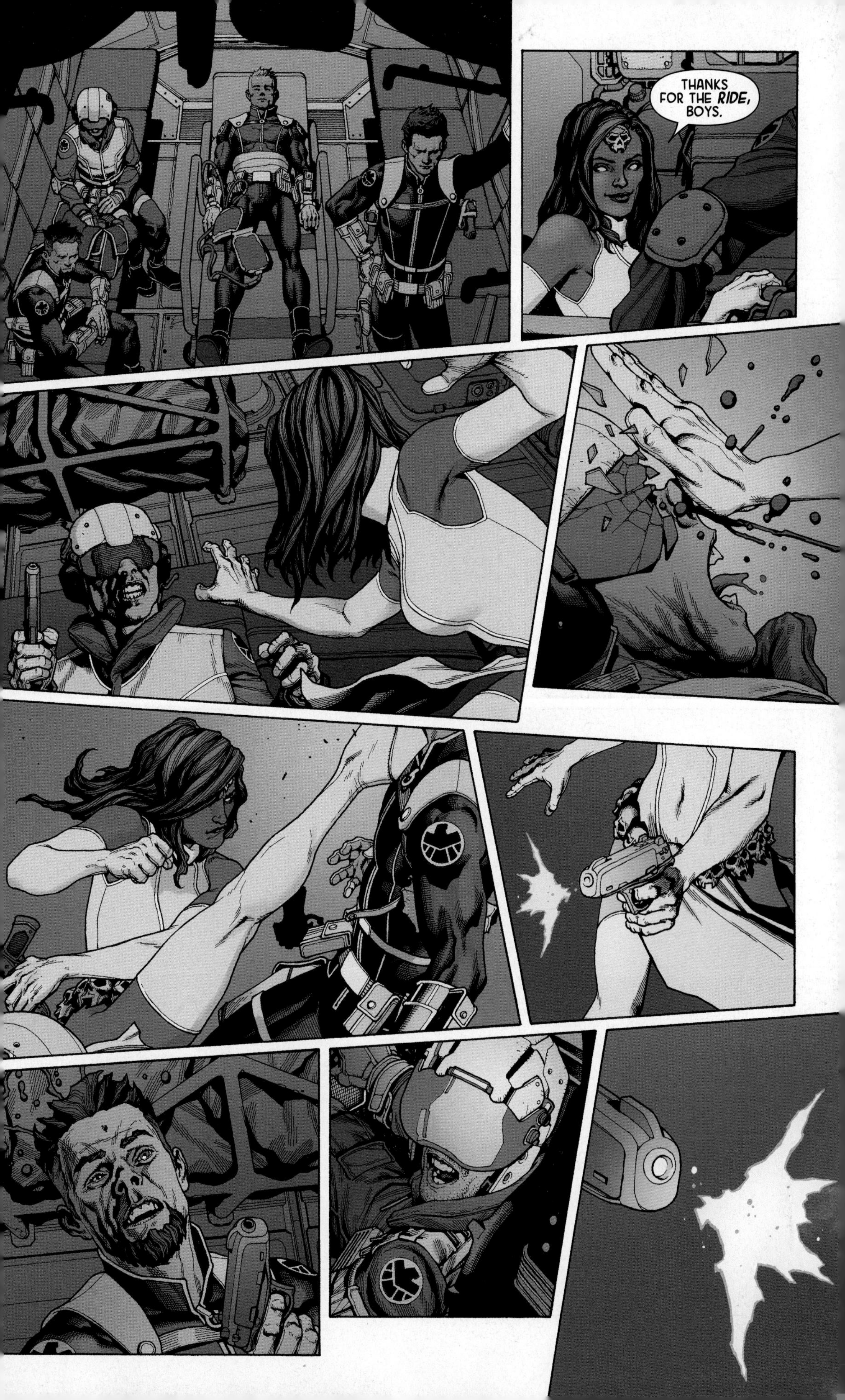
THANKS FOR THE RIDE, BOYS.

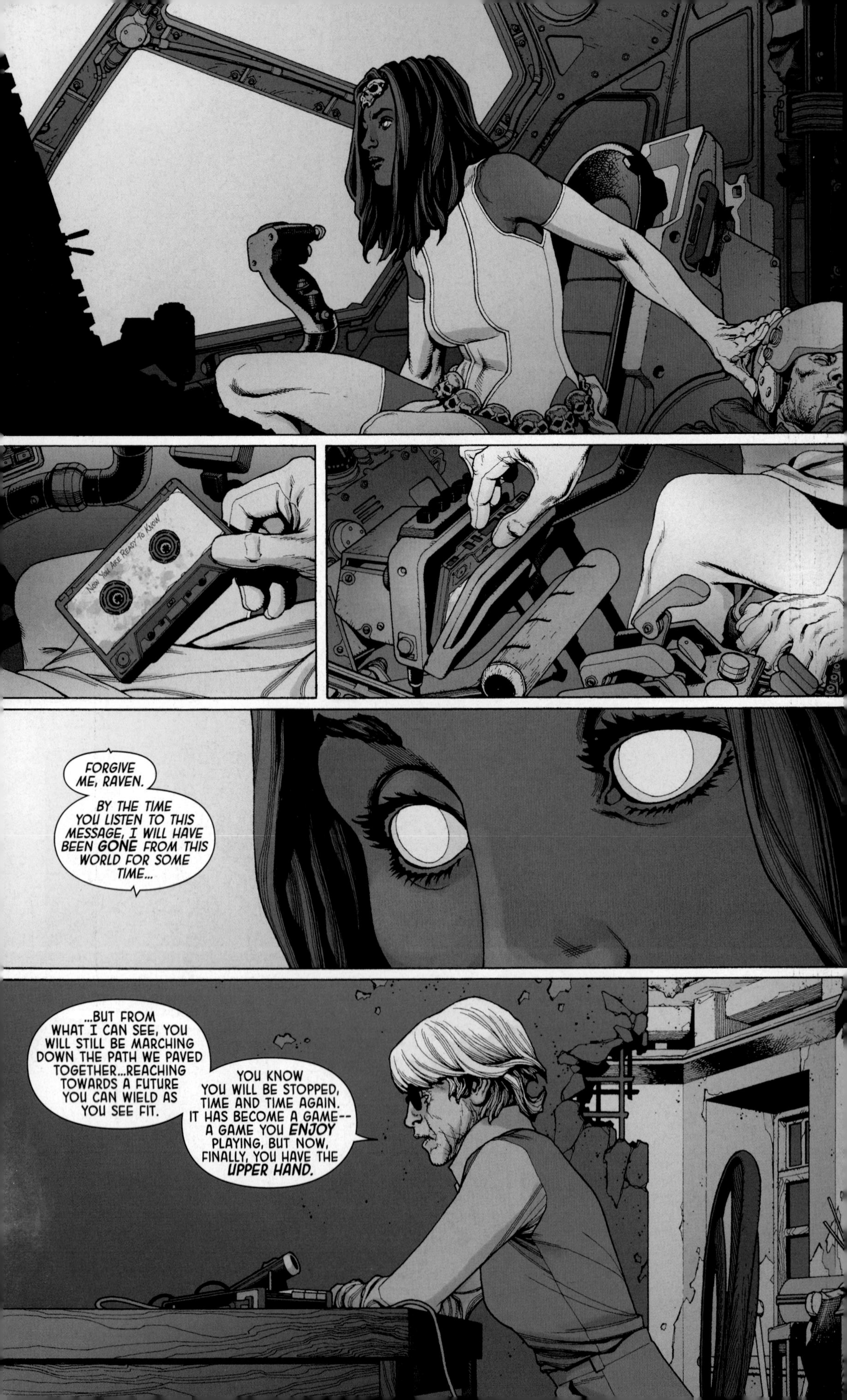
Now You Are Ready To Know
FORGIVE ME, RAVEN.
BY THE TIME YOU LISTEN TO THIS MESSAGE, I WILL HAVE BEEN GONE FROM THIS WORLD FOR SOME TIME...
...BUT FROM WHAT I CAN SEE, YOU WILL STILL BE MARCHING DOWN THE PATH WE PAVED TOGETHER...REACHING TOWARDS A FUTURE YOU CAN WIELD AS YOU SEE FIT.
YOU KNOW YOU WILL BE STOPPED, TIME AND TIME AGAIN. IT HAS BECOME A GAME-- A GAME YOU ENJOY PLAYING, BUT NOW, FINALLY, YOU HAVE THE UPPER HAND.

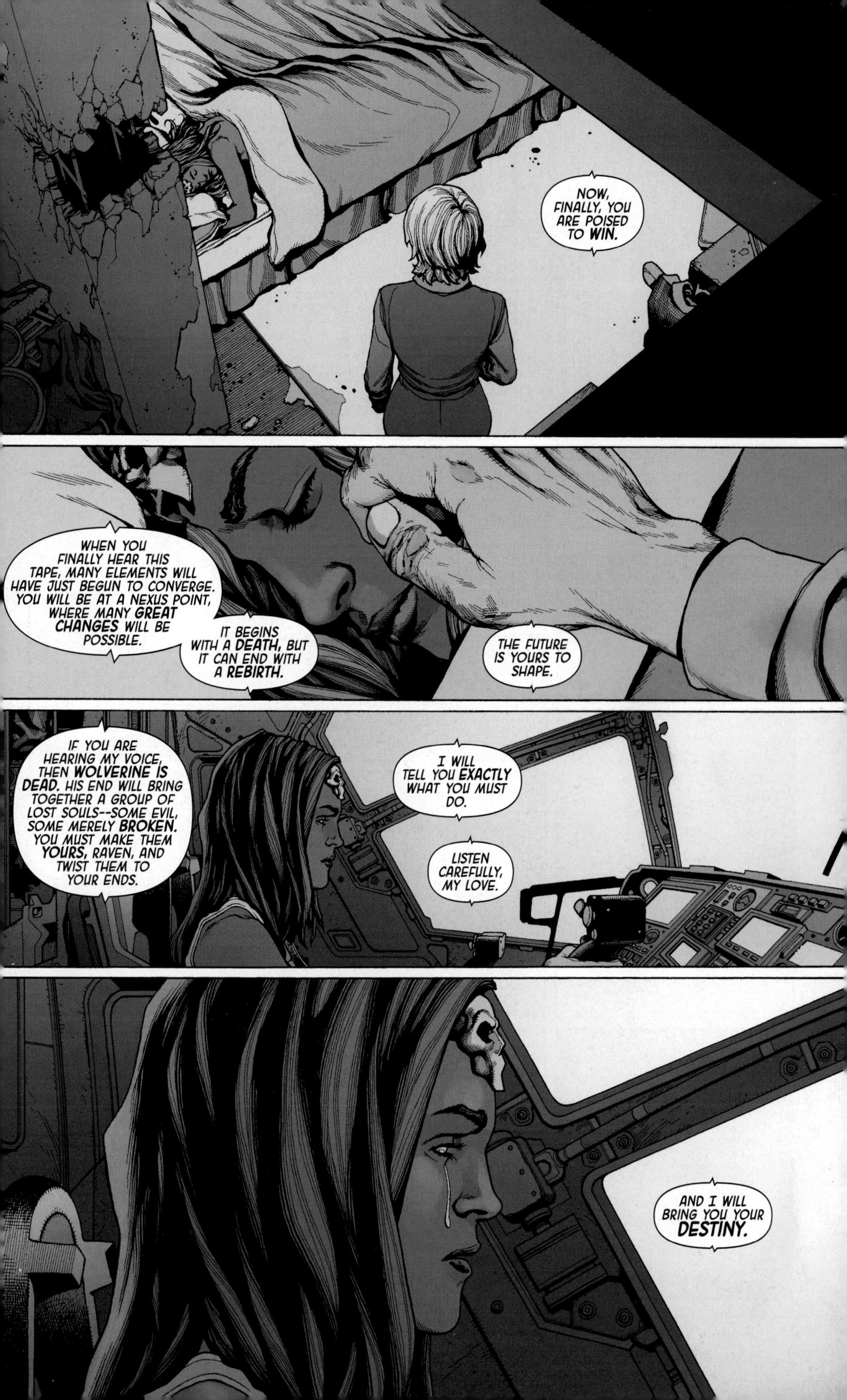
NOW, FINALLY, YOU ARE POISED TO WIN.
WHEN YOU FINALLY HEAR THIS TAPE, MANY ELEMENTS WILL HAVE JUST BEGUN TO CONVERGE. YOU WILL BE AT A NEXUS POINT, WHERE MANY GREAT CHANGES WILL BE POSSIBLE.
IT BEGINS WITH A DEATH, BUT IT CAN END WITH A REBIRTH.
THE FUTURE IS YOURS TO SHAPE.
IF YOU ARE HEARING MY VOICE, THEN WOLVERINE IS DEAD. HIS END WILL BRING TOGETHER A GROUP OF LOST SOULS--SOME EVIL, SOME MERELY BROKEN. YOU MUST MAKE THEM YOURS, RAVEN, AND TWIST THEM TO YOUR ENDS.
I WILL TELL YOU EXACTLY WHAT YOU MUST DO.
LISTEN CAREFULLY, MY LOVE.
AND I WILL BRING YOU YOUR DESTINY.

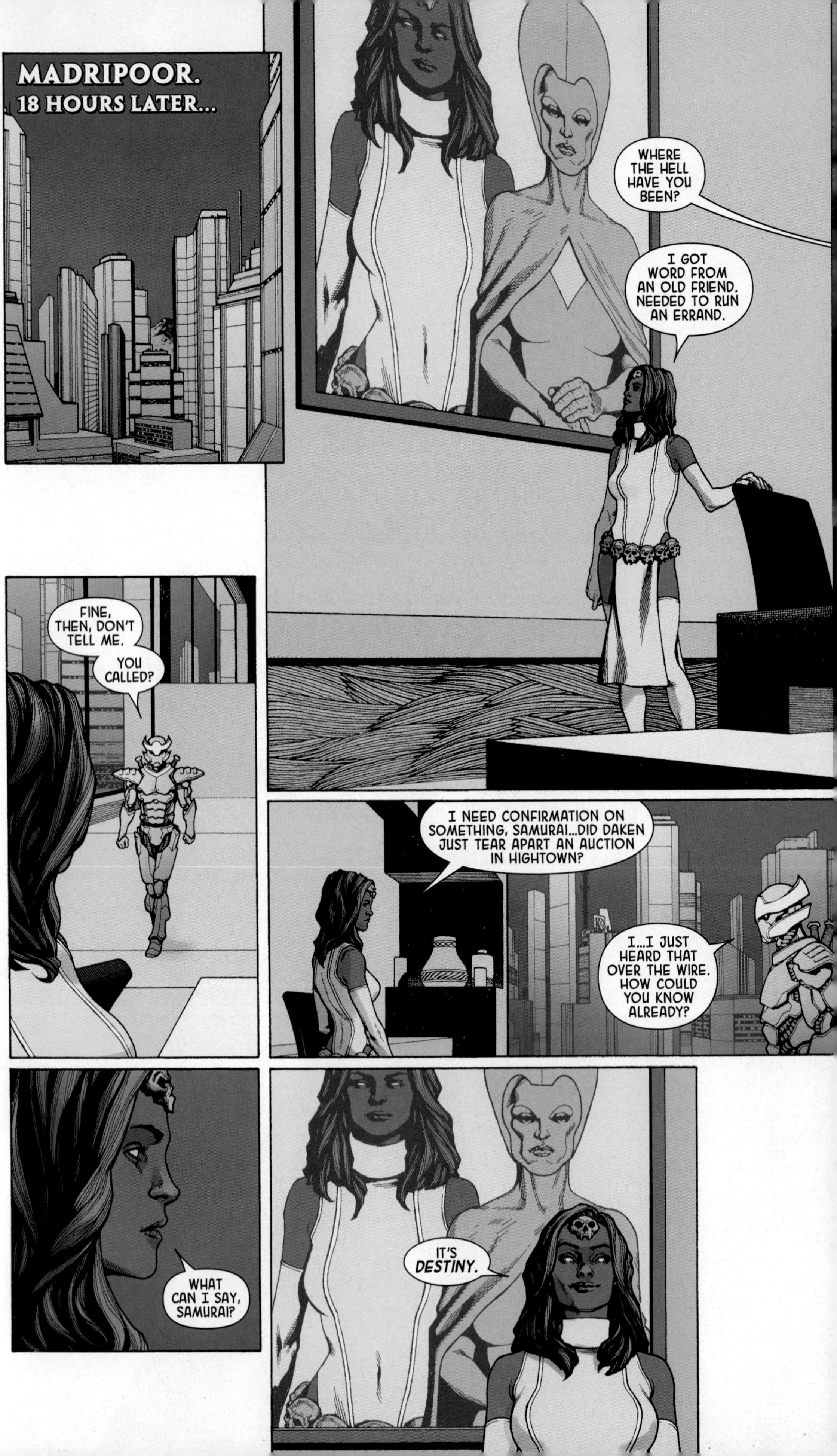
MADRIPOOR.
18 HOURS LATER...
WHERE THE HELL HAVE YOU BEEN?
I GOT WORD FROM AN OLD FRIEND. NEEDED TO RUN AN ERRAND.
FINE, THEN, DON'T TELL ME.
YOU CALLED?
I NEED CONFIRMATION ON SOMETHING, SAMURAI...DID DAKEN JUST TEAR APART AN AUCTION IN HIGHTOWN?
I...I JUST HEARD THAT OVER THE WIRE. HOW COULD YOU KNOW ALREADY?
WHAT CAN I SAY, SAMURAI?
IT'S *DESTINY.*

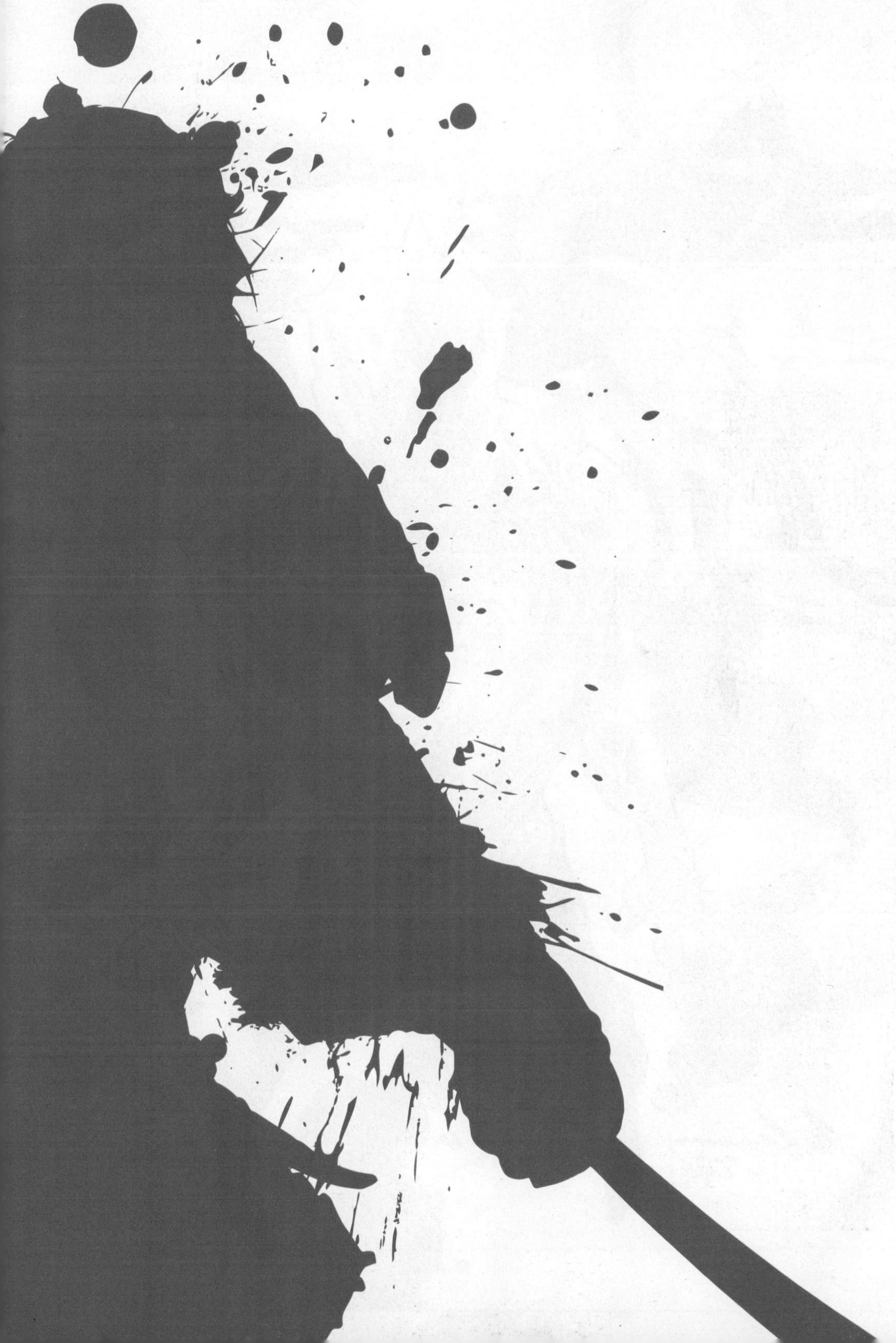

7

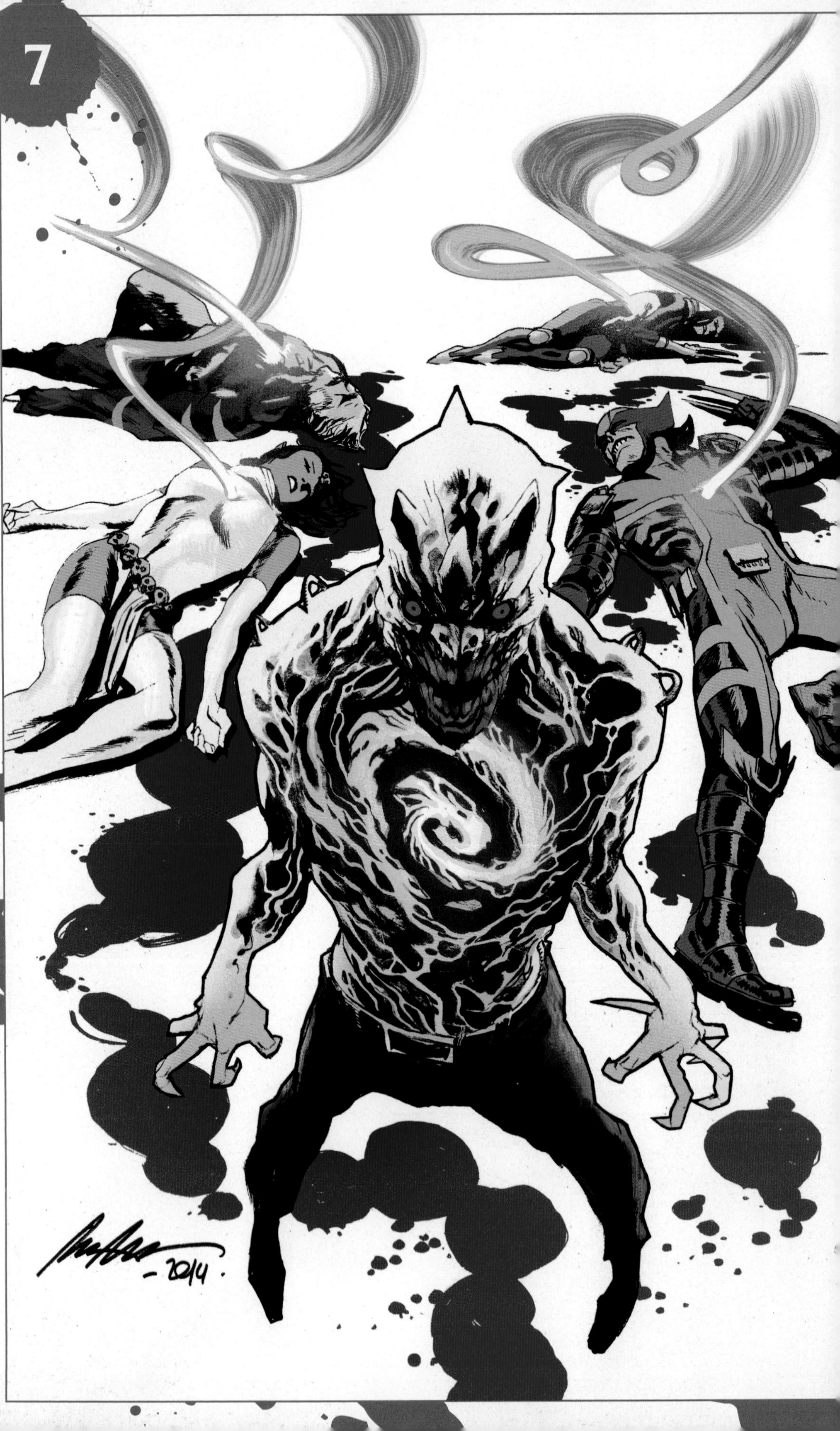
2014

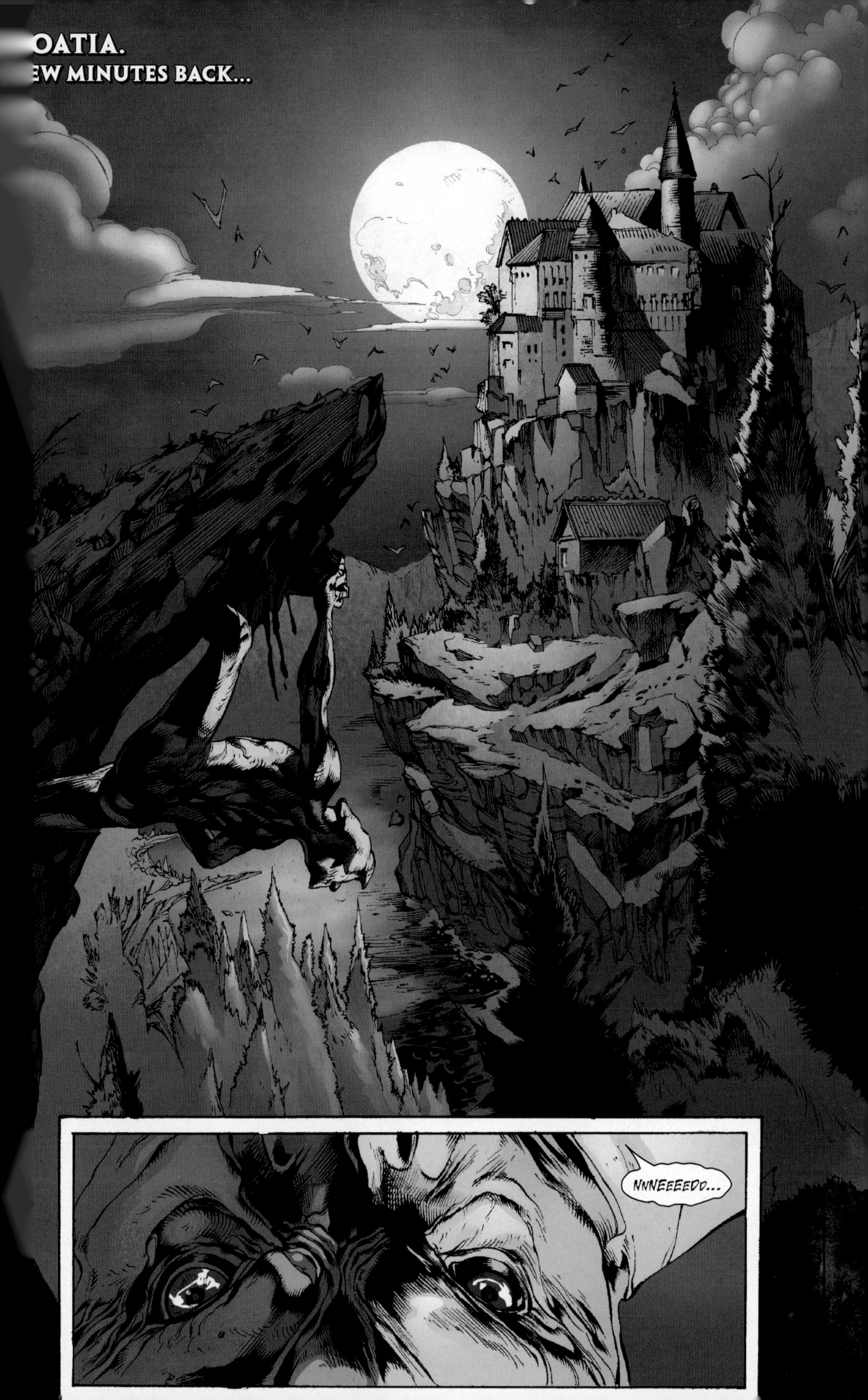
OATIA.
EW MINUTES BACK...
NNNEEEEDD...

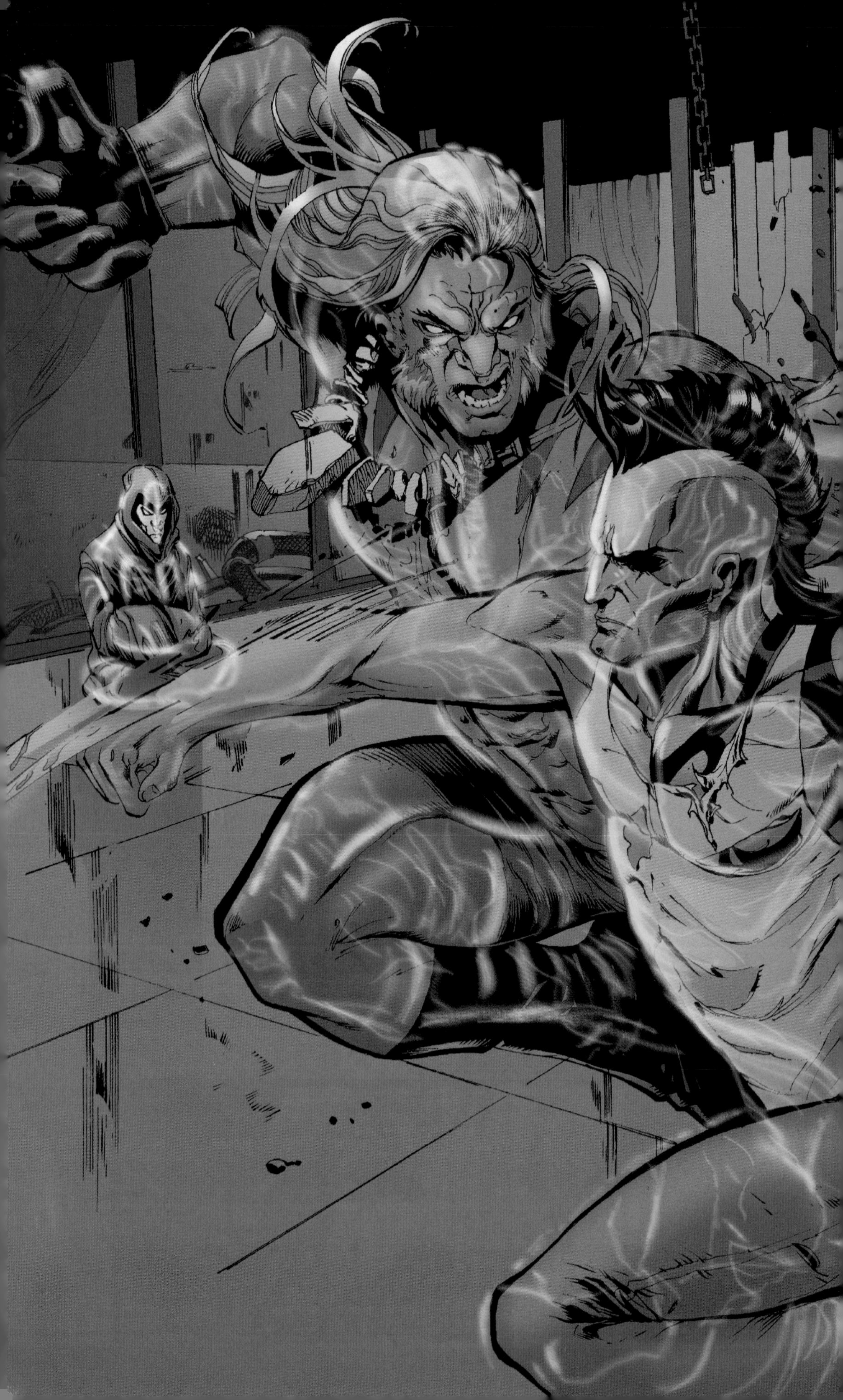

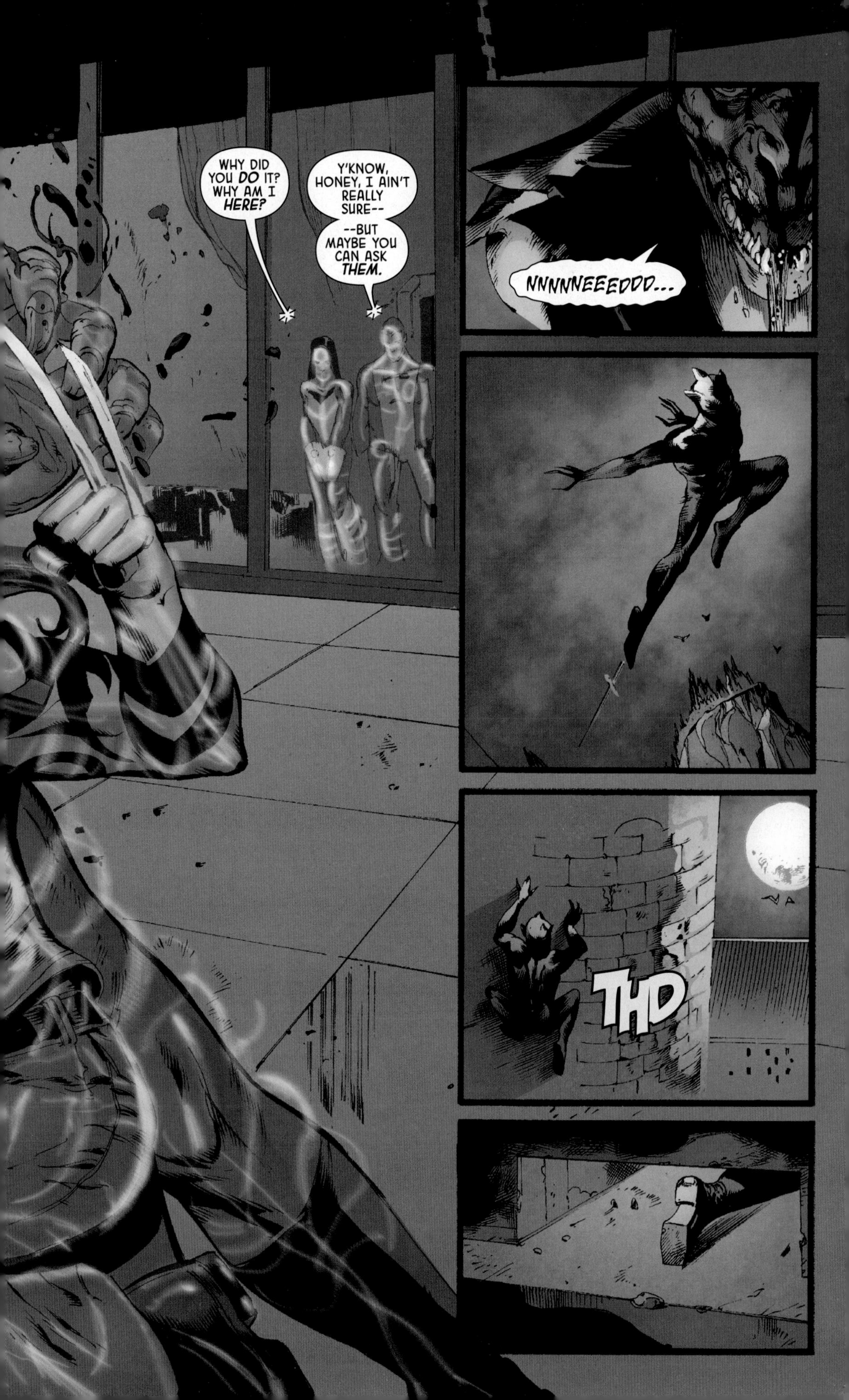
WHY DID YOU DO IT? WHY AM I HERE?
Y'KNOW, HONEY, I AIN'T REALLY SURE--
--BUT MAYBE YOU CAN ASK THEM.
NNNNNEEEEDDD...
THD

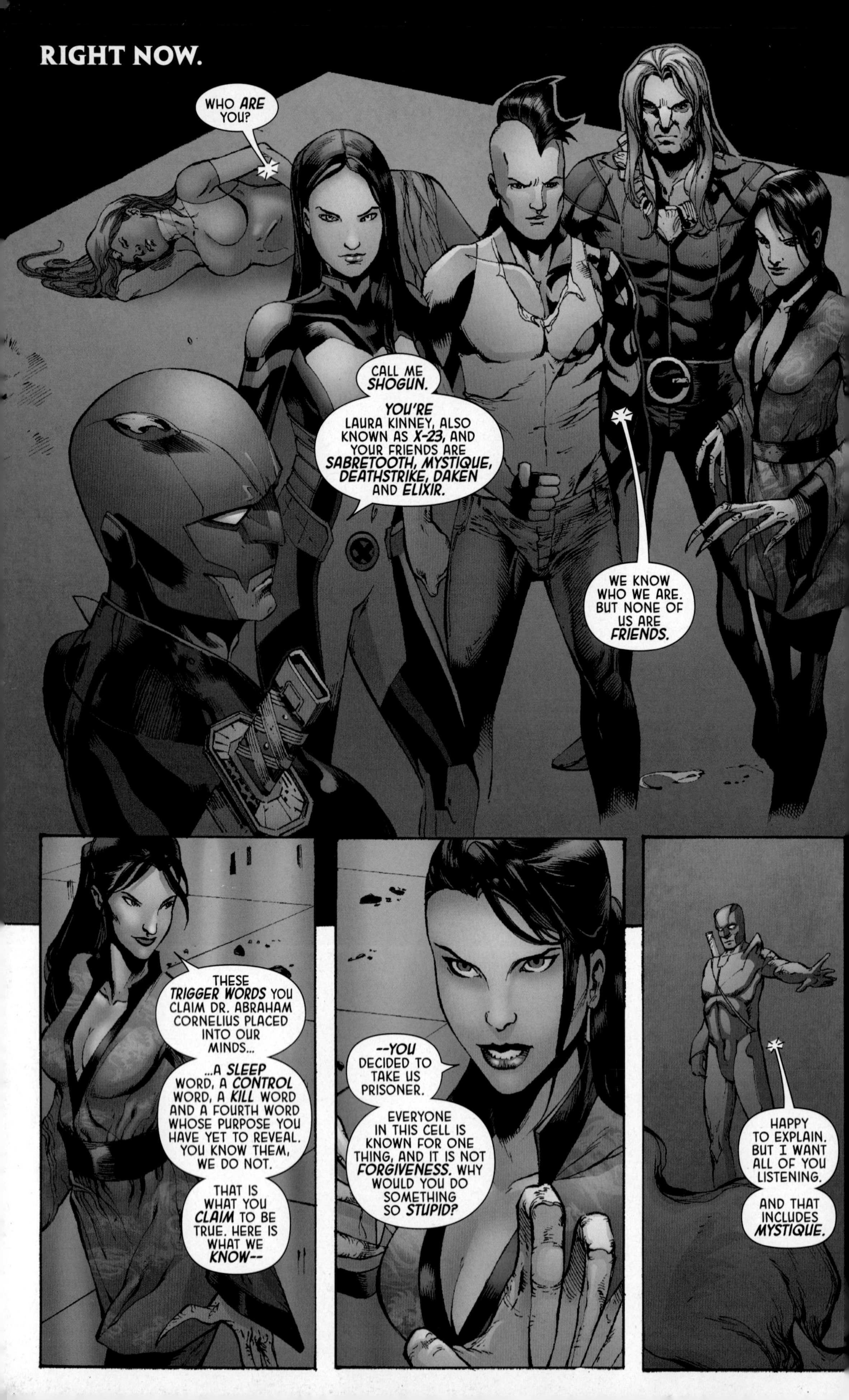
RIGHT NOW.
WHO ARE YOU?
CALL ME SHOGUN.
YOU'RE LAURA KINNEY, ALSO KNOWN AS X-23, AND YOUR FRIENDS ARE SABRETOOTH, MYSTIQUE, DEATHSTRIKE, DAKEN AND ELIXIR.
WE KNOW WHO WE ARE. BUT NONE OF US ARE FRIENDS.
THESE TRIGGER WORDS YOU CLAIM DR. ABRAHAM CORNELIUS PLACED INTO OUR MINDS...
...A SLEEP WORD, A CONTROL WORD, A KILL WORD AND A FOURTH WORD WHOSE PURPOSE YOU HAVE YET TO REVEAL. YOU KNOW THEM, WE DO NOT.
THAT IS WHAT YOU CLAIM TO BE TRUE. HERE IS WHAT WE KNOW--
--YOU DECIDED TO TAKE US PRISONER.
EVERYONE IN THIS CELL IS KNOWN FOR ONE THING, AND IT IS NOT FORGIVENESS. WHY WOULD YOU DO SOMETHING SO STUPID?
HAPPY TO EXPLAIN. BUT I WANT ALL OF YOU LISTENING.
AND THAT INCLUDES MYSTIQUE.

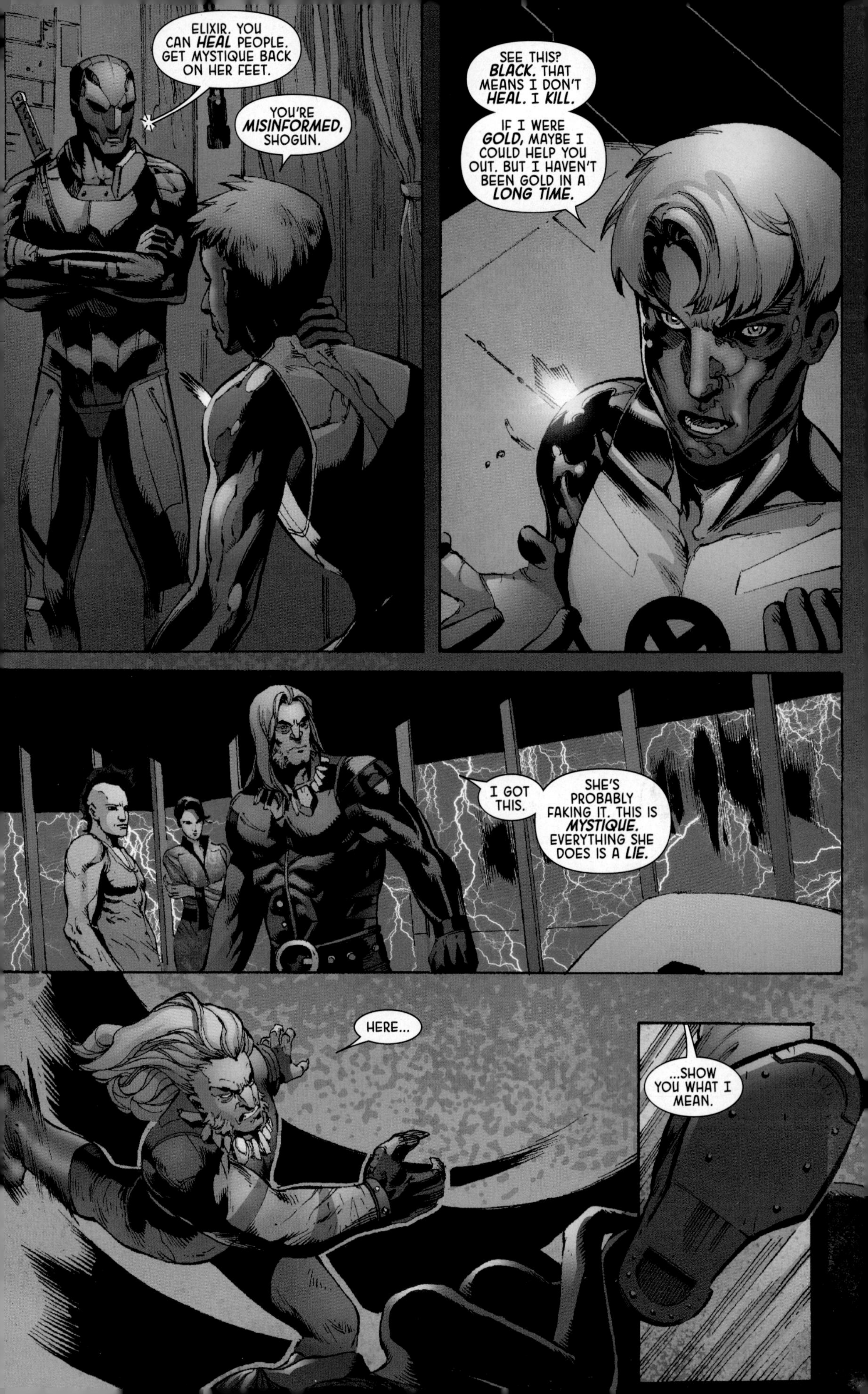
ELIXIR. YOU CAN HEAL PEOPLE. GET MYSTIQUE BACK ON HER FEET.
YOU'RE MISINFORMED, SHOGUN.
SEE THIS? BLACK. THAT MEANS I DON'T HEAL. I KILL.
IF I WERE GOLD, MAYBE I COULD HELP YOU OUT. BUT I HAVEN'T BEEN GOLD IN A LONG TIME.
I GOT THIS.
SHE'S PROBABLY FAKING IT. THIS IS MYSTIQUE. EVERYTHING SHE DOES IS A LIE.
HERE...
...SHOW YOU WHAT I MEAN.

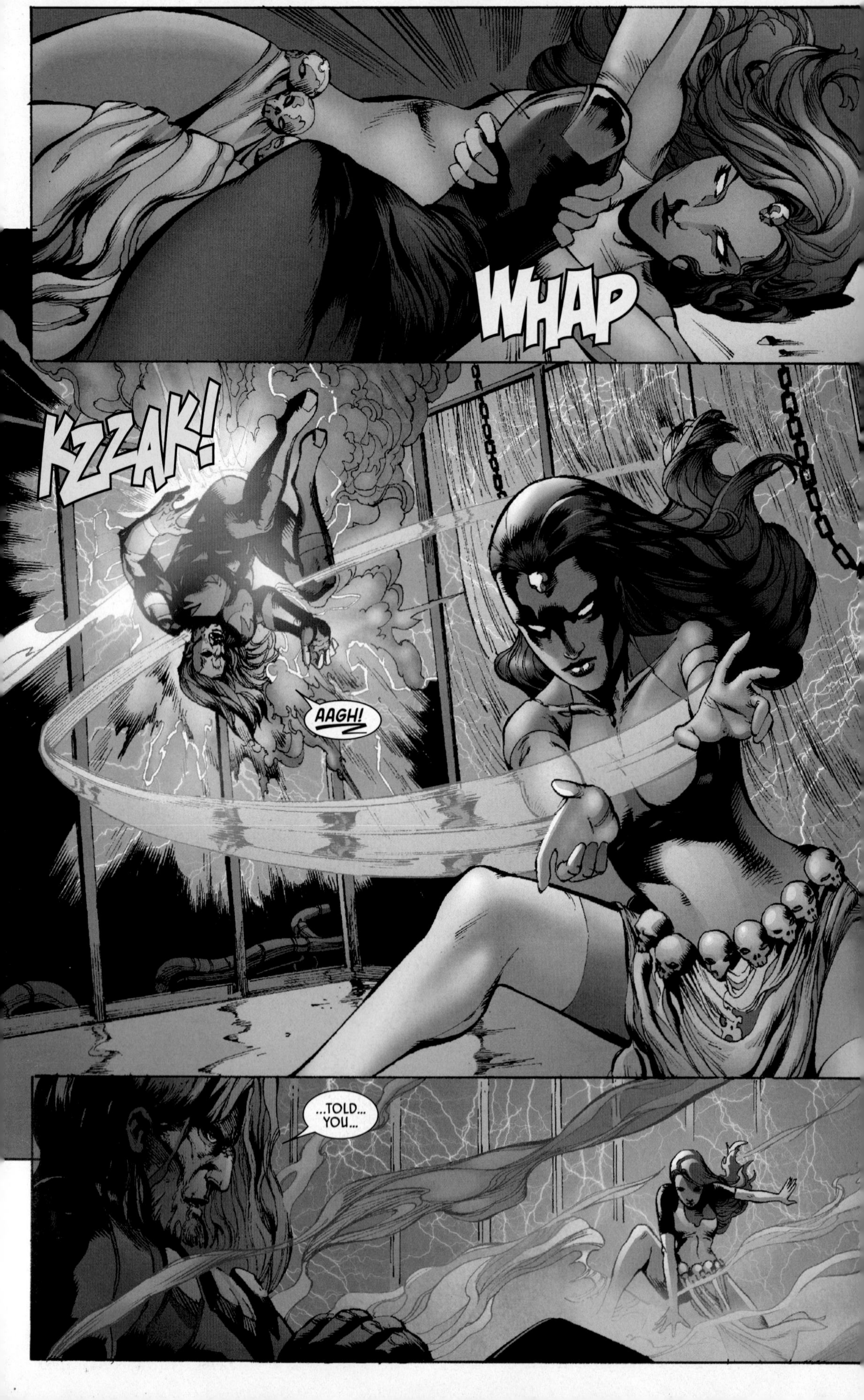
WHAP
KZZAK!
AAGH!
...TOLD... YOU...

GOOD ENOUGH.

THEY READY TO *LISTEN?*

I DOUBT IT. BUT IT'S WORTH A TRY.

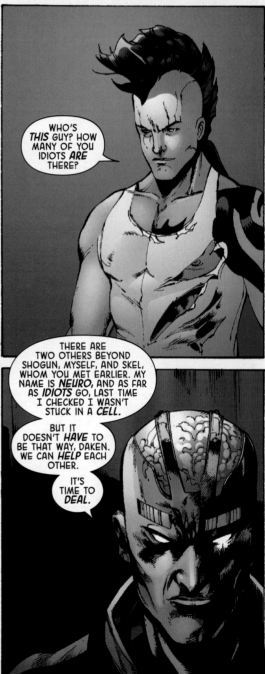

WHO'S *THIS* GUY? HOW MANY OF YOU IDIOTS *ARE* THERE?

THERE ARE TWO OTHERS BEYOND SHOGUN, MYSELF, AND SKEL, WHOM YOU MET EARLIER. MY NAME IS *NEURO*, AND AS FAR AS *IDIOTS* GO, LAST TIME I CHECKED I WASN'T STUCK IN A *CELL.*

BUT IT DOESN'T *HAVE* TO BE THAT WAY, DAKEN. WE CAN *HELP* EACH OTHER.

IT'S TIME TO *DEAL.*

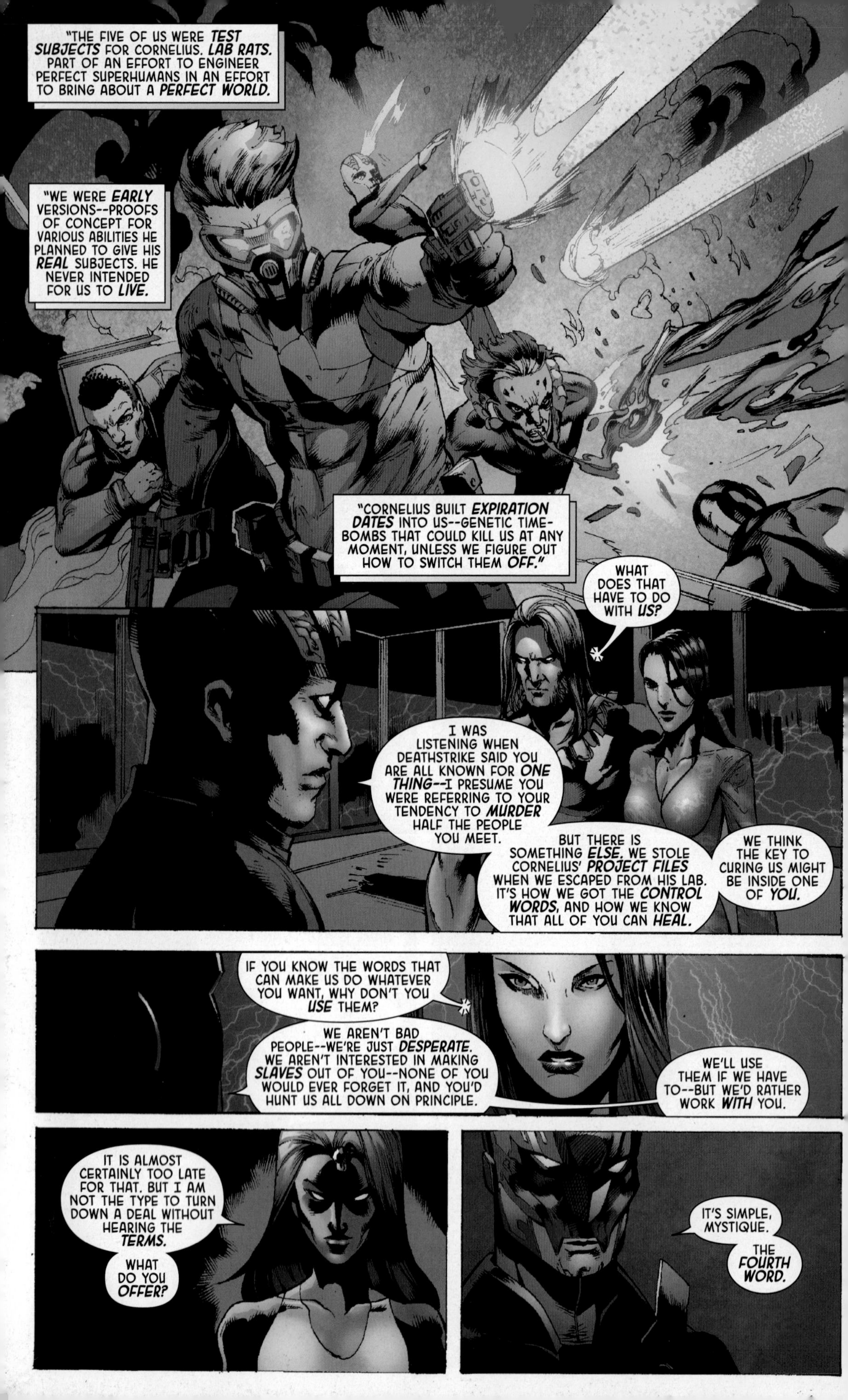
"THE FIVE OF US WERE TEST SUBJECTS FOR CORNELIUS. LAB RATS. PART OF AN EFFORT TO ENGINEER PERFECT SUPERHUMANS IN AN EFFORT TO BRING ABOUT A PERFECT WORLD.
"WE WERE EARLY VERSIONS--PROOFS OF CONCEPT FOR VARIOUS ABILITIES HE PLANNED TO GIVE HIS REAL SUBJECTS. HE NEVER INTENDED FOR US TO LIVE.
"CORNELIUS BUILT EXPIRATION DATES INTO US--GENETIC TIME-BOMBS THAT COULD KILL US AT ANY MOMENT, UNLESS WE FIGURE OUT HOW TO SWITCH THEM OFF."
WHAT DOES THAT HAVE TO DO WITH US?
I WAS LISTENING WHEN DEATHSTRIKE SAID YOU ARE ALL KNOWN FOR ONE THING--I PRESUME YOU WERE REFERRING TO YOUR TENDENCY TO MURDER HALF THE PEOPLE YOU MEET.
BUT THERE IS SOMETHING ELSE. WE STOLE CORNELIUS' PROJECT FILES WHEN WE ESCAPED FROM HIS LAB. IT'S HOW WE GOT THE CONTROL WORDS, AND HOW WE KNOW THAT ALL OF YOU CAN HEAL.
WE THINK THE KEY TO CURING US MIGHT BE INSIDE ONE OF YOU.
IF YOU KNOW THE WORDS THAT CAN MAKE US DO WHATEVER YOU WANT, WHY DON'T YOU USE THEM?
WE AREN'T BAD PEOPLE--WE'RE JUST DESPERATE. WE AREN'T INTERESTED IN MAKING SLAVES OUT OF YOU--NONE OF YOU WOULD EVER FORGET IT, AND YOU'D HUNT US ALL DOWN ON PRINCIPLE.
WE'LL USE THEM IF WE HAVE TO--BUT WE'D RATHER WORK WITH YOU.
IT IS ALMOST CERTAINLY TOO LATE FOR THAT. BUT I AM NOT THE TYPE TO TURN DOWN A DEAL WITHOUT HEARING THE TERMS.
WHAT DO YOU OFFER?
IT'S SIMPLE, MYSTIQUE.
THE FOURTH WORD.

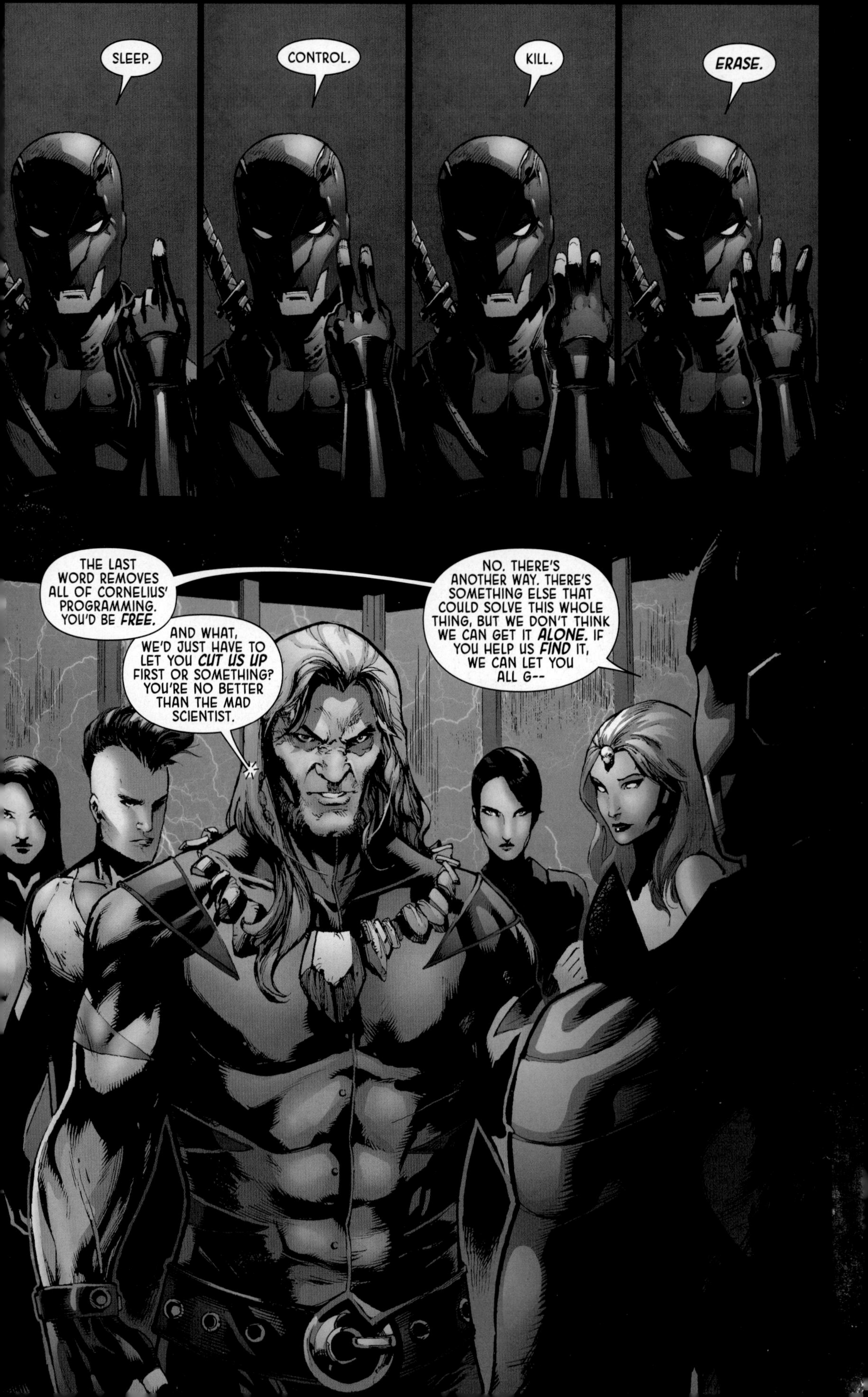
SLEEP.
CONTROL.
KILL.
ERASE.
THE LAST WORD REMOVES ALL OF CORNELIUS' PROGRAMMING. YOU'D BE *FREE.*
AND WHAT, WE'D JUST HAVE TO LET YOU *CUT US UP* FIRST OR SOMETHING? YOU'RE NO BETTER THAN THE MAD SCIENTIST.
NO. THERE'S ANOTHER WAY. THERE'S SOMETHING ELSE THAT COULD SOLVE THIS WHOLE THING, BUT WE DON'T THINK WE CAN GET IT *ALONE.* IF YOU HELP US *FIND* IT, WE CAN LET YOU ALL G--

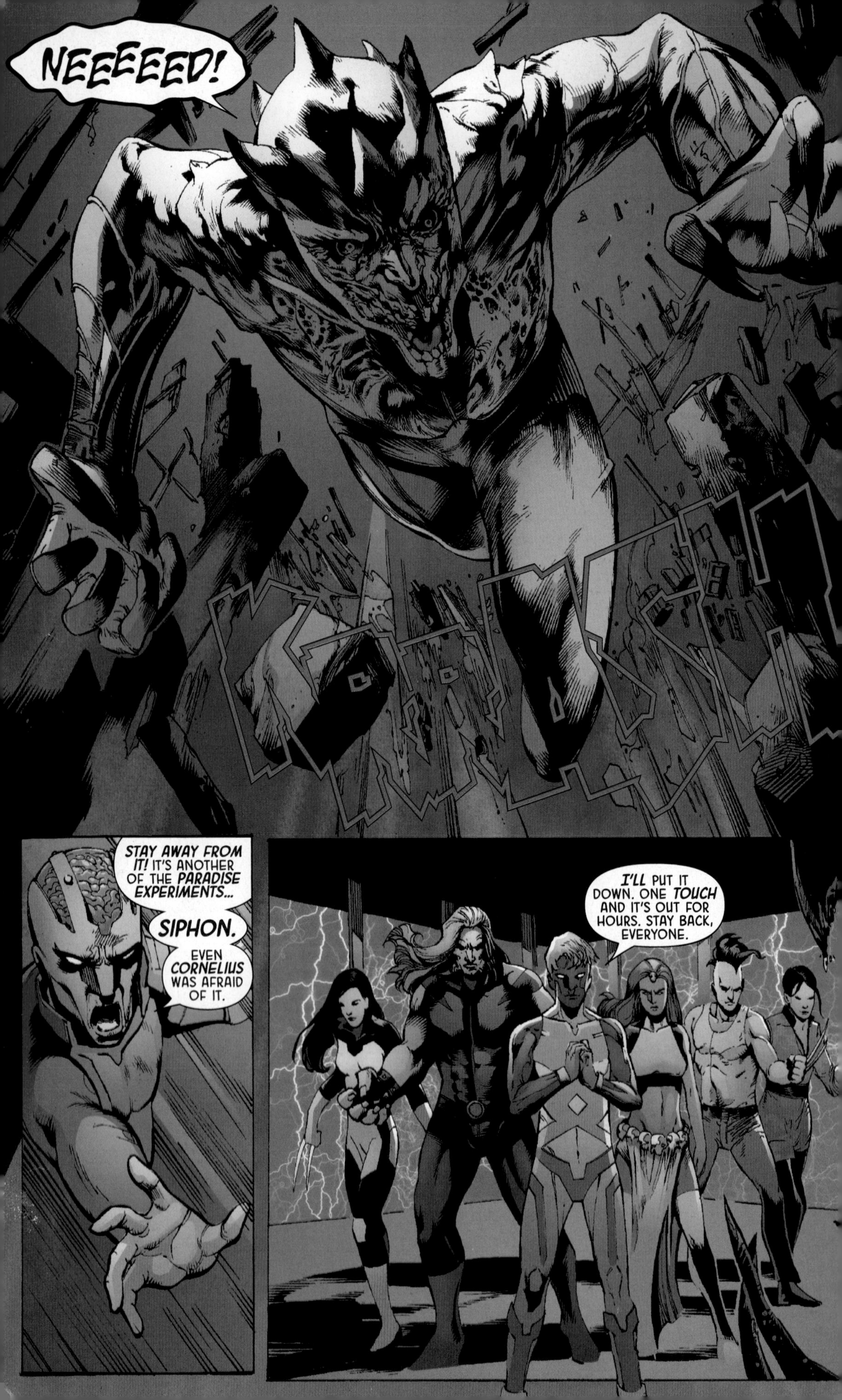
NEEEEED!
STAY AWAY FROM IT! IT'S ANOTHER OF THE PARADISE EXPERIMENTS...
SIPHON.
EVEN CORNELIUS WAS AFRAID OF IT.
I'LL PUT IT DOWN. ONE TOUCH AND IT'S OUT FOR HOURS. STAY BACK, EVERYONE.

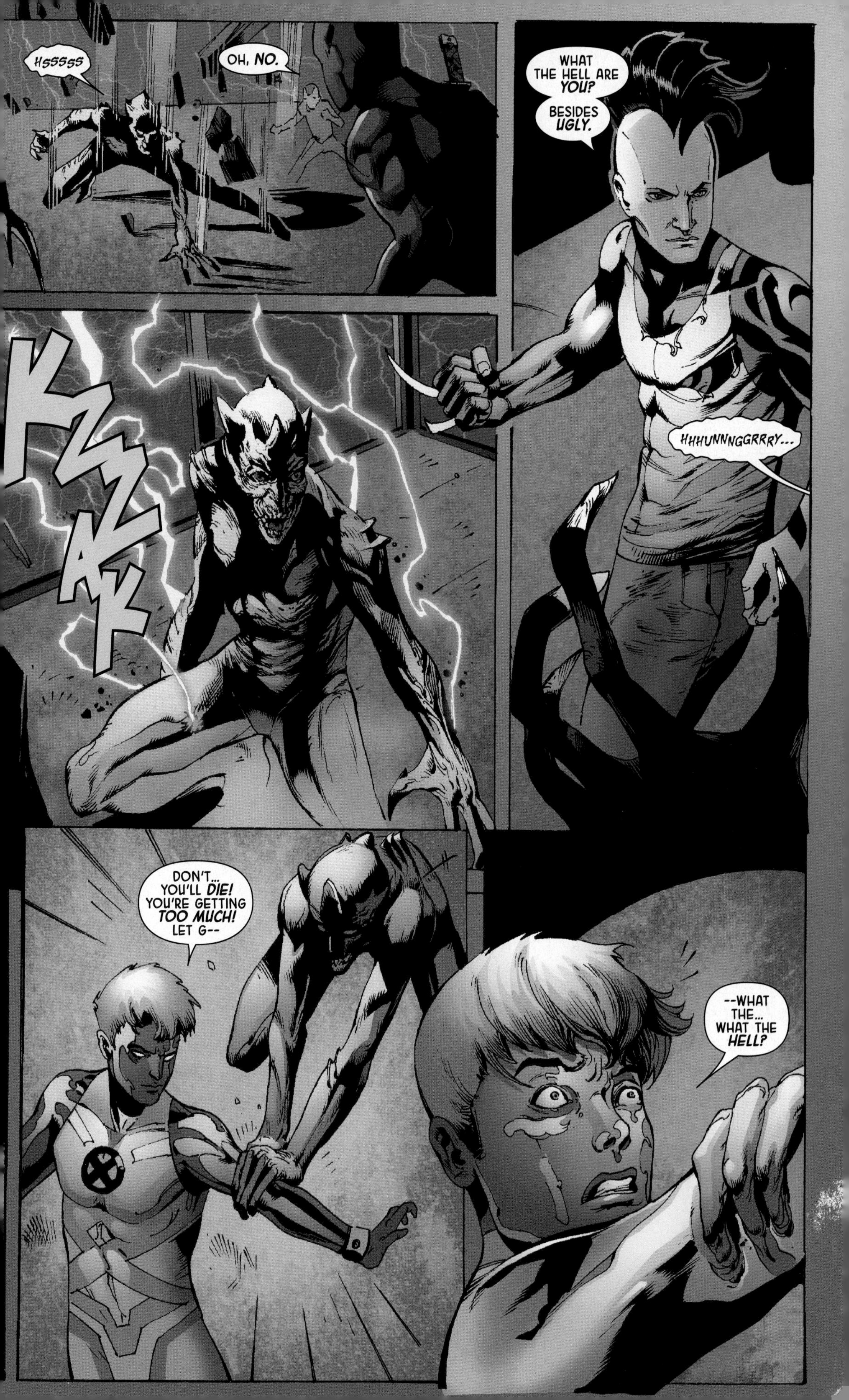
HSSSSS
OH, NO.
WHAT THE HELL ARE YOU?
BESIDES UGLY.
KZZZAK
HHHUNNNGGRRRY...
DON'T... YOU'LL DIE! YOU'RE GETTING TOO MUCH! LET G--
--WHAT THE... WHAT THE HELL?

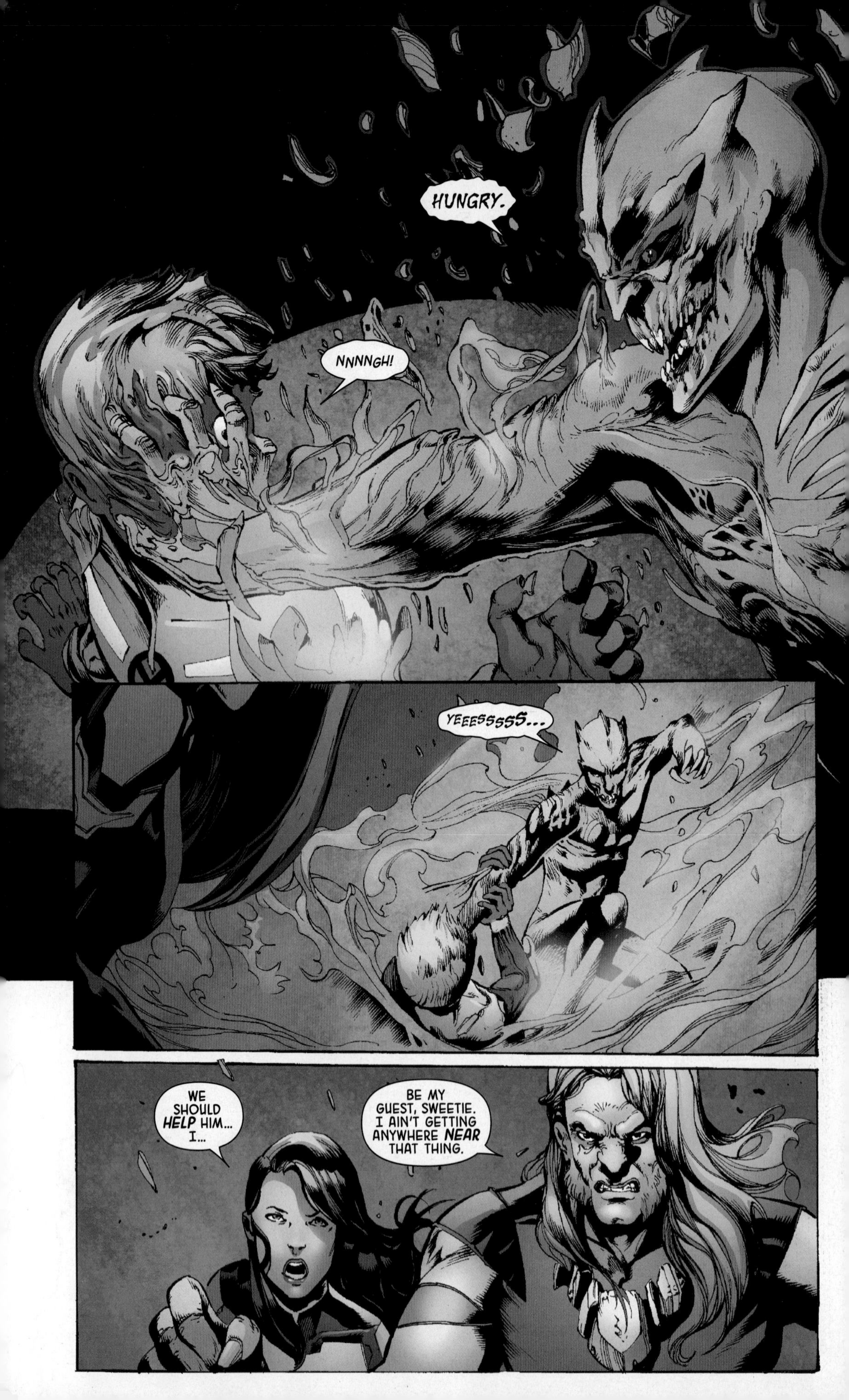
HUNGRY.
NNNNGH!
YEEESSSSS...
WE SHOULD HELP HIM... I...
BE MY GUEST, SWEETIE. I AIN'T GETTING ANYWHERE NEAR THAT THING.

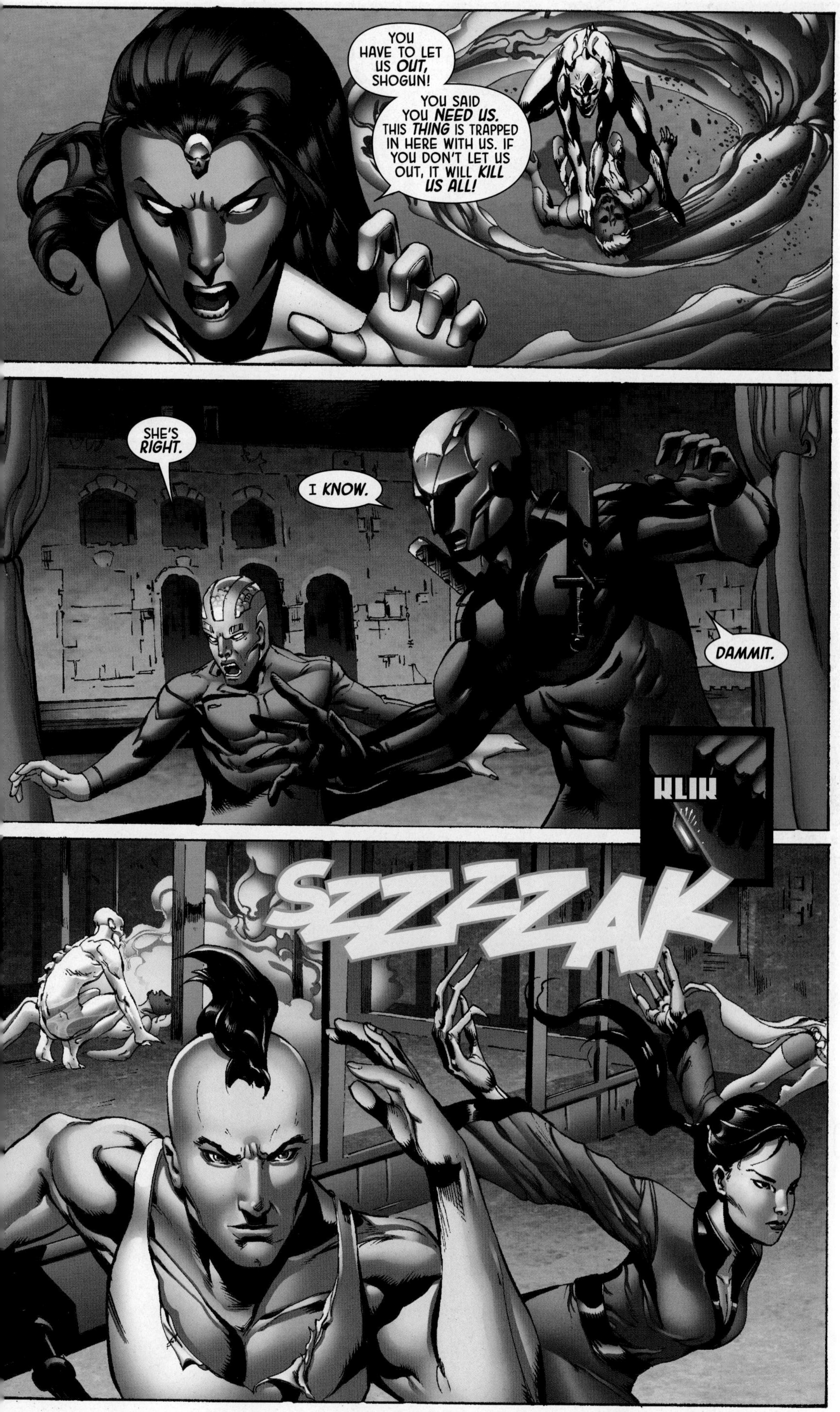
YOU HAVE TO LET US OUT, SHOGUN!
YOU SAID YOU NEED US. THIS THING IS TRAPPED IN HERE WITH US. IF YOU DON'T LET US OUT, IT WILL KILL US ALL!
SHE'S RIGHT.
I KNOW.
DAMMIT.
KLIK
SZZZZAK

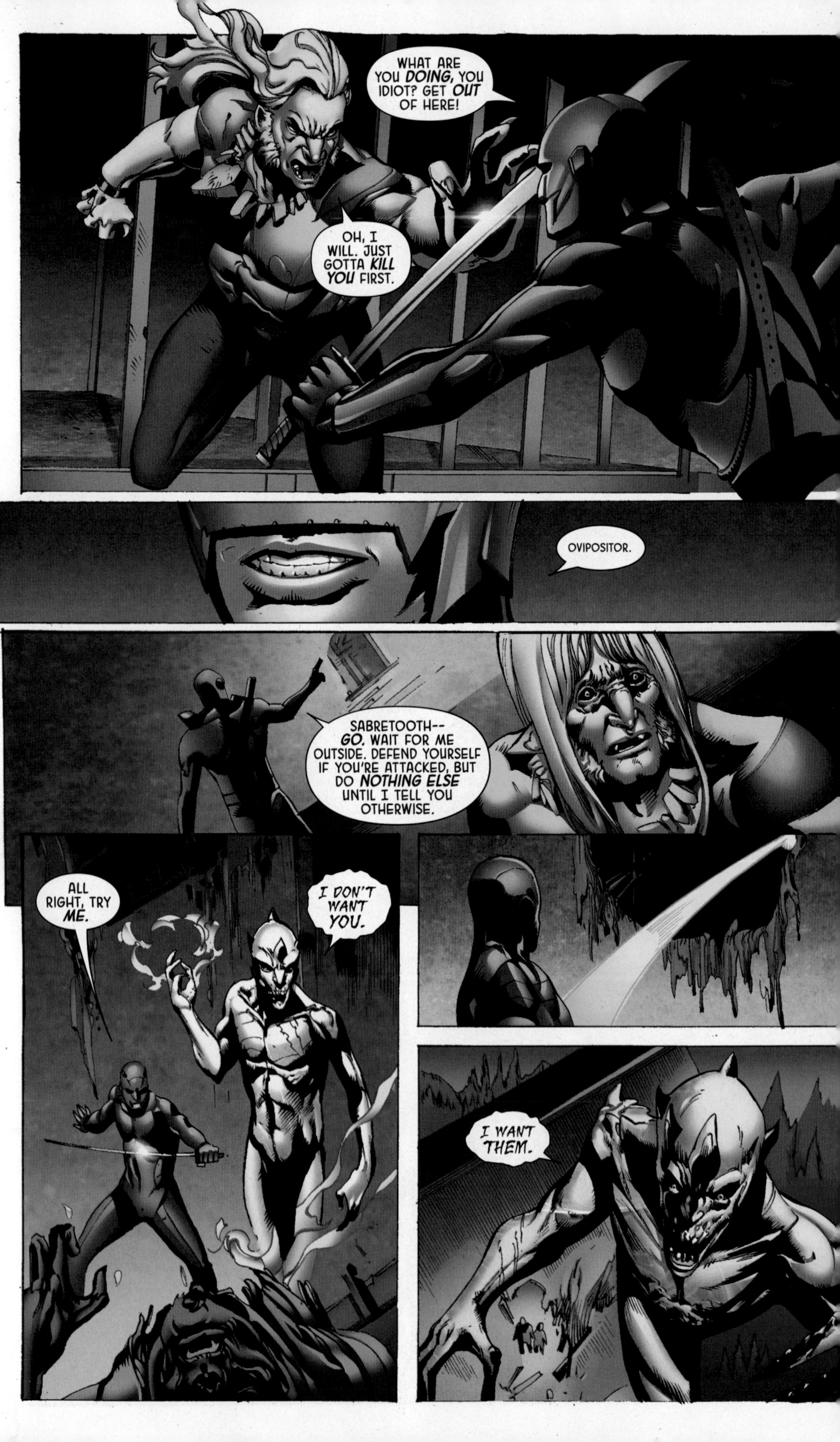
WHAT ARE YOU DOING, YOU IDIOT? GET OUT OF HERE!
OH, I WILL. JUST GOTTA KILL YOU FIRST.
OVIPOSITOR.
SABRETOOTH-- GO. WAIT FOR ME OUTSIDE. DEFEND YOURSELF IF YOU'RE ATTACKED, BUT DO NOTHING ELSE UNTIL I TELL YOU OTHERWISE.
ALL RIGHT, TRY ME.
I DON'T WANT YOU.
I WANT THEM.

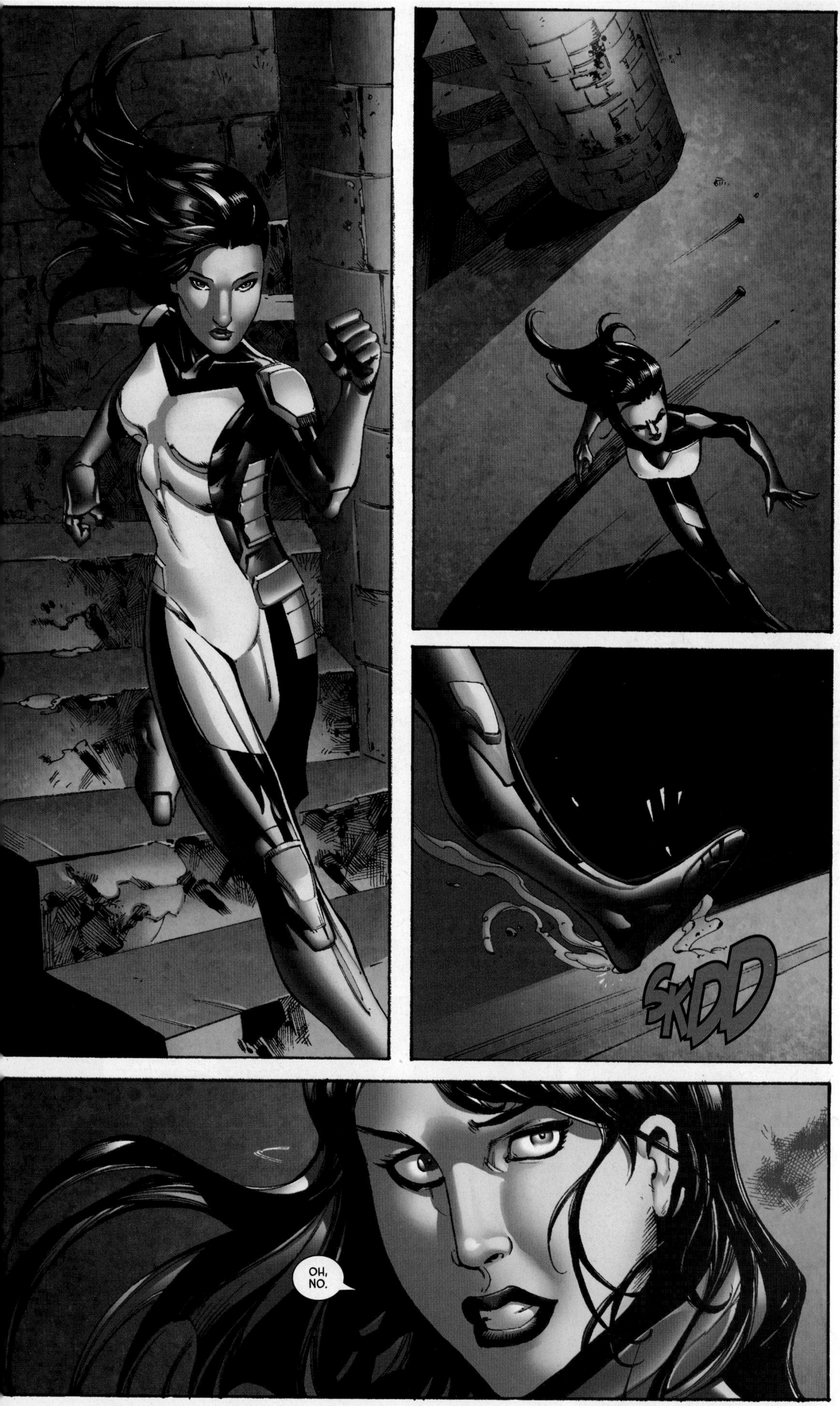
SKDD
OH, NO.

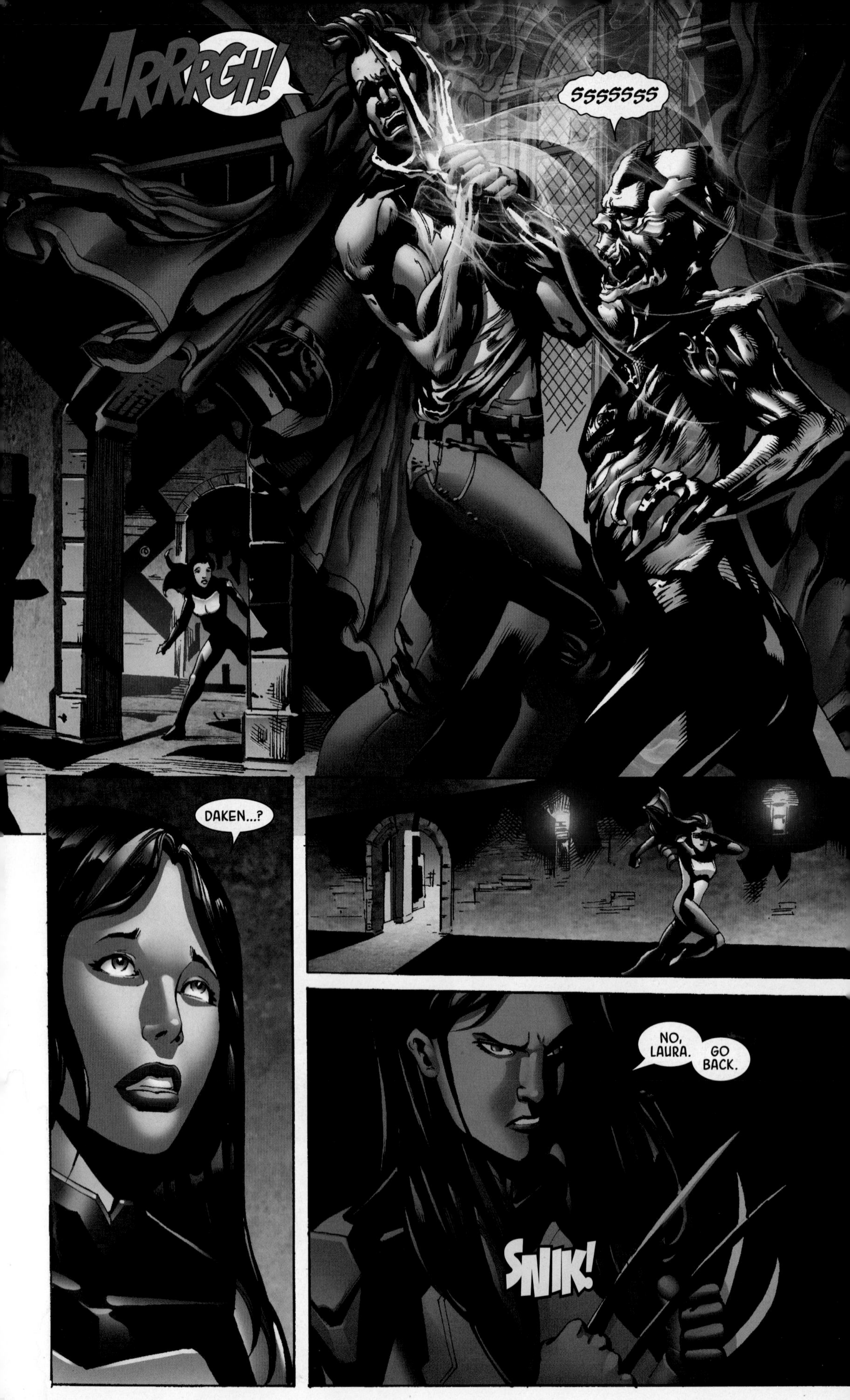
ARRRGH!
SSSSSSS
DAKEN...?
NO, LAURA. GO BACK.
SNIK!

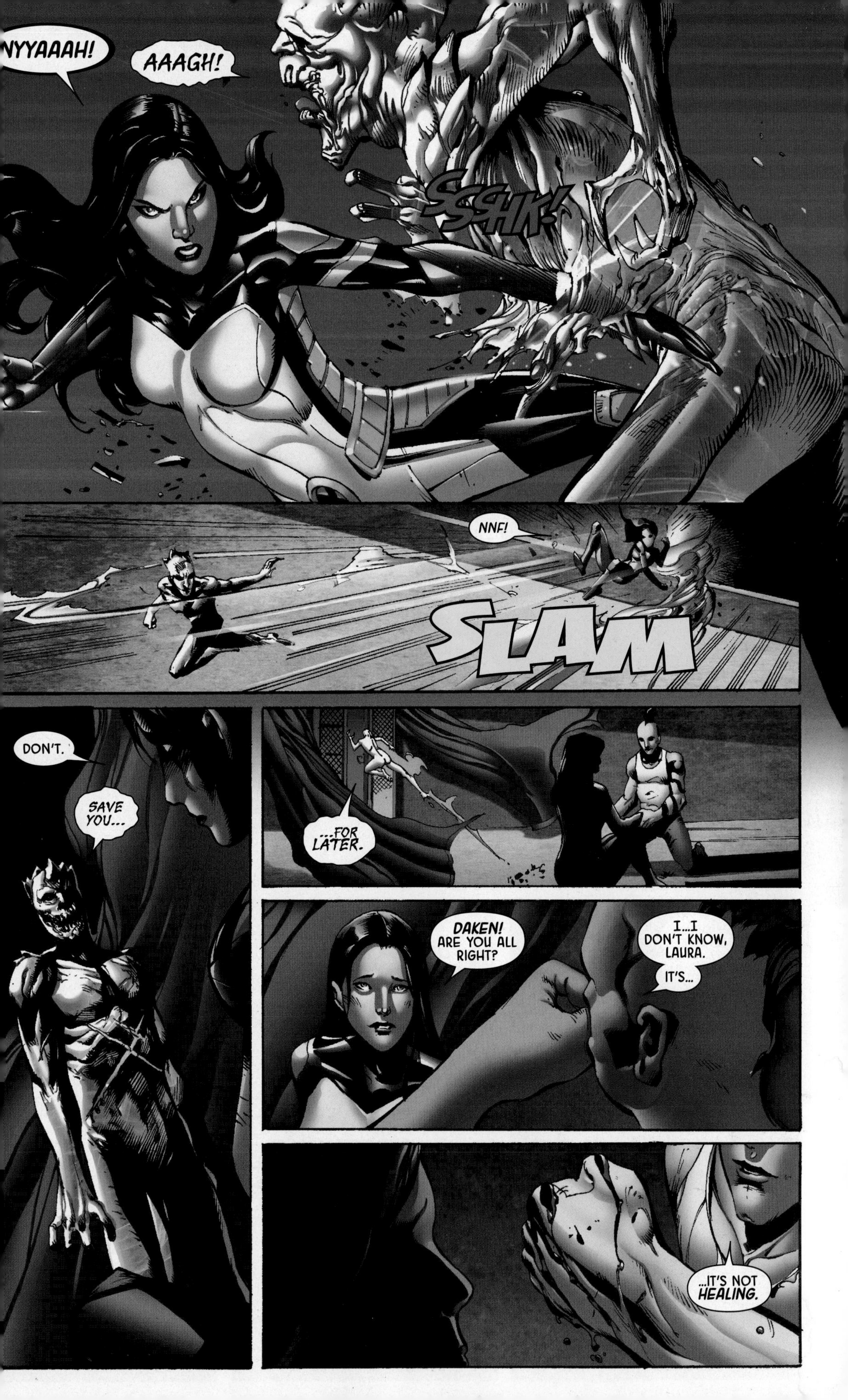
NYYAAAH!
AAAGH!
SSSHK!
NNF!
SLAM
DON'T.
SAVE YOU...
...FOR LATER.
DAKEN! ARE YOU ALL RIGHT?
I...I DON'T KNOW, LAURA.
IT'S...
...IT'S NOT HEALING.

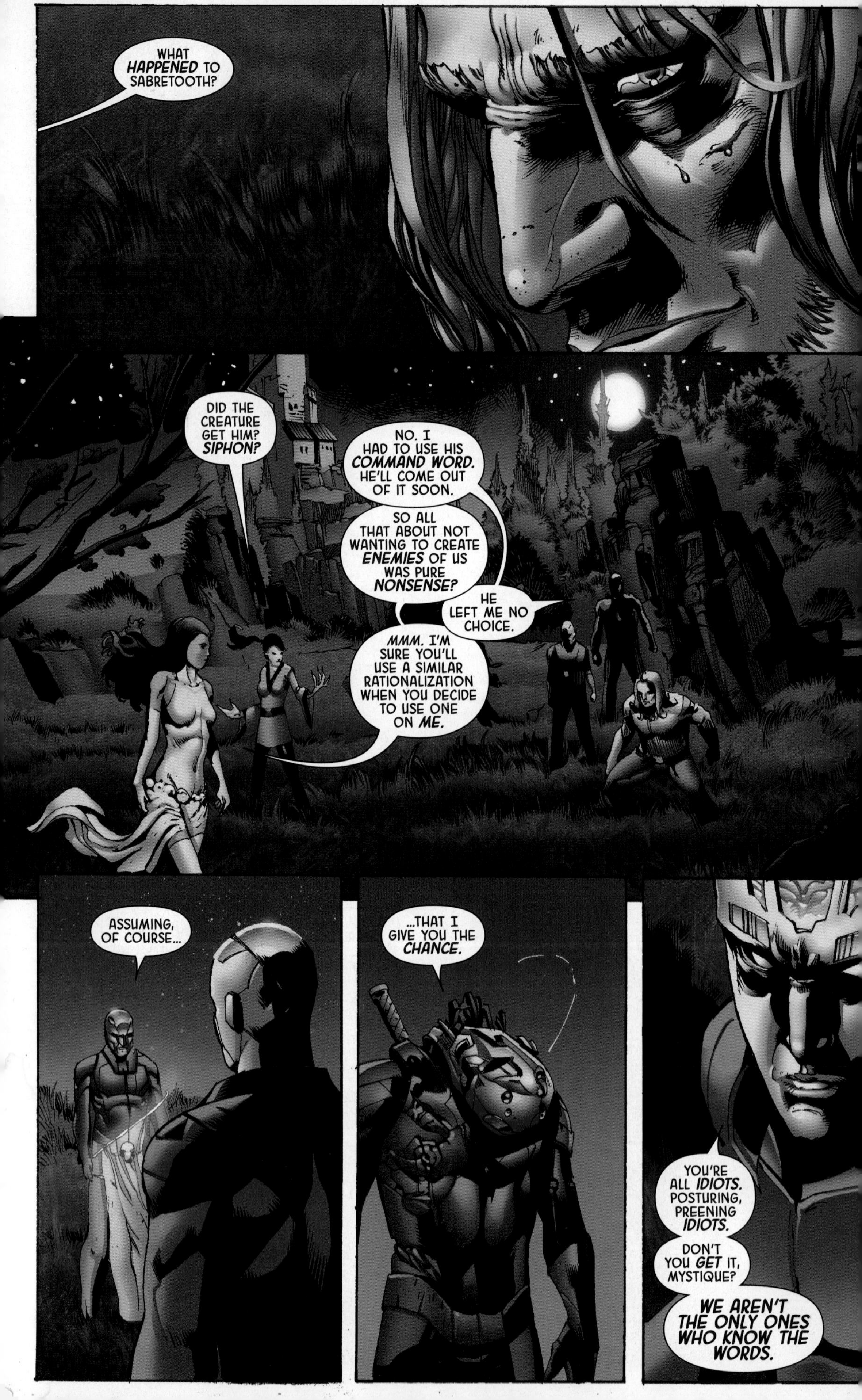
WHAT HAPPENED TO SABRETOOTH?
DID THE CREATURE GET HIM? SIPHON?
NO. I HAD TO USE HIS COMMAND WORD. HE'LL COME OUT OF IT SOON.
SO ALL THAT ABOUT NOT WANTING TO CREATE ENEMIES OF US WAS PURE NONSENSE?
HE LEFT ME NO CHOICE.
MMM. I'M SURE YOU'LL USE A SIMILAR RATIONALIZATION WHEN YOU DECIDE TO USE ONE ON ME.
ASSUMING, OF COURSE...
...THAT I GIVE YOU THE CHANCE.
YOU'RE ALL IDIOTS. POSTURING, PREENING IDIOTS.
DON'T YOU GET IT, MYSTIQUE?
WE AREN'T THE ONLY ONES WHO KNOW THE WORDS.

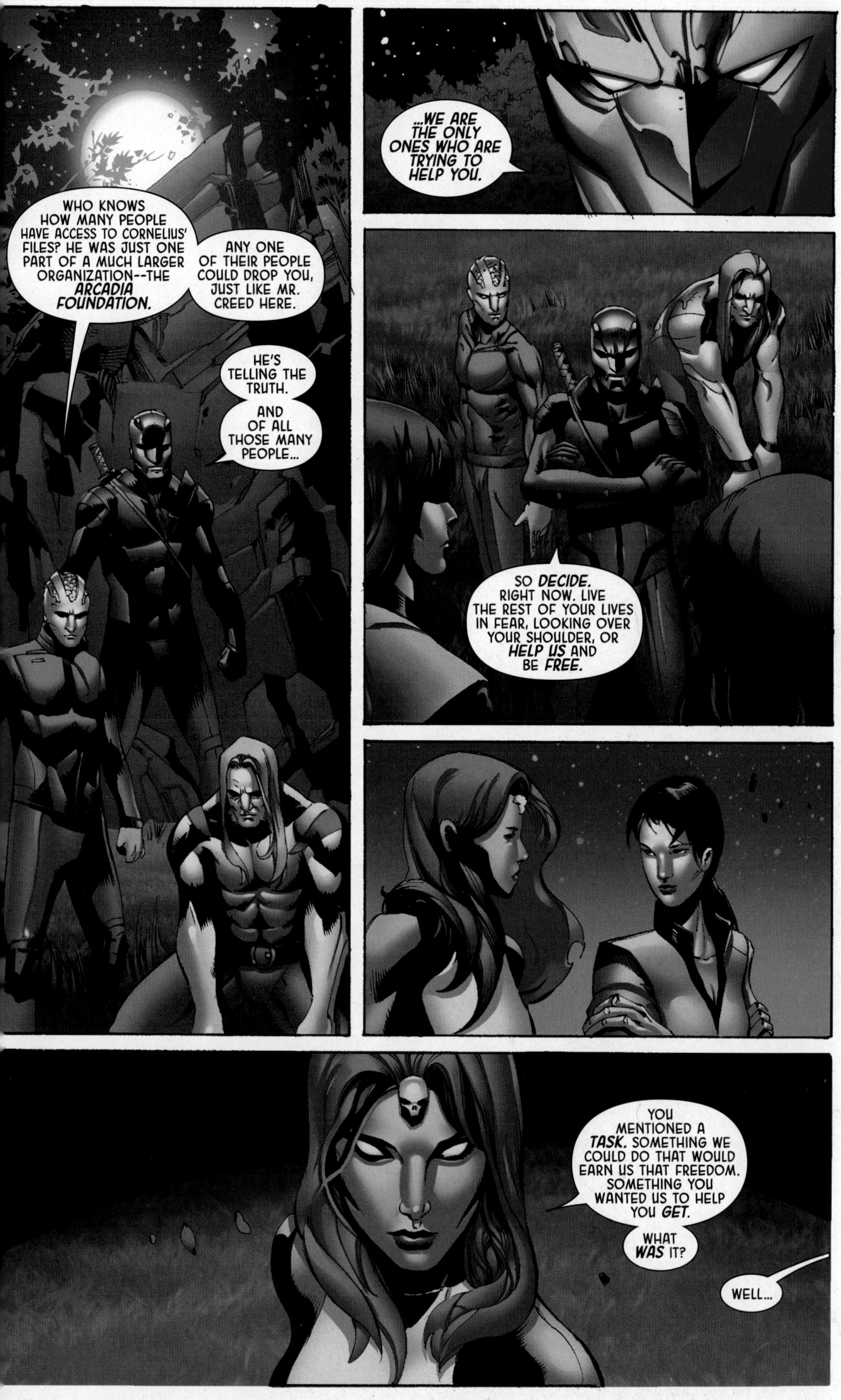
WHO KNOWS HOW MANY PEOPLE HAVE ACCESS TO CORNELIUS' FILES? HE WAS JUST ONE PART OF A MUCH LARGER ORGANIZATION--THE ARCADIA FOUNDATION.
ANY ONE OF THEIR PEOPLE COULD DROP YOU, JUST LIKE MR. CREED HERE.
HE'S TELLING THE TRUTH.
AND OF ALL THOSE MANY PEOPLE...
...WE ARE THE ONLY ONES WHO ARE TRYING TO HELP YOU.
SO DECIDE. RIGHT NOW. LIVE THE REST OF YOUR LIVES IN FEAR, LOOKING OVER YOUR SHOULDER, OR HELP US AND BE FREE.
YOU MENTIONED A TASK. SOMETHING WE COULD DO THAT WOULD EARN US THAT FREEDOM. SOMETHING YOU WANTED US TO HELP YOU GET.
WHAT WAS IT?
WELL...

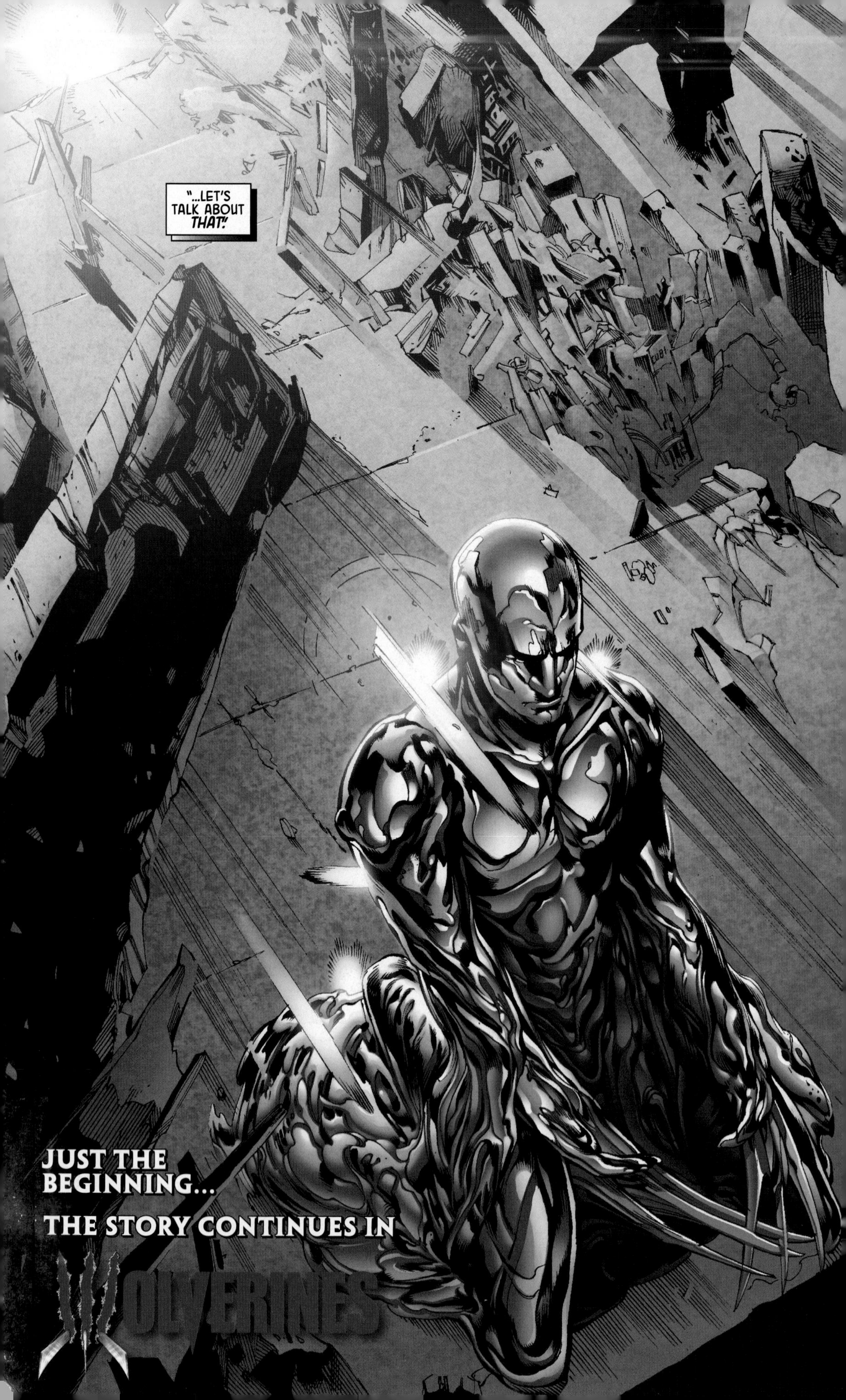
"...LET'S TALK ABOUT THAT!"
JUST THE BEGINNING...
THE STORY CONTINUES IN
WOLVERINES

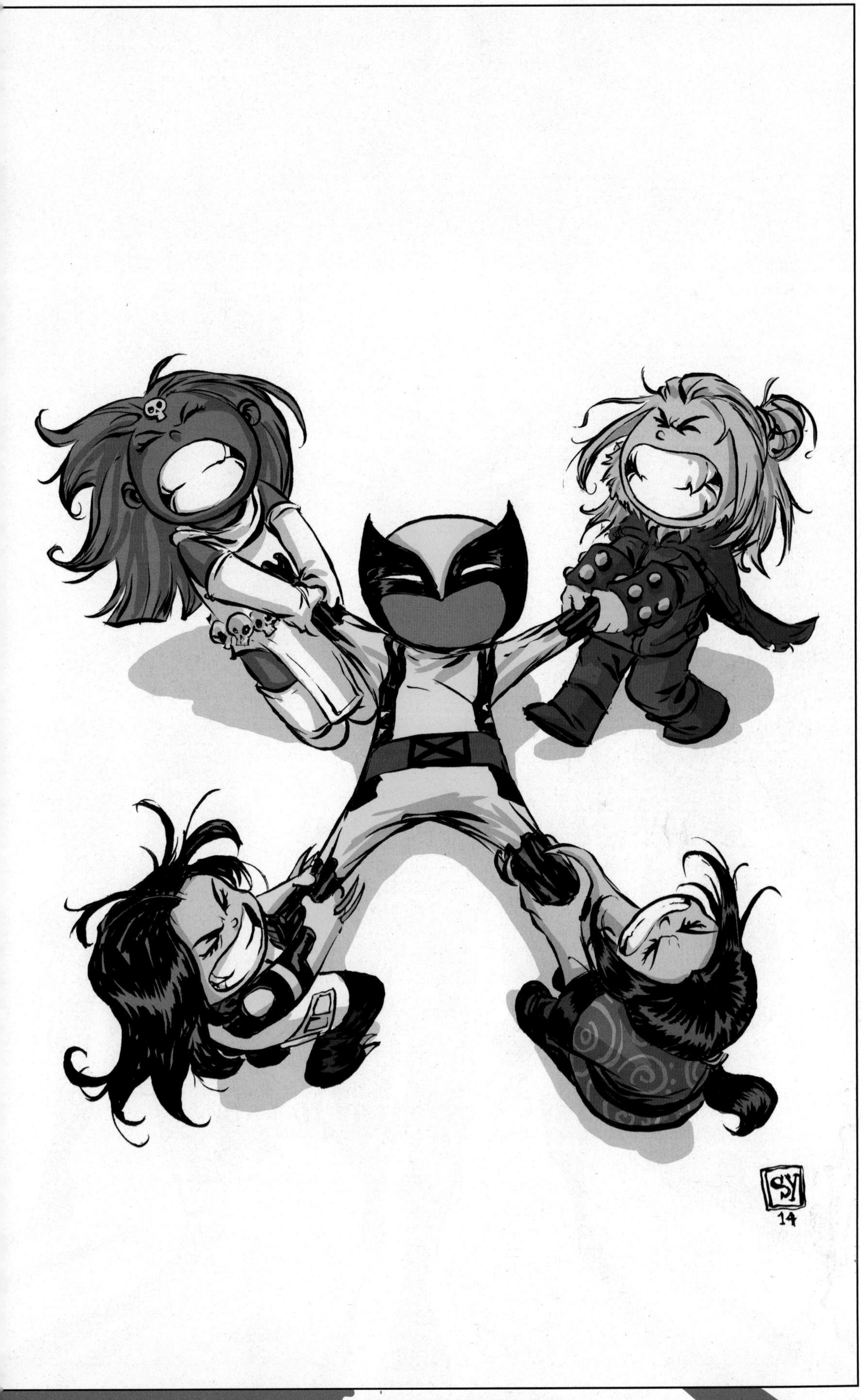
SY
14

#1 VARIANT BY SKOTTIE YOUNG

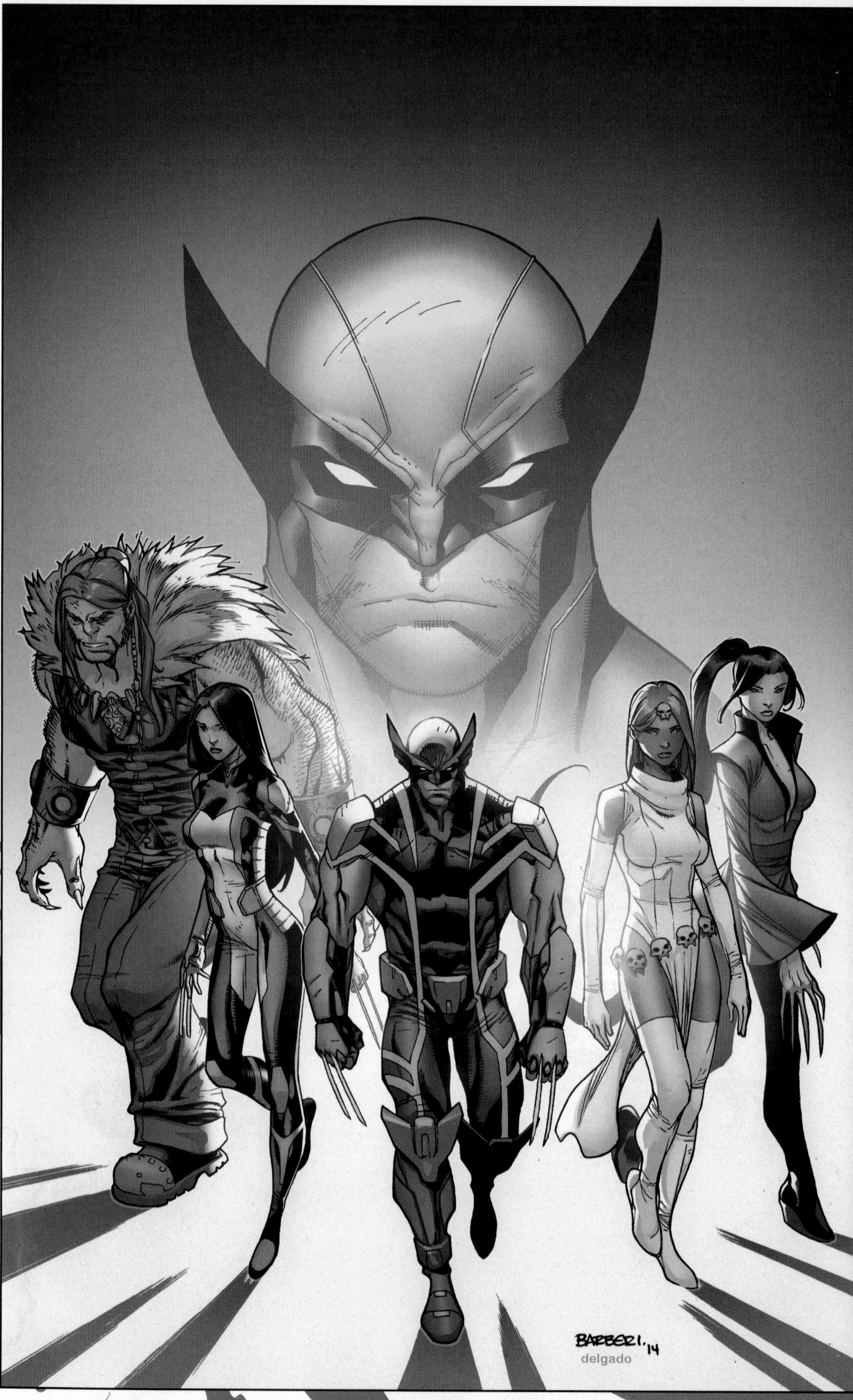
BARBERI. '14
delgado

#1 VARIANT BY CARLO BARBERI & EDGAR DELGADO

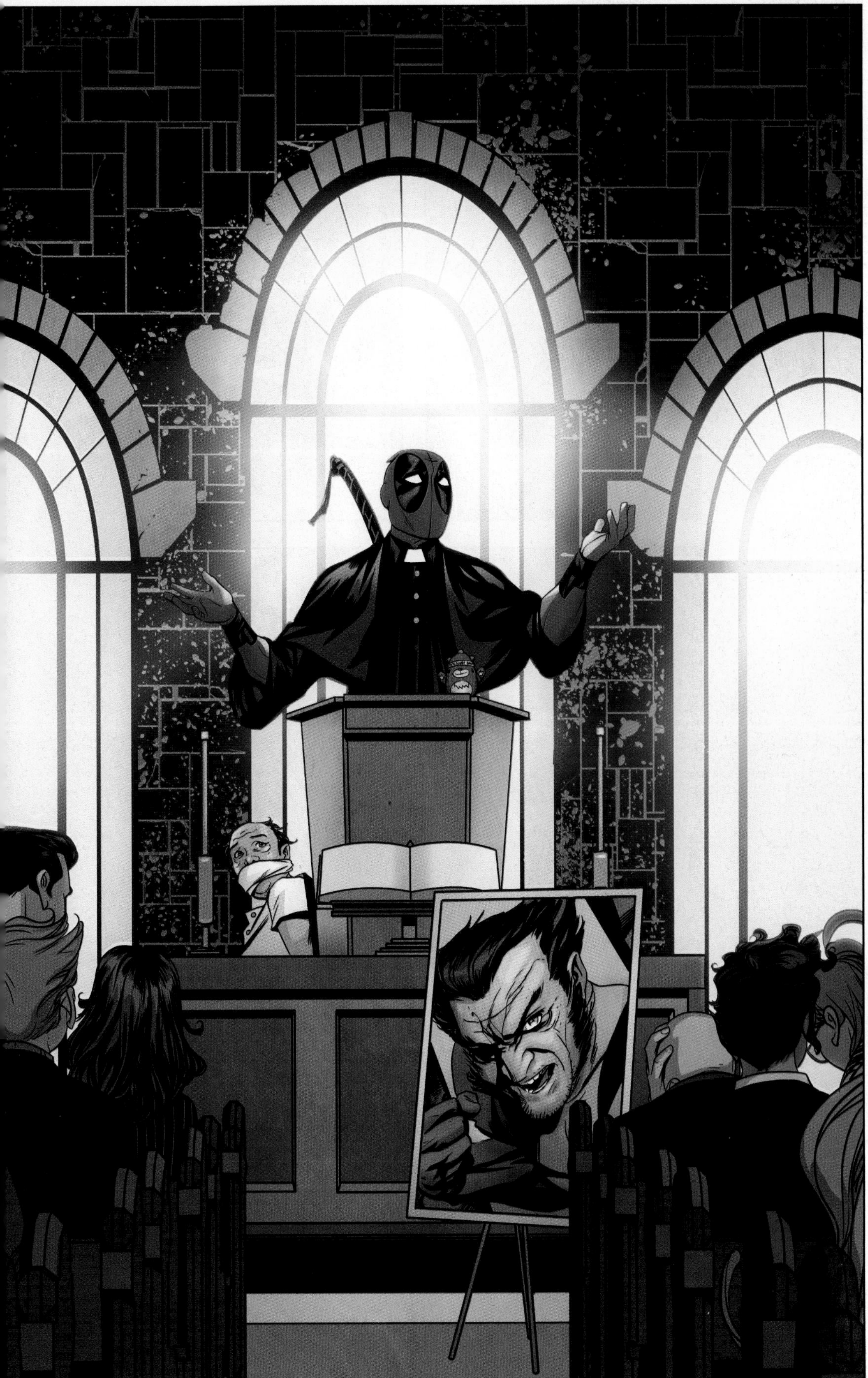

#1 VARIANT BY MIKE MCKONE & JASON KEITH

CANADIAN VARIANTS

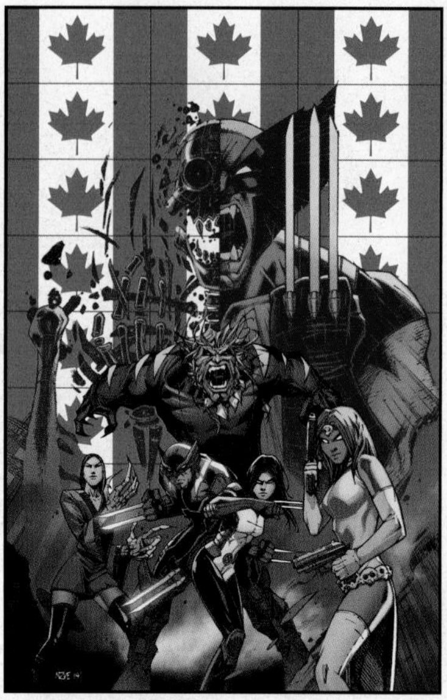

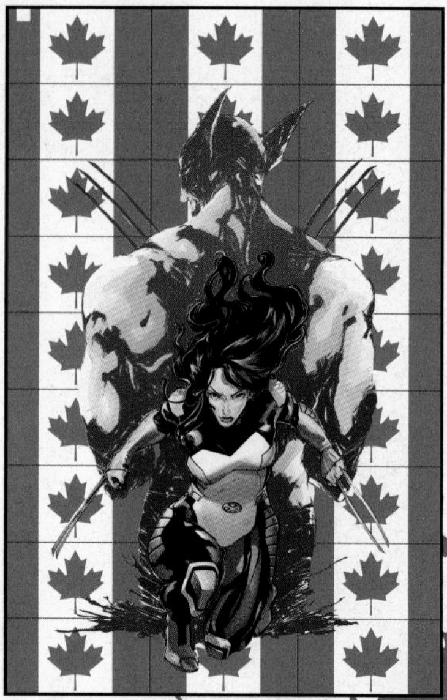

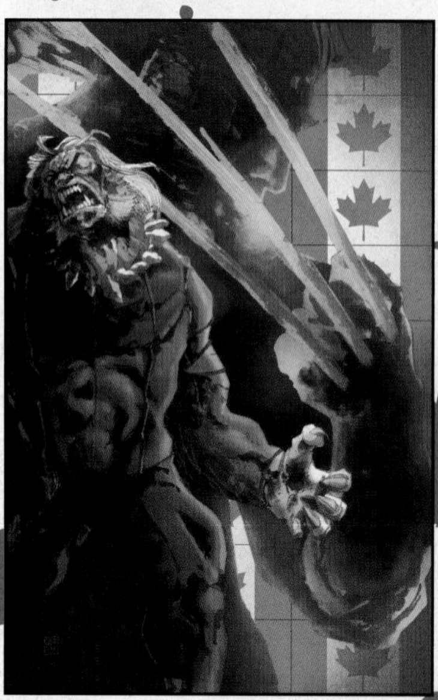

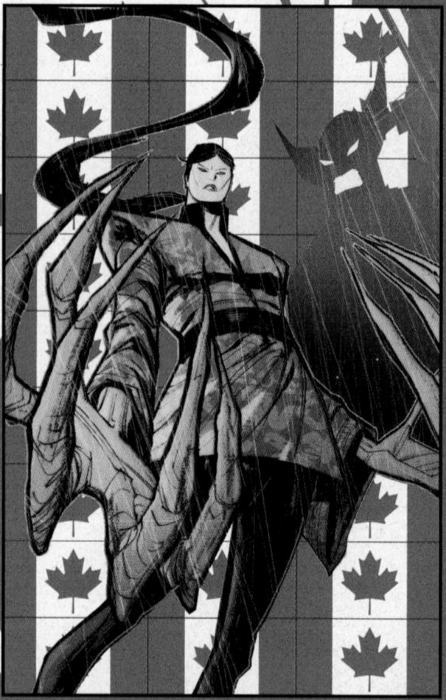

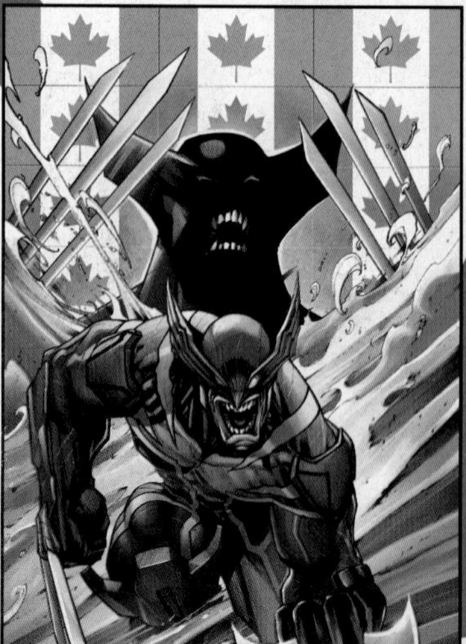

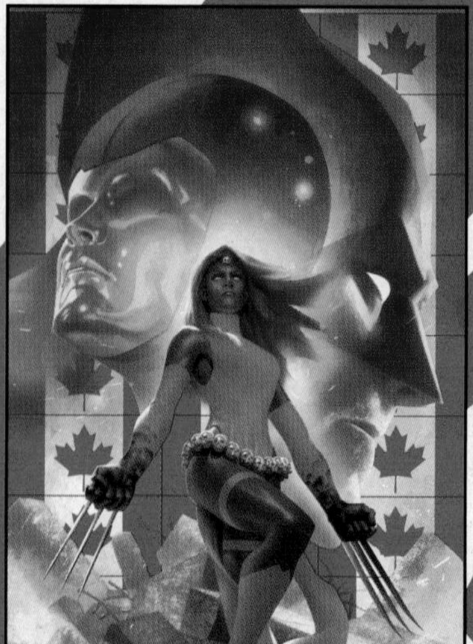

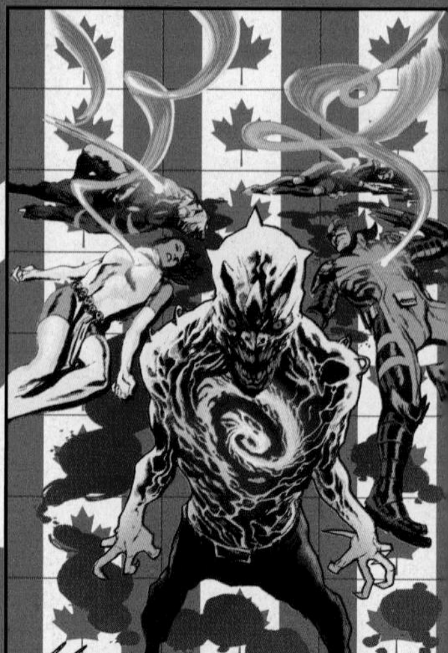

CHARACTER DESIGNS

LADY DEATHSTRIKE BY JUAN DOE

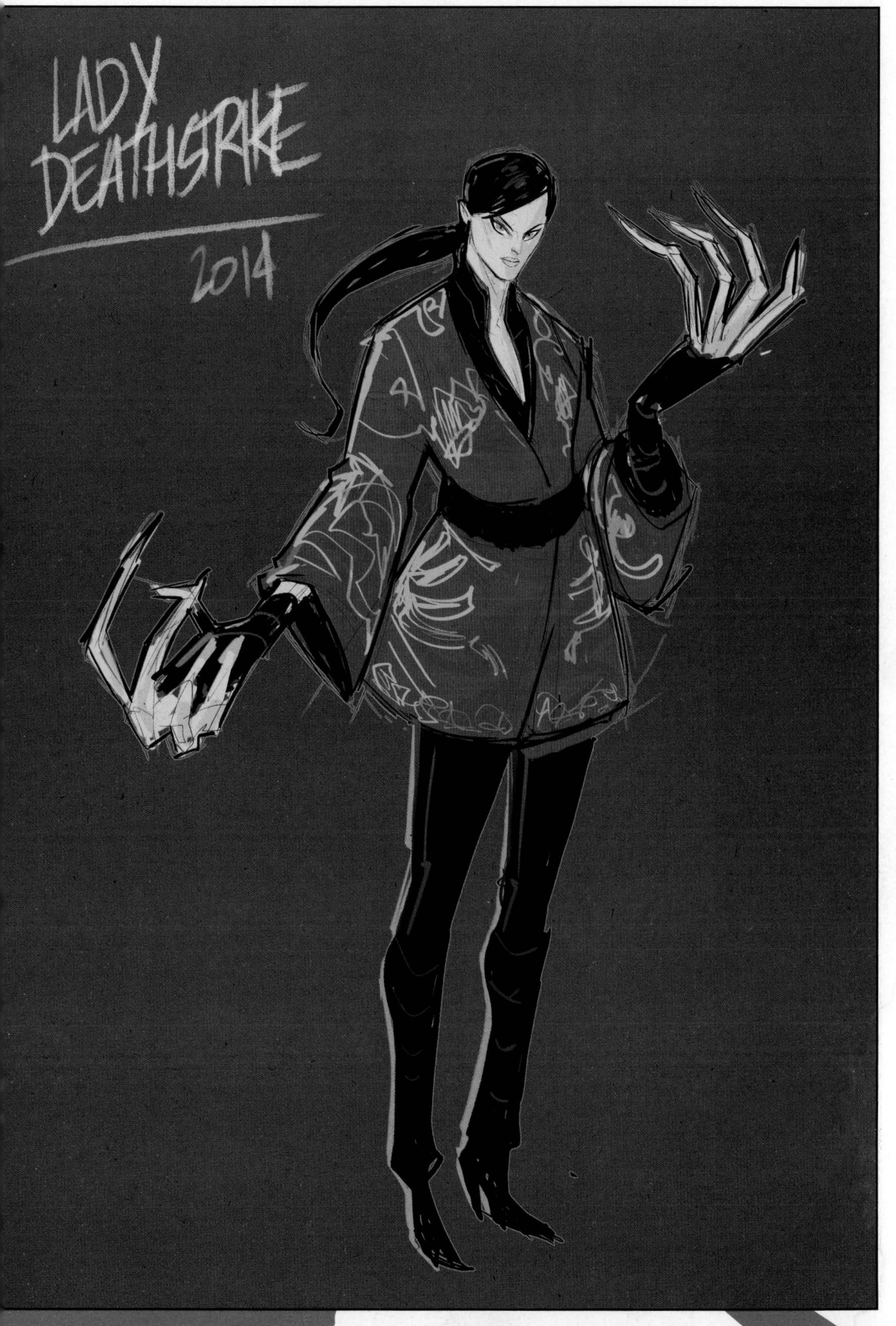
LADY DEATHSTRIKE
2014

CHARACTER DESIGNS

NEURO BY OLIVER NOME

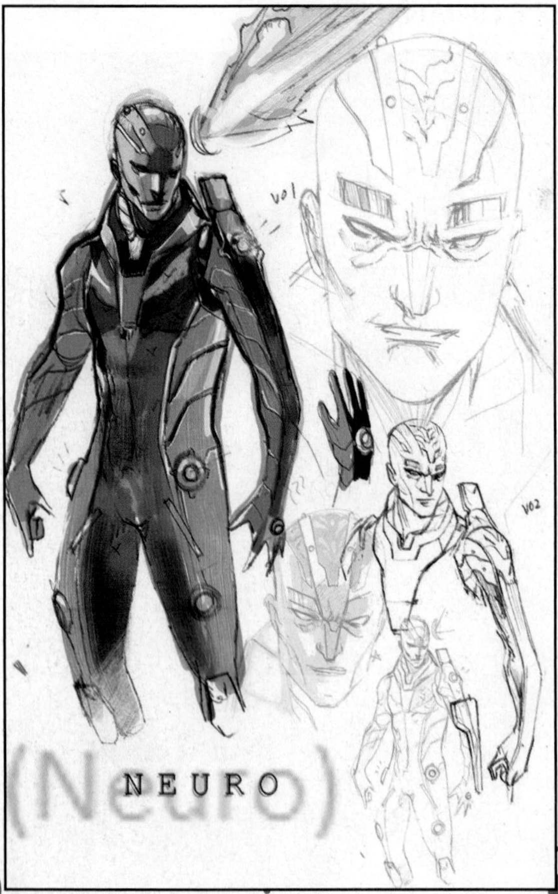
v01
v02
(Neuro)
NEURO

SIPHON BY RAFAEL ALBUQUERQU

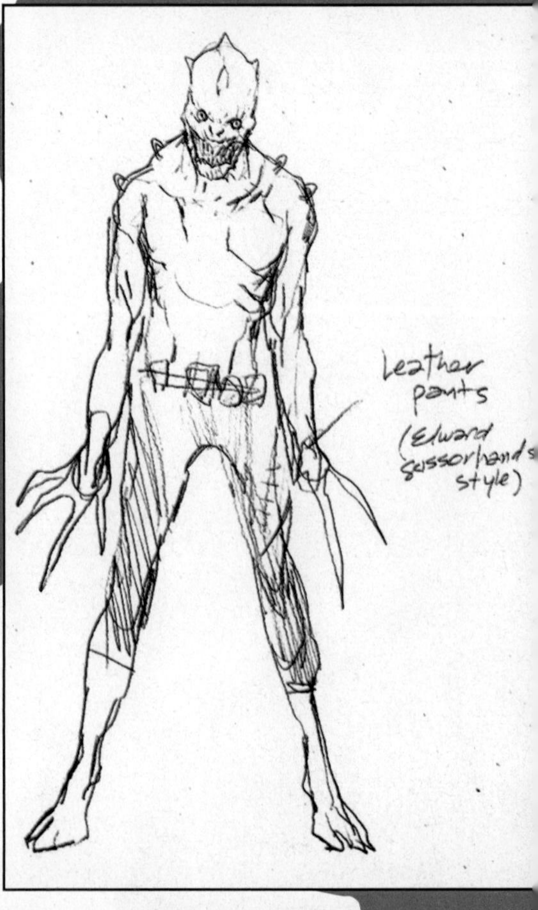
Leather pants
(Edward sissorhands style)

#1 COVER SKETCHES
BY OLIVER NOME

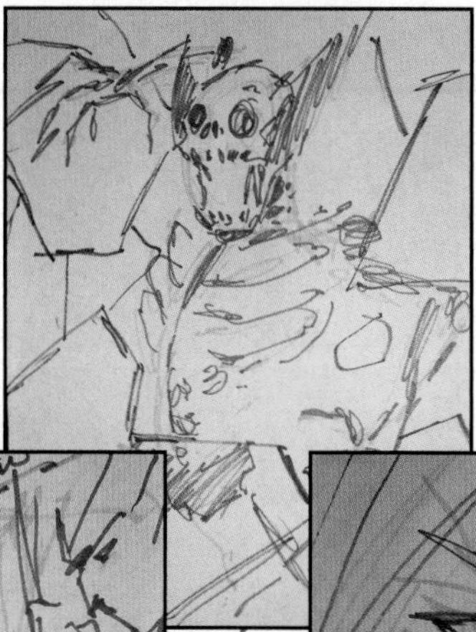

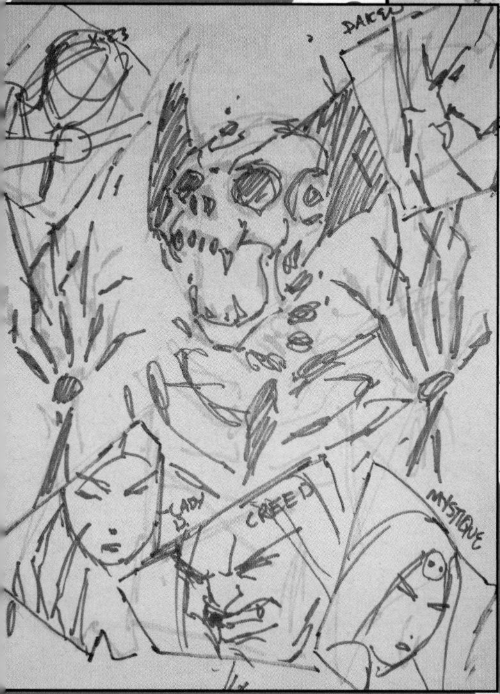
X-23
DAKEN
LADY D
CREED
MYSTIQUE

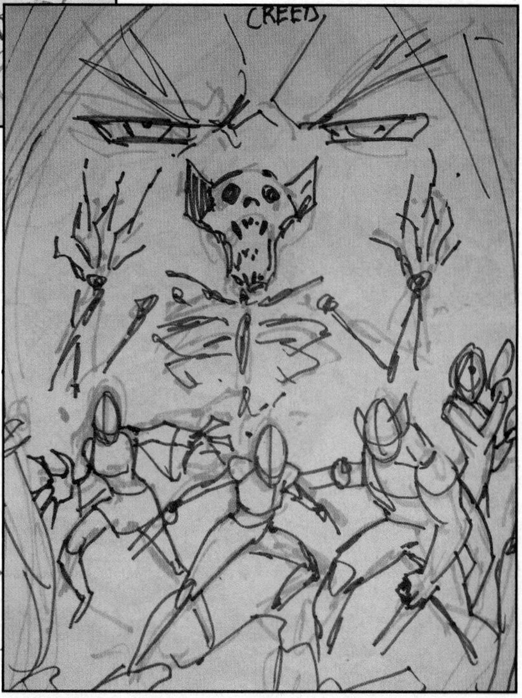
CREED

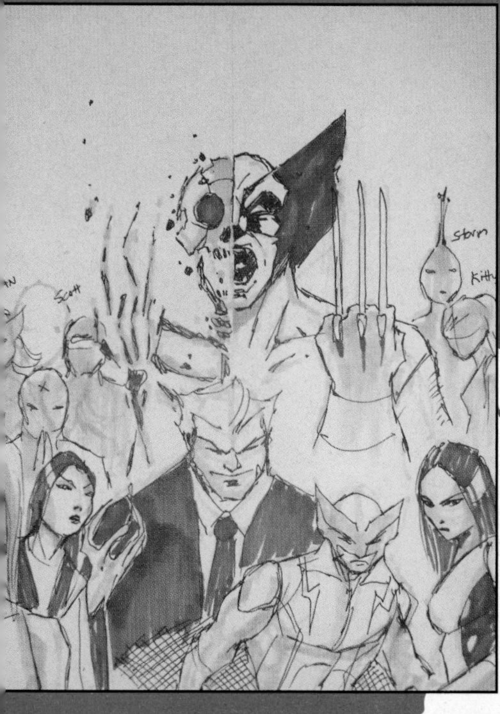
Scott
Storm
Kitty

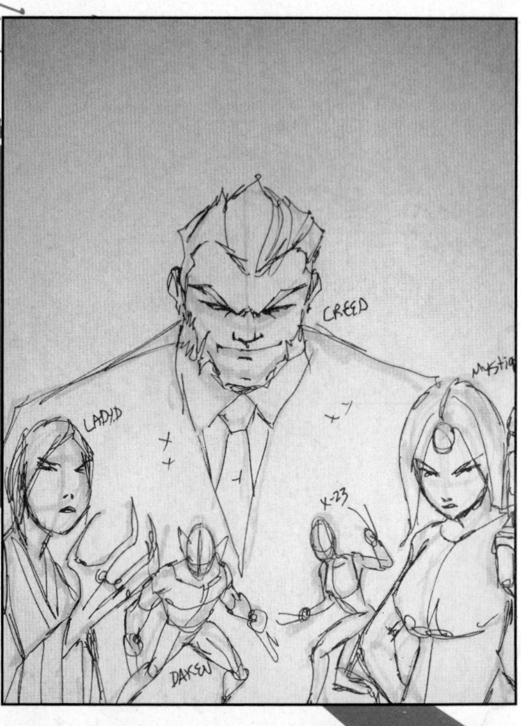
CREED
Mystiq
LADY D
X-23
DAKEN

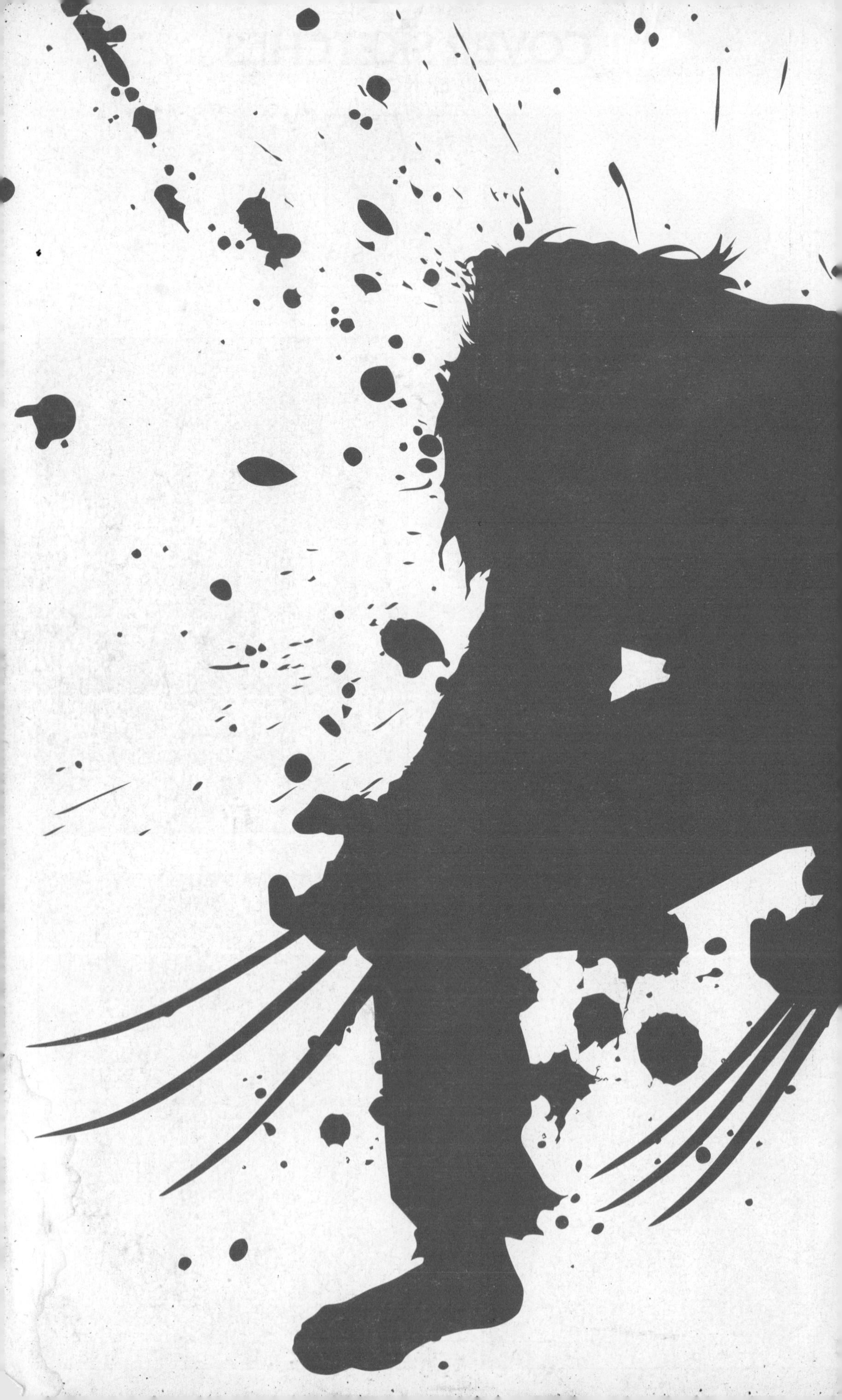